Going Places

The American West in the Twentieth Century

Martin Ridge and Walter Nugent, editors

The cover of a Union Oil Company road map from the early 1950s depicted some of that era's most familiar tourist icons. A similar representation at the dawn of the twenty-first century might also include Las Vegas and Disneyland. Author's collection.

WESTERN UNITED STATES

Road Map

76

UNION

Going Places

Transportation Redefines the Twentieth-Century West

Carlos Arnaldo Schwantes

INDIANA
University Press
Bloomington and Indianapolis

This book is a publication of

Indiana University Press
601 North Morton Street
Bloomington, IN 47404-3797 USA

http://iupress.indiana.edu

Telephone orders 800-842-6796
Fax orders 812-855-7931
Orders by e-mail iuporder@indiana.edu

The paper used in this publication meets
the minimum requirements of American
National Standard for Information
Sciences—Permanence of Paper for
Printed Library Materials, ANSI
Z39.48-1984.

Manufactured in
the United States of America

**Library of Congress Cataloging-in-
Publication Data**

Schwantes, Carlos A., date
  Going places : transportation redefines
the twentieth-century West /
Carlos Arnaldo Schwantes.
      p. cm. — (The American West in the
twentieth century)
Includes bibliographical references and
index.
  ISBN 0-253-34202-3 (cloth : alk. paper)
  1. Transportation—West (U.S)—
History—20th century. I. Title. II.
Series.
  HE210 .S34 2003
  388'.0978'0904—dc21
                      2002006857

1 2 3 4 5 08 07 06 05 04 03

To
Richard W. Schwarz,
Sidney Fine,
Robert A. Henderson,
Richard Maxwell Brown,
Walter Nugent,
and
Mark Burkholder

Six historians who stood at the crossroads and showed me which way to go.

CONTENTS

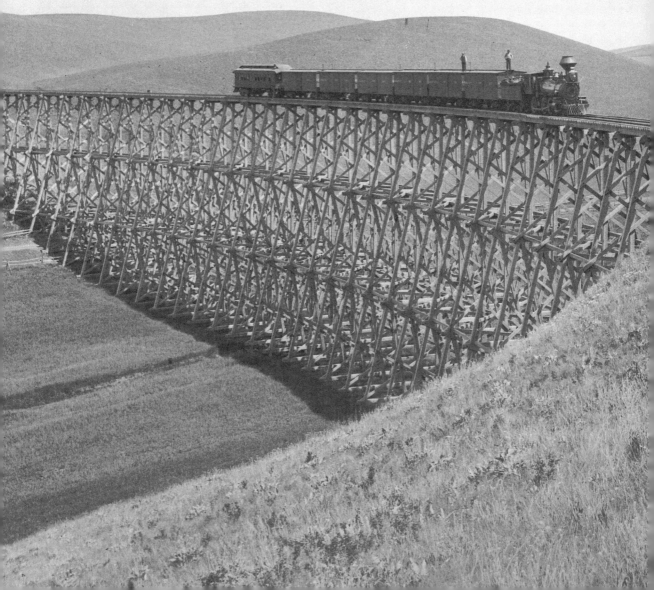

There is, of course, much to be said about views from hotel porches, from automobiles slipping along well-kept roads, from car windows and other vantage points for the luxurious; but the real Simon pure, next-to-nature way to enjoy scenery is on foot; also it's cheaper.

—*Official Guide of the Railways*, June 1916

The unusual phone call I received in 1991 confirmed for me the value of serendipity to help explain the ebb and flow of personal opportunities. What followed was a conversation I had neither expected nor even knew it was possible to have. From my home in Idaho, I listened as an unfamiliar voice from New York City asked if I would participate in a week-long lecture tour called "In the Wake of Lewis and Clark." I would be expected to travel the Columbia and Snake rivers on board a small cruise ship operated by a tour company then called Sven-Olaf Lindblad's Special Expeditions. The proposal sounded exciting, but what was the catch? Somehow it all seemed too good to be true.

Promising a response by the next day, I phoned a local travel agent who aptly characterized the Lindblad enterprise as "the Mercedes-Benz of cruise companies." That was good enough. I phoned Special Expeditions and promptly signed on. Here, at last, was my dream opportunity to run away to sea—if only for short intervals. More than a decade later, and after two dozen cruises on the Columbia and Snake Rivers and another dozen along the Inside Passage of Alaska, I have accumulated at least a quarter of a year's time on board the *Sea Lion* and her sister ship the *Sea Bird*. My time "at sea" proved to be far more valuable than I could ever have imagined. It enabled me to reflect at length on transportation and tourism as a participant, not just as an academic onlooker. The field experience inspired me to write and illustrate a small book on the Columbia

Many years before tour companies began to offer weeklong boat cruises on the Columbia River in the 1990s, Union Pacific streamliners showcased the stunning water-and-mountain scenery of the Gorge area. Courtesy Union Pacific Museum.

River, and it proved invaluable when I researched and wrote a much larger one on the steamboat and stagecoach era in the northern West.

In addition, in 1995 the American Orient Express Railway Company asked me to lecture aboard their cruise train. Thus, to a week or two spent aboard small ships each year, I added a similar span of time aboard a luxury train as it rambled across the United States and Canada. Time spent that way once again provided additional inspiration and amplified what I learned in research libraries.

For instance, during a dozen "American Orient Express" trips, I saw for myself how much cargo crosses the West by train. One April morning as we crossed the high plains of northern New Mexico, I saw workers installing a third track on the busy Chicago to Los Angeles mainline of the Burlington Northern & Santa Fe. When I returned the following year, numerous freight trains occupied all three tracks. Diligently working to keep them all safely spaced were railroad dispatchers in Fort Worth, Texas, who followed the action on gigantic computer screens that showed the track schematics across the western United States. Still other trips on the "American Orient Express" took me across Canada from Vancouver to Montreal, and from Quebec even farther east to Nova Scotia. In Halifax's historic Canadian National Station in 1999, we reached the eastern limits of train travel in North America. I wondered: Where can we go from here?

Human travel, fortunately, is not limited by North America's rail network, extensive though it is, or by its commercially navigable waterways. During the more than three decades I spent in the Far West (from 1969 until mid-2002), I also set forth to explore the expansive regional landscape on foot—and even a few times by raft and kayak. As I grappled with the timeless dilemma posed by so much to see during an average life span, I increasingly enjoyed surveying the West as framed by the windows of trains, planes, boats, and automobiles—especially the latter. Along all but the narrowest and most dangerous stretches of roadway, I could easily stop my car wherever I wanted to take a closer look. During the many meanderings by automobile, I managed to travel to every county in the sprawling region astride or west of the 100th meridian, the invisible map line that bisects the high plains of the United States from North Dakota to Texas into wet and dry sides, more or less. Hence the 100th meridian is one commonly accepted mental divide between East and West.

The opportunity to wonder as I wandered around the West by car provided valuable perspective on a perennially fascinating region. Often the highway itself became my destination for a day or a week as I came to understand how it represented more than a ribbon of asphalt or concrete, or a means merely to drive from one place to another. Long-distance highways like old Route 66 or modern Interstate 80 are twentieth-century equivalents to the dusty trails along which earlier generations plodded west to Utah, Oregon, or California. Modern roads and highways link landscapes both ordinary and sublime for hordes of tourists eager to experience for themselves the scenic splendors preserved within the West's national parks. And those same corridors often leaven despair with opportunity for tormented souls who dream that their cars and geographical mobility will help them locate better jobs or escape corrosive or failed personal relationships. The study of roads and highways reveals how competing modes of transportation noticeably redefined the West during a hundred-year span of time.

It seems difficult even to imagine the modern West without reference to its planes, trains, and automobiles. Freeways define modern Los Angeles just as surely as those same freeways contribute to urban sprawl, traffic congestion, and occasional smog that challenge the "City of Angels" to make itself a livable place. The tall and graceful Space Needle has been the defining landmark of Seattle's skyline since the World's Fair of 1962. It long seemed an appropriate symbol for the hometown of Boeing, a company famous for rockets and various vehicles that transported astronauts into space, and for jetliners like the 707 that redefined space closer to the ground and gave a whole new meaning to commercial travel by air.

However, in early 2001 Boeing announced that it was relocating its headquarters from Seattle, its base since the company's founding as Pacific Aero Products in 1916, to Chicago, in part because traffic congestion increasingly plagued commuters in Seattle, including Boeing's own office workers. Smug and starry-eyed Seattle, it now appeared, had simply been too slow to develop the kind of transportation infrastructure demanded of a modern metropolis. If there is a more ironic case of transportation—or lack thereof—shaping a portion of the modern West, I have yet to find it. But here I am running ahead of my story.

Early on, as I meandered along the roads and highways of the West without a destination clearly in mind, I often felt guilty about the seeming purposelessness of it all. Or worse, was I shirking responsibilities in the office or at home? I admit that there was something nice about a week without any mail or phone calls or gutters to clean at home or papers to grade in the office. All I did was wander by day and read about the West at night. Fortunately, in a bookstore along the way I discovered *Outside Lies Magic*, a thin volume brimming with insight. In this book, Harvard landscape history professor John Stilgoe urges his readers to get outdoors and carefully study the everyday landscape. His preferred mode of travel while making observations was by foot or bicycle, which would certainly be appropriate for intimate spaces; but across the vast distances of the American West, I found an automobile to be more practical. I think the principle is much the same, because along the roads of the West I did discover an abundance of the magic outside that is the subject of Stilgoe's fine book.[1]

Library research became an invaluable addition to my automobile wanderings and vice versa. I would read about a place of historical significance and then venture forth to experience it in person. Alternatively, along the road something would arouse my curiosity, and upon returning home, I would hasten to the university library to learn more.

We humans cannot go back in time, but we can go to places where history happened; and by walking the ground, we intellectually energize ourselves because we experience more fully what took place there years before we were born. At first I sought places clearly recognized for their historical significance, such as national historic sites or the many lesser sites commemorated only by roadside interpretive markers. Gradually, and by what can be described as a purely inductive approach to learning, I came to see that an obvious topic for me to research in this way was the impact of transportation on the twentieth-century West. Thus, by combining two subjects long of interest to me and by blending library and field research, I could perhaps cloak my occasional wanderings with a measure of academic respectability.

On the following pages I offer an extended interpretive essay on transportation and its impact on the modern American West. It is not possible, of course, to confine the story to the West exclusively, because activity on Wall Street or on Capitol Hill or other places outside the West invariably affected the region. Conversely, events in the West sometimes affected the nation as a whole. For example, deregulation of the nation's airlines in 1978, which during subsequent decades rumbled through the industry like a great earthquake to topple one-time giants and give rise to numerous unintended consequences, can be traced back to the intrastate airlines that took to the skies of California in the 1950s and 1960s. The West was the arena in which common American values like a fascination with speed were embodied in bold new ways, such as a long-term national quest to shorten the time it took to travel from one coast to the other. In the 1920s that meant using the most powerful artificial lights on the planet to illuminate a transcontinental airway across Nebraska and Wyoming, and ultimately from New Jersey to California, to keep coast-to-coast airmail on the move around the clock.

Where possible, I intend to relate transportation history to personal observations made during five decades of travel. My very earliest memories, in fact, are all of travel. My parents told me that even as a youngster I refused to sleep in the car during our family's annual automobile excursion between Indiana and my grandparents' home in North Carolina. I remember being "glued" to the windows of our big Hudson—except for brief intervals when my brother Dave and I got bored and wrestled one another (with appropriate sound effects) on its capacious back seat. That drove our parents crazy, and they separated us when they could stand no more. It was back to the car windows for me. The passing landscape became my main source of entertainment. Even today I resent being told by flight attendants to pull down my window shade so that the cabin is dark enough to view the movie. The only "movie" I really care to see is outside and below the wing, and it is definitely not made in Hollywood.

With that background in mind, I have focused on transportation land-scapes already familiar to most observers. For readers who are motorists, such places will be no more exotic than the service stations, motels, and strip malls we drive past each day, each one the result of changing transportation technology. In addition, I want to offer readers easy access to historical materials located in numerous books, essays, newspaper articles, pamphlets, and conference proceedings devoted to transportation. Publications on steam locomotives or Ford Model T automobiles would by themselves fill a small library.

The writing of any book is itself a journey. We choose an intended destination, but it is the research and writing that ultimately get us there, though sometimes we end up far from where we originally intended to go. Regardless of where a journey may lead, an author comes to depend on many people for directions and for various other forms of aid and sustenance. It is easy to accumulate debts, both intellectual and personal, that can never be fully repaid. In addition to everyone I encountered personally during my odyssey, I am intellectually indebted to numerous authors whose research and writing I cite in the "Suggestions for Further Reading."

For their personal help and encouragement, I wish specifically to thank Walter Nugent and Martin Ridge, who with everlasting patience encouraged me to complete this study for their series on the twentieth-century West. David Nicandri, director of the Washington State Historical Society, nurtured my interest in transportation history in a variety of ways. On several occasions he invited me to give public lectures in Tacoma, and always he made the rich collections of the Society available for research. Edward Nolan, the Society's curator, shared and encouraged my enthusiasm for travel ephemera.

Gregory P. Ames, my colleague at the Saint Louis Mercantile Library, graciously shared the extensive knowledge and insight he brings to his job as curator of the John W. Barriger III Railroad Library. I appreciate the support from Ray Mundy, my colleague and director of the Center for Transportation Studies. For all sorts of reasons, I want to thank four more colleagues at the University of Missouri-Saint Louis: John Neal Hoover, director of the Saint Louis Mercantile Library; Mark Alan Burkholder, dean of the College of Arts and Sciences; Louis Gerteis, chair of the History Department; and Blanche M. Touhill, chancellor. Also, I cannot forget two special colleagues at the University of Idaho, Kathy Aiken and Rick Spence, both of them recent chairs of the History Department.

I benefited greatly from a lengthy conversation with aviation historian Robin Higham and from the several articles he sent me afterwards. Likewise, I am indebted to Ron Goldfeder of the National Museum of Transportation, a Saint Louis County park, to the many inquisitive students in my transportation history classes, and to numerous librarians and archivists working behind the scenes. I especially appreciate the help of Daniel Rust, a graduate student at the University of Idaho, who graciously allowed me to use some of his extensive research on the aviator Nick Mamer. I thank my son Ben, a recent history graduate of the University of Pittsburgh and now a doctoral student at the University of Delaware in the history of technology, for letting me test ideas with him during our long walks together.

"All Aboard!" The camera of Richard Steinheimer captured a Northern Pacific conductor in Jamestown, North Dakota, waving "highball" to the locomotive engineer. This time-honored gesture signaled the commencement or continuation of a journey by rail. In the case of the multimodal book that commences on the next pages, I want to say "All Aboard!" as well as "Please Fasten Your Seat Belts." Courtesy DeGolyer Library.

Finally, I dedicate this book to six historians who encouraged me during major turning points in my lifelong love affair with history. Richard Schwarz, my mentor at Andrews University, opened my eyes to what professional history demanded and then steered me in the direction of the University of Michigan and the legendary teacher and scholar, Sidney Fine, who served as graduate advisor for both of us. Robert Henderson recruited me to Walla Walla College by offering me a tenure-track job in 1969. Richard Maxwell Brown at the University of Oregon in 1980 and Walter Nugent at Indiana University in 1984 recharged my intellectual batteries at critical moments by sharing their knowledge and wisdom with me as a member of their summer seminars sponsored by the National Endowment for the Humanities. Finally, and most recently, Mark Burkholder played a key role in persuading me to return home to the Midwest in 2001 by joining the University of Missouri-Saint Louis as the Saint Louis Mercantile Library Endowed Professor of Transportation Studies and the West. Once I jokingly said I needed two business cards to contain a title that long; now I hope this book suggests that combining the two fields does make a great deal of sense. These six historians did their best by me, but in my academic career, as in the writing of this book, I alone take full responsibility for errors of fact or judgment or methodology.

Going
Places

Prologue

The View from
29,000 Feet and Below

The growing air-mindedness of the American people can be taken for granted. No further proof need be cited than the record of Western Air Express. In 1926 we carried 267 passengers, in 1927 the total increased to 400, advanced in 1928 to 6,794 and in 1929 it exceeded 25,000! In other words the passenger travel over one system increased 400 per cent in the last year and over 1,000 per cent in four years. Similar records of other transport companies point toward similar progress.

—Harris Hanshue, president of Western Air Express, in *Aeronautics* (June 1930)

> "Can you tell me," I asked her, "which is the best road to California?"
>
> Without hesitating she answered: "the Union Pacific."
>
> "No, I mean motor road."
>
> Compared with her expression the worst skeptics I had encountered were enthusiasts. "Motor road to California!" She looked at me pityingly. "There isn't any."
>
> —Emily Post, *By Motor to the Golden Gate* (1916)

I prefer a window seat. Any place else on a modern jetliner feels uncomfortably claustrophobic. Besides, on a clear day the price of a window seat includes a free lesson in physical geography. May 3, 2000, was one such day, and our lesson focused on a 600-mile swath of terrain that extended across the Rocky Mountains from Phoenix to Denver.

Clearly visible from 29,000 feet are the impediments that nature shoved in the way of railroaders, highway engineers, and aviators who sought to construct and maintain safe and reliable transportation corridors across the western half of the United States in the twentieth century. Newer corridors frequently used older ones, as when early airmail pilots followed the "iron compass" defined by tracks of the first transcontinental railroad. When low ceilings obscured the way, they flew to the right of the tracks to avoid head-on collisions with mail pilots speeding from the opposite direction.

Automobile versus train. This 1919 image from the mining town of Gem, Idaho, seems to symbolize the epic contest that dominated the history of transportation in the American West during much of the twentieth century. The one thing needed to make the symbolism complete is an airplane overhead. Barnard-Stockbridge Collection, courtesy University of Idaho Library.

Whether their interest lay in planes or trains or automobiles, transportation providers surmounted nature's challenges by using the best engineering know-how and technology of their time, combined with generous measures of common sense and native ingenuity. It is easy to take for granted what they accomplished within the span of just one generation. Only imagine flying between, not above, the peaks of the Rockies in the days before pressurized planes or modern avionics. Likewise, riding aboard a jetliner on which all smoking is banned, I find it amusing to recollect that in 1930 the Department of Commerce, which then oversaw the nation's growing network of airways, fretted about the careless passengers who dropped their still-smoldering cigar and cigarette butts from windows that opened to provide ventilation on low-flying and nonpressurized planes of the era. Over high mountain country they could possibly ignite brush and forest fires on the ground never far below. "Some air transport operators have posted warnings in the cabins of their planes, and in most cases it is effective," noted *Aero Digest*. However, upon investigation Uncle Sam discovered that the worst offenders were stogie-smoking pilots and copilots.[1] Hidden from public view in their sealed and instrument-lined cockpits of today, captains and first officers are presumably models of professional rectitude.

Colorado's boast that more of its terrain extends above 10,000 feet than that of all other states combined (except Alaska) and that a thousand of its peaks reach more than two miles into the sky (about 150 of them topping 13,000 feet in altitude) adds another, rather sobering dimension to recollections of pioneering days of flight. Another peculiarity of the Rocky Mountain country now passing beneath our wings is that the valley bottoms are often higher above sea level than the tops of the tallest peaks east of the Mississippi River.

Such forbidding terrain suggests why any interpretation of how planes, trains, automobiles, and other modes of transportation reshaped everyday life in the American West during the twentieth century must do more than simply amplify the familiar history of transportation in the East. The western half of the United States had a history and geography peculiarly its own, and those combined to distinguish West from East during the twentieth century no less than they had during the nineteenth, when the West was often equated with frontier conditions, and descriptive words like "isolated" or "empty" or "primitive" invited invidious comparisons with the "civilized" East.

Whether the topic is railroad promotion of national parks or how Los Angeles built a network of freeways that fostered suburban sprawl (and smog), it is impossible to grasp how transportation affected residents of the twentieth-century West without first pondering how the region's geographical distinctiveness and its resulting patterns of settlement influenced the evolving ways of moving people and goods from one place to another, activity that provides a good working definition of transportation. It is also noteworthy that for much of the twentieth century there were fewer people and goods to move across the expansive western landscape than was typical for the mature and more densely populated areas of the United States east of the Mississippi River.

Consider that in 1900 more people lived on New York City's tiny and densely packed island of Manhattan than in all of expansive California, which was home then to approximately a million and a half people. Los Angeles in 1900 claimed about a hundred thousand residents, certainly an impressive figure when compared to the rest of the West or to the population of Los Angeles only a decade earlier, but insignificant when compared with the 3.7 million residents of the metropolis in 2000. That same year Phoenix ranked as the nation's sixth-largest city, but it had only 5,544 residents when the twentieth century dawned. The remote Nevada out-

CAÑON OF THE RIO LAS ANIMAS.

William Henry Jackson photographed a Denver & Rio Grande train as it threaded its way along narrow-gauge tracks. Running high above the Las Animas River between Durango and Silverton, it illustrates the ruggedness of Colorado's Rocky Mountain landscape. Courtesy Colorado Historical Society.

DETROIT PHOTOGRAPHIC CO.

post of Las Vegas in 1900 could claim as many as *thirty* residents. Because so few people occupied so much land, "pioneering" and "developmental" were terms still aptly descriptive of transportation enterprises across large parts of the American West in the early twentieth century.[2]

✾ ✾ ✾

In recent years, in-flight magazines have often contained a map of the United States featuring the landscape in various shades of green and brown. The East is invariably tinted green, while most of the West is brown, the latter being an good depiction of the portion of the continent now passing below my window. I know that nature sometimes tints this landscape green too, during the wet weeks of spring, but that is the exception.

The interior portion of the West was (and in many ways remains) an especially harsh and at times unforgiving place. Its climate is far drier and its land surface far more broken, uplifted, and generally incompatible with human settlement than any comparable portion of the United States east of the Mississippi River. For such reasons, major modes of transportation, notably the thousands of miles of canals incised into the well-watered landscapes of New York, Pennsylvania, Maryland, Ohio, Indiana, and other eastern states during the 1820s and the 1830s, were never duplicated across the West. It was not just that the region lacked surface water. Canals for irrigation are a common feature of desert landscapes in the West today, and some of them are quite large. One such waterway in arid California is far longer than the fabled Erie Canal extending 364 miles across upstate New York, and it is nearly as wide. However, by the time a sane person could conceive of building a western counterpart to the Erie Canal—or even a more modest waterway—America's canal technology had been largely superseded by railroads. Unlike canals that froze solid during winter, trains operated year round with the help of snow removal crews and equipment. Only a few short canals for transportation, mainly to connect steamboats that once plied sections of the Columbia River and its tributaries in the Pacific Northwest, were ever built west of the 100th meridian.

Regardless of the technological drawbacks of canals, at the peak of the building craze of the 1830s there were simply too few people living west of the Mississippi River to justify the expense of extending canals or any other mode of commercial transportation across the sprawling region. Not until near the end of the 1840s did mule trains, freight wagons, coastal steamships, river steamboats, and stagecoaches regularly plod, paddle, or bounce their way across the West to provide commercial transportation within the region.

For another two decades, many non-Indian newcomers to the western frontier continued to think of their true homes as located in the East and

Midwest where they had grown up and still had family members. All such places required nearly a month of hard travel to reach by stagecoach from West Coast settlements. The trip from one coast to the other by way of steamships and a portage across the narrow Isthmus of Panama was no faster or easier. Because distances were so great and conditions of travel so primitive, the western third of the United States before the coming of a transcontinental railroad in 1869 might just as well have been located on a separate continent. When a Montana newspaper of the 1860s commonly used the headline "News From America" to share with its readers any bits of information Virginia City residents chanced to receive from the East Coast, it spoke to the territory's remoteness from the nation's main centers of population.[3]

Helping to energize entrepreneurs who struggled to establish and maintain the earliest commercial transportation links across the West were periodic finds of precious metal. No single discovery was more important than the thrilling one that took place in the western foothills of the Sierra Nevada in 1848. California's mineral bonanza would subsequently alter the course of transportation, not just in the "Golden West," but across the entire United States. As one respected investment guide observed in its 1900 issue: "The first great movement in the construction of railways dates from the discovery of gold in California." The impact of California gold on the nation's industrial and commercial development was "prodigious" and had "no precedent in history." *Poor's Manual of Railroads* continued: "All sections were proportionally benefited. The wealth drawn so copiously from the Western part of the continent stimulated to an extraordinary degree the commerce, manufacture, and trade of the Eastern."[4]

Between the California gold rush in 1849 and the onset of a brief but unsettling depression in 1857, construction crews spiked a total of 17,138 miles of new rail line into place across the United States. The figure represented a sizable addition, considering that the entire nation contained just 9,021 miles of track in 1850. However, very little of that frenzied track laying took place west of the Mississippi River in a part of the country too empty and undeveloped to warrant extensive railway construction. California's first tracks (and among the first to be laid anywhere in the West) belonged to the Sacramento Valley Railroad, a 22-mile line that inaugurated service in 1856 between the capital city of Sacramento and gold diggings in the foothills farther east. Given what was to follow, its length was hardly impressive. Nonetheless, from that acorn grew a mighty oak called the Southern Pacific System, its length in 1900 nearly equaling the nation's rail mileage only fifty years earlier.

What the Sacramento Valley Railroad had once portended for transportation in California and the West was not lost on Harris Hanshue, a Los Angeles airline executive. Writing nearly seventy-five years later in *Aeronautics* magazine, he dared to compare his airline, barely four years old, to the state's pioneer railroad, which despite its inauspicious beginnings had become an integral part of an important industry. Hanshue's essay was remarkably prophetic because Western Air Express, the carrier he headed, had recently become the first airline in the United States to make a profit carrying passengers without the benefit of a federal airmail subsidy. The California-based company soon merged to form Transcontinental and Western Airlines, a major coast-to-coast carrier. It retained the familiar TWA initials through its long history, though it later renamed itself Trans World Airlines after extending its reach beyond the coasts of the United States.[5]

A meager portion of Hanshue's old Western Air Express survived on its own to become Western Airlines, a respected regional carrier and the nation's oldest airline in 1986 when Delta acquired it. Using Western's hub in Salt Lake City, Delta almost overnight became a major player in airline transportation across the West and elsewhere. The story of Harris "Pop" Hanshue and Los Angeles's quest for better air transportation is more effectively told elsewhere. But first we need to get the air age's original "iron compass" properly spiked into place.

Well before the 1920s, when Hanshue's generation of dreamers and doers dared to test how air transportation might transform the West, the coming of railroads was certain to inspire plenty of comment. Life after rail connections changed so dramatically that newspapers frequently used the word "magic" to describe the transformation. During an era defined by steamboat and stagecoach transportation—that is, during the three decades from the 1850s through the 1870s—mining settlements scattered throughout the Rocky Mountains experienced distinctive seasonal rhythms. During the summer months in the 1860s, letters from the East Coast might reach Montana in about twenty-two days; but during winter months, when waters of the upper Missouri River froze solid and snowdrifts closed high mountain passes to stagecoach travel, no one dared to predict when any mail "from America" might arrive.

Before the coming of railroads, winter blizzards and ice storms might disrupt communication and transportation across the nation's high frontier for days, weeks, and even months at a time. Quarantined by intense cold and deep snowdrifts, metal miners struggled to survive in their isolated mountain camps. Many a rugged outdoorsman began to suffer from scurvy, a dreaded and potentially lethal disease caused by a diet lacking in fresh fruits and vegetables. Residents of Virginia City, Montana, publicly wept with joy in May 1864 when a long-blocked wagonload of flour at last reached their mountain outpost, where they had been snowbound for five months. Even the residents of accessible Portland, Oregon, the commercial metropolis of the Pacific Northwest, saw the pace of life along city streets slow noticeably during winter months. The coming of railroads redefined the meaning of winter in Portland and every other place their "magic" rails touched.

During the four decades after the Central Pacific and Union Pacific companies first linked their rails in 1869, a benchmark year that marked completion of the nation's first transcontinental railroad at Promontory, Utah, sweating tracklayers spiked seven additional transcontinental lines into place across the western United States. The trunk lines were popularly known as the Santa Fe, Southern Pacific, Union Pacific (via the Oregon Short Line to Portland), Northern Pacific, Great Northern, Milwaukee Road, and Western Pacific (via the Rio Grande and the Missouri Pacific lines). North of the border, the Canadian Pacific completed a transcontinental line to Vancouver in 1885; and unlike the rail companies in the United States, its tracks actually did reach from one coast to the other. Canadians built two additional transcontinental lines that reached across the Dominion in the early twentieth century.

In Canada and the United States, the biggest railroad companies (and many regional and local ones) became household names because in countless ways both great and small they affected every western household. As nothing else, they thoroughly reshaped the West by boosting its economy and reconfiguring its once-open spaces. In fact, most notable changes that occurred in the West during the late nineteenth century were somehow linked to railroads.

From the trunk lines, railroads of the West thrust out branch or feeder lines to develop hitherto untapped sources of mineral, timber, and agricultural wealth. Arizona and New Mexico mines—rich in copper and other base metals but nearly worthless as long as slow and inefficient mule teams struggled to haul heavily laden ore wagons to far off processing plants, some as distant as Kansas City—generated fortunes after the coming of railroads greatly lowered the cost of freight transportation. Not only did an expanding network of tracks bind West and East, but it also linked together once-distant parts of the West. El Paso and Los Angeles, Salt Lake City and Butte, Portland and San Francisco—all of these and many more pairs of growing cities were firmly and efficiently linked for the first time by rail corridors completed during the 1880s.

By the dawn of the twentieth century, railroad alchemy transformed a journey from Omaha to Portland, once a time-consuming ordeal that required four to six months of hard travel along the Oregon Trail, into a pleasure jaunt that could easily be completed within three or four days. A passenger willing to spend additional money could enjoy the experience of crossing the West on board luxuriously appointed sleeping and dining cars, conveyances that boosted personal comfort to a level unimaginable to earlier generations of travelers. Running across the desert Southwest was a Southern Pacific luxury train, the "Sunset Limited," which in 1900 featured a "composite car" that offered indulgences such as a "barber shop, café, library, and smoking-room" in addition to the usual comfort of sleeping and dining facilities.[6]

Freight moved far faster by rail too, and that created all kinds of new business opportunities for westerners. Starting in the 1880s, solid trains of chilled apples from Washington orchards or juicy oranges from newly planted groves in southern California reached markets in the East while

they still were fresh. Neither plodding freight wagons nor the speeding stagecoaches of earlier days had had a significant impact on the nation's eating habits. They simply could not get western produce to distant markets fast enough or without bruising it along the way.

The first refrigerated cars of the Northern Pacific Railroad supposedly hauled ten tons of Chesapeake Bay oysters from Baltimore, Maryland, to Tacoma, Washington, in October 1883, only days after the nation's second transcontinental line was completed at a final spike ceremony in Montana. That was a curious cargo, given that the chilly waters of Puget Sound, so rich in shellfish and other seafood, lapped at Tacoma's own doorstep. No doubt it conferred status on merchants and residents of the "New Northwest" to serve customers or neighbors fresh food that came all the way from the opposite coast. From the other direction, boatloads of tea sailed from China to Tacoma, from where special trains sped it to New York and other East Coast markets. Closer to home, refrigerated cars and the new technique of pasteurization of beer would spell doom for the numerous small-town breweries scattered throughout the West.

As for population growth during the years that followed the famous "wedding of the rails" in 1869, sizeable portions of the West remained remote, hard to reach, and thus only sparsely settled until additional railroad lines opened for business. In fact, but for the significant advances in civil and mechanical engineering that made it feasible for railroads in the 1860s to bore longer tunnels, span wider canyons and rivers, and operate ever more powerful locomotives, many parts of the West would probably have remained isolated outposts served only by the most primitive modes of transportation. Once again, however, the contrast between West and East is noteworthy.

Whatever the mode of transportation, the West did not simply import its technology and know-how from the East. It adapted it. Extending service across the West during the late nineteenth century required railroad companies to reshape existing transportation technology to meet a unique set of regional geographic and environmental challenges. That had been true, too, for early-day providers of steamboat and stagecoach transportation. Some of the best-quality stagecoaches—today a well-recognized icon of the frontier West—came from a manufacturer in Concord, New

(PRECEDING SPREAD) *The Oregon Railway and Navigation Company's bridge across Oregon's Hood River was brand new when Carleton E. Watkins photographed it in 1882 for his illustrated study of the Columbia River. Courtesy Oregon Historical Society.*

The Lewiston, *one of many steamboats that once linked remote northern Idaho with Portland by way of the Snake and Columbia rivers, loads wheat at Illion, Washington, in the early twentieth century. Major Lee Moorhouse Collection, courtesy University of Oregon Library.*

Hampshire; and many a "mountain steamboat" specially designed to ply the shallow waters of the Missouri River between St. Louis and central Montana took shape in boatyards located along the banks of the Ohio River and its tributaries in Pittsburgh and elsewhere. Most early railway locomotives used out West were built in Pittsburgh or Philadelphia. However, all such technologies had to be adapted to meet western conditions, most notably the lack of large population centers and major markets that were needed to generate a volume of traffic railroads required for profitable operation. In the early days, too, they could often afford only modest wooden stations, spindly trestles, and a line of slender rails resting on rough-hewn ties supported by little or no ballast.

In the eastern half of the United States, stagecoaches, steamboats, and railroads connected already-existing centers of population. By contrast, along the original rutted dirt-and-sand trails that extended from Missouri to Colorado, California, or Oregon, there were few towns or villages to connect. Often not even a wayside tavern existed to offer food and drink to weary travelers. Early overland stage lines adapted as best they could. From local building materials, including logs, adobe, and blocks of matted prairie sod, they fashioned crude way stations to permit an occasional change of horses and a modest meal service for passengers. Steamboats churned along the waters of the Missouri River, and except for frequent stops to obtain wood for fuel, they functioned as self-contained machines. When compared to railroad operations, early-day steamboat and stagecoach service was relatively inexpensive to provide. Their support structures required little or no fundamental alteration of the landscape and no great feats of civil engineering. Even so, steamboat and stagecoach companies found it challenging to maintain regular service because of the primitive state of the countryside.

Railroad building, by contrast, required investment capital in far larger amounts than any steamboat or steamboat operator dreamed possible. For example, on average every single mile of the Pacific Railroad extended west from St. Louis in the 1850s cost the equivalent of five or six steamboats and eight to ten stagecoaches and the teams of horses or mules required to pull them. Like expensive steam locomotives that made day-to-day operations possible, much of the money required to build and run railroads came from sources in the East. Early railroads of the West, and especially venture capitalists from outside the region, needed an abiding faith in the future growth of a hitherto remote and little-known part of the United States.

Unlike railroads of the East, those of the West in the nineteenth century needed to extend their tracks across miles of rugged and lightly settled land—all before they could hope to earn a penny's return on investment. Often it seemed that railroaders faced the daunting task of generating freight and passenger dollars by running trains from nowhere in particular to nowhere at all. With generous grants of federal land, Congress helped to underwrite the cost of construction in areas where private investors feared to tread. In this way big railroads of the West acquired the landed empires they held in the twentieth century. But land alone could not overcome all the problems that railroad pioneers faced.

Even after major railroads had been spiked firmly into place, problems unique to the West occasionally plagued their day-to-day operations. For example, along stretches of desert track in the days when steam locomotives ruled the railroad landscape, finding clean water needed to maintain steam pressure presented a serious challenge. If trackside sources of

Before airlines began offering food service aloft, the railway restaurant in Arrow, Colorado, at an elevation of 9,585 feet had to be among the highest points in the United States where a traveler could obtain a hot meal. The long-gone hamlet was located west of the Continental Divide on the Denver & Salt Lake Railroad that linked Denver and northwestern Colorado. Louis Charles McClure Photo, courtesy Colorado Historical Society.

water contained too much alkali, mineral deposits quickly built up and clogged locomotive boiler tubes, often after just a single run. Today, flying high above the West at the dawn of the new millennium in the relative comfort of a Boeing 737, it is difficult to recall the down-to-earth problems that once bedeviled early providers of transportation.

From the plane window I now survey a vast and complex terrain dominated by range after range of towering mountains. This is the roof of the
continent, at least for the lower forty-eight states. Many of the mountains
in central Colorado still wear a mantle of winter snow. Pikes Peak is well
covered. Deep and narrow canyons occasionally knife their way through
the mountain clusters, and railway and highway engineers sometimes used
those natural passageways for their tracks and roads. Southwest of Denver are the several large prairies known locally as parks. The scattered
mineral bonanzas of bygone years encouraged ambitious railroads like
the Denver, South Park & Pacific to extend a line of narrow-gauge tracks
over the mountains to serve mining camps and towns. Most such tracks
were pulled up years ago after the mines played out.

What is remarkable even in the twenty-first century is how few signs
of human habitation the landscape of the interior West reveals, at least
when surveyed from the lofty perspective of a commercial jetliner, even
after a century of population growth. Much of the terrain below clearly
remains part of the aptly named "empty quarter," as the journalist Joel
Garreau described the interior West in his book *The Nine Nations of
North America* (1981).[7]

Just how empty the land truly is depends on how much the beholder
knows of the region's colorful history of mining booms and busts. In ac-
tuality, the tide of population has crested and ebbed several times in the
mineral districts of Colorado. Today the human tide is generally rising
again as vacationers and retirees work hard to relax and play in style and
comfort in the gentrified mountain towns where prospectors and miners
probed and dug for gold and silver in years long past. Some prominent
settlements have evolved into upscale communities—notably the resorts
of Aspen and Telluride—and the railway lines that carried ore to the smelters have since been paved over and turned into jogging paths.

Such communities have not exactly forgotten their gritty history, though
they have turned it into a marketable commodity. Annual miner's day festivities present a great opportunity for local merchants to dig for tourist
dollars. Main street boutiques sell expensive knickknacks that are much
too cute for words (or common sense). This kind of transformation is taking place all over the West, not just in the former Rocky Mountain mining camps, and it contributes to population growth even in remote locali-
ties that were once as dried up and forgotten as scattered tumbleweeds.

Even so, compared to the United States east of the Mississippi River,
large portions of the West do remain very empty. From the air, the most
easily recognizable signs of human habitation below are probably the
threadlike lines scribed by railroad and highway corridors. River highways, on the other hand, are nonexistent. Because the land as a whole is
so brown and dry, any rivers below us leave only small and barely legible

signatures. In fact, direct flights from Phoenix to Denver will never cross a river of any consequence unless an aridity-crazed passenger succeeds in hijacking and diverting the plane in a mad quest to reach a land of greater rainfall.

Aridity is the primary reason so much of the interior West remains so sparsely populated. Many locations are simply too dry or too high to support large settlements. Even some of the West's well-watered anomalies like Portland and Seattle were for years surrounded and isolated by miles of dense forests and difficult-to-cross mountain passes. Whether the land was wet or dry, most westerners at the dawn of the twentieth century still tended to cluster together in a few prominent enclaves. The major metropolitan areas that effectively defined the West in 1900—notably Los Angeles, San Francisco-Oakland, Portland, Seattle, Salt Lake City, Denver, and El Paso—all formed islands of population surrounded by vast oceans of land. Separating any pair of cities were miles of space defined not just by emptiness but also by ruggedness. Transportation links forged by an expanding network of railroad lines during the expansive second half of the nineteenth century enabled these cities to grow, prosper, and thus dominate the small settlements that marked the limits of their often-vast urban hinterlands.

The West's island pattern of settlement served as a visual reminder that the region's economy in 1900 remained closely tied to metal mining or timber harvesting, two extractive activities typically done in remote, nearly inaccessible places. Around ubiquitous deposits of valuable minerals arose one or more centers of population. Some such settlements were located in high mountain country at elevations of ten thousand feet or more where paralyzing blankets of snow often isolated long-suffering residents from the rest of the world from October through May. Agricultural areas, too, often took the form of highly scattered and extremely specialized islands on the land, with raisin or almond or apple production, to name just a few of the West's many crops, dominating a single valley, in contrast to the wheat, corn, or cotton belts that defined broad swaths of farmland extending across hundreds of miles of the Middle West or South. The dispersed pattern of commodity production, no less than its scattered towns and cities, set the West apart from the more densely peopled East and created major headaches for providers of transportation.

Only consider the state of Idaho. Its boundaries in 1900 enclosed a portion of the earth about equal in size to England, Scotland, and Wales combined but containing only 161,000 residents, or about the number who lived in a respectable English city. How so few people could raise enough money to construct and maintain even a modest system of roads and highways offers testimony to ingenuity and perseverance. A further nightmare for aspiring highway builders was that sizeable portions of Idaho were mountainous and unpopulated. They still are. However, across the American West such big transportation headaches are by no means unique to Idaho.

HIGHWAY LOOPS - AFTON, WYO. TO MONT

In the 1920s the camera of Wesley Andrews recorded one of the many looping mountain roads built in Idaho. This one connected the town of Montpelier with Afton, Wyoming. Courtesy Oregon Historical Society.

Few places in the West could boast of a more complex railroad landscape than the mining town of Lead, South Dakota. In this 1902 photograph the lower tracks belong to the Deadwood Central Railroad (affiliated with the Chicago, Burlington & Quincy), the middle tracks to the Fremont, Elkhorn & Missouri Valley (an affiliate of the Chicago & North Western), and the upper tracks to Homestake Mining Company, which used them to haul ore from its metal mines. Courtesy South Dakota State Historical Society.

Even today the corridors forming the nation's latticework of interstate superhighways are widely spaced across the central Rocky Mountains and most other parts of the sparsely populated interior West. From east of metropolitan Phoenix until our flight topped the Front Range near Denver, the only superhighway I spied from the air was Interstate 40, a pencil-thin line running east to west across the high plateaus of northern New Mexico and Arizona. Paralleling the modern expressway are portions of famous old Route 66. Alongside the two highways run the well-maintained tracks of the former Atchison, Topeka & Santa Fe Railway, now merged with other western railroads to form the Burlington Northern & Santa Fe Railway Company. Together with Union Pacific, these two carriers dominate the flow of rail freight across the West today.

I knew the tracks below were well maintained because of first-hand experience, not because I could see such details from a jetliner. Just two days earlier I had bounded along them while serving as a lecturer on board the "American Orient Express," a private cruise train. We were on our way west across the United States from Washington to Los Angeles by way of Savannah, New Orleans, and the Grand Canyon. Our trek took ten days and covered nearly five thousand miles of the South and West. Among the sights along the way, I recall most vividly the polychrome sunset in the Painted Desert west of Gallup, New Mexico, which I watched from the open vestibule of a vintage passenger car.

I hasten to add that train vestibules were not intended for viewing the passing landscape, though many of us enjoy doing just that. They are noisy, breezy, and even dangerous places. The American Orient Express has posted warning signs on all of its cars. The one at my elbow admonished, "Do not lean out of open doors or windows!" Just in case anyone missed the point the next line read, "Do not place any part of your body outside of the windows!" The next said, "Do not throw any objects from the train!" Finally, "Do not throw cigarettes or other burning material from the train!" That caused me to think of those early airline pilots and their smoldering cigar butts.

The main purpose of a vestibule is to allow passengers easy access to individual cars while stopped at stations or to permit them to walk safely between cars while the train is in motion. However, when the upper half of a vestibule's Dutch door is left open, I can never resist the temptation to study the passing scenery from a mobile viewpoint. By combining fourteen trips that I have made thus far since 1995 as a special lecturer on board the American Orient Express, I can claim to have crossed the United States from coast to coast while standing up. Along the way I have enjoyed attempting to read the American landscape like the pages of an open book, its various chapters corresponding to the dark and mysterious bayous traversed along the Louisiana Gulf Coast, the expansive plains and bright blue skies of western Texas, and the ruddy mountain gorges incised by the Colorado River.

Juxtaposing western landscapes as seen from a moving train with those visible from a jetliner helps to underscore how transportation shaped regional landscapes, even as those landscapes (along with changing technologies) influenced both how and what kinds of transportation would likely be provided. It must be emphasized that where the rails or highways run today is not a product of geography alone. Politics, economics, and oversized personal egos also played a role—and that was as true for the little-known highway builders as for the fabled railroad barons. The often-dismal result of mixing ego, politics, and highway construction—that is, placing local interests above the national good—caused one journal devoted to the cause of good roads to complain in 1916 about "the little congressman who has been scheming to build his little road where it will never be traveled by anybody."[8]

Regardless of their inspiration, different modes of transportation shaped the landscape of the West in three distinct ways. First, the machines we commonly call locomotives and trains required visible support structures in order to transport anything. In the case of railroads, steam-powered locomotives required rails and ties, and usually, but not always, ballast to support the track and keep it well drained. Defining the right-of-way were a variety of distinctive structures, including signals, sanding and water towers, roundhouses, passenger stations, freight warehouses, earth fills and cuts, tunnels, bridges, and so forth. Before the invention of mechanical refrigeration, workers standing atop special trackside platforms periodically iced carloads of perishable food.

Conversion from steam to diesel power during the 1940s and 1950s altered the railroad landscape by rendering some of the familiar support structures obsolete, but it did not change the basics. Today's trains still run on rails and tracks, though even those fundamentals of railroading have gained a new look over the years. The water tanks for thirsty steam locomotives may have disappeared, but keen-eyed observers will notice that as freight trains grew heavier in recent years, so did the rails themselves. Many of the newest ties are formed from concrete, not wood. In a real sense, the railroad landscape is always in transition.

So too are the nation's airways. Most obviously, jets have replaced the once ubiquitous DC-3s and other early propeller-driven models on all but the shortest flights. The modern support structures required for commercial flight are often less visible than the airplanes themselves. Contemporary commercial aviation depends on electronic, and hence invisible, signals to guide pilots, though in earlier years rotating beacons visually defined major flight paths across the West. A motorist today will sometimes spot a solitary structure shaped much like an oversize bowling pin. Those are focal points for the system of electronic navigation that has replaced lighted airways. Jet contrails, like smoke streaking from fast-moving steam locomotives, serve to delineate the aviation landscape for

This Milwaukee Road image from 1931 illustrates how the ample windows of a passenger car framed the passing landscape. Courtesy Milwaukee Public Library.

far-off observers. Airports, of course, form a fundamental component of the aviation landscape; and all large ones require major modifications to the landscape on which their runways, terminals, and parking lots are built.

Apart from their own infrastructure, all modes of transportation shape in some way the landscapes over or through which they pass. Railroads, for instance, played an active role in the irrigation of arid western lands by encouraging newcomers to plant both crops and towns. The infamous urban sprawl of Los Angeles—infamous at least in the eyes of Easterners who early developed good systems of mass transit—was a product of where steam railroads first located their outlying stations, then of interurban railroad lines powered by electricity, and finally of widespread automobile ownership. Airports were typically sited beyond city limits, at least initially; yet they invariably functioned as very powerful magnets to pull urban growth relentlessly toward them.

Furthermore, the relatively recent concept of hub airports, a radical (and radial) departure from the linear pattern that prevailed in railroad days and was carried forward through the first half-century of commercial aviation, helped promote the growth of those metropolitan areas most favored by good air connections to other cities of the United States and the world. Among the West's hub cities are San Francisco and Denver for United, Salt Lake City and Dallas-Fort Worth for Delta, Seattle for Alaska, Los Angeles and Dallas-Fort Worth for American, and Phoenix and Las Vegas for America West. Not coincidentally, all these hub cities rank among the fastest growing metropolitan areas of the West.

A third way that transportation shaped the western landscape was by framing it for observers, or even for would-be observers located far outside the West who had not yet seen it for themselves. To that end, the railroads of the West published hundreds, perhaps thousands, of different promotional brochures over the years (with cumulative print runs easily numbering in the millions) to package the western landscape attractively and thus "sell" it to prospective settlers as well as to tourists. Airlines later printed tourist brochures showing the Grand Canyon or the Golden Gate Bridge as seen by passengers peering down through the windows of a plane.

What drivers might see from the windows of their automobiles was not the same West as that framed by windows (or open vestibule doors) of a moving passenger train, and for certain it was not the same West as seen from a high-flying commercial jet. Each perspective involved different degrees of intimacy.

Thinking about the distorted perceptions of the West that travelers gain if they study it only from the windows of a commercial jetliner, I am reminded of the hordes of subway commuters who daily rumble through the dark tunnels beneath the streets of New York or London. They may understand well the neighborhoods where they begin or end their journeys, but the above-ground landscape between subway stations may often

Long before Denver had its first airport, it could boast of a busy railroad station. It is seen here in 1906. Detroit Publishing Company photograph, courtesy Colorado Historical Society.

019514. UNION DEPOT, DENVER, COLORADO.

remain as remote and unfathomable as that flown over by travelers between major airports

The passing countryside appears more coherent when viewed from the windows of a passenger train, but trains must stick to the rail corridors that effectively define the angle of vision of all who ride them. In some places the vista is broad, but often we look out a window and are left to guess what lies beyond the confining hills or canyon walls. Certainly, passenger trains cannot stop or digress to permit travelers to find out what is there, though as one motorist driving my own car, I can easily do so. The writer Emily Post aptly described the United States prior to motoring across it from New York to California in 1915 as "an unopened book," apart from "the few chapter headings that might be read from the windows of a Pullman train."[9]

I sometimes fear that observers aboard a commercial jetliner remain so remote from the West they fly across that any visual clues discernible on the ground can easily deceive them into thinking that the land is so dominant that people—who are always invisible from high above—are only visitors there. For that reason I always want to test what I see from the air against observations I have made during more than thirty years of driving through all parts of the American West in order to gain an intimate perspective on the region.

For instance, if you scan a western landscape carefully from the air, you can often discern a pattern of thin lines that suggests the coming of housing subdivisions to the remote highlands of New Mexico and Colorado. Some curvilinear streets and cul-de-sacs incised by earthmovers into the mauve landscape don't yet have houses on them, but the telltale signatures of residential or recreational subdivisions predict the future with far greater accuracy than tea leaves or crystal balls ever could. All such landscapes need only await the settlers who will surely come.

This pattern of coming settlement is especially visible on the high plains south and east of Denver, a metropolis where tall buildings rise so abruptly from surrounding flatland that when seen from an airplane window they seem to form an enormous three-dimensional bar graph. Beyond the left wing of the jetliner stretches an urban corridor defined by Interstate 25 and the expanding cities of Pueblo, Colorado Springs, Denver, Boulder, Greeley, and Fort Collins; and beyond the right wing are the ranches and farms of the high plains. They meet abruptly where earthmovers and backhoes have scraped away topsoil to sculpt patches of bare land and curvilinear streets that await the homebuilders. The interconnected swatches of brown earth define the intersection—a battle zone, perhaps—between two ways of life and two different ways of using the land of the high plains.

As United flight 2762 gradually descends toward Denver, I observe how the new airport located in farmland some twenty miles east of the Colorado capital functions as a magnet to lure more people into the once-open spaces. Motels and rental car agencies are the vanguard of the urban sprawl sure to follow. "There's a new golf course!" exclaims one enthusiastic passenger ahead of me to his seatmate. I pretend not to hear, and I do not share his enthusiasm.

Muffled bumps tell passengers that the wheels of the Boeing 737 have locked into place in preparation for landing. In the distance the main terminal building comes into view. Its irregular roofline sculpted from Teflon-coated fiberglass is intended to remind observers of a line of snow-covered Rocky Mountain peaks or an encampment of Plains Indian tepees. Others have likened this visually arresting construction to a cluster of circus tents or to massive dollops of whipped cream. This much is certain: as a distinctive architectural statement, there is no comparable airport terminal in the United States. Once criticized but now often ranked among the best such facilities in the United States, the terminal building forms the centerpiece of the vast aviation landscape still emerging from the plains east of Denver. It is a transportation landscape that also extends literally around the globe.

The following chapters offer a fuller examination of transportation landscapes as well as of several major changes wrought by transportation technology, but I will state in advance that this is not always a story of progress. The job of moving goods and people poses a continuing challenge to providers of such services, and often their responses have left shippers and passengers frustrated. Yet transportation, and most notably the joy of travel to some distant and exotic place, has created many fond memories.

One

Transportation Corridors Transform the West

Rutted streaks of red and brown defined the side roads. From these no-name paths across the prairie, an informal caravan of dispossessed Americans steered their old and battered automobiles onto the main paved highway and headed west. They wanted to leave the land of dust behind. By day they traveled along a narrow strip of asphalt and concrete known as Route 66, and by night they camped close beside it—except across the Mojave Desert, where they drove through the night to avoid the searing heat of the sun.

Night or day, the highway corridor became a nurturing presence, the "mother road," in the words of John Steinbeck; and like any good mother, she offered her children the promise of better days ahead. The rearview mirror reflected a ribbon of pavement unspooling to the eastern horizon—back to the "dust-bowl" country of Oklahoma. Back even farther to Joplin, Saint Louis, and Chicago. The highway ahead extended west to the possibility of a better life in California. Route 66 was literally a corridor of hope.

When migrants like Steinbeck's fictional Joad family in *The Grapes of Wrath* traveled west along Route 66 in the late 1930s in search of opportunity on America's West Coast, the journey was hard. The main highway linking Oklahoma and California ran through mile after bone-wearying mile of high plains and desert. The desiccated landscape frightened the impoverished pilgrims and tested the stamina of their aging vehicles.

In his saga of the Joad family, Steinbeck quietly highlighted a revolution in transportation that profoundly reshaped the American West during the first third of the twentieth century and continued to do so for decades to come, though the

States of the West did not welcome migratory workers during the 1930s. The ubiquitous New Deal photographer Arthur Rothstein recorded this image in 1936 as uniformed members of the Colorado Militia waited at the state's southeastern border to discourage migrants heading north from Oklahoma and New Mexico. Courtesy Library of Congress.

most noticeable changes took place during the 1920s. That was when growing legions of auto owners of all income levels participated, if only unintentionally, in a bloodless coup that surprised and upended the once-mighty railroad industry. For Cimarron, Wagon Mound, Fort Sumner, and numerous other cattle, farm, and oil communities strung along its tracks like pearls on a steel necklace, the Atchison, Topeka & Santa Fe Railway—a network of 13,452 miles of track in the late 1930s—had served as the "mother road" of earlier years. In many ways the railroad still was the mother, though this mother had a fist of steel in her velvet glove and had not always bothered to conceal it. Neither had other big railroads. "You cannot turn in any direction in American politics," wrote the economist Richard T. Ely back in 1890, "without discovering the railway power. It is the power behind the throne."[1]

The transportation revolution of the 1920s changed that. By the beginning of the twenty-first century, although railroads hauled more tons of freight across the West than ever before, competition with other modes of transportation was much more intense. No longer did railroads dominate state legislatures and community councils as they once had, no longer did their passenger stations function as centers of town and village life, and no longer did their prestige luxury trains form highly visible symbols of railroad power.

The road-and-highway network of the West, which had expanded impressively during the two decades bracketed by the world wars (1919–39), ranked alongside the automobile as the foremost contributor to the twentieth-century transportation revolution that made it possible for the Joads and their numerous real-life counterparts to drive cars of their own westward to California, Oregon, and Washington in the late 1930s. Only twenty-five years earlier, a cross-country trek by automobile would have been newsworthy and nearly impossible for all but the most determined and affluent drivers; and only twenty-five years later, famed Route 66 was itself antiquated. By the early 1960s the latticework of limited-access interstate highways expanded rapidly to accommodate a swelling flow of automobile and truck traffic, and Route 66 eventually became a casualty of the change.

In their day, sojourners like the Joads represented the latest generation of Americans to confront the peculiarities of the nation's western landscape. Route 66 in the 1930s epitomized the most recent of many transportation corridors that over the years had threaded their way across the landscape of the American West and through the pages of its history. So much of the history of the region could be written in terms of those early-day corridors—some synonymous with power, as railroads were in their heyday, or with powerlessness, as Route 66 was when Steinbeck immortalized it during the Depression Decade.

A century earlier when American pioneers plodded west in the early 1840s in covered wagons, they followed another set of corridors, the now-famous Oregon and California trails. The daunting landscape between the Missouri Valley and the Pacific Coast formed an abiding presence during journeys that extended across a four-to-six-month span of time and at least two thousand miles of nearly empty terrain. The West's mountain-rimmed valleys and the panoramic vistas defined by distant mesas and buttes may have entranced later generations of tourists, but the pilgrims of the 1840s and 1850s were travelers, not tourists, a distinction that dust-bowl refugees of the 1930s would have appreciated. To travelers, whether they set forth in covered wagons, stagecoaches, or private automobiles in later years, it was significant that the West contained so much space, so few people, and so little water. Their only hope, it often seemed, was to stick to the known corridors.

There were exceptions to the land of little water, of course. Exceptions, contradictions, and ironies have long defined the region. The arid West—that is, the bulk of the countryside that receives less than twenty inches of rainfall a year, or the amount of moisture required to grow corn, wheat, and other common crops—was not the whole West. Nine months of drizzle and mist nurtured dense stands of Douglas fir in portions of Oregon and Washington west of the Cascades, yet just east of the mountains stretched plateaus far too dry to sustain anything taller than sagebrush and bunchgrass. Years later, when the same land was planted in wheat, the rolling plains in July and August resembled an amber ocean as gusts of wind rippled across their surface.

East of the Rocky Mountains, the waters of the Missouri River during spring and early summer usually flowed deep enough to permit a fleet of shallow-draft steamboats to muscle their way across the sandbars and other shallow places to climb from Saint Louis to central Montana in the 1860s and 1870s—the gold rush years before the long-awaited coming of the railroads. A journey up the river corridor required about two months; and if the boatmen were lucky, they loaded the valuable cargoes that made their effort worthwhile and steamed rapidly back to Saint Louis, Sioux City, or other home ports. But if the water level fell too soon, it could strand them on the high plains, perhaps until next year's spring rains or snow melt.

On the opposite side of the Rockies, a considerably greater volume of water gained Portland, Oregon, access to landlocked Idaho by means of steamboats that plied the Columbia and Snake Rivers. Steamboat paddles also splashed across San Francisco Bay, Puget Sound, and several large lakes of the mountain West. Again, those were the exceptions in a region defined by its aridity. If anything, they served to illustrate how the combination of too little water, too few people, and too much space defined much of the western landscape elsewhere. Travelers who used their own animals and wagons to cross the West during the nineteenth century ignored the region's geographical peculiarities at their peril. Those same defining features certainly had to be uppermost in the minds of business pioneers who risked precious venture capital to forge commercial transportation links across so formidable a terrain.

The western landscape, or at least vast expanses of it, intimidated both the travelers and the early transportation entrepreneurs. Yet depending on how and when a person crossed it—whether by stagecoach in the 1850s or by railroad Pullman car in the 1920s—the identical landscape might be perceived as lethal or beautiful, challenging or nurturing, a risky venture

View of Tonopah from Railroad Depot.

A typical island of population in a harsh and seemingly empty landscape. J. E. Stimson positioned his view camera at the railroad depot in 1905 to survey the new mining settlement of Tonopah, Nevada. Courtesy Wyoming State Museum.

Not all migrants to the West Coast in the 1930s headed west along Route 66 in search of work in California. This man was among the many "Dokies" who left the dry Dakotas and migrated west in search of greener pastures in Oregon and Washington. Arthur Rothstein photographed him near Missoula, Montana, in July 1936. Most likely he had followed federal highways 10 or 12, two unsung corridors extending across the West. Courtesy Library of Congress.

or a moneymaking opportunity. The fact that Route 66 was in place and available for the Joads to use in their late 1930s trek to California was itself a tribute to the basic development work done by providers of commercial transportation during the previous century. Without the pioneering activities of railroads, it would be impossible to account for the explosive growth of southern California beginning in the 1880s or the rise of commercial agriculture both on the Pacific Slope and the Great Plains, or even the creation of a highway network itself.

Never forget that during the 1930s, as refugees from the Great Plains motored west in search of a better life (and whether they were fully conscious of it or not), it was railroad power that essentially shaped the West they and their parents knew best. Now that was changing. It was the highway they followed west to the Pacific Coast, and the world of motorized transportation increasingly defined their lives—and not just as modes of travel. During World War II many recent emigrants to the West Coast traded picking beans, tomatoes, and oranges for good-paying jobs in the aircraft factories and shipyards, which supplied two basic types of transportation needed to win the war. After that conflict ended in 1945, a growing number of former refugees from the dust bowl and their children moved to new suburbs defined by automobile ownership and a new set of transportation corridors, the freeways expanding across southern California. After 1956 the newly established Interstate Highway System promoted a similar transformation nationwide. Once again it would be transportation corridors that defined and redefined many fundamental aspects of life in the twentieth-century West.

Transportation pioneers of the 1840s and 1850s used mule trains, freight wagons, stagecoaches, steamboats, and other relatively inexpensive and utilitarian conveyances to link together the small and isolated settlements typical of the West at the time. The main exceptions, and the region's only significant population centers in those early years were San Francisco, Salt Lake City, Denver, and Portland. Occasionally a mining camp would mushroom suddenly to prominence, and then disappear almost as fast.

The goal of all transportation pioneers was to haul people and goods across the sparsely populated West as cheaply as possible—and "haul" is truly the appropriate word to describe conveyances aboard which luxuries of any kind were hard to justify. Only the elegant river steamboats offered a rare exception to the unadorned fare typical of pioneer years. Most purveyors of transportation simply did not have any extra dollars to spend on elaborate support structures or on pampering their passengers. As much as possible they sought to adapt transportation to the land or waterways as they found them, and thus they seldom worked to alter the landscape itself in any fundamental way.

Then came the railroaders. They literally restructured the landscape of the West. To a much larger extent than was true in the East, the West was a hard place made livable and productive by various types of technology—dams, irrigation systems, even the self-leveling combines that harvested wheat on rolling hillsides. But ranking foremost among all such technologies was the railroad.

Beginning mainly in the 1860s, railroad companies built bridges and bored tunnels, sliced massive cuts and piled up impressive fills to provide

To provide a good right-of-way for its trains between Portland and Spokane, the Oregon Railway and Navigation Company dramatically reengineered the rolling landscape of eastern Washington. Courtesy University of Oregon Library.

a foundation for their tracks. With sufficient money and engineering know-how, they intended to triumph over all impediments that nature placed in their path. They also nurtured the growth of the settlements served by their tracks and trains, a good many of which the railroaders themselves had originally helped to plant.

The next group to reshape the landscape of the West to meet the needs of transportation were the highways builders, those dreamers and doers whose persistent efforts led to the creation of a nationwide network of numbered federal roads in the mid 1920s, among them Route 66. Still later came freeways and superhighways. At first glance it may seem that no group did more to shape the distinctive features of the twentieth-century West than the highway builders. Where railroad builders had earlier created a rigidly defined grid of corridors—and major development of the West during their era had invariably occurred within sight of their tracks—highway builders greatly augmented what the railroaders had begun and made it possible for development to take place anywhere their roads ran, and even in anticipation of roads soon to be built.

Ironically, the highway builders were successful only because the railroad builders had done such a good job first. The chronological relationship between the two modes of transportation is important. Nothing the highway builders did would have been possible, at least initially, without the pioneering development work done by the railroaders. In a figurative sense, the roads and highways of the West rested upon a firm foundation laid initially by the railroads. In some instances that was literally true, as in the mid-1920s when builders of a scenic highway across the Continental Divide west of Colorado Springs used more than fifty miles of right-of-way abandoned by the Colorado Midland Railway. It has been estimated that it would have cost nearly three million dollars to duplicate the roadbed, bridges, and tunnels donated to the state by shareholders of the dismantled railway.[2]

Every metropolis of the modern American West, with the notable exception of Las Vegas, had already become a prominent population center when highway builders extended their ribbons of gravel, asphalt, and concrete in the early twentieth century—tentatively at first but then with seemingly unstoppable force. In less than a generation, motorized transportation not only changed the landscape but also altered long-standing patterns of living, working, and shopping. If highway builders did not invent suburban settlement—in the greater Los Angeles area the steam and electric railroads had done that—they nonetheless encouraged suburbs to expand and fill in empty spaces until their boundaries fused to form an undifferentiated mass now best described as urban sprawl.

As for aviators who pioneered commercial flight in the 1920s, they used new technologies to leapfrog the mountain-and-desert landscapes of the West. Initially their open-cockpit planes attained so little altitude and used such primitive instruments of navigation that pilots had to thread their way visually through mountain passes. In many parts of the West

tion to reach. In addition, travelers might use horses and buggies—and, as a last resort, their own two feet. Practically speaking, however, the vast majority of westerners overcame problems posed by distance and a sparsely populated countryside by traveling aboard steam-powered trains. The same was true for hauling their freight.

Fortunately, because North American railroads were so highly organized, it is possible today to reconstruct the approximate whereabouts of every scheduled limited or local passenger train operating in the United States or Canada and also to know exactly where the railroad corridors themselves ran, the only exceptions being some commuter and electric interurban lines. Such information is readily accessible because every month, beginning in June 1868, the railroads of North America published their current passenger schedules between the covers of a massive periodical known as *The Official Guide of the Railways and Steam Navigation Lines of the United States, Porto [sic] Rico, Canada, Mexico, and Cuba.*[4]

The bulky *Official Guide,* which was at one time the world's biggest monthly publication, has been aptly described as "the book that gathers no dust" because for years it enjoyed such heavy use in railroad ticket offices. But there was far more to the *Official Guide* than timetables used one month and quickly forgotten the next. "Its files present a faithful history of railroad building—first of individual lines, then their consolidation into large systems, which later were partially broken up into their constituent parts, and finally the taking over for war purposes of all roads by the Federal Government," reminisced its editors on the occasion of the publication's fiftieth anniversary in May 1918.[5]

The inaugural issue of what was christened the *Traveler's Official Railway Guide* contained 280 pages, but in January 1930, when it attained its greatest bulk, the *Official Guide* contained 1,796 pages. The June 1868 guide listed approximately 5,100 railroad stations in the United States and Canada. A little more than sixty years later the jumbo *Official Guide* of January 1930 listed approximately 76,000 stations. The publisher truthfully claimed that "the files of *The Official Guide* contain almost the only record of many phases of transportation development, particularly in the combination of through routes, the accelerated time of trains, the improvement in the comfort of equipment, and many other features which distinguish American travel."[6]

For good reason the book became commonly known as the "Railroad Man's Bible." Once, as the result of a proofreader's error, the *Official Guide* showed a train stopping at a station where the railroad had not officially scheduled it. According to a popular story that circulated through the rail industry, when someone called the mistake to the attention of the head of the railroad's passenger department, he roared, "Dammit, if the *Official Guide* says that train stops there, have it stop."[7]

Each month's *Official Guide* featured an extensive collection of timetables designed to provide information required by the army of ticket agents who formed the vital connecting link between North American

they navigated by following railroad tracks. So vital were the rails to early aviators that one aeronautical engineer suggested in 1930 that railroads "be induced to paint the name of the road at intervals between the rails on the roadbeds of their lines." He believed that such markers "would constitute excellent aids to direction-finding for pilots who have maps which show the names and lines of the various railroads."[3]

Like early-day pilots who navigated across the West by following rail corridors, the road builders often chose to locate their early highways near the tracks; and like the railroad builders, they sought to take full advantage of nature's engineering wherever possible. It made sense to let a river excavate a right-of-way. It was less expensive and far easier to build roads and railroads that way, but by following existing rail corridors, the early highway builders gave the impression that they hoped to maintain contact with kindred spirits in an exceedingly lonely landscape. Highways in the twentieth-century West extended the work originally begun by railroads to develop the countryside.

Climbing to a high plateau located west of Albuquerque, New Mexico, Route 66 closely paralleled the main tracks of the Atchison, Topeka & Santa Fe Railway, though the modest two-lane highway must have at first appeared to be a poor relation compared to the transcontinental railroad whose steel rails, burnished by the wheels of frequent freight and passenger trains, shimmered in the bright New Mexico sun. Here the premier trains of the Santa Fe thundered along main-line tracks that formed a corridor of power between Chicago and Los Angeles. Until the 1930s steam locomotives had hauled them all, and a lingering smudge of coal or oil smoke along the distant horizon graphically heralded the passing of another train. That changed in 1937 when the Santa Fe introduced its diesel-powered "Super Chief" to set a new standard for speed and luxury. The streamliner raced from Lake Michigan and the Pacific Ocean in a mere 39 and ¾ hours, and its state-of-the-art locomotives left scarcely a trace of smoke behind.

The "Super Chief" featured air-conditioning, a recent innovation, throughout its cars and all-private bedrooms, in contrast to the old-fashioned, open-section sleeping cars found on most trains in the United States. Also available were on-board valet, barber, and maid-manicure services; daily market reports; and news bulletins. The dining car featured Fred Harvey meal service, which ranked it among the nation's finest restaurants. The elegance and speed of the "Super Chief" ("Extra Fast—Extra Fine—Extra Fare") helped make the train a favorite of Hollywood moguls and movie stars as well as of more ordinary mortals who had money to spend for such luxuries during the Great Depression years.

Perhaps passengers aboard the Super Chief noticed the road-weary travelers heading west by automobile along Route 66 west of Albuquerque, but probably not. There and elsewhere, when a lengthy stretch of paved highway and railroad paralleled one another, passengers often noticed motorists trying to race the train; but wherever roads and tracks

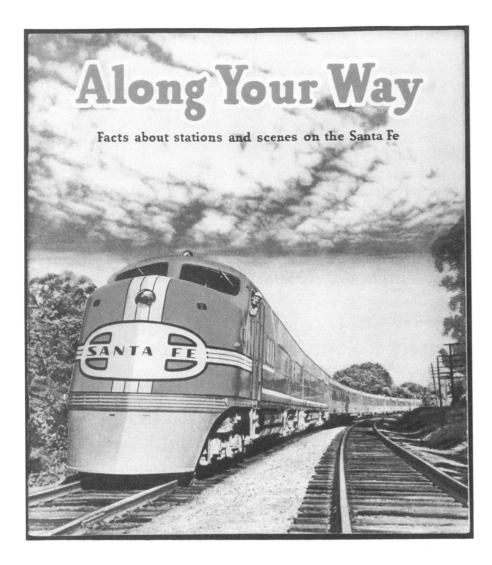

Along Your Way

Facts about stations and scenes on the Santa Fe

The front cover of a post–World War II brochure prepared for travelers depicts one of the newest additions to the Santa Fe's growing fleet of diesel-powered locomotives. Inside is a map and essay drawing an explicit parallel between the historic Santa Fe Trail across the American Southwest and a new one represented by the railroad. Author's collection.

intersected, the speeding train always prevailed. That was one small manifestation of railroad power that any passenger riding aboard an express train could enjoy personally.

Motorists may have paused to watch as one of the Santa Fe's big freight trains steamed ponderously through Laguna Pueblo or as the "Super Chief" flashed briefly into sight and then quickly disappeared over the

horizon. In parts of northern New Mexico and in several farther west in Arizona and California, the rail and highw so similar in some ways and yet so fundamentally different, leled one another and then diverged again—much like thei twentieth-century West.

☙ ☙ ☙

Today it is hard for most people to envision where ra ran in the opening years of the twentieth century. Man have been abandoned and their rails pulled up and sold All that remains of many former right-of-ways is a fain landscape. Even that may have vanished after having be paved over. The many miles of track that do remain company to another as the result of a series of merger often-confusing changes of names. Today's Union Paci out doubt the longest-surviving name in the history of portation, includes sizeable carriers that were themse names—such as Missouri Pacific Lines and the Wester But those two and many more are all but forgotten e and die-hard students of rail history. Likewise, durin membered era a century ago, hundreds, if not thou trains steamed along railroad corridors at any given

Long-distance travel across the American West years of the twentieth century—that is, during the intercity travel by automobile became common—ty ney by train. In a few locations—most notably ale including the sheltered waters of Puget Sound, Sa navigable stretches of the Columbia and Sacrame might choose, for the sake of variety, cost, or conve a scheduled steamship or steamboat. A number offered such service in 1900. Another alternative to was the West's new electric interurban lines; but at few such carriers extended a significant distance city into the countryside, and no interurban railr network of tracks totaling more than a hundred

Except on scattered electric interurban lines ar of the Great Northern Railway across the Cascac where smoke-free electric locomotives kept tra mountain tunnels starting in 1909 (or on the M 1915), thousands of steam locomotives of vario of 37,663 for the United States in 1900) hauled e train that served the West in the opening year: Located beyond the sound of a locomotive wh lets that required a bumpy stagecoach ride fro

railroads and their many passengers. Most casual travelers never gained access to copies of the *Official Guide,* nor did they want to. The massive compilation normally remained well out of their reach behind the wood-and-metal wickets where passengers lined up to buy tickets. But ask a ticket agent a question, and he might moisten an index finger and quickly leaf to the correct page in the *Official Guide.* That feat was not as easy as its sounds. Until recent years, railroad companies were grouped according to "the community of interest" rather than listed in alphabetical order, yet an experienced agent knew exactly where to look. A beginner could, of course, use the *Guide's* comprehensive index of stations.

Month after month for well over a century, the pages of the *Official Guide* faithfully chronicled the expansion, consolidation, and contraction of the railway network across North America. The massive *Official Guide* issued for June 1916—1,600 pages of densely packed information—was typical of the publication during the heyday of railroad passenger service. Today no other single source of information offers a better snapshot of the railroad network across the United States at the time it attained its greatest mileage or does so much to refresh the modern memory about that vanished era.

Statistics compiled annually by the Interstate Commerce Commission (ICC) recorded that as of June 30, 1916, the railroad network of the United States had climbed to a total of 254,251 miles, up 462 miles from the previous year. Until then, the nation's rail mileage had expanded each year since the federal regulatory agency issued its first statistical report in 1888. No one realized in mid-1916 that the nation's rail network had reached a milestone by recording its all-time high. Before another year passed, the United States was at war in Europe, and rails from lightly used or redundant lines were being removed and sold as scrap metal to armament manufacturers.

An earlier issue, the *Official Guide* for January 1900 (1,024 pages long), offers an excellent portrait of the West's web of rail corridors at the dawn of the new century. (The editorial pages of the issue, by the way, discussed at length whether the twentieth century actually began that January or in 1901. Proper timekeeping was long a major concern of the *Official Guide,* and its editors stood at the forefront of the movement that established standard time zones on the railroads of North America in 1883 and hence for the general public of both Canada and the United States.) In January 1900 the track network of the United States totaled 190,833 miles, of which the seventeen contiguous states along or west of the 100th meridian accounted for 51,931 miles, or approximately 27 percent of the whole. The rail network of the East had basically matured by that time, while railroads of the West continued to add track. They accounted for the bulk of the 63,418 miles of new line added in the United States between 1900 and 1916.[8]

The five major railway companies serving the West in 1900 were commonly recognized names—like Ford, Disney, and Microsoft are today—

and their main lines fairly pulsed with the economic energy that defined the rapidly growing region. The January 1900 entry for Southern Pacific Lines in the *Official Guide* totaled eleven pages densely packed with information, which included a detailed map of the sprawling system (8,207 miles long). The tracks of the Southern Pacific, which allowed the company to dominate transportation in California and several other states of the Far West, formed a corridor of power extending from Portland all the way to New Orleans by way of San Francisco and Los Angeles. Another corridor linked San Francisco and Ogden, near the remote Utah site where grandees from the Central Pacific and Union Pacific lines had driven a final, or golden spike, in 1869 to complete the nation's first transcontinental railroad. Numerous additional miles of branch track extended from the Southern Pacific's main lines in 1900.

The *Official Guide* listing recalls that the president of the Southern Pacific Company in early 1900 was Collis P. Huntington, one of the original Big Four, who along with Leland Stanford, Mark Hopkins, and Charles Crocker organized the new Central Pacific. Huntington, the last of a generation of transportation pioneers, died during the first year of the new century, and with him one era closed.

The Northern Pacific Railway (4,620 miles long) dominated a broad corridor of track and land extending across the plains and mountains of the northern West between Saint Paul, Minnesota, and Puget Sound. In 1883 it had become the nation's second transcontinental railroad, and the first built by a single company. The self-proclaimed "Yellowstone Park Line" required six pages to list its passenger timetables in 1900, most of them recording the comings and goings of branch line locals that linked towns and villages in its sparsely populated service territory. The Great Northern Railway, which paralleled the Northern Pacific but at a more northerly location, also required six pages to cover its 4,969 miles of track. On April 25, 1901, the Great Northern and Northern Pacific, two distinct railroads but both controlled by James J. Hill, acquired the Chicago, Burlington & Quincy for $200 a share and thereby gained access to Chicago from Saint Paul.

The Union Pacific System, which billed itself as the "World's Pictorial Line," was in 1900 in the process of trying to rebuild itself after a period of bankruptcy that had seen several former subsidiaries pruned away. Though it had officially shrunk to 2,985 miles of track, the Union Pacific still needed nine pages to list its trains that united Omaha and Kansas City with Portland and Seattle, and with numerous settlements in between. The *Official Guide* published separate listings for the Oregon Short Line Railroad, the Oregon Railroad & Navigation Company, and the St. Joseph & Grand Island Railway, all of which soon returned to the Union Pacific System then being reassembled by financier Edward H. Harriman.

The last of the original Big Five railroads of the West was the Atchison, Topeka & Santa Fe (8,198 miles long in 1900). Its *Official Guide* entry totaled fourteen pages of schedules and other information pertaining to

Commercial photographer Asahel Curtis captured the elegance typical of railroad dining cars in the 1920s. Courtesy Washington State Historical Society.

its trains serving a broad corridor between Chicago and southern California. In addition, a full-page announcement stated: "Shortly after February First 1900 the Atchison, Topeka & Santa Fe Rwy. Co. will announce the completion of its own line to San Francisco." The historical significance of the notice was that the "upstart" Santa Fe (a newcomer when compared to the Southern Pacific, a venerable California institution and truly the most significant power operating within the state's borders) was poised to

Transportation Corridors Transform the West • 47

invade the Southern Pacific's San Francisco stronghold and headquarters city.

In 1900 it seemed likely that the Chicago, Milwaukee, & St. Paul would reach west to the Pacific from the end of its track in South Dakota. Already it had extended 8,760 miles of track across the grain, timber, and mineral-rich belts west and north of Chicago and grown exceedingly prosperous as a result. Perhaps the 8,322-mile Chicago & North Western Line would reach west from the end of its track in central Wyoming; or the Chicago, Rock Island, and Pacific (3,819 miles long) would do so from New Mexico. A dark horse in America's ongoing transcontinental sweepstakes was the St. Louis–San Francisco, which reached west from Saint Louis into Oklahoma; but in 1900 any movement toward its stated goal had stalled a long way from the Pacific Coast.

Of this group of potential transcontinental railroads in 1900, only the Chicago, Milwaukee & St. Paul actually made it to the Pacific. It publicly announced its intention in late 1905 and completed a line to Puget Sound four years later. The other "missing link" finished after the start of the twentieth century was the Western Pacific Railway, which on August 22, 1910, commenced service between Salt Lake City and Oakland to form a new transcontinental corridor between Oakland and the East Coast by working closely with the Denver & Rio Grande and other existing railroads. In reference to the impressive trackside scenery through California's Feather River Canyon, it boasted that it ran "one hundred miles through Wonderland."

Supplementing the biggest transcontinental railroads, systems, and aspirants were middle-sized regional carriers like the 1,142-mile Colorado & Southern Railway and the Denver & Rio Grande Railroad, the self-styled "Scenic Line of the World," which operated 1,673 miles of track—both narrow-gauge (3 feet between the rails) and standard-gauge (4 feet 8 ½ inches between the rails)—in mountainous country west of the Colorado capital. Finally, there were several dozen short-line railroads of varying lengths.

It is difficult if not impossible to generalize about the mixed bag of short-line railroads that once linked the West's interior mining and sawmill towns and farm centers to the metropolitan corridors formed by main-line carriers. Many of their corporate titles proclaimed grand ambitions that they seldom had the resources to realize. For instance, the Wyoming & Missouri River Railroad in 1899 opened an 18-mile line of track due west from Belle Fourche, in South Dakota's Black Hills country, to serve the coal camp of Aladdin, Wyoming; but its trains never did run anywhere near the Missouri River.

Maps in the *Official Guide* reveal that from the latticework of main-line corridors, branch tracks reached out to serve any settlements of consequence. The major railroads owned some of these, while others were small and independent, at least initially. Perhaps typical of the various short lines serving the West's outback was the Santa Fe, Prescott & Phoenix Railway, which operated its freight and passenger trains between the Santa Fe main line at Ash Fork and the desert outpost of Phoenix, Arizona, a distance of 196 miles. The Santa Fe, Prescott & Phoenix used its full-page listing in the *Official Guide* of January 1900 to boast that the copper mines of Arizona "are being demonstrated as the largest and richest producers in the World." Elsewhere it bragged that "health seekers and tourists" would find the Salt River Valley to have a mild, dry climate "where flowers bloom out doors and vegetation is green during the winter." It praised the area around Phoenix as a land with "no snow, no freezing weather, and very little rain."[9] The Santa Fe, Prescott & Phoenix Railway, like many similar carriers in 1900, would one day be acquired by one of the region's transcontinental giants.

Most of the important railroad corridors extending across the western portion of the United States in 1900 ran from east to west. The main north-south exceptions were the lines that linked Salt Lake City with Butte, Montana; Omaha and Kansas City with Billings and the far Northwest; and Los Angeles, San Francisco, Portland, and Seattle. However, not until late March 1901 did the Southern Pacific's newly completed Coast Line connect San Francisco and Los Angeles by way of San Jose and Santa Barbara. "It passes through some of the most beautiful coast and mountain scenery in California, through the celebrated resorts of Santa Cruz and Monterey, and near various other points of interest including Stanford University, the Big Trees, the Santa Cruz Mountains, the Lick Observatory, and numerous Old Missions founded by the Franciscan Friars in their early settlement in California, and it opens up a country famous for its fruit and dairy products."[10]

Before this, the sole rail link between San Francisco and Los Angeles had passed through the state's San Joaquin Valley. The trains traveled at such a leisurely pace that coastal steamships offered vigorous competition to the Southern Pacific—at least those steamships that the railroad did not already own. The January 1900 *Official Guide* listed a fleet of coastal steamers that since the 1850s had maintained dependable service between the ports of California and the Pacific Northwest. One of them, the Pacific Coast Steamship Company, could boast of a corporate name even more venerable than that of the Great Northern Railway or the Atchison, Topeka, and Santa Fe. In 1900 several ocean-going carriers competed with railroads for coastwise passenger and freight traffic, though typically the Pacific Coast Steamship Company did more business than its several maritime rivals combined.

Commencing in 1915, two luxury liners of the Great Northern Pacific Steamship Company, the *Great Northern* and *Northern Pacific,* sailed between San Francisco and Astoria, Oregon, near the mouth of the Columbia River, where trains sped passengers to and from Portland. The railroad owners of the "Twin Palaces of the Pacific" boasted that both vessels were "luxuriously furnished and have many comfortable public halls and lounges, including a smoking-room with an open fireplace and

Beyond the totem pole, long a landmark in Seattle's Pioneer Square, a two-car interurban train pauses in the heart of the city's commercial district in 1904. The photographer, Asahel Curtis, did not record whether it had arrived from Tacoma, at the other end of the line, or was soon headed there. Courtesy Washington State Historical Society.

a large amount of deck room." They featured "palm garden verandas, sun parlors, glass-enclosed promenades." Their staterooms were "large and comfortably furnished, many of them have iron beds and private baths, and there are several commodious suites." Travel time between San Francisco and Portland was slightly more than thirty hours, which in 1915 compared favorably with the Southern Pacific trains that linked the two cities in twenty-six hours. The fare by ship was the same as by train, but it included meals and a sleeping berth. Likewise, the fastest trains on the Southern Pacific's Coast Line required about fourteen hours to complete a trip between San Francisco and Los Angeles, while the steamships *Harvard* and *Yale* required nineteen hours to complete the same journey overnight.[11]

For all its bulk and wealth of details, the *Official Guide* in the early twentieth century overlooked some modes of transportation. It clearly favored steam-powered railroads. As service areas of the West's major electric interurban railroads expanded during the decade after 1900, some of them—most notably the Oregon Electric Railway, linking Portland with Eugene and numerous towns of the Willamette Valley in between; the Spokane and Inland Empire Railroad, extending service across the rolling wheat fields of eastern Washington between Spokane and Moscow, Idaho; and the Pacific Electric Railway, blanketing the greater Los Angeles area— eventually listed their passenger schedules in its pages, but timetables for most of the West's several dozen interurban lines never appeared in the *Official Guide*. Absent too are listings for hundreds of local stagecoach lines that once supplemented railway service. In several places by 1916 operators ran motorized stages, but in some remote parts of the West horse-drawn conveyances prevailed into the 1920s.

All in all, the *Official Guide* was far better at recording change and continuity within the railroad industry than in anticipating any future trends in the competitive mix of transportation of all types. In January 1900, for instance, the *Official Guide* listing for the Colorado & Southern Railway noted: "The season at the famous Winter Resorts of the South and Southeast is at hand." The railroad main line linked Colorado and Texas with standard-gauge tracks, though the Colorado & Southern also operated diminutive trains on several narrow-gauge branch lines extending southwest from Denver to serve isolated mountain mining camps such as Breckenridge and Keystone. Those two places and many others later became famous ski resorts, but in 1900 the Colorado & Southern ignored the powder snows of the Rocky Mountains in its advertisements. At the time, snow of any type was nothing but an operational headache. Likewise silent on the attraction of Rocky Mountain snows was the Denver & Rio Grande Railroad, which ran narrow-gauge trains to several additional mining camps west of Denver.

Only after World War II did the mountain mining towns of Colorado become world-class winter resorts. Like the future appeal of the Sunbelt, the joy of vacations spent frolicking in Rocky Mountain snows had yet to be invented—or at least popularized. Railroads in the early twentieth century did promote a "See America First" campaign that sought to generate passenger traffic by "systematic exploitation of American scenery." A focal point of these campaigns was the West's several national parks and monuments, notably Yellowstone, Yosemite, Grand Canyon, Glacier, and Mount Rainier. Each one had a major railroad to promote it as a tourist destination.[12]

For more than two generations, railroads wielded power to define major aspects of life in the United States and Canada. Perhaps for that reason, no rail executive in 1916 could fully anticipate the competitive jolt soon to be administered by a rapidly expanding network of all-weather roads and highways and an ever-increasing number of people traveling in their private automobiles. Even so, the portents of disturbing trends ahead were obvious from hindsight. Consider only this one statistic: during 1915 alone, railroad companies mired in receivership accounted for some 42,000 miles of line, or fully one-sixth the entire rail mileage of the United States. Financial misfortune of this magnitude had never before occurred in the history of American railroads.

Another statistic of significance was that during 1915 the average price of a new automobile fell below $2,000 for the first time since the young industry attained national stature. Some new models sold for less than $400. In addition, for the first time in modern history Congress in 1916 provided federal dollars to states to encourage them to build better highways to accommodate the growing number of automobiles. In 1915 a total of 2,446,000 motorcars and trucks were registered in the continental United States. Just five years later, despite major disruptions caused by war, the number had swelled to 9,232,000. Railroad power would never be the same, and neither would the familiar transportation landscape of the West. Already by the early 1920s a network of road and highway corridors was expanding rapidly across the region.

In their own way, the nation's highways came to serve as significant corridors of power, though initially they were certainly unimpressive when compared to the main lines of the railroads. Early roads, some of them more fittingly called trails, frequently ambled across the open landscape of the West with no discernable goal in mind—at least none that lay beyond the borders of a particular city or county or congressional district. At the city limits or county lines or state boundaries, a good paved road might abruptly degenerate into a mediocre gravel path. Early roads were the products mainly of local interests, local politics, and local minds.

The *Rand McNally Auto Road Atlas of the United States* (first issued in the mid-1920s) visually delineated the rapid evolution of America's highway corridors, much as the *Official Guide* did for the railroads. The 1926 *Auto Road Atlas* graphically depicts a jumble of roads and highways of varying quality and meandering configuration, all of which said a great deal about the intense localism and "pork barrel" politics that too often prevailed in those early years.

If highways of the West did eventually evolve into true corridors of power, it was only because of the power of individual motorists multiplied many millions of times until the aggregate, the "motoring public," made its collective voice heard clearly in state legislatures and on Capitol Hill. The result was more and better highways to serve the always-growing number of motorists waiting impatiently for ribbons to be cut so that they could zoom along new corridors in the latest model cars. Curiously, and to bring the cycle of popular demand and government response back to where it began, it became common for individual motorists to imagine any new stretch of highway had been constructed expressly for them. Drivers seemed to bond personally with the nation's highway network in the 1920s and 1930s, something train travelers frequently found impossible to do with large and aloof railroad companies.

While individual automobiles were at first unimpressive machines of change, in the aggregate the American automobile acquired a truly awesome power to influence the national economy and humble the once all-powerful railroad industry. That reversal of fortune was as unthinkable at the dawn of the new century as passage of a law requiring speeding passenger trains to halt for any motorist who dared to cross the tracks ahead of a locomotive.

Route 66, like the tracks of the Santa Fe Railway, linked Chicago and Los Angeles; but highway travelers were typically a more plebian crowd than folks who crossed the West in the lap of luxury aboard the "Super Chief" and the other premier trains. Regardless of the railroad, all transcontinental limiteds featured elegant dining cars, club cars, and sleepers. On the other hand, for motorists on Route 66, long-distance travel typically meant commonplace lodging, service stations redolent with the odor of grease and gasoline, and roadside cafes—places often synonymous with the breakdowns, heartburn, and heartbreak that defined a highway habitat. Nonetheless, there was something so magical about Route 66 and its "grassroots democracy" that it became the quintessential road trip for two generations of Americans.

In a post–World War II song recorded by more than two hundred artists, most notably Nat "King" Cole, the entertainment industry advised Americans to "Get Your Kicks on Route '66." During the 1960s a popular television series called *Route 66*, which featured catchy theme music by Nelson Riddle, gave the highway an added boost. Back in the mid-1930s, however, the music appropriate to the Joad family and their real-life counterparts struggling to reach California was Woody Guthrie's dust-bowl ballad that began, "So long, it's been good to know you."

It should be noted here that many dispossessed or jobless people bidding "so long" to rural Oklahoma and other hard places in the 1930s

"'BOES" BEATING THEIR WAY TO N. DAKO
ON A C. & N.W. FREIGHT

Crowded atop the freight cars of a Chicago & North Western train, migratory workers are headed to the grain fields of North and South Dakota during August 1914. War is imminent in Europe. Only later would some of these men likely follow the harvest in their automobiles. Courtesy South Dakota State Historical Society.

88742

PHOTO BY
HERSEY & HERSEY
HECLA, S. D.

TRAIN AUG. 13–1914

traveled in search of more promising locations by rail, much as earlier generations had done, by stealing aboard empty boxcars or huddling together in open gondolas. Steinbeck's impoverished Joad family were actually better off than sojourners by rail because they drove an automobile of their own to California. In fact, the number of motor vehicles registered in Oklahoma between 1930 and 1935 dropped by almost 50,000, from 550,000 to 502,000. The state of Oklahoma accounted for nearly one-seventh of a nationwide decline of 314,000 registered vehicles. The Joads motoring west could be thankful for small blessings.

Owning an automobile, even a well-used one, made a symbolic statement, much as was true also for Route 66 or the best passenger trains of the railroads of the West. As nothing else, an automobile was a token of status to the many dispossessed people who owned none at all.

Driving along Route 66, no less than luxuriating aboard one of the passenger trains of the Atchison, Topeka & Santa Fe Railway, was never simply a matter of basic transportation, as vital as that feature of the journey was. During the final years of the nineteenth century, a growing web of rails also refashioned the West into expansive new landscapes of production. Far more than was typical either of the East or South, the post–Civil War West became whatever railroads willed for it; and big companies transformed the everyday lives of westerners more fundamentally than early-day operators of freight wagons, stagecoaches, and steamboats had ever dreamed of doing. As late as the 1930s, the American West remained heavily dependent on railroads, and that included ports of the Pacific and Gulf coasts, where the trains and ships exchanged their cargoes.

Railroads defined the region's modern landscape, not just by where they located (or failed to locate) their tracks, as obvious as that impact was; but they also stirred the popular imagination by issuing numerous promotional brochures and pamphlets, all intended to sell the West to prospective settlers and tourists. The West of the 1920s and 1930s was still a product of railroad politics, finance, engineering, and marketing ingenuity, as it had been for the previous sixty years, though the relentless growth of highways and skyways steadily undercut that power. Even so, no matter how automobiles or highways or even transcontinental skyways entered the national consciousness or what they foreshadowed, railroad power continued to define major aspects of life in the West at least until after World War II. That was the era when railroads ruled.

The cover of a Northern Pacific brochure that in the early 1930s advertised the "Scenic Route Across America." The rear platform offered passengers the best vantage point from which to view the passing landscape. Author's collection.

Two

When Railroads Ruled

The mountainous Bitterroot divide separating Montana and northern Idaho is a very lonely place today. It was not always so. Massive electric locomotives—"the largest of their class in the world"—once hauled heavy freights of the Milwaukee Road upgrade and through a 1.7-mile-long tunnel bored beneath St. Paul Pass. Through here ran the "Olympian" and the "Columbian," two premier passenger trains between Chicago and Tacoma and Seattle on Puget Sound. In their heyday, railroad dining cars brought to this remote place a display of elegance usually found only in posh hotels or restaurants. Today my lunch choices are simple. I can feast on the trail mix I brought along in my backpack, or I can go hungry.

In former years the loud hum of electric locomotives grinding slowly upgrade broke the mountain stillness, and flanged wheels squealed as long freight trains rounded a horseshoe curve that helped them gain elevation within the narrow confines of the valley. That hum was once the sound of what the railroad grandly advertised as "The Dawn of the Electrical Era in Railroading." [1] The loudest sound I hear today is that of mountain bike tires crunching along a gravel path. In some places I also can hear mountain water cascading downhill to the St. Joe River on its way to the Columbia River and the Pacific Ocean. Bonneville and other dams will use it to generate electrical power ("white coal"), though nearly three decades have passed since it last energized the trains that passed through here. There are plenty of other markets for electricity, however.

The first thirteen miles of the Hiawatha Trail were opened to the public on May 29, 1998. Exactly two years later I biked with my family along the former railroad right-of way. The route, which descended gradually from the snow-blanketed peaks of the Bitterroot Range into the upper valley of Idaho's

High in the Bitterroot Mountains where the Hiawatha Trail extends today, an enthusiastic Warren G. Harding played railroad engineer in 1923 as he eased the gargantuan electric locomotives of his Presidential Special downhill into Avery, Idaho. The talented photographer Asahel Curtis recorded the scene, never to be repeated because Harding died unexpectedly in San Francisco on his way back to the White House from Alaska. Courtesy Washington State Historical Society.

St. Joe River, passed through several abandoned tunnels and over high steel trestles. Biking along the old right-of-way some twenty years after the last freight trains thundered down this grade, I ponder the financial reverses that humbled a once-mighty railroad—the Chicago, Milwaukee, St. Paul & Pacific—and what that story of decline revealed about railroad power in the twentieth-century West. I need to understand railroad power in the broadest sense of the word as well as what it means in terms of watts and volts that energized locomotives and trains.

For that reason, remnants of a once-extensive overhead electric system that powered Milwaukee Road locomotives for more than fifty years particularly fascinated me. Beginning in late 1916, seven years after the line reached the shores of Puget Sound, electric locomotives began to haul passengers and freight over the mountainous stretch of track between Montana and Idaho. The Milwaukee Road bragged that it was "offering to tourists a novel attraction in its electrified service across the Rocky Mountains for 230 miles." [2] That proved just the beginning. The railroad electrified additional miles of track through the Rocky Mountains as well as through the Cascade Mountains farther west.

The state-of-the-art installation and a radically different kind of locomotive—"It uses no coal, requires no water and has no ashes to dump; it carries no tender and has no boiler, and will run indefinitely at a uniform rate of speed"—formed the centerpiece of the world's most extensive railroad electrification project at the time. Its completion thrilled regional promoters, jaded travelers, and even science fiction writers. "That this great project has excited universal interest," noted the *Official Guide,* "is evidenced by the fact that the Russian Government Commission on its recent trip to Washington [1917] chose this route across the continent in order to observe the electrification." [3]

The Milwaukee Road prepared "motion picture films and stereopticon slides" to show to audiences in "motion picture houses, schools, colleges, churches and fraternal society entertainments." The first of these, known as the "Electrification Film," dealt with its stretch of wonder railroad through the Rocky Mountains. In addition, there was "a film describing a trip through the Cascade Mountains and a series of stereopticon slides, 100 in number, which take one on a trip from Chicago to the western terminals of the road at Seattle and Tacoma. Any of these films and slides [would] be cheerfully loaned for exhibition purposes" upon application to the general passenger manager of the Chicago, Milwaukee & St. Paul Railway at its Chicago headquarters. [4]

Viewing the former right-of-way as a secluded hiking and biking trail, it is difficult to recall that the Rockefellers with their oil-soaked millions were once major investors in the Chicago, Milwaukee & St. Paul. That was back in the early twentieth century when the anticipated return on investment from the railroad's projected extension to the Pacific seemed as good as gold in the bank.

What went wrong was that the railroads of the West roared into the twentieth century propelled as much by a full measure of confidence as by steam. The industry had every reason to be supremely confident. During the last third of a century since the end of the Civil War in 1865, railroads had done nothing less than refashion the landscape of the American West, and in 1900 they seemed poised to do still more of the same. Why not? At the dawn of the new century there remained much land and few people in the West. The need to develop the region seemed clear to anyone even remotely interested in railroads as blue-chip investments.[5]

The railroad in 1900 continued to be the most advanced technology capable of taming the West. By contrast, the automobile was still basically a toy of the rich. There were only eight thousand automobiles in the entire United States in 1900 and only about 150 miles of paved roads for them to use. No wonder the railroads remained unchallenged as the dominant transportation technology as well as the biggest business in the United States.

In every western state, railroads individually and collectively wielded enormous power. They dominated the constitutional conventions of the newest states and had no misgivings about flexing their corporate muscles to cajole legislators into writing laws favorable to them. The popular expression "to be railroaded" connoted their impressive political and economic power. Railroad power also generated sizeable fortunes for astute investors.

At the dawn of the new century there was every reason to believe that railroad power would continue indefinitely. So much remained to be done to develop the land—to "win the West" as it was popularly phrased. Railroads were there to do the job—for a price, of course. Not everyone was happy to pay that price. Farmers had complained for years about high railroad freight rates, yet no one could deny that in much of the West the railroads made commercial agriculture viable or that they nurtured the rise of impressive new cities.

∗∗∗ ∗∗∗ ∗∗∗

The Chicago, Milwaukee & St. Paul was fated to be among the last lines to push west to the Pacific coast of the United States and thereby join the ranks of the big transcontinental railroads, though few observers then foresaw the end of an era. In 1905, when the St. Paul (as it was popularly known) made its ambitious plans public, it was a long-established, exceedingly prosperous Midwestern carrier. There was justification for the Rockefellers and other moneyed people to invest their dollars in such a well-regarded enterprise. Its common stock sold for almost $200 a share that year and returned a solid dividend to investors. "As a dividend earner," observed the respected financial analyst Carl Snyder in 1907, the St. Paul had a record "unsurpassed" by any western railway. He was cautious about endorsing its Pacific extension, yet he concluded that it was "absurd" to fear that the likely cost "could seriously cripple so rich and prosperous a road as the St. Paul."[6]

Reaching for the Pacific from a point near Mobridge, South Dakota, on the Missouri River, the St. Paul aimed for Seattle, 1,489 miles away. Its leaders seemed determined to spare no expense as they built a solid, well-

No 8 ROUND HOUSE AVERY IDAHO,

Wesley Andrews photographed the roundhouse in Avery, Idaho, in the 1920s, where the Milwaukee Road's steam and electric locomotives exchanged their loads. The town was named for Avery Rockefeller, a member of the oil-rich family that had invested in the railroad. Courtesy Oregon Historical Society.

engineered line. Instead of the cheap wooden trestles used to support the first transcontinental railway, they invested in heavy steel and concrete bridges—the same massive ones that now seem so ludicrously overbuilt for bicycles using the Hiawatha Trail. The St. Paul celebrated the opening of its Pacific extension in 1909, almost exactly forty years after dignitaries drove a last spike to complete the nation's first transcontinental railroad at Promontory, Utah.

There was no compelling reason in 1909 to think that America's railway age would end, at least not in the foreseeable future. So great was the confidence of St. Paul executives in continued prosperity that in 1913 they announced plans for a technological feat almost as breathtaking as their original push to the Pacific. They planned to electrify mountainous portions of their line, something no other trunk line elsewhere in the world had attempted on so grand a scale. Management was certain that operation of passenger and freight trains by electricity instead of steam would save it considerable money. "It is calculated that the economies of operation will be effected as a result of this electrical installation sufficient to pay for the cost, $15,000,000, in five years and to increase the capacity of the track to an extent equivalent to that of a second track over the entire distance."[7]

Who in 1913 could foresee both the corporate and personal grief caused by the soaring cost of financing the Pacific Coast extension and its electrification—or, worse, the unexpectedly low revenues the new line generated? Commodity traffic heading east from Puget Sound failed to grow as management originally anticipated primarily because an enormous amount of that freight instead sailed by ship through the Panama Canal after it opened for traffic in 1914. Likewise, Milwaukee Road executives failed to anticipate how rapidly or easily a growing fleet of private automobiles could, like a great army of termites, eat gaping holes in their passenger revenues.

Weighted down by its accumulated troubles—some self-inflicted and others wholly impossible for management to anticipate—the Milwaukee Road in 1918 failed to pay a dividend on its common stock for the first time since 1892. The economic slump that affected the collective pocketbook of the Pacific Northwest in the early 1920s added to the railroad's woes. Shocked and angered by its unending financial plight, onlookers pointed accusatory fingers in all directions. The supposed villains ranged from deceitful management to incompetent government regulators.

As the price of St. Paul common stock trended ever lower between 1916 and 1925, it traced the sagging fortunes of a once-mighty company. Unable to pay $48 million worth of bonds when they matured, the railroad passed to the hands of receivers. It was the largest business failure in the history of the United States to that time. A share of its common stock sold for the almost unbelievable low price of 3¼. The debacle that occurred in March 1925 turned out to be only the first of three episodes of bankruptcy for the troubled enterprise.

When the railroad emerged from receivership two years later as the Chicago, Milwaukee, St. Paul & Pacific—or simply the Milwaukee Road —it remained financially the weakest of the nation's transcontinental railways. Finally, as the 1970s gave way to the 1980s, a once-again-bankrupt Milwaukee Road chose to dismember its line west of Miles City, Montana. Its last freight train ran east from Tacoma in March 1980.

Bicycling today along the Hiawatha Trail through the Bitterroot Mountains, one finds it hard to believe that this gravel path essentially offers a history lesson, a corporate case study of the type taught in business schools. It is equally hard to recall how tracks laid in this remote place once connected with a steel network that encompassed many portions of the American West—each such corridor enabling railroad power to pulse between the region's major metropolitan centers as well as outward from cities to energize numerous jerkwater hamlets, the out-of-the-way places tucked deep in the mountain canyons of Colorado or Idaho or elsewhere. The term "jerkwater," it should be noted, derives from the large water tanks that steam railroads once located at intervals alongside their tracks. At such places, engine crews paused and jerked down a large spout to replenish the water supply required by thirsty locomotives. In time "jerkwater" became a synonym for remote and insignificant communities, many of which, if they managed to survive in the latter twentieth century, were no longer even served by railroads.

Whether in hamlets or cities, railroad stations represented the most important links between communities and the "metropolitan corridor," as the Harvard landscape historian John Stilgoe aptly characterized the rail network.[8] Moreover, the day-to-day activity that took place in railroad stations showcased the power of paper. That is, though the well-known metal steel provided a popular metaphor for railroad power, the power of western railroads was never merely a matter of iron and steel, coal and oil, or muscle and brains. It was also a matter of paper.

Running a railroad required a veritable mountain of paper. Apart from paper money itself, there were ornate stock certificates issued to investors, timetables, waybills, employee timecards, ledgers, reports, and so on. To operate successfully, even a small company used many different forms of paper, and larger lines generated many tons of it annually. An article called "The Red Tape Worm," written by an employee of the San Pedro, Los Angeles & Salt Lake Railroad, described how federal regulators in the pre–World War I era required railroads to generate paper documents, "all part of the unnecessary 'red tape'" that had been "crowded upon railroad management by the exacting requirements of Governmental commissions."[9]

The form of railroad paper most familiar to the traveling public was probably a ticket, followed by the timetable. Railroad companies typi-

F. Jay Haynes photographed Northern Pacific locomotive 140 taking on water at Livingston, Montana, in 1886. Courtesy Montana Historical Society.

cally maintained well-stocked racks of timetables outside the ticket windows of their stations. Timetables were free for the taking. In addition, besides displaying the timetables issued by dozens of different carriers, they often stocked their racks with railroad promotional brochures. The array of timetables and brochures available at any time varied widely from station to station, but in the early-twentieth-century West no federal or state organization worked harder than the railroads to advertise the region to would-be settlers or to lure travelers to experience for themselves its scenic splendors.

The San Pedro, Los Angeles & Salt Lake Railroad passenger timetable issued in 1915 was typical of its genre in that it contained schedules not only for that company but also for the various subsidiaries, connecting railroads, and electric interurban lines that fed traffic to it. The folder offers a good promontory from which to view key aspects of travel in the West at the height of the railway era. In mid-1915 the "Salt Lake Route," as the San Pedro, Los Angeles & Salt Lake popularly billed itself, used its public timetable to advertise summer trips to the Panama-Pacific Exposition in San Francisco and the Panama-California Exposition in San Diego—"the most beautiful of world's expositions." It advised travelers that "the entire Pacific Coast is prepared to entertain a multitude of visitors during the year 1915, with the best of accommodations at reasonable rates."

One item conspicuously missing was any mention of Las Vegas as a tourist destination. At that time it certainly was not. Las Vegas was only a stop on the way to someplace else. "Stopovers of ten days at Las Vegas, Nev., will be allowed on all classes of westbound tickets from the East, to afford passengers an opportunity to visit the various mining districts reached via the Las Vegas & Tonapah R. R. and connecting lines." Among the named trains pausing in Las Vegas for servicing were the "Overland Express," the "Colorado-California Limited," and the "Pacific Limited," a misnomer because that slow train made nearly all stops along the 811 miles that separated Salt Lake City and San Pedro. The railroad's flagship was the "Los Angeles Limited," which operated between Chicago (via the Union Pacific and Chicago & North Western) and its namesake city in California. It featured an observation club car, "free reclining chair car," dining car, "electric lighted drawing room," and sleepers in a variety of room configurations. "News bulletins and stock reports are posted in observation cars en route."

The Salt Lake Route invited travelers to stop over at Riverside, California, to see orange groves—"thousands of acres of golden orange trees representing an investment of millions of dollars. From these same trees are shipped oranges to all parts of the world." Also of interest in southern California was Universal City, "the greatest photoplay city on earth; 10 miles north of Los Angeles by electric railway or automobile. Built and operated by the Universal Film Co., occupying hundreds of acres, with permanent concrete buildings. Visitors are welcomed and given an opportunity of seeing pictures made by several different companies of players."

The 1915 timetable of the Salt Lake Route listed station elevations— 4,260 feet for Salt Lake City and 267 feet for Los Angeles—and populations for each stop. Los Angeles had 550,000 residents, Salt Lake City 125,000, and Las Vegas a mere 1,500. San Pedro, the city at the end of the line, had 8,500 people. It was important to the railroad because it was a major port serving southern California.

The Salt Lake Route offered frequent commuter service between Los Angeles and San Bernardino, a testimony to growing suburban sprawl in the area defined by Pomona, Ontario, and Riverside, as well as Los Angeles itself. Conversely, the 1915 timetable addressed the opposite end of the settlement spectrum by listing "Stage and Automobile Connections" to a host of tiny towns in Nevada and Utah outback. And while in Utah, "Don't fail to visit Bingham Copper Mines." Perhaps that advice was to be expected of a railroad financed in part from copper dollars. "Real mining camp life may be seen at this greatest copper producing camp in the world. Visit the mine and the mammoth smelters near Garfield." This "wonderful scenic trip" required an hour's ride from Salt Lake City and could be reached via Salt Lake Route and the Bingham & Garfield Railroad. The railroad also invited travelers to Salt Lake City to "hear the great organ in the Mormon Tabernacle. Free recitals at noon."

As was typical for timetables issued by railroads serving the Pacific Coast in the early twentieth century, the Salt Lake Route advertised coastal steamship service. Its preferred carrier was the Pacific Navigation Company, which operated the steamships *Yale* and *Harvard* from Los Angeles to San Diego and San Francisco. "Luxurious and fast." Railroads hoped that such timetables would not only serve as valuable souvenirs of a trip but also provide an inducement for readers "to go and see for themselves."[10]

Among the timetables that might be found on a typical station rack was an especially colorful one issued in 1902 by the Colorado Midland Railway, which billed itself as the "Pikes Peak Route." Its striking cover featured an Indian warrior astride a white stallion looking down the tracks to Pikes Peak. On the inside pages a publicist extolled the scenic appeal of Hagerman Pass—"The Crowning Glory of all the Wonders of the Rocky Mountains."[11] The 310-mile Colorado Midland Railway was in many ways no different from other small to medium-sized carriers that supplemented service by the major railroads across the West. What set the Colorado Midland Railway apart was that its unkind fate foreshadowed the troubles that lay ahead in the 1920s for railroads of the American West. In 1917 it became the first railroad line of any consequence in the United States to be completely abandoned. Never before had so much standard-gauge railroad track simply been pulled up and sold for scrap.

Just seventeen years earlier, few prophets would have predicted such a thing. Ever since the famous "wedding" of the rails at Promontory, Utah, in 1869, railroad mileage in the West had increased every year. After a four-year lull in construction activity caused by the nationwide depression that began in 1893, the pace of track laying picked up again in 1897. Animated by the optimism derived from observing all the positive changes rails had wrought in the hitherto "empty" landscapes, railroad executives extended still more corridors. Nothing seemed likely to slow the pace of construction.

Railroad empire builders continued to battle one another for control of valuable territory. Among the railroad barons of legendary status were James J. Hill and Edward H. Harriman, who sparred with one another all across the Pacific Northwest. Spurred on by oversized egos as much as by hard data that led them to aggrandize their holdings, Hill and Harriman between them gained control of the bulk of the railway mileage across the American West.

The Canadian-born Hill had extended the tracks of his Great Northern Railway between Saint Paul and Seattle in 1893, but for two more decades he worked to fill in the gaps, to develop the land through which Great Northern tracks passed. In the process he earned the laudatory title of "Empire Builder." Harriman won control of the financially ailing Union Pacific shortly before the dawn of the new century and rebuilt it from the roadbed up. Furthermore, after the death of Collis P. Huntington in 1900, Harriman gained control of the Southern Pacific System, which included steamship lines in the Gulf of Mexico and on the Pacific Coast. For a time, Harriman controlled the world's largest railroad empire.

That said, it should be noted that in 1900 the assessed value of railroads of the United States totaled slightly more than $31 billion, of which the states and territories located west of the Mississippi River (including Minnesota, but not Louisiana, Alaska, or Hawaii) accounted for a mere 20 percent. Nonetheless, the railroad industry loomed exceedingly large in the West in 1900 because the region was so sparsely populated and so ripe for development, at least in the eyes of the railroaders and their allies.

Every major railroad listed in the *Official Guide* included a roster of its top executives. Despite the undeniable power that names like Harriman and Hill connoted, the Hills and Harrimans of the railroad industry represented only the proverbial tip of the iceberg in terms of the great armies of employees that made freight and passenger service possible. Travel by train was an almost universal experience in the turn-of-the-century West, and aboard any of the region's hundreds of daily passenger trains travelers had a chance to observe first hand the hierarchy of railroad power.

On board any train the most visible representative of the enterprise that ran it was the conductor. Resplendent in his uniform—a blue broadcloth coat trimmed with shiny brass buttons, a dark vest, watch pocket and gold chain, and black trousers—and looking very much like a ranking military officer, a conductor represented the power and majesty of the railroad company when he collected a passenger's ticket.

Furthermore, the conductor, not the locomotive engineer, was the employee officially in charge of the train; and every train, whether it hauled passengers or freight or both (mixed trains were commonly found on lightly patronized branch lines), had its own conductor. Standing behind him on all but the shortest railroads was an army of workers, their collective responsibility being to see that his train operated on time and reached its destination safely. In 1900 the legions of railroad employees in the United States had for the first time topped a million people. More specifically, those ranks included a total of 29,957 conductors; 42,837 enginemen; 44,130 firemen; 50,789 switchmen, flagmen, and watchmen; 26,218 telegraphers, operators, and dispatchers; and many more.

Peter Britt, a photographer and artist based in southern Oregon, immortalized a conductor on the Rogue River Valley Railroad. Prominently displayed are his pocket watch and signal lantern, two key tools of his trade. Courtesy Southern Oregon Historical Society.

Uppermost in the mind of every conductor was the question of time, and the big brass pocket watch that he often consulted was an integral part of his uniform. In the West especially, where railroad lines typically consisted of a single track with sidings (or turnouts) spaced at intervals to permit two trains to pass one another, safety demanded accurate time-keeping. Safe operations required all railroad conductors and engineers to obey thick books of rules, employee timetables, and special orders and to pay attention to time accurate to the minute. Meeting places of trains had to be designated precisely in terms of hours and minutes to prevent collisions.

Accident-free operation further demanded that train crewmembers carefully synchronize their watches at the beginning of each run. For that reason the boundary lines between standard time zones invariably coincided with places where crews paused to hand off train operations to one another. Railroad towns like Mandan, North Dakota, on the Northern Pacific; North Platte, Nebraska, on the Union Pacific; and Dodge City, Kansas, on the Santa Fe marked the boundary between the Central and Mountain Time zones.

Time zones were themselves a railroad invention. None existed in any part of the West before November 18, 1883, the "day of two noons," when major railroads across the United States and Canada reset countless watches and clocks at high noon and thereby arbitrarily reduced at least forty-nine different time standards used by railroads into five standard zones (including Atlantic in eastern Canada), all without any authorization from state, provincial, or national governments. "God Almighty fixed the time for us," thundered one opponent of the change; and he complained that "a lot of railroad superintendents had fixed this new time to suit themselves." On the other hand, when it came to resolving local confusion about time, "the people will be as much if not more benefited by the change than the railroads," noted the *Pittsburgh Leader*. No national time legislation followed until 1918, when Congress passed legislation to save daylight and thus conserve valuable fuel need for the war effort and to "provide standard time for the United States," thereby validating what the railroads had done four decades earlier.[12]

After railroads became the masters of time keeping, their push for standardization did not stop there. Once railroads had been willing to tolerate a five-minute variation in watches worn by train crews, but no more. "Watches which are liable to vary as much as five minutes a day are not fit for use," and any such laxity in time keeping was "unworthy of the present age of railway management," warned the *Official Guide* in 1889. To make certain that accurate time prevailed on railroads everywhere, at least four thousand watch inspectors and their assistants checked and rechecked approved timepieces in the 1920s.[13]

In their passenger timetables, too, the nation's time moguls standardized to the minute the distance that separated metropolitan centers as far apart as Chicago and Los Angeles. In January 1900, for instance, the

Chicago & North Western crews use a rotary snowplow to clear the tracks near De Smet, South Dakota, in 1916. They are working just west of the Big Cut area that Laura Ingalls Wilder immortalized in one of her books about pioneer life on the prairie. Courtesy South Dakota State Historical Society.

Atchison, Topeka & Santa Fe allotted exactly 67 hours and 50 minutes for its "California Limited" to sprint across the 2,265 miles that separated those two cities. The Southern Pacific defined the distance between New Orleans and Los Angeles as 59 hours and 20 minutes, and that between San Francisco and Portland as 37 hours and 10 minutes.

After equating distances precisely with hours and minutes, railroads did all in their power to enforce those schedules, even if that meant defying the unpredictable forces of nature. Deep winter snows that once had slowed or halted stagecoaches and delayed delivery of the mail for days and even weeks had to be muscled aside by railroad plows or kept at bay by the lengthy snowsheds that covered sections of track through the Cascades and the Sierras. Only adding to railroad woes was the fact that steam power and sub-zero temperature were about as compatible as water and oil. In addition to blowing and drifting snow, and ice-encrusted rails and switches, icicles "grew like fangs in the mouths of poorly drained tunnels and were a serious threat to safety in low-clearance areas," notes Gregory Ames in his essay on the winter operation of steam locomotives. The engineer and fireman occasionally crouched low behind a locomotive boiler "when entering tunnels to protect themselves from icicles crashing through cab windows."[14]

Regardless of the workaday problems, any delay was intolerable. Thus, in its daily operations a big railroad functioned much like a finely tuned watch; and every time a conductor consulted his own watch, it reminded him that his train was but one cog in a large and complex transportation machine.

Railroads were obsessed with time and the good order it signified. Thus, it was natural that the old General Time Convention, founded in 1872 and largely responsible for establishment of standard time zones in 1883, should formally transform itself into the American Railway Association on April 8, 1891. Just as its predecessor organization had worked to codify railroad timekeeping, it now sought to devise a "Standard Code of Train Rules" to govern all aspects of railroad operation. The ongoing activity of the American Railway Association soon resulted in thick books of industry guidelines.

Attention to detail was not only good for business, but it was vital to maintaining the kind of industrial discipline necessary to ensure the safe operation of trains. Even in the best of times, railroading was extremely hazardous work. During just twelve months from July 1899 through June 1900 a total of 2,550 railroad workers died from job-related accidents, and another 39,643 suffered injuries. Helping to humanize those numbers was an engineer on the Illinois Central named "Casey" Jones, who died in a smashup on April 30, 1900.

Given the grim statistics, it should not be surprising that among the more prominent advertisements published in the January 1900 *Official Guide* was one for A. A. Marks' "Patented Rubber Feet"—with more than "22,000 in use." The text noted that "although a man may meet with the misfortune of having both of his legs severed from his body, it does not necessarily imply that he will never be able to walk and get about as other persons do." The Marks company advertised its prosthetic devices in the June 1900 *Official Guide* with pictures of railroad workers standing atop steam locomotives and a caption that read: "He has two good legs. One made by nature, the other by Marks."[15]

"A perfect railway organization is akin to that of the United States army," noted one industry observer in 1893, and not just because of danger or discipline. The need for organization dictated that military-like hierarchies must prevail on all the large carriers: "The officers of the traffic

This allegorical image dating from 1894 uses a railroad metaphor to discourage the consumption of alcoholic beverages. Courtesy Library of Congress.

and operating departments are major-generals or brigadier-generals according to their respective responsibilities. The colonels, captains, and lieutenants are synonymous with railway officials of lesser positions." [16] To continue this line of thought, the conductors perhaps corresponded to sergeants, and locomotive engineers, firemen, and brakemen to corporals—very brave corporals because of all railroad employees they were exposed to the greatest dangers. Thick books of rules, similar to military field manuals, governed all aspects of train operations. "Rule G," for example, prohibited employees from drinking on the job or when on call. Even entering a saloon or tavern might lead to a railroader's dismissal.

During an ordinary journey the employees most likely to be encountered by passengers were the station agents and conductors. They were the most visible links in a chain of command that extended along the tracks and telegraph wires to various division offices and finally to the headquarters of the railroad companies. Top executives of the Atchison, Topeka & Santa Fe Railway were based in Chicago, the nation's railroad capital and home also to the Chicago, Milwaukee, St. Paul & Pacific; Chicago, Rock Island & Pacific; Chicago & North Western; and several other railroads. The Union Pacific maintained its home offices in Omaha, as it still does today. Both the Great Northern and the Northern Pacific, which developed a close working relationship in the days of James J. Hill, were based in an office building in Saint Paul, Minnesota. The Southern Pacific defied convention, as it often did, and maintained its headquarters on the West Coast in San Francisco.

In truth, certain major decisions did not originate even at the desk of a railroad president. Because of the way western railroads had raised needed capital, every major carrier was enmeshed in a web of financial and political connections that extended east all the way to Capitol Hill, Wall Street, and big banks in New York, Philadelphia, and Boston. The relationship was not always congenial. Arthur Edward Stilwell, who built or headed several railroads radiating out of Kansas City, once complained bitterly that the "Money Trust" was so autocratic that it wielded as "great a power as the Czar of Russia." [17] Often the network of financial connections extended beyond the East Coast and across the Atlantic Ocean to investors in Germany, the Netherlands, and Great Britain. All such financial links helped to underscore the power of paper.

⚜ ⚜ ⚜

It was paper above all else that made it possible for railroads to advertise the West. Together with the obvious physical and economic changes wrought by the rails themselves, such promotional activity transformed the landscape and hence formed an integral part of the "magic" popularly attributed to railroads. Perhaps there was no more graphic display of railroad power across the West than their several landed empires and how they promoted them to prospective settlers.

Because of their inordinately great need for capital, and to provide an acceptable return on the money of investors, railroads of the West worked diligently to coin land into money. All along their tracks they sought to transform prairies into farms and ranches by luring settlers, even as they later turned mountains into scenery to attract tourists. The challenge for promoters was to take a landscape that onlookers found unappealing, even frightening in its austerity and transform it so as to excite the imagination. To that end railroads used paper and ink and artistic creativity.

Railroad development activity required a great deal of faith in the future, though the results inevitably seemed worth the effort, at least to many enthusiasts. "It is wonderful the transformation a railroad will make in a country in a few months, changing trackless prairies into settled farms,

Otto C. Perry photographed a Northern Pacific freight train near Marshall, Washington, in 1938. His image provides an evocative portrait of a railroad landscape typical of the time. Apart from the train itself are a water tower in the distance, semaphores for signaling, and numerous wires for communication along the right-of-way. Courtesy Western History Department of the Denver Public Library.

fields of grain, and prosperous towns," noted an excited correspondent in the *Lutheran Observer,* whose words of praise were reprinted in the *Official Guide* of February 1888. "At every station the best buildings are those built by the railroad companies. They become the civilizing power, pushing their forces of men and construction trains in advance of civilization, giving work to the homesteader and bread to his hungry wife and children, while the prairie is bringing forth its crop." The railroad was "the poor man's friend, the country's treasure, and our best help in the work of home missions."[18]

As time went on, advertising became increasingly important to the general well-being of railroad companies across the West, especially after 1900 and in response to a thickening web of government regulation. The passenger traffic manager of the Union Pacific System observed at a convention of advertisers in mid-1914 that the value of rail publicity activity had only increased as state and federal regulators limited the industry's earning power. Nonetheless, he urged railroads to carefully focus their efforts. "I doubt whether a hundred thousand dollars expended in advertising freight service would cause two kegs of nails to be shipped where one was shipped before, and I think it may truthfully be said that advertising will not create freight traffic. Advertising of luxurious passenger service may stimulate travel, but to a limited extent only." At the time there was no competition for such business in most parts of the United States, and hence no need for railroads to advertise for it.[19]

However, he continued, "all forms of publicity which depict in truthful terms the wonderful health and pleasure resorts of our continent are of incalculable benefit" to everyone. "The public owes much to the transportation companies for their exploitation of Yellowstone National Park, the Adirondacks, California, the Canadian Rockies, Florida, the Yosemite, the Grand Canyon, etc." Likewise, he emphasized the importance of advertising settlement opportunities for homeseekers, the result of which is the "constant recession of the world's frontiers, the conquest of new countries and the trite but pleasant occupation of developing two blades of grass where one grew before."[20]

Railroads of the West wholeheartedly agreed, and thus they emerged as major publishers. The total output for a promotional campaign mounted by a single large railroad might exceed ten million brochures. Prospective tourists and homeseekers obtained most such publications for the cost of a postage stamp, or they could pick them up free at their local railroad station. In 1914 the Northern Pacific offered at least twenty-five separate booklets on development topics such as "Suggestions to the Dry Farmer" in addition to its tracts and leaflets boosting specific areas and communities. The Denver and Rio Grande published a lavishly illustrated booklet in 1909 called "The Fertile Lands of Colorado." Railroads increasingly promoted the Centennial State, long favored for its mineral resources, in terms of its agricultural possibilities. The railroad updated "The Fertile Lands of Colorado" annually for several years to provide "a concise description of a vast area of agricultural, horticultural and grazing land in Colorado and New Mexico," and to give "full information for intending settlers as to lands remaining open for entry or for sale."[21]

Apart from their numerous publications, several railroads operated special demonstration trains. To showcase the resources of the Pacific Northwest, the Northern Pacific Railway periodically outfitted special cars to carry exhibits featuring fish, timber, and mineral resources as well as the products of farms, orchards, and gardens. "In the season, fresh apples, pears, plums, cherries, peaches, prunes, grapes, melons, roots, and garden vegetables will be brought from the north-western States daily for exhibit." Over the years the various railroads serving the West operated "Better Farming Trains," "Good Seed Trains," "Beef Production Trains," and even a "Sugar Beet Special."[22]

Western railroads in the early twentieth century opened booths in eastern cities and flooded the United States with increasingly vivid promotional literature. In 1902 alone, the Great Northern hired thirty-four agents to work in the rural heartland east of Chicago. They typically gave illustrated lectures in country schools and offered samples of actual produce to excite the interest of agriculturalists in the new Northwest. Agents might also attend county fairs and circuses where they slipped bundles of Great Northern booster literature under the seats of farmers' wagons.

To share ideas and coordinate publicity efforts, the company-paid boosters formed the American Railway Development Association in the early twentieth century. At such gatherings professional railroad publicists discussed in private as well as public sessions the best kinds of settlers to seek, and hence railroad companies helped determine the racial and ethnic makeup of the regions they served. "All races and nationalities have their good and bad traits, and one is best suited for one line of work, another for a totally different," explained one publicist at a 1922 meeting of the Association in Denver. In the remote and frontier-like upper peninsula of Michigan served by his employer, the Duluth, South Shore & Atlantic, he continued, "the Northern European is best suited for settlement."[23]

Professionalizing their publicity campaigns did not stop railroads of the West from competing vigorously with one another for more settlers. The Kansas City Southern Railway, which boasted in a passenger timetable issued November 1911 that it served the "Land of Fulfillment," observed with pride that many people immigrating to Louisiana came from the Pacific Northwest. It added, as a timeless come-on to would-be settlers: "The day of cheap land is rapidly drawing to a close. The small amount of it left is fast being grabbed up by the men who see and realize future conditions. It will be a mighty scramble for the next generation to obtain agricultural land at any thing like it can be procured for now."[24]

By the early twentieth century, railroad promotional pamphlets had evolved into works of art designed to appeal visually and emotionally to prospective settlers from a variety of backgrounds. A 1910 railroad brochure promoting the community of Hood River, Oregon, featured full-sized Red Spitzenburg apples in color. Just a few months earlier the Southern Pacific's passenger department published a pamphlet titled "Eat California Fruit: By One of the Eaters," which described that state's wondrous fruit culture. Imaginative readers could almost taste tangy fresh oranges and grapefruits.[25]

Railroad tourist guides, as distinct from guides promoting agricultural settlement, were popular too. Over the years, companies issued brochures to draw attention to every conceivable natural attraction—from Yosemite and Yellowstone National Parks to the Great Salt Lake, the beaches of coastal Oregon, and trout streams in mountain Idaho—as well as to urban amenities. Among the latter titles was "Bungalow Life in California," issued by the Union Pacific to showcase "charming homes, covered with vines and roses, where one may spend a winter in a climate which insures sunshine and balmy air every day."[26]

Appealing to devotees of a more rugged lifestyle was a brochure titled "Finned, Furred, Feathered," which described the resorts, the fish and game, and numerous other outdoor attractions located along the Western Pacific Railway in northern California in 1914. Its pages featured "many illustrations of scenes of outdoor life, hunting, fishing and camping, which show also the magnificent mountain scenery of the region. A compact statement of the game laws and season is also included." At much the same time the Denver & Rio Grande Railway published "Outdoor Life in the Rockies." The Rio Grande Western Railway in 1900 published "Utah —A Peep into a Mountain-Walled Treasury of the Gods."[27]

Scenery was an asset, and western railroads of the early twentieth century worked hard to coin as much of it as possible into dollars. "Picturesque Colorado," issued by the Colorado & Southern Railway in 1912, described "some of the most remarkable parts of the Rocky Mountain region accessible to tourists using its trains." Among those were the Garden of the Gods near Colorado Springs, Estes Park, and the historic gold camps of the Cripple Creek area. The same railroad also issued "several dainty booklets devoted to especial features." Among the available titles were "Out Doors in Colorado," "Trouting in Colorado," "The Pikes Peak Region," and "One-Day Mountain Excursions."[28]

In several of its publications, the Colorado & Southern called attention to a scenic stretch of track called the Georgetown Loop, which suggests that the railroad landscape itself could be successfully promoted as a tourist attraction. "This trip is known alike for the weird beauty of that wonderful gorge and the engineering features by which the railroad has been enabled to ascend it." It represented, said the *Official Guide,* "one of the cases where science seems to have forced an issue with nature to see which is master." Naturally, proclaimed the *Official Guide,* "the engineer has triumphed," and the looping mountain railroad track became acclaimed as "one of the engineering curiosities of the West."[29] At one point Colorado & Southern trains climbed a series of switchbacks as they sought to access alpine country 14,007 feet high, said to be the highest point on earth to be reached by a regular railway. "An admirable feature of the trip is the fact that it can be made within one day from Denver, a day which will be long remembered by those who participate in it."[30]

Few parts of the West were as spectacular as the Rocky Mountains, but the region's railroads knew that passengers enjoyed looking at the passing scenery at least part of the time. Thus, every transcontinental railroad published special folders or guides, many of them elaborately illustrated with color maps, photographs, and drawings to help passengers pass the time by identifying rivers, mountain ranges, towns, tunnels, and other features in the passing landscape, and gave them away to travelers. Such pamphlets often included news of business opportunities in the towns along the way.

So important did railroads think the passing landscape was to passengers that some companies did far more than encourage them merely to read about it. They sought to make it visible even after nightfall. The Chicago, Milwaukee & St. Paul equipped its "Fast Mail" in 1913 with a large marine searchlight, "which throws a stream of light for a distance of three miles. The searchlight is on the observation platform, and is in charge of an experienced operator. It can be swayed 90 degrees from right to left and 45 degrees upward. This road parallels the Mississippi River for over one hundred miles, and the illumination of the scenes along the river banks, the boats, passing trains, etc. will be an amusing feature of a trip on this train."[31]

In July 1899 the passenger department of the Union Pacific issued what must surely rank among the most unusual publications in the annals of railroad literature. Its title was "Some of Wyoming's Vertebrate Fossils." The *Official Guide* noted that "these original inhabitants of Wyoming are attracting great attention from all geologists and paleontologists, and the new discoveries that are constantly being made there are adding materially to scientific knowledge." The Union Pacific "has contributed to this end by publishing the illustrated pamphlet above referred to, and also by issuing invitations (including transportation) to the heads of the scientific departments of the various universities of the country to bring parties to the field for purposes of exploration." Whether the pamphlet was generally available on board its several daily passenger trains across Wyoming was not clear, but a copy could easily be obtained by writing the company's home office in Omaha, Nebraska.[32]

Onboard handouts of all types formed an essential part of the popular reading material available in coaches and sleeping cars that long-distance passengers commonly used to fight boredom. In the late 1920s, for instance, the Union Pacific furnished travelers on its westbound "Gold Coast Limited" between Omaha and Los Angeles with copies of "The Overland Mail" as they entered the dining car for breakfast. "There are three editions of this train 'newspaper,' one for each day of the trip, and each dealing with the section of the route traversed on that day." The publication

01716   DEVIL'S GATE BRIDGE, GEORGETOWN, COLORADO

*The Georgetown Loop,
located fifty miles west of
Denver on the Colorado &
Southern Railway, was for
many years a tourist marvel.
Courtesy Colorado State
Historical Society.*

"furnishes information regarding the principal towns, scenic features, and points of historic interest along the line and describes the various vacation regions served by the Union Pacific System; it also gives particulars of the several side trips which may be availed en-route."[33]

The *Official Guide* once editorialized that "the pleasure of traveling is greatly enhanced by a knowledge of the history of the country through which one is passing, and a description of the interesting points which appear in the landscape." Annotated public timetables often served that purpose. Railroads, in fact, packed so much information into a typical public timetable that it became a catalog of the company's stock in trade. These became a venerable staple of travel, but some passengers found them very confusing. In the mid-1930s the trend was toward greater simplification. Frequent photographs that illustrated various features of passenger, freight, and other services often replaced "prosy reading matter."[34]

Finally, in a special category of published items were calendars, playing cards, baggage stickers, and picture postcards that railroad companies gave away freely. The Northern Pacific Railway once issued a set of colored postcards that reproduced "historic photographs of Indians, buffalo, covered wagons and other interesting pictures of the old West."[35]

※ ※ ※

Many scenic wonders of the West were framed for passengers by the open windows of a moving train, yet some spectacular ones lay off the main lines—and often well away from the tracks themselves. In January 1900 no tracks threaded their way to the south rim of Grand Canyon or Yosemite or the geysers of Yellowstone. Yet railroads of the West rapidly extended spur lines to transport tourists to the major national parks or encouraged feeder railroads to do so.

In mid-1907 the tracks of the Yosemite Valley Railroad extended to El Portal, where they offered "an easy means of access to that region of wonderful beauty. Under the present schedule passengers are landed at El Portal, the entrance to Yosemite National Park, in the evening, where excellent hotel accommodations may be had over night, and the stage ride through the park commenced the next morning." Before this, tourists had usually reached the national park by stagecoach from the nearest railroad station in Merced.[36]

The national parks of the West became popular tourist destinations after transcontinental railroads realized their potential for generating passenger dollars. The Northern Pacific was fortunate that the first national park, Yellowstone (established in 1872), could easily be reached by stagecoach from its mainline at Livingston, Montana. In 1903 the railroad extended a 54-mile branch from Livingston to Gardiner on the park's northern boundary. From there it was a mere five miles by stage to Mammoth Hot Springs Hotel.

The Northern Pacific could never hope to monopolize passenger traffic to Yellowstone. In the early twentieth century, competition between railroads dominated by the Harriman or Hill interests resulted in the Union Pacific's extending a branch line north from St. Anthony, Idaho, to Yellowstone, Montana, which it opened for traffic in 1908. Five years earlier, the Union Pacific and Chicago & North Western lines had joined forces to organize and conduct escorted tours through Yellowstone and Rocky Mountain Parks.

In time, four different railroads, including the Chicago, Burlington, & Quincy at Cody, Wyoming, and the Milwaukee Road at its Gallatin Gateway station in Montana, competed for summer vacationers to Yellowstone National Park. At no other park was the competition so fierce. The Union Pacific long considered building a grand hotel for its guests in Yellowstone Park but dropped the idea in the early 1920s because statistics revealed that nearly two-thirds of all visitors by that date arrived by private automobile.

Southern Pacific advertisements sought to promote Oregon's Crater Lake National Park as a tourist destination that it alone served. The Southern Pacific began conducting tours to Crater Lake from its tracks at Medford after the park was created in 1902. In Arizona the Grand Canyon Railway made it easy for vacationers to reach its scenic namesake.

The West has often been described both as a place and as a state of mind. Disentangling the two was not easy, thanks in no small measure to the region's many dedicated promoters, many of them employed by railroads. While it might be possible to dismiss regional boosters as basically harmless souls, not unlike carnival barkers, in some instances their artistic license took the form of grossly exaggerated claims that in the end produced unhappy—and, in some cases, disastrous—results. A prime example can be found on the high and often dry plains of eastern Montana, where railroad promotions lured thousands of naïve settlers with the claim that rain invariably followed the plow. In other words, if you plowed the arid land, life-giving rain was sure to follow.

A spectacular land rush commenced in 1909 that during the next eight years transformed twenty-nine million acres of eastern Montana prairie into thousands of new farms. One particularly vivid enticement, a cover illustration on a Milwaukee Road promotional brochure, showed a farmer plowing large gold coins from the rich Montana soil. Employing similar allurements, the Northern Pacific Railway sold 1.3 million acres of Montana land during 1916 alone. Across the state the number of farms increased from 7,000 at the turn of the century to 46,000 twenty years later. The Great Northern Railway joined the effort to sell Montana by launching a major promotional campaign of its own that included running a

Another graphic illustration of railroad power: this image from Kansas shows what often happened to aspiring settlements on the Great Plains when bypassed by the life-giving tracks. Courtesy Library of Congress.

special advertising car around the United States in 1910 to show skeptics the wonders of the territory it served. The mobile display was widely believed to have accelerated immigration to Montana.[37]

Many prospective immigrants understood clearly that "boosting" the West involved a generous measure of faith, but others apparently did not. Newcomers lured to the high plains of Montana by assertions that rain followed the plow were often too eager to believe that the claim was a matter of scientific certainty. At first the rain gods humored the silliest of boosters and their pathetically deluded converts, but after a decade of extra-abundant moisture, they sent little or no rain to revive the parched Montana earth in 1917. That was the start of the longest and most brutal drought in the state's history. During the first sixteen years of the new century, Montana's farms had averaged twenty-five bushels of wheat per acre, but during the hot and dry summer of 1919 that average plummeted to one-tenth the supposed normal amount. That year the continuing drought cost Montana agrarians an estimated $50 million.

Further battered by a worldwide decline of farm prices, more than half of Montana's commercial banks collapsed between 1920 and 1926. Across some of the state's heavily mortgaged farmlands there were actually more foreclosures than farms, hard as that is to imagine. "Foodless, seedless, landless, and moneyless," in the well-chosen words of Montana historian K. Ross Toole, many a recent settler simply walked away from his scorched fields and moved elsewhere. The state's population declined by about 75,000 residents between 1919 and 1926, the troubled times that Jonathan Raban explored in his 1996 book *Bad Land: An American Romance*. Perhaps as nothing else, the shrill boosterism of the early twentieth century showcased the power of railroads to "win the West"—at least temporarily in the case of Montana's high and dry plains.[38]

Three

Copper Connections and the Last Transcontinental Railroad

The railroad campaign to package and sell western landscapes to prospective tourists and settlers marched ahead with confidence during the first fifteen years of the twentieth century, as did the construction of new lines. Steam railroads accounted for much of the added mileage, but some new track belonged to electric interurban railways, a fresh technology that heralded the coming age of competition.

Hindsight suggests that interurbans occupied the middle ground between steam railroads and automobiles in terms of convenience and service. Electric cars that ran at frequent intervals and were easily boarded almost anywhere made journeys of even thirty miles easy and convenient. Contemporary observers, however, had no reason to regard them merely as a transitional form of transportation, a perky technological newcomer that anticipated the freedom a personal automobile had to offer. To most observers they were just another kind of railroad. The electric interurban lines certainly left their imprint on the landscape, and none was more impressive than that of the Pacific Electric Railway, a leader in promoting the growth of greater Los Angeles.

Curiously, a common thread running through accounts of western railroads, both electric and steam, at the height of their power during the first twenty years of the century, was fashioned, not from iron or steel or even paper, but from copper. The red metal made the wonders of the electrical age possible, and it generated millions of investment dollars required to build America's last transcontinental railroads. This is a story of the copper connection and how it influenced transportation in the early-twentieth-century West.

❧ ❧ ❧

Construction of the first transcontinental railroad is a well-known story. Classic photographs of the festivities at Promontory, Utah, in May 1869, show the Central Pacific and Union Pacific locomotives facing one another as dignitaries wait to drive a last spike to open a long-awaited line between Omaha and Sacramento. The National Park Service carefully preserves the final-spike site today. Well before the memorable events of 1869, however, other celebrations had marked the completion of significant railway lines, such as the one when the Baltimore & Ohio and affiliated railroads opened the first line from Chesapeake Bay to the Mississippi River at Illinoistown (now East Saint Louis) in 1857.[1]

Worth remembering too is that the first-advertised price of a one-way rail ticket across the United States from New York to Sacramento in 1869, a journey of 3,377 miles, was $190.35. Even if that sum is unadjusted for inflation, it is still almost twice a much as a $99 coast-to-coast ticket occasionally offered by Southwest Airlines at the dawn of the twenty-first century. Yet compared to the discomfort of a journey west by stagecoach or covered wagon, a coast-to-coast trip by rail in 1869 was worth every penny of the ticket price. That was something worth celebrating.[2]

Curiously, the two companies traditionally commemorated as forming the first transcontinental railroad did not actually extend their tracks across North America or even come close to serving both coasts. Until a bridge at last spanned the waters of the Missouri River, trains of the Union Pacific terminated on its west bank, and passengers and freight continuing from Omaha to East Coast destinations crossed the river by ferry and rode aboard the trains of at least two additional railroads. The first transcontinental rail line in the Americas was actually completed from coast to coast across the Isthmus of Panama in 1855. Even though the Panama Railroad was located well outside the United States, Yankee investors financed the 48-mile link and reaped a rich and steady harvest of dividends from the heavy flow of traffic to and from golden California during the 1850s and 1860s. Thus "transcontinental" is a slippery term when applied to the early railroads of the Americas.

Even more likely to spark an argument is the identity of the *last* transcontinental railroad to cross the United States. Its builders, of course, could not realize that they were laying a last transcontinental rail line except by hindsight. Among the several candidates for that dubious honor are the Chicago, Milwaukee & St. Paul Railroad, which completed its ill-fated extension to the Pacific Northwest in 1909, and the Western Pacific, which began service between Salt Lake City and Oakland in August 1910 to form a through line across the United States using several different carriers.

J. E. Stimson photographed the "Overland Limited" at Omaha, Nebraska, in 1906. The Union Pacific's bridge over the Missouri River featured a bison's head, one symbol of the railroad's role in "winning the West." Flushed with patriotism during World War II, the Union Pacific contributed the massive bronze sculpture to the war effort. Presumably it ended up as metal for armaments. Courtesy Wyoming State Museum.

To this short list, and for the sake of illustrating the traumas that turned a once-comfortable world upside down for western railroad executives by 1920, I add the name of a third and extremely unlikely aspirant, the El Paso & Southwestern System. It extended tracks across a lightly populated but mineral rich swath of New Mexico and Arizona before it paused in Tucson in 1912 as company executives prepared to continue all the way to Los Angeles. Only recently they had acquired land on which to build the railroad's Pacific terminus (an area occupied today by the Los Angeles Union Passenger Terminal used by Amtrak). With the finish line in sight, the El Paso & Southwestern had only to extend its tracks across a few hundred miles of virtually empty desert land west of Tucson to forge a new rail link between Chicago (in partnership with the Chicago, Rock Island & Pacific) and southern California.

Why the El Paso & Southwestern never reached Los Angeles says much about what happened to American railroads during and after World War I and why they would never again dominate transportation across the West. It speaks volumes, too, about the making and breaking of the copper connection.

⚜ ⚜ ⚜

Metals of all types have figured prominently in the history of western railroads. There are, of course, the metal rails themselves, fashioned in early years from iron (or even from wooden rails topped with a thin bearing surface of iron) and later from durable steel of steadily improving quality. Nothing was more fundamental to a railroad than its rails, and yet rails would only rust in the sun unless the trains passing over them had something to haul. In the case of many western railroads, that was metal itself or the wealth of traffic that one of the region's metal deposits generated.

Gold and its energizing impact on California and the West Coast was a primary reason to build the nation's first transcontinental railroad. Fittingly, it was a golden spike that the dignitaries tapped into place at Promontory to celebrate completion of the project. Silver played a role too. During the 1850s it was the discovery of silver that made Nevada's Comstock Lode famous; and the prosperous mines of Virginia City were located within easy reach of Reno, where starting in 1872 the Virginia & Truckee Railroad exchanged passengers and freight with Central Pacific trains running between California and Utah. Prospectors during the 1870s and 1880s unearthed still more deposits of precious metal that caused railroaders to run tracks into the mountain mining districts of Colorado and other western states.

Copper was one more metal that energized railroad-building projects across the region, but apart from its electrical conductivity, its full importance to western railroads may not be obvious. Gold and silver always ranked as glamour metals, but starting in the 1880s, when the West emerged as a major producer of copper, that base metal generated more wealth than gold and silver combined. Centuries earlier, imaginative Romans had equated the beauty of copper with that of Venus, both the goddess and planet; while in the Middle Ages, the secret formulations of alchemists had continued that tradition by designating copper with the astrological symbol for Venus. That, incidentally, was a circle with a cross attached below (today the familiar biological symbol for female).

Copper remained a beautiful metal in the late nineteenth century, but by then its beauty lay mainly in its value, not its appearance. Many astute investors in America built family fortunes from copper deposits unearthed in the West. Until the 1880s, copper had been used mainly to make pots and pans, to roof public buildings, and to protect wooden hulls of sailing ships from destructive marine organisms that lurked beneath tropical seas; but then dawned the age of electricity. Without copper—literal mountains of it mined, purified, and drawn into wire to carry electricity—the technological revolution in light and power that transformed America and Europe during the 1880s and 1890s, and later the whole world, might well have been short-circuited.

The growing abundance and declining price of copper wire encouraged the electrification of railroad main lines like that of the Milwaukee Road across the Rocky Mountains and Cascades, and the Great Northern through the Cascade Range. Countless miles of wire used as overhead power conduits and as windings in electric generators and motors spurred the development of a whole new kind of railroad, the trolley line. These diminutive carriers extended tracks from the city center to nurture the growth of suburbs. Sometimes they evolved into electric interurban railroads that reached across the miles of countryside to link one city to another.

Interurban lines extended thousands of miles of track across the United States from the 1890s until the eve of World War I, with largest carrier in the nation being the Pacific Electric Railway, which blanketed the greater Los Angeles area with tracks. The Pacific Electric, in contrast to the typical interurban, featured "well ballasted track, heavy rail, interlocking switches and block signals. The equipment is substantial, modern and comfortable. For the longer trips, reserved seats may be required." During the summer of 1915 more than "two thousand regular scheduled trains are run in all directions. There are also a number of personally-conducted trolley trips to points of interest, to Mount Lowe, to the Old Missions, and an all-day ride through 'The Orange Empire,' one of the most comprehensive, in the matter of scenery, in the world."[3]

However, the full story of king copper in the early-twentieth-century West involved more than electricity and transportation, vital as those industries are. Just as gold and silver deposits had spurred builders of western railroads during the second half of the nineteenth century, copper deposits did likewise in the 1880s and 1890s as well as in the first years of the twentieth century. Butte, Montana, fast emerging as the world's greatest single producer of copper ore, was a goal of James J. Hill's Great Northern Railway as it extended west from Saint Paul in the 1880s. A short time after its tracks reached the mines of Butte, Hill's railway pushed its main-line tracks farther west to Spokane, Seattle, and the Pacific Coast, which it reached in 1893.

A decade later, executives of the Chicago, Milwaukee & St. Paul made certain that their new extension to the Pacific Coast also served the mines of Butte, which were the primary source of copper later used to electrify its main line. Therein lies another of the many explanations for the proud railroad's humiliating bankruptcy in the mid-1920s. The villain in the scenario was John D. Ryan, the sole westerner to sit on the Milwaukee Road's board of directors and a man who pushed hard for its electrification, though not from a disinterested point of view. He not only organized the Montana Power Company, which proposed to sell electricity to the railroad, but also presided over the Anaconda Copper Mining Company, which by dominating production in Butte became one of the world's major suppliers of copper. Electrification of the Pacific extension thus provided Ryan a ready market for both surplus power and copper, some twelve thousand tons of which he ultimately sold to the Milwaukee Road. The obvious conflict of interest later haunted the beleaguered carrier.

Copper and copper-based fortunes played a crucial role in several other major railroad-building projects across the twentieth-century West, both the electrification of existing lines and the building of new ones. Remember that western railroads were not undertakings typically financed by a handful of wealthy local investors. Except for the shortest and most rudimentary lines, railroads were large-scale industrial enterprises that required vast amounts of capital to build, equip, and operate. Launching a company of any size might take years and require an investment of many millions of dollars, much of it coming from outside the capital-starved West.

One moneyed easterner who helped bankroll western railroads in the early-twentieth-century West was Arthur Curtiss James, a reclusive person notable because he was popularly acclaimed to be the largest individual investor in railroad securities in the world. A handsome man whose bearded likeness invited favorable comparison to his contemporary, King George V of England, James nonetheless liked to work without any newspaper fanfare. Thus, he remained unknown to the public at large. Equally unknown was that the investment capital James used to underwrite his several railroad construction projects originally came from western copper.

Listed in the June 1916 *Official Guide* among the officers of the 1,000-mile-long El Paso & Southwestern System is the name A. C. James, a vice president. Entered just a few lines above James's name is that of the railroad's president, James Douglas. A nearly identical hierarchy is listed for the Morenci Southern Railway Company in eastern Arizona and the Nacozari Railroad in northern Mexico. The principal offices for all three companies were based in New York's Lower East Side at 99 John Street, an unassuming address as unlikely to signify anything to the public as the name Arthur Curtiss James.

When the *Official Guide* celebrated its fiftieth anniversary in May 1918, its editors explained the human dimension of the rosters of railroad officers that regularly appeared on its pages: "To a young man entering upon railroad work, it has been one of the first signs of success when he achieved a rank which entitled his name to appear in the *Official Guide;* and as he advanced his name mounted, until many times it has reached the top line. The climb of their names toward the top of the page has been among the satisfactions which have come to successful railroad officers."[4] Quite true, but the personnel hierarchy listed in the *Official Guide* in no way explains the significance to railroad building in the twentieth-century West of either Arthur Curtiss James or James Douglas.

Hidden behind their modest entries was a powerful but largely invisible copper connection. The 99 John Street address, it is worth noting, was for many years the home office of Phelps Dodge Corporation, an old New York mercantile partnership that in the late nineteenth century evolved into a mining company as a result of the fortune it made in Arizona copper. Phelps Dodge, now headquartered in Phoenix, is still not a household name, but today it ranks as the largest investor-owned copper producer in the world.

A century ago it was Phelps Dodge copper that underwrote the cost of building the El Paso & Southwestern and its several allied railroads and provided Arthur Curtiss James with the investment capital that made him such an influential figure in railroad circles in the West. For his original millions he could thank his grandfather and great-grandfather, who were among the founding partners of Phelps Dodge in 1834. The president of Phelps Dodge in the early twentieth century was James Douglas; and he, along with his ally Arthur Curtiss James, played a notable if unsung role in forging a complex new landscape of production across the American Southwest.

Any examination of the copper connection and its role in funding railroad construction in hitherto remote parts of the United States should also include William Andrews Clark, a contemporary of Arthur Curtiss James. It was Clark, a copper king who amassed a fortune from the metal mines of Montana and Arizona, who in the opening decade of the twentieth century forged a missing rail link across the desert landscape that separated rapidly growing Los Angeles from the main line of the Union Pacific Railroad in northern Utah.

One event that spurred Clark to build the San Pedro, Los Angeles & Salt Lake Railroad was the recent rush of fortune seekers into southern Nevada following discovery of several major gold and silver deposits there. What Clark could not foresee was that after the heyday of Goldfield, Tonopah, and other mining camps and towns spawned by the 1900 rush, an unremarkable jerkwater railroad town located alongside his tracks in southern Nevada would produce a bonanza of another sort. That place, of course, was Las Vegas. Clark, who died in 1925, did not live long enough to see it transformed into a gaming and entertainment metropolis, but his name lives on in Clark County, where Las Vegas is the seat of local government.

Not Clark, but Salt Lake City figured prominently in the aspirations of the Western Pacific Railroad, another major transportation link forged during the early years of the twentieth century. It formed an indispensable connection in the grandest, yet weirdest transcontinental railroad scheme yet proposed.

By winding along scenic Feather River Canyon, Western Pacific tracks breached the Sierra Nevada to join railroads converging at Salt Lake City with the port of Oakland on San Francisco Bay. The mountains proved less of an obstacle to the new railroad than the Southern Pacific's determination to block an upstart competitor from reaching west to the Golden State, and particularly its headquarters city of San Francisco, where it was to monopolize rail traffic until the early twentieth century.

When completed in 1910, the new Western Pacific line extended the reach of the Denver & Rio Grande that already linked Denver and Salt Lake City. Originally, these sister carriers were expected to form a crucial part of the transcontinental railroad system being assembled by George Jay Gould, eldest son of the well-known railroad baron Jay Gould. To understand what young Gould—who was still in his thirties in 1892 when he inherited his father's railroad and telegraph empire, part of a family fortune worth at least $70 million—sought to accomplish with his impressive burst of railroad building activity, it is necessary to recall that the term "transcontinental railroad" had always been a bit of a misnomer. Yet it had long been applied to the original Union Pacific-Central Pacific line between Omaha and San Francisco Bay as well to the rail companies that later connected Saint Paul with Puget Sound and New Orleans with Los Angeles.

In fact, until the twentieth century no one in the United States had yet assembled a true transcontinental railroad, a one-management system that actually joined the nation's opposite seacoasts. That was what George Gould aspired to do by becoming the nation's newest colossus of roads, a towering figure with one foot of his rail empire planted firmly on the Atlantic shore and the other on the Pacific. He was, in the words of a Wall Street observer, an extravagant and self-indulgent man, who had great confidence in himself and in "the boundless power of the Gould millions."[5]

From his father, the younger Gould gained an 11,000-mile system that stretched across the Midwest from Buffalo, New York, to Pueblo, Colorado, and as far south as El Paso, Texas. To extend his Wabash and Missouri Pacific holdings farther west, he added the Denver & Rio Grande and Rio Grande Western lines in 1901, which allowed him to reach across the Rocky Mountains to Salt Lake City and Ogden, Utah. However, young Gould's ego was far from satisfied. In 1902 he gained control of the Western Maryland Railroad, which ran from Baltimore through its namesake state to West Virginia. A year later he gained control of an as-yet-unbuilt railroad, the Western Pacific, which promised to extend a line of tracks all the way from Salt Lake City to San Francisco Bay, a distance of 924 miles when the line opened in 1910. In the end, all that stood between Gould and the realization of his transcontinental dream was a deceptively short stretch of track in the Pittsburgh area required to join the opposite ends of his empire together. Work crews had begun forging the missing link even before Gould launched Western Pacific construction in 1905.

In early 1902 the passenger department of the Wabash Railroad published an illustrated folder highlighting the railroad's proposed entry into Pittsburgh. "An excellent map appears in this folder showing the lines of the 'Gould System' extending westward to Ogden and southward to New Orleans, Galveston, Laredo and El Paso, which will be brought into touch with Pittsburgh by the completion of this line." [6] The Pennsylvania Railroad, which gained wealth and power by dominating Pittsburgh's considerable steel traffic, was just as determined to prevent that from happening. Helping the Pennsylvania maintain its near monopoly was the maze of hills and valleys that surrounded the city and created a construction nightmare for latecomers who aspired to extend a railroad line into Pittsburgh after all of the best approaches had been taken.

Gould, seemingly motivated more by ego than financial good sense, incorporated the Wabash Pittsburgh Terminal Company and spent $50 million to reach Pittsburgh. For that money he gained a first-class rail line that included eighteen double-track tunnels and dozens of heavy bridges, most notably a massive cantilever structure, the second longest of its type in the world, that stretched across the Monongahela River to the palatial station he erected in the heart of Pittsburgh's business district.

On July 2, 1904, his railroad commenced through passenger service between Pittsburgh and Saint Louis, heart of the sprawling Gould system and the site of that year's World's Fair. A Pittsburgh band saluted the first passenger train to depart for the Missouri metropolis, 710 miles and 18 hours away, by playing that year's hit song, with its chorus, "Meet Me in St. Louis, Louie, Meet Me at the Fair." For passengers entering downtown Pittsburgh at night through the railroad tunnel bored under Mount Washington, the lights of the city must have been as spectacular back then as they are for motorists today arriving by way of the nearby Fort Pitt Tunnel.[7]

Caught up in the euphoria of the moment, Gould stepped up work on the Western Pacific. Once its tracks were in place on the Pacific slope, all he required to reach from one ocean to the other was a connection between Pittsburgh and Cumberland, Maryland. Gould confidently expected to close that tiny gap of 129 miles out of 3,276 miles in a short time.

The keystone of Gould's transcontinental system was the Wabash, but it was as amazingly weak as it was critical to his success. The stock analyst Carl Snyder noted that it had never paid a dividend. He further observed

Great Northern President Ralph Budd (left) enjoys a light moment with Arthur Curtiss James during a visit to Portland, Oregon, in the early 1930s. At the right is W. F. Turner, president of the Spokane, Portland & Seattle Railway from 1920 to 1932.
Courtesy Oregon Historical Society.

with a large measure of incredulity that despite this dismal record, the Wabash still could claim 1,974 stockholders, "a fact which illustrates the propensity of the public to buy most anything that is offered to it." Those acerbic words reflected Snyder's low opinion of Gould and his strange assemblage of rail lines, and events soon proved him right.[8]

In the aftermath of the devastating financial panic that swept across the nation in November 1907, components of Gould's railroad empire sank into bankruptcy one by one. The Wabash Pittsburgh Terminal led the procession on May 29, 1908. Anticipated steel traffic had never materialized after Pittsburgh producers succumbed to arm-twisting by the Pennsylvania Railroad and backed out of earlier agreements with Gould. A little more than three years later, on December 26, 1911, the Wabash itself joined the gloomy procession of Gould railroads entering receivership. "George Gould had made many enemies, and when the final break came he had no friends to come to his aid," one of his contemporaries later wrote.[9]

Though the Gould rail empire soon vanished along with the family fortune, the Western Pacific lived on. In 1926 the ubiquitous investor Arthur Curtiss James gained a controlling interest in the railroad and took his seat as chairman of its board. At the same time, he grew heavily involved with the Great Northern Railway—some contemporaries claimed he was the largest individual stockholder in the company—and thus he figured prominently in a successful project to extend two hundred miles of Great Northern and Western Pacific track across the deserts of central Oregon and northeastern California to link the two railroads and forge an important new corridor called the "Inside Gateway." Arthur Curtiss James was among the Western Pacific and Great Northern dignitaries who attended the last-spike ceremony in late 1931. "To Mr. James too has likely fallen the distinction of having completed the epoch of major railway construction in the United States," observed the *Railway and Marine News* of Seattle.[10]

Despite its troubled beginnings, the historic Western Pacific line is today a healthy component of the Union Pacific Railroad, and the rocky outcroppings along the Feather River Canyon reverberate frequently to the sound of heavy freight trains on their way to Salt Lake City or Oakland. Additional trains travel to or from Oregon because the "Inside Gateway" is still used today for freight traffic between California and the Pacific Northwest.

The Great Northern anticipated that passenger service between Minnesota and California would begin during the spring of 1932, but it never did. The Great Depression upended those plans. The "Inside Gateway" remained the last new railroad corridor to be built on the Pacific slope. However, in the Mountain West, the 38-mile Dotsero Cut-off between Orestod (Bond) on the Denver & Salt Lake Railway and Dotsero on the Denver & Rio Grande Railway opened with appropriate fanfare on June 16, 1934. The new line shortened the rail distance between Denver and Salt Lake City by 173 miles and made through service via Moffat Tunnel to the Pacific Coast possible for the first time. Neither of these construction projects actually required laying many additional miles of track, but together the "Inside Gateway" and the Dotsero Cut-off represented the end of an era in terms of rail corridors across the West.

Among the several transcontinental railroads of the United States, the tracks of James J. Hill's Great Northern ran farthest north and closest to the international boundary with Canada, Hill's homeland. Curiously, another son of Canada, James Douglas, the president of Phelps Dodge, successfully built the railroad line farthest south and closest to the border with Mexico. In fact, Douglas and the El Paso & Southwestern System sought to forge an additional transcontinental link until the United States abruptly marched off to fight World War I in April 1917, effectively halting new railroad construction for several years.

Unlike Hill or Harriman or even the luckless George Gould, Douglas —like his business associate Arthur Curtiss James—kept an exceedingly low profile among America's railroad builders. Douglas, like his fellow copper magnate William Andrews Clark, had originally entered the railroad business because of an interest in mining. They had first crossed swords back in the late 1880s when both Clark and Douglas sought to buy the same Jerome, Arizona, copper property—a property owned at the time by the family of Jenny Jerome, the American-born mother of Winston S. Churchill. When Douglas hesitated to close the deal because of a troubling ethical issue, Clark seized upon the delay to acquire the United Verde Copper Company in a deal that made him a multimillionaire. For the stoic Douglas—a noticeably pious man originally educated as a Presbyterian theologian at the University of Edinburgh—the lost opportunity proved only a temporary setback along a winding road that ultimately led to success and personal fortune in the mining business.

Along the way, Douglas came to realize that the only way to mine copper ore successfully in the unforgiving deserts of Arizona and New Mexico was to organize a complete landscape of production. That meant building a railroad system across the Southwest to supply a veritable forest of timber required for supports in underground mines as well as the coal needed for power and coke for smelters. The processed copper must then be hauled to distant markets as efficiently and inexpensively as possible, else the purified metal would remain virtually worthless. Good transportation was the key to success in western copper, and all mining men knew it. Beginning in the late 1880s with a tiny seedling of a railroad that linked copper mines in Bisbee, Arizona, with Southern Pacific tracks in nearby Benson, James Douglas expanded the various railroad holdings of Phelps Dodge until they matured into the El Paso & Southwestern System in the early twentieth century.

The carrier did not result from any grand design either on the part of Douglas or Phelps Dodge to build a railroad empire. Rather, it was the product of numerous small and often uncoordinated business decisions. Just the same, its tracks eventually ran west from El Paso to Tucson, Arizona, and northeast across New Mexico in the other direction from El Paso to link with the tracks of the Chicago, Rock Island & Pacific. This deal offered convenient connections to Kansas City, Saint Louis, and the nation's rail hub of Chicago. This competitive edge benefited the copper giant when it sought to negotiate favorable freight rates with other railroads.

In this way too, Phelps Dodge became the second-largest industrial owner of railroads in the United States (after United States Steel). The day came when James Douglas could speed across the deserts of New Mexico and Arizona in style aboard his private railroad car, the "Nacozari," and

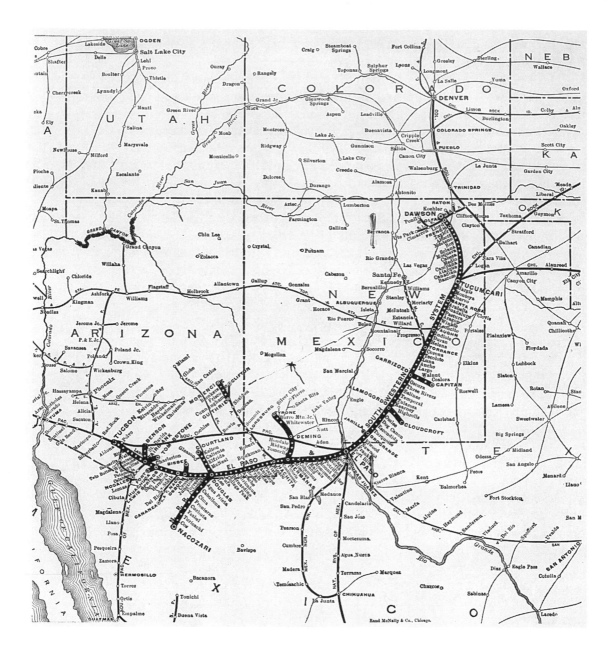

The El Paso & Southwestern System knitted together a mining empire
and later aspired to form an additional transcontinental railroad.
Courtesy University of Arizona Library.

dream of building an even bigger railroad. The imposing railroad station
that the El Paso & Southwestern opened in Tucson, Arizona, late in 1912
suggested that the railroad aspired not merely to knit together scattered
segments of Phelps Dodge's own copper kingdom in the Southwest but

also to build a link for freight and passenger traffic between Chicago and Los Angeles.

Douglas, in fact, planned to extend the tracks of the El Paso & Southwestern System west from Tucson across the Sonoran Desert to the copper mines of Ajo, Arizona. There he planned to use already existing tracks of the Tucson, Cornelia & Gila Bend Railroad for about forty miles before reaching west to Los Angeles. Well before the gaps could be filled in or a station erected in Los Angeles, however, the Great War intervened. Though that cataclysm lasted only from April 1917 until November 1918, at least when measured in terms of formal United States participation, it changed forever how American railroads did business. James Douglas, who died in 1917, never saw what happened to the El Paso & Southwestern system, the fate of which illustrated how different the railroad world was in 1921 than in 1917.

⚙ ⚙ ⚙

When the nation marched off to war in April 1917, American railroads faced "the largest movement of troops in the history of this country." In addition, they had to haul a crushing load of military freight to East Coast points of embarkation as well as move the usual nonmilitary freight and passenger traffic. "Some conception of the magnitude of the task confronting the railroads of the United States may be gleaned from the fact that to move merely one field army of 80,000 men requires 6,229 cars made up into 366 trains, with an equal number of locomotives and train crews," observed the *Official Guide*.[11]

The unprecedented flow of freight traffic hopelessly snarled tracks and bottlenecked the railway yards serving the ports of the East Coast. Cars laden with supplies needed to win the "war to end all wars" ground to a halt in the East, while the railroads of the West sought in vain to locate empty freight cars in which to ship lumber, apples, potatoes, and other commodities vital to the United States and its new military allies in Europe.

America's railroads worked hard to unsnarl the transportation tangle, but the traffic jam in the Northeast and the dearth of freight cars in the West only grew worse. As the volume of traffic surged to new highs, the shortage totaled 164,000 cars in May 1917 alone. After that it fell slightly, only to climb again later that year. As a result, numerous mills shut down their machines because they lacked raw materials, perishable articles spoiled, and coal failed to reach electric power plants, thus raising the specter of blackouts. With the onset of winter, New Englanders worried about a shortage of coal they needed to heat their homes.

The worrisome car scarcity was hardly the fault of the railroads alone. As the new century progressed, federal and state officials wove such a constrictive web of rules and regulations around the railroad industry that fewer and fewer investors found it an attractive prospect. Without financial incentives or a steady infusion of capital needed to modernize their

The camera of J. E. Stimson immortalized a group of "Union Pacific Girl Laborers." The date was May 29, 1918, less than six months before the armistice that ended World War I. During a time of labor shortages, women replaced men in a variety of railroad jobs, but only temporarily. Courtesy Wyoming State Museum.

facilities, railroads struggled to operate trains and maintain the support structures that grew ever more antiquated or simply wore out. One notable result of the financial anemia was the mess the United States and its railroads faced in 1917.

November's shortage of 150,000 freight cars was one reason why at noon on December 28, 1917, President Woodrow Wilson by executive proclamation took over operation of the railroads for the duration of the war. Congress hastened to respond with legislation creating the United States Railroad Administration. Its creation was a controversial step, to be sure, as was Wilson's choice of his son-in-law, Secretary of the Treasury William Gibbs McAdoo, to run it.

Many railroad leaders fumed about the possibility of permanent government ownership or inadequate compensation for the lines when and if they were returned to private hands. "With the exception of the declaration of war," noted the *Official Guide,* taking a measured view, "the step taken by the President in taking over for the Federal Government the control of the railroads is in its effects the most far-reaching act in the history of the Government. Whatever the outcome may be, the action unquestionably afforded relief to a situation which was becoming intolerable and for which radical measures were required."[12]

One result of federal control was to halt new railroad construction such as that proposed by the El Paso & Southwestern to reach Los Angeles. The law of the land now proclaimed: "The construction of new lines or branches or extensions of existing lines shall not be entered upon or contracted for without the Director General's approval." Standardization was the order of the day, and it went far beyond anything railroads had previously done themselves. Something so basic as the form of a standard waybill was now regulated by Uncle Sam, who proclaimed that "a waybill form must be printed on paper approximating in weight 80 pounds, N. 1 Manila, 24x16."[13]

Though an armistice ending the war was declared November 11, 1918, members of Congress dithered for more than a year before deciding to return the nation's railroads to their private owners on March 1, 1920. That was twenty-six months after Uncle Sam nationalized them and after losing a billion dollars during federal operation. Even back in private hands, all was not well with the nation's railroad industry.

The Transportation Act of 1920 formally ended direct federal control, but government regulations only multiplied and further diminished the industry's appeal to investors. In all, the number of federal rules regulating railroad freight tariffs probably totaled in the trillions. There were so many that no one could ever hope to know or fully understand them all. Making this sad state of affairs all the more galling to railroads, a host of new and largely unregulated competitors took aim at their freight and passenger business.

At the same time, the rail industry grappled with the rapidly rising cost of material, taxes, and labor, all part of wartime inflation that by 1920 had pushed the cost of living 70 percent higher than it had been in 1913. Inflation took a big bite out of railroad revenues and employee wages alike. Half a decade of worker unrest culminated in a walkout of members of the shop craft unions on July 1, 1922. Although organized workers lost the strike, the bitter conflict was one more of a succession of blows that left the rail industry both dazed and confused.

By the early 1920s the ability of highway competitors across the West to gnaw vigorously at railroad revenues had become all too apparent. Thus, it made absolutely no financial sense for the El Paso & Southwestern System to continue its planned line west across the desert to Los Angeles. That was why the Phelps Dodge Corporation in 1924 disposed of its controlling interest in the El Paso & Southwestern to the Southern Pacific for a total of $64 million in common stock, bonds, and cash. It was a profitable deal for the big copper company.

James Douglas's son Walter remained a director of the Southern Pacific for several years to come. Curiously, the Southern Pacific's largest individual stockholder was Arthur Curtiss James, his father's business colleague who in the late 1920s found himself at odds with the railroad's directors as they battled to prevent the Western Pacific and Great Northern lines from forging the "Inside Gateway" and competing with it for traffic between California and the Pacific Northwest.

⁂ ⁂ ⁂

Not to be overlooked in any account of this troubling time of transition for American railroads was what happened to the electric interurban lines. They had been a key component of the electrical revolution of the 1880s and 1890s that made the West's copper deposits such valuable investments in the first place and provided a foundation for railroad construction and improvement projects. The interurban interlude dates from the electric streetcar craze that swept across the United States after 1888, the year that Frank Sprague's trolleys went sparking down the rough tracks of the Union Passenger Railway in Richmond, Virginia. The success of the nation's first electric streetcar system soon inspired emulation in other communities, many of which turned to Sprague, the genius behind the meteoric rise of the industry.

(NEXT SPREAD) *Workers construct a streetcar line through downtown Salt Lake City. Paving materials will cover their handiwork except for the rails themselves. Courtesy Utah State Historical Society.*

Trolley cars, so named because a broomstick-like "troller" conducted power from a bare copper wire overhead to an electric motor onboard the car, appeared in all major cities of the West—and also in minor ones like Douglas, Arizona, the copper smelting community named for the Canadian responsible for fashioning a landscape of production to link Phelps Dodge mines and processing plants located along the international border in the Southwest. In Douglas, as elsewhere, trolley lines functioned not merely as public conveyances intended to lessen urban congestion but also as sources of community pride and status symbols of modernity.

The big-league cousin of the ubiquitous trolley sparking along city streets was the electric interurban railroad that reached out into the countryside from the edge of the city to link several settlements together. Interurban cars were typically larger and swifter than city trolleys. Among the nation's earliest so-called interurban lines were the Newark & Granville Street Railway in Ohio in 1890 and the Fidalgo City & Anacortes Railway in the state of Washington in 1891. Probably the first incontestable interurban line was the East Side Railway opened between Portland and Oregon City in 1893. By the end of the decade, the new-fangled electric interurban lines radiated out from many of the West's big population centers. In time, Seattle, Spokane, Portland, Oakland, Los Angeles, Salt Lake City, Denver, and Dallas-Fort Worth all served as hubs for expanding networks. Electric interurban railroads attained the height of their popularity during the first two decades of the twentieth century.

One reason for their appeal was that electric railways typically built their physical plants to less costly and demanding standards than those of steam railroads, and thus their tracks were far less expensive to extend into the countryside. They charged lower fares and offered more frequent passenger service than did steam railroads. Because a traveler could typically wave an interurban car to a stop almost anywhere, they became known as "people's railways."

Most steam railroads initially snubbed the electric lines as "hayseed" carriers. Some operations did fit that description, but no generalization adequately applies to all. Henry E. Huntington's sprawling Pacific Electric Railway was anything but a "hayseed" carrier. At its peak, Pacific Electric operated more than a thousand miles of line that knit together Los Angeles with at least fifty distinct suburban communities—from San Pedro and Long Beach to Pasadena, Burbank, and San Bernardino. In addition to conveying passengers, the Pacific Electric accomplished a feat most interurban lines conspicuously failed to do, and to their detriment: it developed a thriving freight business; and for years it hauled numerous carloads of citrus fruit and oil from the Los Angeles basin and returned with merchandise for the city's fast-growing population. As a rule, the more heavily any interurban depended on passengers to generate revenue, the earlier it succumbed to the automobile. Freight traffic made the Pacific Electric a long-term survivor.

By contrast, most of the West's interurban railroads lived precarious lives and died prematurely, at least when measured by the historic life spans of most other modes of transportation. The typical interurban line was relatively short and heavily dependent on local passenger traffic. A person riding one of its electric cars as it ambled through the countryside from one stop to another—or worse, riding to work aboard a slowpoke streetcar—had only to notice his neighbor speed by in an automobile to be motivated to purchase one just as good or better for himself.

Despite the convenience of interurban travel, few if any modes of public transportation rose and declined more quickly. The heyday of the electric interurban railroad lasted a scant two decades, from the dawn of the twentieth century, when a case of interurban fever agitated the United States, until automobile fever did likewise during the years following World War I. Thousands of miles of interurban line were constructed mainly during two spans of intense construction activity, 1901–1904 and 1905–1908, with each one halting during a nationwide financial panic. Although some lines were finished after 1908, the frenzied construction boom of earlier years was clearly over.

Already by 1914 growing automobile traffic began to cut deep into interurban profits. The Oregon Electric Railway Company, which served the Willamette Valley, went into the red for the first time that year as a result of highway competition, which only grew worse in the succeeding years. By 1915 state roads paralleled practically the whole Spokane & Inland Empire System, and businessmen in eastern Washington who had helped to bankroll the interurban soon found their investments to be worthless.

Electric railway mileage in the United States peaked in 1917 at 41,447, up from 21,682 miles in 1902. The lines shrank rapidly during the 1920s and 1930s. Though no new interurban track of consequence was laid following World War I, many lines already in place continued to haul passengers (and sometime freight), though the weeds that often crowded their right-of-ways revealed as much about the precarious state of their finances as did their formal balance sheets. Rising competition from private automobiles, buses, and trucks drove most of the West's remaining interurban lines out of business during the interwar years.

A few of the West's steam railroads electrified portions of their main lines, although their technological innovations followed a pattern different from that of the region's interurban lines. Steam railroads generally used electrification to solve vexing operating problems, and thus they never generated the kind of grassroots enthusiasm that buoyed interurban builders. The Baltimore & Ohio Railroad completed the nation's first main-line electrification in 1895 through the 1.5-mile Howard Street tunnel running below the streets of Baltimore. The deadly possibility that smoke-belching steam locomotives could suffocate train crews and passengers in long tunnels encouraged the Great Northern to electrify its 2.63-mile bore through the Cascade Range.

The Great Northern increased that total to about six miles of electrified tracks and yards in and around the tunnel in July 1909, but the high mountain country and its killer avalanches continued to challenge safe operations. That was why officials of the Great Northern decided in 1925 to relocated some forty miles of track by abandoning the scenic but hazardous mountain heights and boring 7.7-mile Cascade Tunnel under Stevens Pass. On January 12, 1929, the Great Northern opened what was then the longest railroad tunnel in North America by staging a gala celebration. It included a radio hookup that reached an estimated fifteen million people. The notable participants included Great Northern president Ralph Budd and President-elect Herbert Hoover, himself a mining engineer by training. Clean hydroelectric power generated by the Pacific Northwest's many mountain streams and rivers energized Great Northern trains from 1909 until mid-1956, when modern diesel locomotives ran through Cascade Tunnel to make electric operations obsolete.

Electricity began powering the locomotives of the Butte, Anaconda & Pacific Railway in May 1913. The Montana line had opened in 1893 to connect copper mines at Butte with a smelter complex located twenty-five miles west at Anaconda. Building on its experience with electric machinery in the mines and the Great Northern's operation at Cascade Tunnel, the Butte, Anaconda & Pacific electrified its railroad to take advantage of the economies that seemed certain to result. Electricity powered its trains for more than forty-three years, but changes at the Anaconda smelter decreased business for the railroad. The company removed the wires in 1967 after diesels replaced electric locomotives to haul whatever freight traffic remained.

It was at a time when electricity clearly seemed to be the wonder technology of the future that the Milwaukee Road adapted a system almost identical to that of the Butte, Anaconda & Pacific to two long portions of its Pacific Coast extension. The Milwaukee Road initially estimated that powering trains by electricity through the mountains of the northern West saved it more than twelve million dollars. But overshadowing any good news was the worrisome burden of debt dating from construction of the original Pacific Coast extension and its subsequent electrification.

Adding to the railroad's financial troubles, its leaders failed to anticipate the devastating financial impact of two new modes of competition. One was the swelling volume of automobile and truck traffic, which hurt railroads of the West most noticeably after World War I. Even earlier, competition came from steamships plying the Panama Canal to haul commodities from West Coast ports—lumber from the Pacific Northwest and oil from southern California—to East Coast markets. They offered shippers lower rates than the railroads could because federal bureaucrats kept rail rates artificially high instead of allowing competitive conditions to prevail.

The $463 million Panama Canal, which was built and maintained by federal dollars, had been in the works for a long time, but railroaders of otherwise good judgment initially discounted its competitive potential. The industry soon changed its mind, however. The *Official Guide* described the inauguration of ship traffic through the canal as "the most important event in the recent history of transportation," and it wondered aloud what impact the new waterway might have on prevailing patterns of trade: "What those effects may be upon any city or locality or country no man can surely predict."[14]

During its first years of operation, the Panama Canal actually had deceptively little impact on the transcontinental freight traffic carried by western railroads, although the Milwaukee Road badly needed every bit of traffic it could solicit. As late as 1921 a mere 15 percent of the canal's cargoes traveled from one coast to another, the other 85 percent being traffic from abroad. However, during the following two years, domestic shipments jumped to 52 percent of all freight traffic through the canal. "These figures show that the increase of the coast to coast traffic has been enormous and beyond all previous estimates or expectations," observed the *Railway and Marine News* of Seattle in 1924. President H. E. Byram of the Milwaukee Road complained to a Puget Sound audience that because of the Panama Canal "our railroad, well equipped, operated economically and efficiently, barely has been able to keep house in the last few years."[15]

That was not all. Apart from the Panama Canal, freight traffic by ship along the Pacific Coast soared during the 1920s as well. Gregory Lee Thompson in *The Passenger Train in the Motor Age* (1993) notes that by 1921 "the overwhelming majority of freight leaving Los Angeles and San Francisco went by water." He adds that by 1927 fully 60 percent of all freight between California and Oregon traveled aboard coastal steamers.[16]

In one sense, the railroads of the West had been too successful. For decades they had worked to develop the West and thus increase their own attractiveness as investment opportunities. Their expanding network of tracks made many parts of the region far more accessible than ever before. They issued publicity brochures to lure immigrants to farm the West's new agricultural lands and tourists to gaze at its scenic wonders. Railroads had fostered the growth of towns and cities and new forms of commerce and industry.

This group of workers paving a section of roadway near Bothell, Washington, in 1912 was typical of their counterparts elsewhere, a conquering army who won the West for the automobile. Courtesy Special Collections Division, University of Washington Libraries.

Ironically, as cities of the West grew in population and as the countryside developed and prospered, the region gained valuable resources it needed to build the roads and highways that in time challenged the dominance of railroads. They continued to boost the attractions of the West by issuing still more publicity brochures; but alas for the railroads, the brochures and advertisements that made by far the biggest impression on readers during the years after 1910 were those that promoted new models of automobiles.

For railroads of the West, the most surprising thing about automobiles was how popular they became in a relatively short time and that highway traffic could offer serious competition. Railroads had for years earned money by delivering a steady stream of new automobiles to local dealers by train, and they had been avid supporters of good roads. In fact, their freight trains had hauled much of the construction material used for improved roads. What most astonished railroaders, as well as other observers, was that some roads evolved into all-weather long-distance highways instead of remaining the modest farm-to-market links they originally envisioned—links that would greatly benefit the railroads. That the nation's first transcontinental highway followed soon after its last transcontinental railroad was not coincidental.

Four

Roads Stretching from Farm to Market, but Seldom Beyond

By the early twentieth century the Oregon and California trails were no more. Two generations of immigrants had followed those pathways to the Pacific, but after railroad builders had essentially paralleled them with tracks, the old trails fell into disuse. Freight wagons and stagecoaches lived on in memory and in occasional Hollywood epics devoted to the frontier, but what remained of the trails themselves often consisted of little more than ruts tracing a faint path across a sagebrush plain.

By 1900 the most popular way West—indeed, in most areas the only practical way to cross the West from any direction—was by rail. An eccentric individual might choose to walk across the West. Far more popular were the steamships that regularly plied the coastal waters linking California and the far Northwest. Rural dwellers used farm and ranch wagons to haul crops and livestock to the nearest siding or to the stock pens, grain elevators, and produce warehouses that lined the tracks of a nearby town. From there they still depended on railroads to reach distant markets.

Barely worth mentioning as an alternative to the railroad at the dawn of the century was a new invention called the automobile. Besides being mechanically balky, it required passable roads to use, and those were few beyond the city limits. It was far more difficult to travel west by road in 1900 than it had been in 1858, when overland stages first bounced across the deserts of Arizona and New Mexico to connect California with the rest of the United States, or when rails

Country lane or major highway? It really did not matter because in eastern Washington, as elsewhere, motorists in 1910 faced the same muddy challenges after a rainstorm. Courtesy Eastern Washington State Historical Society.

connected the two in the 1860s. "It is just forty years since ground was broken west from Omaha for the Union Pacific railroad," wrote an early-twentieth-century good roads enthusiast. "The history of those forty years in the development of our material resources has never had an equal in the world's annals, but as the wealth has increased and with it in equal pace all the other comforts of life, the average standard of the transcontinental highway has gradually declined."[1]

To most observers, an "automobilist" who proposed to motor across the rural West for any distance in 1900 seemed just as eccentric as a walker who sought to cross the continent by foot. Any motorist who dared to venture beyond the city limits quickly discovered that his choice was between "bad roads and worse," declared the automobile manufacturer Albert Pope in 1903.[2]

The typical country road amounted to little more than a meandering dirt path. Even the best roads were paved mainly with good intentions. In the early days, good intentions sometimes amounted to little more than covering the deepest or muddiest ruts with wooden planks or attempting to fill them with a thick blanket of straw. Straw roads apparently originated in the Sacramento Valley of California, but farmers and ranchers in rural eastern Washington quickly adopted the technique to improve the dirt paths used by their loaded wagons. "They are simply marvelous," claimed an observer in *Good Roads* in 1905. "The tractive capacity of the animals is at once increased, sometimes as much as one hundred per cent. The dust is no longer in evidence, filling the eyes and hair and destroying the clothes, as well as impeding the efforts of the animals."[3]

Though beneficial to agrarians, straw roads created a problem for early motorists. It was all too easy for steam-propelled vehicles, once a very popular type of car among wealthy Californians, to set the surface of a rural straw road ablaze. That in itself was a crime in most counties, but perhaps even worse for a luckless chauffeur was to collect straw in the chain drive next to the flames that heated the boiler. That might set an expensive vehicle ablaze as well as char a perfectly good stretch of straw road. A more common hazard was a section of mud or sand that merely trapped an unwary automobilist in muck up to the axles, fortunately without the incendiary side effects of a straw road.[4]

Regardless of whether the region's roads were paved or graded or even barely passable in good weather, they seldom connected to form transportation corridors for motorists to use for overland travel. Likewise, something so basic as finding directions remained a major challenge for long-distance motorists until Gulf Oil began to distribute free road maps at its gas stations in 1913. Giveaway maps were commonly available at service stations until the 1970s.

Before free maps, motorists purchased guidebooks, though such publications covered mainly the eastern states. There were occasional direction signs, but like the roads and the roadside amenities, they varied from poor to nonexistent. A lost motorist often found it impossible to obtain good directions from residents living along a country road. Most people knew little or nothing about the condition of the road only five or ten miles away or even beyond the next hill or stand of trees. Early motorists often paused every few miles to seek further directions or else remained hopelessly lost.

The publisher Rand McNally responded with what it called "photo-auto guide books." The bulky and expensive guides displayed photographs overlaid with arrows to show motorists which way to go through confusing road and highway intersections. A descriptive text further assisted lost and baffled travelers. Not until the mid-1920s did highway officials number federal roads to greatly improve navigation for cross-country motorists.[5]

Because early roads across the West presented so many challenges, the region's pioneer motorists had to be an intrepid group unless they limited their driving to an area close to home. Travel any distance by automobile required a person to prepare for almost anything, including the common hazard of abrupt changes in the quality of road surfaces. As early as 1912, venturesome American motorists might drive along some two and a half million miles of road, though a mere 7 percent of the total had a graveled surface or at least nominal grading. Pioneer motorists typically bounced through the countryside along dirt paths that twisted this way and that and were impassable during wet weather.

Despite the challenges, something about a road trip was appealing even in the early days. As automobile ownership became more widespread with each passing year, the Sunday afternoon pleasure drive evolved into a popular form of recreation, and an overnight excursion of any length became a personal adventure. As for the romance of the open road, an aspiring young novelist named Sinclair Lewis captured it in *Free Air,* a book published in 1919 that spins a story of love and misadventure along the way from Minnesota to Seattle. Lewis and his wife made such a journey in their Model T Ford in 1916.

⚜ ⚜ ⚜

As has been noted, in their heyday the railroads of the West produced many regional boosters, or "empire builders," both prominent and unsung. These development-minded individuals labored tirelessly to increase the West's population, to popularize its resources and scenic attractions, and thereby to increase railroad passenger and freight traffic. They continued to promote regional development during a time of rising highway competition in the 1920s and 1930s.

Despite the obvious benefits railroads and their numerous development activities conferred on westerners, they also created new forms of dependency. Their freight rates often determined which of the region's commodity-producing industries prospered and which languished because they were unable to compete successfully in distant markets. A railroad timetable fixed the times of the arrivals and departures of local passenger trains, which for many towns located away from busy main line tracks meant just one local train a day each way. Few of these unpretentious trains were convenient or comfortable, and they became even less so

In contrast to a big-city hotel, personal independence and a rough democracy prevailed at a typical auto camp. Harrison's, which was located in the Columbia River Gorge near Wyeth, Oregon, offered more elaborate accommodations than most such facilities, including the cabins it rented for a dollar apiece in the 1920s. Courtesy Oregon Historical Society.

when they had to compete with automobiles that came and went as their drivers pleased. In fact, a primary reason automobiles grew so popular so quickly was that they freed travelers from the tyranny of railroad time-tables, especially for short-distance trips; and a long family trip by car usually cost less than travel by train.

Not surprisingly, at various times and places western railroads and their power to bless or blight communities by where they located a new line of tracks or by how high or low they set their freight rates became the focus of all-consuming popular animosity. Few people could hope to own a passenger train or even a modest streetcar, but Americans wanted the freedom to travel quickly, at a time of their own choosing, and at the lowest possible cost. As one magazine advertisement for Chevrolet automobiles aptly phrased it in 1924: "Every owner [is] in effect a railroad president, operating individually on an elective schedule, over highways built and maintained chiefly at the expense of himself and his fellow motorists."[6]

Automobiles addressed the popular desire for greater individual control over travel better than any previous mode of transportation technology, including the once-ubiquitous horse and buggy, which had at best a limited range and suffered from the drawbacks common to animal power. That said, an honest appraisal of automobile ownership must admit that it created its own subtle forms of dependency. Today if a light on the instrument panel flashes "Check Your Engine," the owner of the latest and most sophisticated automobile is dependent on expensive computer diagnostics and the knowledge of trained mechanics to remedy the problem. Perhaps it is no exaggeration to claim that the American West entered the twentieth century as the often petulant child of the steel rail, but it left it a somewhat perplexed hostage to the automobile.

Railroad power in its myriad forms and responses to it by other transportation technologies, notably the West's growing legions of private automobiles and fleets of intercity trucks and airliners, shaped the region's transportation history during much of the twentieth century. Initially, however, the several challengers appeared weak and insignificant compared to the almighty railroads, and that—at least in the eyes of smug railroaders—did not seem likely to change.

Highways easily ranked as the least impressive corridors ever extended across the western landscape, at least in 1900. In fact, the term "corridor" hardly seems appropriate to describe most of the early ones. At the dawn of the new century, when paved streets extended to the edge of town and no farther, a city motorist who dared to proceed into the country had better be prepared for all kinds of adventures certain to lie ahead.

As early as 1901 one observer noted that "automobile touring" on the

No wonder travel by automobile was so slow in the rural West in 1910. This Oregon sign warns, "$25 Fine for Riding or Driving over This Bridge Faster than a Walk." Courtesy Oregon Historical Society.

Pacific Coast was a far different matter from that of "tooling about the East." East of the Rocky Mountains the United States had bad roads aplenty, but it had nothing like the "giddy mountain grades," "unbridged rivers," and "wide sand 'washes'" that made the typical road trip "a nightmare" in California—the state, incidentally, which probably could claim to have the best roads in the West in 1900. However, as anyone attempting to drive along them soon realized, that wasn't an impressive claim: "California roads have a way of losing themselves in great barley fields or coming out on the remains of a boom town and going no farther." Along the coast it was not uncommon for a reasonably good road to deteriorate gradually until "it finally comes out on the beach and if it is high tide ends right there."[7]

Not surprisingly, a distance of seventy-five miles usually constituted a reasonable day's drive. Not only were country roads rough, but early-day motorists also experienced frequent delays caused by flat tires and balky engines. The primitive motor vehicle laws of the early twentieth century made for slow going, too. One law enacted in Oregon in 1905 limited the top speed for each of its 218 registered motor vehicles to eight miles per hour in the country when approaching within a hundred feet of any vehicle powered by horses. Not surprisingly, as late as 1908 or 1909 a road trip from Portland to nearby Mount Hood was an all-day adventure by automobile, and that was during summer when Northwest weather was at its best.

In Oregon and most other states, the use of an automobile during cold winter months was simply not feasible until the advent of enclosed vehicles and antifreeze. Before World War I, 90 percent of all car owners stored their automobiles for the winter and returned to horse or steam or electric transportation. The most conspicuous exception was balmy southern California, one of the few places where year-round motoring was possible in the early twentieth century. The mild climate and general prosperity led to the building of many miles of wide, straight boulevards across greater Los Angeles to accommodate the motoring public, but in the nearby countryside the problems were much the same as elsewhere.

An early motorist attempting to drive between Los Angeles and San Diego, a distance of approximately 160 miles (and easily spanned today by multilane freeways), had better be prepared to surmount numerous steep grades interspersed with many miles of lonely landscape. One turn-of-the-century auto adventurer recalled roads in San Diego County that ran along hilltops hidden by clouds: "I experienced the novelty of wheeling for hours among the clouds, selecting the early morning hours for this purpose, in order to avoid teams. Fortunately we chose Sunday, and so got over the worst grades without meeting a team. This will be better understood when one realizes that for miles and miles the grade is only wide enough for one team and this narrow roadbed is cut out of the side of the mountain, dodging into the hollows and shooting 'around the horn' in a way that fairly makes one dizzy if he looks either ahead or behind." Despite the hazards, when measured by the unsophisticated standards of 1901 the road between Los Angeles and San Diego was actually better than most of its counterparts across other parts of rural California. Even in those early days of motoring, speed was important to residents of southern California. The same automobilist observed in 1901 that his best mileage between Los Angeles and San Diego was "85 miles a day on two different days. The last day we made 60 miles in 4½ hours. On a previous trip, made over better roads, we covered 160 miles in 10 hours and 12 minutes running time." [8] The desire for greater speed gave early motorists a reason to demand better roads and highways, and so too did the ordinary hazards of a journey.

On the coastal route from San Diego, "all one day was used in crossing a big ranch, and we passed but two houses during that time. This ranch, which is a Spanish grant, is about the size of Rhode Island, and midway across it we broke a front spring. The nearest village was fully 30 miles away with some wretched roads intervening." The writer further warned readers who dared undertake an automobile tour of rural California that "one thing is necessary above everything else, which is to have a machine able to climb 40 percent grades. If your carriage will not do that you must stay in the towns. Of those automobiles that have gone into the Yosemite Valley only two have come out with their own power." [9]

Early motorists who aspired to drive from Los Angeles or San Francisco all the way to Yosemite National Park, the crown jewel of the rugged Sierra Nevada, seemed about as daring as if they had chosen to climb hand-over-hand up the rocky face of El Capitan itself. As for anyone hoping to drive east from California across the deserts of Arizona or Nevada, it was best to pack along a block and tackle at a minimum—and a generous measure of courage. Better yet, why not take a train and forget about risking life and limb in a foolish attempt to motor across the continent?

❧ ❧ ❧

Any comeback for long-distance trails or roads across the West would have to result from the marriage of technological innovation and promotional activity—the same kind of boosterism that railroads had used so successfully to sell the region to prospective tourists and settlers. Prominent among several early groups promoting better rural roads in the United States was the League of American Wheelmen, founded in 1880 by bicycle enthusiasts. This organization became a mainstay of the national Good Roads Movement by which riders sought to promote improved surfaces to make their bicycle outings more enjoyable. Bicycles were all the rage during the late nineteenth century, and even at the start of the new century more than three hundred manufacturers built more than a million bicycles a year.

New Jersey led the nation toward better roads when its state government, in 1889, permitted individual counties to issue bonds to pay for local construction projects. Two years later, New Jersey established the first state highway department in the United States, largely in response to pressure from bicycle enthusiasts. In 1893 Massachusetts became the second state to shoulder a portion of the hitherto local and county burden of providing money to build good roads. The trend toward state support for improved roads picked up speed in 1895 after Connecticut and California (the trendsetter in the West in motoring) joined the movement, and again in 1898 with the addition of Vermont and Maryland. By 1910 twenty-six states had highway construction and maintenance departments. Further contributing to the nation's growing interest in good roads was the advent of Rural Free Delivery of mail.

With few exceptions, responsibility for building and maintaining roads in late-nineteenth-century America had rested on the narrow shoulders of local governments and their often-parsimonious taxpayers. During the first two decades of the twentieth century, roughly three-quarters of all money required to finance highway construction was raised by property taxes. It was common for cities to use those dollars to hire trained engineers to design good roads and then hire a small army of workmen to construct them. But rural dwellers, accustomed to an economy based largely on barter and credit, preferred to work off whatever road taxes might be levied on them. Gathering from time to time for what amounted to a daylong social occasion not unlike a barn raising, farmers used their own teams of draft animals, their own scraping equipment, and their own muscle to shovel dirt into sloughs or mud holes or to level high spots in the primitive pathways that connected their farms and ranches to nearby villages.

Their concern was not the automobile and its driver, who was often a city dude expensively clothed in a linen duster, scarf, visored cap, and goggles. In the sound of their noisy gasoline engines and in the great clouds of dust they raised, these gadabouts showed how alien they were to the slow and measured pace of rural life and how their speedy automobiles might endanger slow-moving farm animals in the road. By contrast, the typical farmer or rancher wanted only to make the rural roads passable for his own plodding horse-drawn wagons. It is worth recalling that at the dawn of the new century approximately two-thirds of all Americans lived in rural areas.

The primary purpose of a country road was to link farms with markets as represented by nearby railroad connections. These dirt paths typically extended from towns into the surrounding countryside like spokes radiating from a hub, and thousands of individual hubs dotted the rural landscape from Maine to California. Seldom did the spokes link together in any meaningful way. Most rural Americans did not need a more extensive or sophisticated network of roads and highways at the turn of the century.

For that reason, battles for good roads were not easily won. Advocates of good roads had to expend "a tremendous amount of argumentative energy" to persuade state lawmakers to make even the most grudging appropriation for highway construction.[10] The rural-dominated legislatures typical of the early twentieth century saw no good reason to squander tax dollars to benefit a few city dwellers and their noisy automobiles. At best they appropriated only tiny amounts of money for any project likely to benefit bicyclists and city motorists—or, more likely, to benefit crafty politicians who wanted mainly to impress hometown voters. Pork-barrel politics, not the logic of geography or civil engineering, typically determined where scattered sections of improved roadway would be built. Because politics figured so prominently in early construction projects, lobbying organizations grew important in the nation's quest for improved roads.

One early promoter of better roads was the Automobile Club of Southern California. Established in 1900, it was two years older than the American Automobile Association (today's AAA), itself a venerable organization. Apart from a handful of automobile social clubs, those two associations were without peer in the early twentieth century. During the decade of the 1920s, the Automobile Club of Southern California figured prominently in the ongoing work of charting and marking automobile trails across the West from Los Angeles to New York City and Washington, D.C. Even with novel forms of boosterism, during the first quarter of the twentieth century the task of building better roads across California and the rest of the West lurched forward mainly by fits and starts, like an automobile with a badly tuned engine.

Road-building activity as a rule was most impressive in metropolitan areas where enthusiastic lobbyists worked closely with sympathetic governments. In rural areas it barely inched ahead until a self-taught mechanic named Henry Ford popularized reliable and inexpensive cars more effectively than any of his numerous contemporaries. Ford introduced his Model T on October 1, 1908. It was the first of fifteen million vehicles of that designation, a record surpassed in the United States only by the original Volkswagen "Beetle."

An early Model T straight from the factory was a basic machine unburdened by the apparent frills of a gasoline gauge, speedometer, oil gauge, or temperature indicator. It had no self-starter, no bumpers, and no choice of color except black. There was no accelerator pedal either. There were three pedals on the floor, however, that a driver pumped to shift into low or high gears or reverse. He manipulated two levers on the steering column, one to control the amount of gas fed to the engine and hence set the speed, and the other to adjust the spark. Finally, the intrepid driver of a Model T had to climb in and out over a fake door.

Despite its idiosyncrasies, a Model T in operation proved as indefatigable as a well-constructed work boot, and its down-home qualities quickly endeared it to farmers and ranchers. Nothing did more to increase the pressure on legislatures to provide better roads than the ever-widening circle of automobile owners, though as late as 1912 nearly half of the states still lacked highway departments and hence any coordinated response to the needs of a growing legion of motorists.

As for federal dollars to improve the nation's poor-to-nonexistent network of roads and highways, the prevailing interpretation of the Constitution effectively tied Uncle Sam's hands and kept him from becoming

During a get-together called a "Sociability Drive," these proud owners array their Model T Fords along the main street of Dayton, Washington, in 1913. Courtesy Oregon Historical Society.

directly involved in any form of road building. The Good Roads Movement nonetheless helped spur Congress to establish the Office of Road Inquiry within the Department of Agriculture in 1893 to provide expert advice to any state and local official interested in learning how to construct an improved farm-to-market road. Congress appropriated $10,000 to pay for the newly created office but forbade employees from challenging state sovereignty by seeking to influence road policy within an individual state or county in any way. Despite its obvious limitations, the Office of Road Inquiry functioned in a tenuous manner as the granddaddy of the Federal Highway Administration created later.

Federal officials worked closely with the National Good Roads Association and the Illinois Central Railroad to sponsor the first "Good Roads Train," which in 1901 ran between New Orleans and Chicago. At various stops along the way the cadre of experts gave public lectures and occasionally took time to help build short sections of what were commonly labeled "object-lesson roads." However, not until 1916 did Uncle Sam aspire even to junior partner status with individual states in road-building projects, even those of obvious national importance.

For most members of Congress, the twin concepts of good roads and national interest long remained mutually incompatible. They were not deaf to the rising public clamor for good roads, however. Among the most compelling arguments was that they would help reduce rural isolation, especially in winter and spring when unimproved roads often were impassible, and make it easier for Uncle Sam to deliver mail regularly to the nation's sizeable farm population. Nonetheless, only after lawyers found a Constitutional loophole that permitted federal involvement did a majority in Congress respond with the first of several measures intended to aid highway construction across the United States. Even so, in the landmark highway legislation of 1916, Uncle Sam contributed dollars only in the guise of lending a helping hand to farmers and other rural dwellers. Such limits prevented knowledgeable federal officials from becoming directly involved in building improved urban roads and highways until many years later.

As long as good roads remained synonymous mainly with forging a series of better links between farm and market—and as long as any truly regional or national highway system remained nonexistent—America's railroads stood at the forefront of a movement they believed would benefit them by improving the flow of goods and people throughout rural portions of the United States. Across a vast swath of the rural West accurately described as "Union Pacific country," one such advocate of improved country roads was Edward H. Harriman, the railroad's chairman. Farther north another supporter was Harriman's arch rival, James J. Hill. As the chairman of the Great Northern Railway emphasized as recently as 1910, "I know of no material aid to the farming population so important as the creation and maintenance of good roads."[11]

A year later when the Minnesota State Automobile Association held its third annual endurance run from Saint Paul to Helena, Montana, officials of the Great Northern Railway arranged for a special hotel train to meet the "autoists" at the end of each day to attend to the needs of the "road-weary party." At that time there were no tourist courts or motels across rural Minnesota, North Dakota, and Montana, and "autoists" welcomed the railroad's hospitality. The Great Northern train consisted of two dining cars, a garage car filled with auto supplies and spare tires, and five sleepers lighted by electricity, cooled by electric fans, and kept dirt and dust free by vacuum cleaners (all such conveniences being relatively new themselves). In the observation car a modern "Victrola" offered music to soothe tired motorists.

That was not all. The Great Northern train included a physician "as well as typewriters for all the newspaper correspondents in the cars, a barber shop, a clothes pressing establishment for both men and women on the auto tour, and a photographic dark room." Suggesting just how important the annual "motor safari" was in the eyes of railroad executives, the hotel train included two business cars, one belonging to Louis W. Hill, president of the Great Northern Railway, and the other to John Ringling, president of the White Sulphur Springs & Yellowstone Park Railway. In short, the Great Northern offered a good solution to "one of the chief difficulties that the autoists find, and it was the center of many pleasant social evening entertainments after the day's run."[12]

Although a few venturesome motorists could brag about driving from coast to coast across the United States in the early twentieth century (a daring feat that always attracted considerable newspaper coverage), even rail executives as astute as Edward H. Harriman and the Hills, James J. and his son Louis, failed to anticipate that automobiles and trucks might one day, and without any fanfare, emerge as serious competitors to their railroads. Who could blame them? Rural residents of the West might bounce over rutted dirt roads in horse-drawn wagons to haul crops to the nearest railroad station, but when they wanted to travel even to an adjacent county seat, the preferred mode of transportation was probably the passenger train.

Despite the obvious shortcomings of the West's early automobiles and highways, there was always an adventuresome soul ready to attempt something new simply because no one had done it before. One such individual was Dr. Horatio Nelson Jackson, a young physician from Vermont, who won a measure of fame when he completed America's first transcontinental automobile trip on July 26, 1903. With his own money and car, Jackson and a mechanic from Tacoma, Washington, named Sewall K. Crocker left San Francisco on May 23 and piloted a two-cylinder, twenty-horsepower Winton touring car across the United States to New York City.

Their roundabout route took them east by way of Idaho's Snake River plain, southern Wyoming, and the Platte River Valley of Nebraska. Across much of Wyoming they paralleled the old Central Overland route last used some thirty-five years earlier by transcontinental stagecoaches. The halfway point of their journey found them bouncing through rutted sagebrush outside Rock Springs, Wyoming.

In all, the two adventurers crossed nearly 6,000 miles, or nearly double the recorded distance from the Pacific to Atlantic coasts, because they made lengthy detours to avoid impassible and flooded areas. Among the equipment they took with them was a block and tackle, which came in handy when the pair repeatedly became stuck in muddy buffalo wallows as they struggled across Nebraska. In all, they completed the trek from San Francisco to New York in sixty-three days, 12 hours, and 30 minutes. That was a record time for automobiles, though it might be worth noting that back in the 1860s a stagecoach could do the same thing in half as many days. It is worth mentioning, too, that Nelson and Crocker of necessity spent nineteen of their days on the road idle, usually waiting for rail shipments of replacement parts.[13]

Records of any type always challenged others to better them. Already by 1905 it could be reported that the "record for the trip from San Francisco to New York stands at present at thirty-three days, made last August by a light touring car of ten horse power and weighing but twelve hundred pounds." That was about half the time it took Jackson and Crocker in 1903. A motorist in 1906 took just fifteen days to drive from one coast to the other, but that record soon fell too. By 1916 it was possible for a lucky motorist to zip across the continent in just five days, a time that approximated the speed of the best passenger trains.[14]

Record-breaking or not, a transcontinental road trip was not for the faint of heart, and commercial road transportation of any type was out of the question. Not until 1927 would the first transcontinental buses commence regular operation. During a span of nearly sixty years—from the last run of the overland stagecoach in 1869 until the start of coast-to-coast bus service—the only commercial passenger transportation by land across the United States had been by train. By the same token, no long-haul truck lines extended across the continent until the late 1920s.

The team of adventurers who dared to drive a loaded freight truck across the Southwest from Pueblo, Colorado, through Santa Fe and Phoenix to Los Angeles in 1911 faced many of the same obstacles that deterred motorists a decade earlier. The challenge of covering 1,450 miles in 66 days (not all of them spent in travel) was accomplished by a four-cylinder, 37-horsepower, gasoline-engine-powered truck. Swiss-made and licensed by the Saurer Motor Company of New Jersey, this rugged vehicle was aptly termed the "Pioneer Freighter."

Ironically, its 14,000-pound payload consisted mainly of heavy lumber planks required to bridge creeks and soft sections of ground. Its aver-

A sightseeing bus and its intrepid tourists pass the Brigham Young Monument and the Mormon Temple in Salt Lake City on a cold day in the early twentieth century. Courtesy Utah State Historical Society.

age speed was barely more than three miles per hour, or about as fast as a man could walk. Yet to a growing band of enthusiasts, the journey of the "Pioneer Freighter" anticipated the day when heavy-duty trucks matured into true long-distance freight haulers. That same year, 1911, America's first Motor Truck Show was held at New York's Madison Square Garden. One of the vehicles on display was the "Pioneer Freighter," shipped by rail from Los Angeles back to Pueblo, from where it plodded east over the primitive roads leading toward New York.

The widespread use of automobiles and trucks outside the urban West remained unthinkable to most observers, at least until manufacturers built better cars and roads for the masses. Until then, most automobiles remained seasonal playthings of affluent city dwellers who had money and time enough to occasionally challenge the "frontier" in their cars.

Paralleling the quest for more powerful and reliable automobiles was an ongoing search for better quality road surfaces. Not uncommonly early roads of the West abruptly degenerated into two muddy ruts extending across a field. Countless other miles of dirt road were simply scraped from the land, and when wet became deeply rutted, if not impassible. During the dry seasons those same pathways were marked by contrails of swirling dust created by the passing of an occasional automobile. Something so basic as drainage culverts remained virtually unknown. Not until 1911 did Columbia University offer what was apparently the first college degree in highway engineering.

Like many other facets of the automotive revolution, the pursuit of better pavement originated in the city and seeped into the surrounding countryside, where at the turn of the century the very best rural roads in most places consisted of crushed rock. In many a city the first modern paved surfaces were made of cobblestones, bricks, and even special wooden paving blocks. Cobblestones and gravel remained the favored paving materials for city streets until the 1890s because their rough surfaces provided needed traction for horses' hooves at a time when many animals hauled heavy wagons. That seemed more essential than providing pampered bicyclists and motorists smooth surfaces beneath their tires. Those paving materials also helped diminish the clouds of dust raised by early automobiles.

Road builders first used a promising new material called Portland cement in Bellefontaine, Ohio, in 1891 to pave streets surrounding the Logan County courthouse. Two years later, also in Ohio, they pioneered the use of bricks to surface a rural section of the Worcester Pike in Cuyahoga County outside Cleveland. Workers finished the nation's initial section of brick road successfully at a cost of approximately $16,000 a mile, although its main impact seems to have been to encourage the paving of city streets, where such work went rapidly forward. By the time of America's entry into World War I in April 1917, cities had paved their main thoroughfares, although many side streets were still dirt.

Beyond the city limits, progress toward paved roads and highways was generally uneven and slow. With asphalt and concrete, the two most common paving materials today, still so little used in the early twentieth century, the best a motorist could expect was a hard surface of bricks, a few hundred bumpy miles of which were scattered around the United States. Some short sections of highways in the timber-rich Pacific North-

*Motoring through the Mitchell Point Tunnel, one of many scenic
attractions on Oregon's Columbia River Highway.
Courtesy Oregon Historical Society.*

west were originally paved with stout wooden planks. As late as 1914 less
than one percent of the nation's surfaced rural road mileage was paved
with anything as durable as concrete.

One state that took several bold steps to lift America out of the mud
was Oregon. At first it was no different than most other states, though in
1910 Governor Oswald West had proclaimed the state's entire Pacific
coastline to be a public highway. In that way he preserved beach scenery
for future generations to enjoy as they drove along what is now Highway
101. Only in 1913, by which time approximately ten thousand motor
vehicles were already in use throughout the state, did the legislature for-

mally promote the building of better roads. Before that, Oregon had only city or county-sponsored roads.

One valuable thing that Oregon's newly created highway commission did was to plan a truly statewide system of highways for the first time. Financed by a one-quarter-mill levy on all property, Oregon's highway measure raised $700,000 during its first year and focused attention on improving a trio of routes most likely to benefit drivers. Those three were the Coast Highway; the Pacific Highway, completed from Portland through the Willamette Valley in 1922 and fully paved to California in 1926; and the Columbia River Highway between Portland and eastern Oregon. More than any of its contemporaries in the West, the Columbia River Highway gained world renown as a model of what skilled road builders might accomplish.

Samuel Christopher Lancaster, the consulting engineer on the Columbia River Highway project, envisioned a road that was scenic as well as functional because it could showcase such natural wonders as Multnomah Falls and Oneonta Gorge. Farther east was Mitchell Point, where Lancaster designed the road to thread its way through one of the first major automobile tunnels in the United States. After it opened on November 10, 1915, the tunnel became a scenic attraction of the early highway age. Located five miles west of the town of Hood River and bored nearly four hundred feet through a promontory of basaltic rock, Mitchell Point featured five expansive windows that opened through the rocky hillside to provide motorists an awe-inspiring panorama of the Columbia Gorge.

Closer to Portland was Crown Point, a lofty promontory topped by the Vista House from which it was possible on a clear day for motorists to survey fifty miles of the Columbia River as it coursed through the Cascade Mountains. In addition, there was the visual thrill of the road itself. "In many places while spiraling down, the roadbed is supported upon rock shelves, doubling back along the mountainous cliff five times in a double figure 8, before passing at the level of the river through a region abounding with twenty-four rushing waterfalls."[15]

Not surprisingly, when the first section of the Columbia River Highway opened to traffic in 1915, the festive occasion was not unlike one of the final spike ceremonies that railroads of the West had regularly staged during the previous century. The celebration did not mean that construction of the Columbia River Highway was finished, however. Many challenges remained. At one narrow point east of The Dalles, the builders used a block and tackle to hoist men, tools, and explosives to a rocky face 120 feet above railroad tracks, where they incised a ledge for the highway. "The workmen labored in what is known as a boatswain's chair, and all holes were drilled with 7/8-inch steel and single jack hammers. Great caution was necessary in shooting the holes, as trains were constantly passing on the mainline directly under the cliff."[16]

That was the final obstacle that stood in the way of the first modern paved highway in the Pacific Northwest. By late 1921 the work was done and the highway open to automobile travel from Astoria and Portland through the Columbia Gorge to Pendleton, a distance of approximately 365 miles. Beyond eastern Oregon, a motorist could continue into Idaho, Utah, and Wyoming by following the general course of the old Oregon Trail on relatively good roads in the 1920s.[17]

Road builders in Oregon and elsewhere consciously sought to identify their modern handiwork with historic corridors. This appeared to give legitimacy to their creations. "The highways of the country are something more than a commercial asset to the state through which they run. They are sometimes the symbols of visions, hardships and achievements; and the Old Oregon Trail is one of the greatest examples of that symbolism."[18]

One of the last official acts of President Warren G. Harding before his sudden death in 1923 was to attend a history pageant held at the summit of the Blue Mountains east of Pendleton, Oregon. The event attracted almost 30,000 onlookers. Its main purpose was to draw an explicit parallel between the original Oregon Trail and the Old Oregon Trail Highway. It was easy for highway enthusiasts to lapse into overwrought prose to describe the occasion: "To thousands of motorists who had traveled scores of miles in a few hours, over broad, smooth highways flung like ribbons of satin across the country, the spectacle of the jolting, rumbling, creaking wagons, creeping and swaying top-heavily down the wooded hillside through the uneven meadow, and fording the streams to the accompaniment of shouts and cracks of whips, was a sight not soon forgotten, and brought home to everyone present the blessing of highways that have abolished most of the discomforts of overland travel."[19]

Across parts of the American Southwest, highway builders consciously sought to pay homage to the old Butterfield stagecoach trail that in the late 1850s had linked Saint Louis and San Francisco. "The old stage stations will be preserved—what remains of them—and the nation will be reminded of an adventure unparalleled in history." The stagecoaches that used the route "were handled by horsemen who were the 'Lindberghs' of the period, except that they made their passages many times and attempted to maintain schedules."[20]

The reference to Charles A. Lindbergh, the young aviator who made history in 1927 by flying solo across the North Atlantic, suggests that highway enthusiasts did not need to rummage through history seventy or eighty years old for their inspiration. Along a portion of the modern Imperial Highway across southern California in the mid-1930s, motorists could see sections of an old plank road that stretched through the sandy dunes near the Salton Sea just a decade earlier. It became an historic artifact when Henry Ford removed part of the old plank road to display in his museum in Dearborn, Michigan. It was one example of how rapidly a modern road and highway system took shape across the West between 1915 and 1930, a time when transcontinental corridors like the Lincoln Highway and Route 66 knitted local and regional segments into a truly national network.

Back in 1832, a physician named Charles Caldwell had predicted that in time a network of railway lines would join the United States into one "mighty city." [21] Indeed, by the dawn of the twentieth century that bold prophecy had been fulfilled. The rails formed what John Stilgoe later labeled the "metropolitan corridor," a term equally well suited to characterize Caldwell's one "mighty city" of a nation. Moreover, as a result of the frenzied pace of construction activity during the 1920s, all-weather roads and highways extended across the United States to form yet another type of metropolitan corridor that united the nation as never before. No longer were these merely the farm-to-market roads originally envisioned by railroad supporters. They were beginning to challenge the primacy of the railroads.

Five

The Emergence of New Corridors of Power

Modern transportation was a keynote of the Saint Louis World's Fair held in 1904. Only agriculture claimed more pavilion space that year. Four-fifths of the sixteen acres of transportation displays were devoted to railways, with the remainder given over to a mixed assortment of buggies, wagons, and automobiles. Although this was the first international exposition held after the Wright brothers' successful flight in late 1903, neither the Wrights nor anyone else put an airplane on display. Cigar-shaped dirigibles attracted the most attention from fairgoers and seemed to represent the future of aviation.

Bicycles, which had been plentiful at the World's Columbian Exposition held in Chicago in 1893, had passed "out of vogue" by the 1904 Louisiana Purchase Exposition. Astute fairgoers may have noticed that while not one automobile had been on display in Chicago, at least 140 automobiles were exhibited in Saint Louis only a decade later. The number of automobiles bounding—or more likely, bouncing—along the rough highways of the West would increase noticeably each year, especially after the end of World War I. Many additional miles of highway crisscrossed the landscape in an attempt to keep pace with the growing number of automobiles. Highway pavements grew better too—though how much better remained a matter of intense public debate.

Americans recalled both the highways and the automobiles of those years in highly personal terms. Aviator Charles A. Lindbergh recalled that when his father brought a Ford Model T home to the family farm in Minnesota in 1912, his mother christened the newest member of the household "Maria." For young Lindbergh, "Maria brought modern science to our farm, and nothing else attracted me as much, or was as chal-

Don't allow your hogs to get out and root up the grade, causing it to wash. Don't drink "white mule" and get in your automobile and go down the road showing the people you have the fastest car in the country.

—from "Observations of a Highway Patrolman," *Highway Magazine,* March 1921

137

ALSEA BAY BRIDGE - 3028 FEET LONG - OREGON CO

HIGHWAY, OREGON.   W·312.

The Oregon Coast Highway was one of the West's new corridors of power in the 1920s, and few highways offered motorists more impressive scenery. Wesley Andrews photographed its graceful bridge across Alsea Bay. Courtesy Oregon Historical Society.

lenging or as symbolic of the future." The lad learned to drive "Maria" at age eleven, and three years later, in 1916, he motored west with his mother to California to spend the winter. Their trip from Minnesota took a full month because the roads were so bad.[1]

A decade later Lindbergh graduated from the Army's flying school in San Antonio, Texas, and moved to Saint Louis, where he became the first pilot to fly the mail between there and Chicago. In the Missouri metropolis he came to know an automobile-enthusiast-turned-aviator named Albert Bond Lambert, a pharmaceutical manufacturer whose best-known product was an antiseptic mouthwash called Listerine. Lambert developed such a passion for aviation that he bought a biplane from the Wright brothers in 1909 and took his first flying lesson from no less an authority than Orville Wright himself. Nearly two decades later Lambert pooled some of his Listerine dollars with contributions from other Saint Louis industrialists to buy the plane that "Slim" Lindbergh flew from New York to Paris in 1927—and into the pages of history. No event did more to make the United States "air-minded" than the record-breaking flight of the "Spirit of St. Louis." It is fitting that modern Lindbergh Boulevard and Lambert-St. Louis International Airport intersect, just like the careers of these two automobile and aviation enthusiasts back in the 1920s. So, too, did the history of the nation's highways and skyways intersect.[2]

Compared to the technical sophistication and organizational maturity of the nation's railroad industry, transportation by road or air still seemed crude and primitive when World War I ended. That was an age of youthful exuberance for motorists and aviators alike—of joyriding on the ground and barnstorming in the sky. It was hard to imagine how either technology would become the basis for major new corridors of power by the end of the 1920s.

※ ※ ※

One highly publicized event, the United States Army's First Transcontinental Motor Convoy, exposed the shortcomings of postwar highways across the West and of motor transportation in general. Crossing the continent by private automobile was no longer a novel feat in 1919, but a proposal to cross it with a convoy of Army trucks did attract public attention. That was why, on July 7, 1919, just eight months following the armistice that ended World War I, a crowd of onlookers collected near the White House to watch as the drivers of a convoy of fifty-six military vehicles started their engines and plodded across the District of Columbia and west toward San Francisco.

As a military maneuver, what was about to take place was without precedent in United States history. The Army intended to use its First Transcontinental Motor Convoy to test the reliability of motorized military vehicles and to train the officers and enlisted men it assigned to maintain and drive them, a total of 209 soldiers. Without doubt the railroad gridlock that occurred during the first nine months of war in 1917 had caused Army brass to think about logistics and various forms of alternative transportation.

The convoy stretched a full two miles and included trucks of various sizes and manufacture. One pulled a trailer on which the Army had mounted a large searchlight; another hauled an armored tank, one of the fearsome new motorized vehicles to appear on the battlefields of Europe during the Great War. The procession included ambulances and motorcycles. Tagging along in shiny automobiles decorated with a variety of flags and banners was a group of civilians who had personal stakes in the convoy's success. These included representatives of several tire, automobile, and truck manufacturers as well as journalists eager to record a good adventure story. Thanks to the boosterism of Frank Seiberling, longtime head of Goodyear Tire and Rubber, that company's fifteen-member band rode merrily along for a short distance in its own special truck.

One last-minute recruit to the Army's transcontinental venture was Dwight D. Eisenhower. The young lieutenant colonel considered himself fortunate to have been selected to make the journey—at least until its long season of troubles began. Years later in a published memoir, Eisenhower described the experience as traveling through "darkest America with truck and tank." The roads east of the Mississippi River presented few obstacles, though Eisenhower recalled that on occasion "the heavy trucks broke through the surface of the road and we had to tow them out one by one, with the caterpillar tractor."[3]

The trucks themselves frequently proved as mechanically balky as the proverbial Army mule. Along the way the convoy experienced an endless series of tribulations that included broken fan belts, snapped steering gears, stuck valves, and sputtering magnetos. Each new malfunction caused another delay. The convoy suffered no flat tires, but only because the Army's heavy trucks rode on solid rubber tires. The pace of travel became dishearteningly sluggish, but in every town along the way crowds gathered to cheer the soldiers along—or, more likely, to slow them down further by crowding into the roadway to gawk at the brave soldiers and their war machines.

West of the Mississippi the pace of travel slowed still more. In Iowa the physical condition of the main road west seemed to deteriorate with each passing mile. Billowing clouds of dust became a constant companion along dirt roads over the high and dry plains, and a major annoyance to the soldiers, but nothing irritated them more than the rickety condition of many bridges they encountered along the way west. These jerrybuilt structures could easily support the weight of ordinary automobiles, but the heavy military vehicles often shattered the weather-beaten timbers and landed in the shallow streams or thick mud below. All other vehicles ground to a halt as soldiers sweated and strained to reclaim their temporarily immobilized trucks.

In California the highways were the best of the trip, and spirits soared. In Sacramento Governor William D. Stephens compared the soldiers to the "Immortal Forty-Niners." Cheers, fireworks, and showy speeches that "ran on and on, in a similar vain," in Eisenhower's words, greeted the Army convoy as it limped the last few miles into San Francisco's Lincoln Park on September 7, 1919. Indeed, there was reason to cheer. The soldiers had at long last achieved their objective, though during an odyssey that stretched across sixty-three days and a total of 3,310 miles they had averaged only five miles an hour and suffered at least 1,900 mechanical breakdowns.[4]

The transcontinental trek proved slow going, too, because heavy vehicles had broken through the decks of at least a hundred bridges. The Army carefully repaired all of them to a higher standard than before. In this way Uncle Sam contributed to an infrastructure of better roads across the West that benefited the civilian motorists who came later in their own automobiles.

The long journey made it obvious to Army brass—and perhaps even to the most mulish members of Congress—that if the United States became entangled in future wars it needed a rationally planned and solidly constructed national highway system, which the nation conspicuously lacked in 1919. Perhaps of even greater importance in the long run, what lieutenant colonel Eisenhower observed about the close relationship between good highways and a strong national defense made him a dedicated advocate of the Interstate Highway System, the greatest road-building commitment in American history, which he helped to launch as President Eisenhower in 1956.

Uncle Sam still played a modest and somewhat ambivalent role in national road building when young Eisenhower bounced to San Francisco along the wretched roads of the West with the Army Transcontinental Motor Convoy in 1919. Only three years had passed since Congress enacted the first modern measure to aid road construction in the United States, though that landmark legislation was badly flawed because it failed to encourage construction of a comprehensive national network of highways. Nonetheless, the Federal Aid Road Act that President Woodrow Wilson signed into law on July 11, 1916, marked the reemergence of Uncle Sam as a road builder after an absence of several decades, even if it took him a while to flex his muscles.

His return was "the subject of many dismal prophecies of the probable waste of public funds, of shiftlessness—in a word, of the 'pork barrel.'" But supporters of the federal government's new departure reminded critics of some "of the work that Uncle Sam put through with credit to himself. The Panama Canal stands first, but it is by no means alone. Our life-saving, geodetic survey, reclamation, and fish-culture service need no defense or apology."[5]

The 1916 measure gave $75 million to the Secretary of Agriculture to fund improvements to rural post roads during the next five years. He granted money to individual states on the basis of a 50-50 match. Because the dollars were restricted to states already having highway departments in place to supervise construction, the six holdouts scrambled to create departments in order to get their share of the federal appropriation. The first highway segment completed under the 1916 act was a 2.6-mile project in Contra Costa County, California, which cost federal and state taxpayers approximately $21,000 a mile, including concrete pavement for two lanes of roadway and drainage culverts.

Unfortunately, the 1916 act failed to mandate that federal dollars be used to promote construction of an interconnecting system of highways to benefit the entire nation. Thus, individual states, motivated by local politics and lacking any sort of comprehensive vision, typically spent federal dollars to improve geographically scattered segments of the main intercity highways. The result was a hodgepodge of short and separated fragments of good roads. A motorist cruising blissfully along an improved highway might discover only too late that the section of good pavement abruptly ended in a mile or more of axle-wrenching mud holes.

Furthermore, in the near term, any federal encouragement of state highway construction was effectively nullified when the United States entered World War I the next year. Even so, the 1916 act was important for the precedent it set, and supporters of good roads never underestimated its importance. The magazine *Better Roads and Streets* published a full-page cartoon in May 1916 showing a "Good Roads" wedge being driven into a stubborn log called "Congress" by a powerful mallet called the "vote." It titled its cartoon "The Entering Wedge"—and what an important entering wedge the 1916 measure ultimately proved to be![6]

The decade from 1910 to 1920 was particularly important in the history of highways and automobiles in the American West. Not only did the 1916 highway measure set an historic precedent by involving the federal government directly in road building for decades to come, but during that span of time a growing number of middle-class Americans also discovered the pleasure of automobile ownership, something that had been limited mainly to the wealthy in earlier years. One reason was a drop in the price of cars that made it possible for more people to afford one; and as cheap used cars became available, the circle of automobile owners further expanded. Automobiles grew in popularity not merely because they were functional but also because they provided an appealing new type of family recreation. Like streetcars in the previous era, automobiles and good highways became symbols of modernity. Never could the two technologies be effectively separated.

Scarcely had the guns of war fallen silent in November 1918 before officials of the Department of Agriculture hastily transferred $140 million worth of surplus military equipment to individual states to use in building and maintaining their roads. The gifts included some 27,000 motor vehicles as well as countless hand tools that could be used to help accelerate postwar road-building projects. The federal largesse gave momentum to the ongoing crusade for better roads.

Moreover, wrote Ernest Flagg Ayres, "With the war over, the boys came home, shed their uniforms, and demanded jobs. Idaho responded to the full limit of her resources." The most extensive program of public works "which the state had ever undertaken was soon underway."[7] The job that Idaho tackled in 1919 was repeated throughout the West. There was much to do, as the slow trek of the Army's First Transcontinental Motor Convoy reminded newspaper readers in 1919.

As of the following year, almost three million miles of roads and highways stretched across the United States, though many were suitable only for horse and buggy travel. In fact, only about 36,000 miles had all-weather surfaces able to sustain the wear and tear caused by growing automobile traffic. A motorist who attempted to drive across the Mojave Desert between California and Arizona in the early 1920s still must expect to surmount one challenge after another. "Signs of civilization are left behind with the crossing of the Southern Pacific Railroad tracks, and soon the car is again laboring through heavy sand." Large dunes stretched across the California landscape in every direction. "Just as the tourist begins to wonder whether or not it will be possible to go any farther, something new in the line of road construction looms up ahead of him. It is the famous Holtville-Yuma plank road, an innovation in highway building that was completed shortly before the nation entered the late war." The road consisted of two by six planks held together by strap iron to form a narrow pathway. The California Highway Commission was responsible for maintaining "the West's most unique highway."[8]

Important as various forms of federal aid were during the immediate postwar years, it was the states that discovered a magical new tax lever that helped to push their road-building programs steadily ahead through the 1920s and 1930s. In sharp contrast to forward movement by fits and starts that had typified highway building in most states of the West during the prewar years, the 1920s witnessed the emergence of a truly national network of federal and state highways. Between 1921 and 1937 the various governments in the United States spent no less than $19 billion for new roadways or improvements and another $12 billion for maintenance, or a total of $31 billion—a sum greater than the total capital investment in railroads of the United States in 1939.

Gas stations across the West once featured many distinctive designs. This one was located in downtown Portland. Even today the state of Oregon does not allow motorists to pump their own gas. Courtesy Oregon Historical Society.

The critical component that made steady highway progress possible during the interwar decades was a state tax on gasoline. The Oregon legislature blazed the way in 1919 when it imposed the nation's first such levy, a penny tax on every gallon of gasoline a motorist purchased. Automobile owners saw the tax as a painless way to pay for more miles of good roads. With its ingenious new source of construction dollars and a rallying cry to "Lift Oregon out of the Mud," contractors soon blanketed the Beaver State with hundreds of miles of improved highways. New Mexico and Colorado quickly followed Oregon's lead. Within a decade, every state had imposed a tax on gasoline that ranged from two to six cents a gallon.

By 1928 gasoline taxes nationwide generated approximately $300 million a year for improved roads and highways. "The trend toward 'bigger and better' gasoline taxes is the outstanding recent development in highway financing," said *Highway Magazine*.[9] Automobile license fees added another $325 million. Still more highway money came from Uncle Sam and from state highway bonds. The revenue generated by gas taxes remained high even during the Depression and helped to fund many additional miles of new or improved roads and highways. Congress imposed a one-cent-per-gallon levy on gasoline in 1932, but originally it was not dedicated solely to highway construction.

During the 1920s the states of the West expanded their highways at a rate never before or since equaled, and for the first time many of them were paved with something more substantial than good intentions. All records for road construction in the United States were surpassed during the fiscal year of 1922, according to the annual report of the Bureau of Public Roads. During that period 10,000 miles of federal-aid roads and more than an equal mileage of highways without federal assistance were constructed.[10]

Road builders opened up many a remote and once nearly inaccessible corner of the western landscape located far beyond existing railroad corridors—a fact that alarmed a young conservationist named Aldo Leopold. In a 1925 article, the future author of *A Sand County Almanac* observed, "We are building good roads to give the rancher access to the city, which is good, and to give the city dweller access to recreation in the forests and mountains, which is good, but we now, out of sheer momentum, are thrusting more and ever more roads into every little remaining patch of wilderness, which in many cases is sheer stupidity. For by so doing we are cutting off, irrevocably and forever, our national contact with the Covered Wagon days." Leopold went on to note that "the good roads mania, and all forms of unthinking Boosterism that go with it, constitute a steam roller the like of which has seldom been seen in the history of mankind."[11]

Even as individual states rushed to build more and better roads and highways, most Americans continued to think mainly in local terms. Given the nature of American politics, it was a rare mind indeed that conceived of a truly national highway system or even of a single all-weather highway that linked one coast with the other. As for federal authorities, who likely had the broadest vision of any highway planners, before the early 1920s they did not involve themselves directly in building good roads across the United States—or in any region of the country. Until that happened, it was private associations and visionary individuals who dared to dream the biggest dreams.

The American Automobile Association had envisioned a transcontinental highway as early as 1902, but another decade passed before anything concrete happened. That was after prominent Indianapolis industrialist Carl Graham Fisher, founder of the Prest-O-Lite Company, manufacturer of auto headlights that for the first time made it possible for motorists to drive safely after dark, dared to suggest an improved road—a "Coast-to-Coast Rock Highway"—in 1912. Perhaps more importantly, he also proposed a way to finance it. From time to time visionaries had projected roads across the map of the United States, but Fisher was a tough-minded businessman who had made a personal fortune in various enterprises related to improvements of the automobile. His proposed transcontinental highway was only a dream, to be sure, but he had a good-as-gold record of making dreams of all types come true.

For instance, Fisher was among the founding fathers of the Indianapolis Motor Speedway (home today of the city's classic Indianapolis 500). In like spirit, he dared to think that ordinary motorists might someday drive from New York to California without having to brave muddy streams or repeatedly free cars stuck to their axles in sand traps. Fisher's first *Ocean-to-Ocean Highway Bulletin* appeared in the fall of 1912. He expected the publication to heighten popular enthusiasm for his pet project and recruit new members to its cause. On its front cover he printed a map of the United States showing various other highway routes that proposed to cross it—the Northwest Trail and the Sunset Trail, for instance. But Fisher cleverly did not reveal even an approximate location for his dream highway. He wanted its mystery location to excite still more popular interest in his project.[12]

So compelling was Fisher's promotion of a "Coast-to-Coast Rock Highway" that within thirty days of his first public announcement, he already had in hand pledges for at least a million dollars. He also gained valuable publicity from around the nation. Among his most loyal backers were automobile manufacturers based in Indianapolis, who at that time competed successfully with their rivals in Detroit. Regardless of which place had the better claim to the title of "motor city," automakers both of Indianapolis and Detroit understood that additional miles of improved highways helped boost car sales. Moreover, the idea of actually driving your own automobile across the United States along a good road excited the public imagination because in 1912 a trip of that distance remained an elusive dream.

Fisher's transcontinental highway boosterism won pledges not just from auto industry leaders but also from ordinary Americans who grasped the full significance of what he and his prominent backers were proposing. The dream evolved, in 1913, into the Lincoln Highway Association, which boldly proposed to construct a modern all-weather highway from New York to San Francisco as a patriotic tribute to the martyred president. Among the Lincoln Highway's principal business backers, in addition to Fisher of Prest-O-Lite, were Henry B. Joy of the Packard Motor Car Company and Frank A. Seiberling, who had founded the Goodyear Tire and Rubber Company in 1898 with a loan of $3,500. However, more than profits alone motivated the captains of industry to back the Lincoln Highway. In common with the general public, the impressive scale of the project fired their imaginations.[13]

The proposed route of the Lincoln Highway stretched west 3,389 miles from Times Square in New York City to the Pacific Ocean in San Francisco. The intended highway bent southwest through Trenton and Philadelphia and then west to surmount the Allegheny Mountains on its way to across Pennsylvania to Pittsburgh. It linked together the Midwest cities of Canton, Fort Wayne, and South Bend before bypassing Chicago to the south and west.

It cut across northern Illinois and Iowa before reaching Omaha, Cheyenne, and Salt Lake City. Skirting the southern shore of the Great Salt Lake, the proposed road dashed across the sparsely populated desert country to link several Nevada mining towns with Reno. It topped the Sierra Nevada at historic Donner Pass before dropping down to Sacramento and California's broad Central Valley. Bending south through Stockton, the Lincoln Highway planned to enter San Francisco aboard ferryboats that spanned the bay from Oakland. "Let's build it," Fisher urged his loyal supporters, "before we're too old to enjoy it."[14]

From its inception, the Lincoln Highway Association had pursued a secondary goal of educating the motoring public to support better roads in all parts of the United States. That in itself was a bold ambition because when Fisher first proposed his coast-to-coast highway, the nation had no improved long-distance highways. The Lincoln Highway thus served to showcase better road construction, albeit in short and often widely dispersed segments at first.

Proponents of the coast-to-coast link initially hoped at least 25,000 motorists could drive their own automobiles west to the Panama-Pacific International Exposition held in San Francisco in 1915. In fact, orders for new cars were sometimes based on completion of the highway in time for the purchasers to drive them cross-country to the World's Fair. That proved impossible for most people because long-distance motoring west of Omaha remained a pioneering venture for many more years to come. Across the Nevada desert an improved highway route was not formally launched until 1925, and it remained a graded but unpaved corridor for another fifteen years.

During the years before World War I, "Lincoln Highway" became a household name. As early as 1915 its boosters produced and sold a *Complete Official Road Guide of the Lincoln Highway*. During the following years the Lincoln Highway Association raised money by selling buttons, pennants, maps, paperweights, and radiator emblems to motorists and businessmen—even to wide-eyed schoolchildren. After all, they were the motorists of the future.[15]

The proposed transcontinental highway, like similar roadways envisioned for the twentieth-century West, may have represented a grand dream, but it was the task mainly of local communities to knit its various

A sign-posting crew from the Automobile Club of Southern California pauses near Salt Lake City in July 1918. They are marking a section of the Lincoln Highway through this part of the West. Courtesy Utah State Historical Society.

sections together. They originally paid for many needed improvements with donated dollars from their own pockets plus any spare money from county and state budgets. Most local upgrades were low cost and consisted mainly of installing culverts, building embankments, and reinforcing bridges. To help dry the highway's muddy surface after an occasional rain, farmers dragged their own scrapers along it to fill ruts and encourage evaporation.

In an effort to make the transcontinental route easy for ordinary motorists to follow, the Lincoln Highway Association hired a small army of painters to emblazon telephone poles along the route with official markers consisting of bright bands of red, white, and blue over which they stenciled a large letter "L." Further helping to reinforce its location in the nation's collective consciousness was the name "Lincoln Highway," which appeared on numerous hotels, cafes, and garages along the way.[16]

🙢 🙢 🙢

By the time the United States entered World War I, boosters of the Lincoln Highway could brag about several paved stretches along its most populated portions, most notably east of Chicago and in California, but in Iowa and numerous areas farther West the route had not changed much since the Lincoln Highway Association was born in 1913. When Carl Fisher first proposed his coast-to-coast highway, there was no hint of the numbered nationwide grid of two-lane, all-weather federal highways first forged in the mid-1920s, and to believe that a limited access superhighway might someday extend east to west across the spacious landscapes of Wyoming or Nevada stretched the limits of science fiction.

Where, for instance, distances were great and population centers small and scattered, it was difficult to raise public money to build good sections of highways; but private associations like the one promoting the Lincoln Highway helped boost local and regional consciousness of the need to do something positive. Such associations aroused the competitive spirit of westerners, as happened after the Lincoln Highway bypassed the states of Kansas and Colorado, much to the dismay of their governors and residents in general.

Professional highway boosters learned to capitalize on the public anxiety aroused by being left off a main highway corridor. Likewise, they became masters at whipping up community pride in anticipation of being located along a named route. This group of fast-talking, glad-handing, and highly persuasive individuals did not differ much from the railroad promoters of an earlier era. All any highway booster needed to do was sketch a proposed route on a map of the United States, give it an impressive sounding name, and then travel from town to town along the way to persuade merchants and local chambers of commerce to subscribe to the new highway association. The promoter, of course, received a portion of any money raised this way.

If inspirational words alone failed to elicit the desired response, a gentle form of extortion might change a merchant's mind. A booster had only to mention casually that the proposed road could easily be rerouted through a neighboring town. In some places a clever highway promoter doubled his take by offering one or more alternative routes and thereby added subscribers. Local eateries and garages, even whole communities, derived pride and profit from advertising that they were located "on the Lincoln Highway" or any other named route. Of course the Lincoln Highway received a special publicity boost in 1919 when the Army's First Transcontinental Motor Convoy followed it west much of the way from the White House to the Golden Gate.

The Lincoln Highway was, in fact, one of approximately 250 special "highways" promoted by private associations across the United States. Some such routes remained basically short and local, while others aspired to cross the continent. By the early 1920s the Theodore Roosevelt International Highway had begun to take shape along a corridor between Portland, Maine, and Portland, Oregon; and the Yellowstone Trail reached out likewise to connect Boston and Seattle. The Pikes Peak Ocean-to-Ocean Highway linked New York City and Los Angeles—at least on paper—though in reality it shared sections of the roadway with the Lincoln Highway between New York and Philadelphia. South of the Lincoln Highway corridor, the Bankhead Highway sliced across Dixieland and the rest of the United States between Washington, D.C., and San Diego. The National Old Trails Road ran through the nation's midsection between Baltimore and Los Angeles, while the Old Spanish Trail roughly skirted the Gulf of Mexico to join Saint Augustine, Florida, with San Diego.

The inaugural convention of the National Old Trails Road (Ocean-to-Ocean Highway Association) was held in Kansas City in April 1912. Its five-hundred delegates spent little time on arcane discussions of how they expected to construct their road, but instead devoted a great deal of time to recounting the histories of the various trails they sought to knit together for the automobile age—the National Road between Cumberland, Maryland, and Vandalia, Illinois; and the Santa Fe Trail between Franklin, Missouri, and Santa Fe, New Mexico.

In its patriotic and historical fervor, the National Old Trails Road conference resembled a meeting of the Daughters of the American Revolution —and, in truth, that patriotic organization was one of its sponsors. An official map of the proposed route emphasized that the favored route would traverse thirteen states and touch five state capitals, ninety counties, and seventy-one county seats. Mrs. Hunter M. Meriwether of Kansas City, a representative of the Daughters of the American Revolution, proclaimed to the assembled delegates that the nation needed "an historic ocean-to-ocean road that will bring into prominence the towns through which it passes, also opening up to the public and to the tourist the great treasure house of historic interest in the West and Southwest, which, in point of age, greatly antedates anything in our Eastern colonial and revolutionary history."[17]

Besides giveaway maps for motorists, all any self-respecting highway association needed to put itself on the map was to paint special color-coded stripes on the occasional telephone poles or fence posts that stood by the road. The color codes, not numbered signs, guided motorists. "It was not an era in which to be color-blind," recalled George R. Stewart, who wrote the classic text on Route 40, which in many locations superseded the National Old Trails Road.[18]

Color-coded direction signs became especially confusing where several routes overlapped. As the number of marked "trails" multiplied and private highway associations ringed roadside telephone poles with color stripes extending nearly from top to bottom, directional markers intended to aid motorists served only to perplex them. The problem of coding caused the *Times* of Louisville, Kentucky, to grumble, "The harmless tourist in his flivver doesn't know whether he is going or coming, whether he is a hundred miles from nowhere or on the right road to a good chicken dinner and a night's lodging." [19] Furthermore, many sharp-eyed motorists noticed that the marked highways added to their motoring woes by occasionally meandering the long way around in order to cater to towns and merchants whose dollars had originally helped to underwrite private highway associations.

Under the circumstances, motorists found guidebooks to be valuable companions in the days before a numbered grid of federal highways. Their advice when reread today reveals some of the idiosyncratic features of early auto travel across the West. The Lincoln Highway guidebook for 1916 described the J. J. Thomas Ranch in the Great Basin desert west of Salt Lake City, Utah, with these words: "Ranch meals and lodging. Hot sulphur springs close to ranch. If trouble is experienced, build a sage brush fire. Mr. Thomas will come with a team. He can see you 20 miles off." [20]

⚙ ⚙ ⚙

Even if motoring around the West remained challenging and confusing in the early 1920s, the automobile itself continued to stir the popular imagination. It changed the social habits of a generation of Americans, and that included how they spent Sunday leisure hours or even how they courted. Automobiles allowed city dwellers to commute ever-longer distances between homes and jobs, and it helped end isolation for a nation of farm dwellers. These revolutionary changes increased the popular pressure building on Capitol Hill for Uncle Sam to fund better roads.

Lawmakers responded by passing the Federal Highway Act of 1921. Like the landmark 1916 act, the new measure provided $75 million in federal funds to be matched by state money on an equal basis. However, unlike the earlier legislation, which funded federal highway projects with $75 million spread over five years, the far more generous 1921 act provided an average of 75 million *each year.* Also unlike the 1916 act, which permitted states to build or improve highways essentially as they themselves saw fit, the 1921 act for the first time promoted the creation of a nationwide grid of about 200,000 miles of interconnected "primary" highways. Only those portions of a state's highways that clearly fostered the national grid or that could be constructed in a reasonably short span of time would be eligible for matching federal grants. Within two years the nation had in place for the first time the framework for a comprehensive network of highway corridors.

The 1921 act thus broke free entirely from the traditional vision of farm-to-market feeder roads favored by railroad executives and for the first time promised them direct highway competition. "But now the highway engineer is building a network of roads to connect the important towns, to reach points not reached by the railroads, to meet the demand for a kind and class of transportation not furnished by the railroads," *Highway Magazine* proclaimed in 1925.[21]

Among the original beneficiaries of the swelling stream of federal and state dollars to pay for improvements were the various named highway associations. Better than most states, which tended naturally to look only within their own borders, booster groups had long recognized the need for interregional routes and a uniform way to direct motorists along them. By the early 1920s, however, the private promotion movement had largely run its course. The inefficiency of multicolored route markers and the potential for "honest graft" among paid promoters increasingly irritated the nation's growing cadre of highway professionals, the officers and engineers of state highway departments and the United States Bureau of Roads, who were responsible to taxpayers for spending their dollars wisely.

In 1922 General John J. Pershing, the commander of American troops in Europe during World War I, submitted a map proposing what would become the nation's first integrated highway system based on consistent criteria. Some 200,000 miles of highways on the Pershing map were designated part of the Federal Aid System and thus could gain financial support from Congress under the 1921 legislation. Meanwhile, the American Association of State Highway Officials, an organization founded ten years earlier and composed of government professionals, grew increasingly wary of private promotional groups and recommended a course of action consistent with the Pershing plan. At their annual meeting in San Francisco in 1924, its members urged Secretary of Agriculture Howard M. Gore, whose department contained the Bureau of Public Roads, to appoint a Joint Board on Interstate Highways. This proposal represented another landmark in the nation's quest for better roads.

Members of the new board chose sections from the hodgepodge of named trails and roads for inclusion in a proposed federal highway system. Representatives from the private promotional associations lobbied hard for inclusion of their routes in the grid, and individual states voiced strong preferences too. The report issued by the Joint Board at the 1925 meeting of the American Association of State Highway Officials formally proposed that a logical and nationwide grid of numbered highways replace the increasingly quirky system of color-marked "trails." Many states had already developed similar systems of numbered highways within their borders.

According to the 1925 proposal, shield-shaped signs would identify U.S. highways that extended across state lines, with each such corridor given a new and distinctive number. On November 11, 1926, a special committee composed of federal and state highway officials assembled at a Pinehurst, North Carolina, resort to sign off on numbered interstate routes across all forty-eight states. The result was a nationwide grid of numbered two-lane federal highways intended to interconnect every city having more than 50,000 residents, much like the Pershing map had originally proposed.

The Emergence of New Corridors of Power • 153

Photographer Arthur Rothstein in 1940 captured the isolation of the location in Sweetwater County, Wyoming, where U.S. 30 crossed the Continental Divide. Here the modern transcontinental route followed a portion of the old Lincoln Highway and also paralleled the tracks of the Union Pacific Railroad. Courtesy Library of Congress.

Odd numbers designated highways that extended in a north-south direction, beginning with U.S. Route 1 on the East Coast and ending with U.S. Route 101 on the West Coast. Even numbers designated east-to-west corridors, beginning with U.S. Route 2 located south of the Canadian border and ending with U.S. Route 90 originally running between Mobile, Alabama, and the Pacific Coast along a corridor paralleling the Mexican border west of El Paso. In addition there were various diagonal routes, most notably Route 66 between Chicago and Los Angeles. The new federal system used a standard black and white shield emblem containing the state name and the highway number.

The numbering system doomed the original Lincoln Highway Association, which simply disbanded in the mid-1930s. The era of private promotion left behind a legacy of evocative route names and the pioneering efforts that resulted in the creation of interstate highway corridors. On the other hand, the new numbered system gave rise to such well-known east-to-west routes as U.S. Route 30. That coast-to-coast highway more or less followed the original Lincoln Highway as far west as northern Utah, from which point Route 30 steered north to retrace the general route of the Oregon Trail to Portland.

Located farther south was Route 40, a highway that followed the route of the original National Road much of the way from Maryland to Illinois. That was one reason why eastern portions of this route had earlier been color-coded as the National Old Trails Association Highway, or merely the National Old Trail. West of Salt Lake City newly designated Route 40 tended to follow the route of the former Lincoln Highway. After official promulgation of the numbered national grid in April 1927, most highway promotional groups faded away along with the colorful route markings that once festooned roadside telephone poles.[22]

Some newly numbered federal highways, notably Route 66, became intimately associated with the golden age of highway travel across the West, much like the North Coast Limited, Sunset Limited, and other luxury trains were with a golden age of rail travel in the years after 1900. Over time, Route 66 attained a measure of popularity that clearly transcended its function as a transportation corridor. On the other hand, Route 666, a minor north-to-south federal highway that meandered across the mountains and desert of eastern Arizona, created contention because its number corresponded to that of the beast identified in the Bible's apocalyptic book of Revelation. In more recent years the "Devil's Highway," as it was locally nicknamed, was renumbered U.S. Route 191.

Despite the nostalgia that Route 66 invokes—and many books today attest to enduring memories of lost times and places along the roadway between Chicago and Los Angeles—no highway corridor has been studied more intensely than that defined by U.S. Route 40. Helping to inspire scholars was a book-length essay combining the words and photographs of George R. Stewart, a Stanford University professor of English, who in the early 1950s carefully traced the route across America. In truth, while U.S. Route 40 was numbered from coast to coast, most motorists who used it probably never thought of it as a transcontinental route. As was true for all other federal highways, they typically drove only relatively short portions of Route 40 on a regular basis—mainly the busy sections that linked Columbus and Indianapolis or Saint Louis and Kansas City. Motorists usually thought of their familiar highways, even nation-spanning ones, mainly in local terms.

Like its many siblings in the 1920s, Route 66 was essentially cobbled together from sections of earlier named roads and highways, including the Ozark Trail, Grand Canyon Route, National Old Trails Highway, and the Will Rogers Highway. Bits and pieces of the old roads had evolved from an even earlier series of trails, traces, farm-to-market roads, and even a few early-day stagecoach routes. That this hodgepodge could be welded together to form any type of through route was a tribute to intense lobbying by a booster organization known as the Route 66 Association.[23]

Starting in Grant Park, near the shores of Lake Michigan, the "mother road" stretched southwest for 2,400 miles before it ended at the intersection of Santa Monica Boulevard and Ocean Avenue in Santa Monica. Along the way to California it crossed three time zones, eight states, and dozens of counties. It became known as the "Main Street of America" because it passed through the centers of so many small towns that typified the United States.[24]

❊ ❊ ❊

Including Route 66, the mileage of surfaced highways in the United States doubled between 1920 and 1930, and it doubled again by 1940. Across the West the boom in highway construction resembled that in mining and timber during earlier years. In the 1920s the amount of money spent on streets and highways easily ranked among the largest expenditures by state governments.

More than anything else it was the rapidly expanding network of roads and highways that encouraged westerners to own cars. By the mid-1920s the automobile was no longer regarded as a useless "go-devil," as some farmers had originally scorned it. A car had now become a necessity of life, especially for rural dwellers. When the weather was good and country roads were dry, an automobile transformed a trip to town from a daylong ordeal into a quick and pleasant jaunt.

Highway construction and better automobiles went hand in hand. First the machine took the lead, then the support structure, but always they aided one another. As a writer in the *Kansas Farmer* noted in 1916, "When it takes four horses to pull an empty wagon to town and wheat is going off in price each day; when the mail carrier gives up in despair and the children cannot get to school, the farmer cannot help wondering how much this condition is costing him each day." In short, "road improvement is a business proposition—a matter of dollars and cents."[25]

During the early years of the Lincoln Highway, a scattered set of "seedling miles," or sample sections of good concrete road, were built along the route. Over such stretches of good pavement local motorists enjoyed speeding along in their automobiles, though in wet weather they found it impossible to reach the good sections because deep mud often blocked access at either end. There, as elsewhere, a motorist bogged down to the axles in gumbo became an instant and passionate convert to the popular cause of improved roads and highways.[26]

Progress in both machines and support structures made it common by the late 1920s for motorists of the West to drive as many as four hundred miles in a single day. Mile after mile, construction crews labored to pave, widen, strengthen, and straighten the highways to improve motoring speeds and safety—but motorists only clamored for more. "It can truthfully be said today as in 1920 or 1925 that the highway industry is still in its swaddling-clothes," enthused the editor of the *Highway Magazine* in January 1930. "The United States, with 46 percent of the total world's road mileage, has improved but 20 percent of its 3,000,000 miles." The sole thing that could halt the road-building boom, he believed, was a decline in "the financial ability of a prosperous consuming public to pay for the motor cars and roads that have now become an established part of its economic life."[27]

He was wrong. In depression as in prosperity, the work of building and improving roads went relentlessly forward. When times were hard, it seemed good public policy to put unemployed men to work building roads; and when times were prosperous, the swelling ranks of motorists demanded more and better roads. And so the work continued year after year. During a span of time nearly two decades long, from the passage of the Federal Aid Highway Act in 1916 through 1934, a big-hearted Uncle Sam gave states approximately $2 billion to help them build better roads. Said one writer: "This makes the Panama Canal authorization of $300,000,000, which threatened many of our leading citizens with hysterics a generation ago, look like chicken feed."[28]

In response to the Great Depression, many thousands of miles of farm-to-market roads were built or upgraded, even as work continued on the nation's network of primary roads. In 1930 President Herbert Hoover increased federal highway aid from $75 million a year to $125 million, but that was a paltry sum compared to the $2.8 billion the New Deal pumped into various road and highway construction projects between 1933 and 1940 to provide employment for both jobless industrial workers and drought-stricken and desperate farmers.

The number of miles of good hard-surfaced highways grew from a meager 387,000 in 1921 to a million miles on the eve of Pearl Harbor twenty years later. However, despite the impressive progress, as late as the attack on December 7, 1941, it was impossible for a motorist to cross the United States by a rational route that was fully paved. As for rural roads, these numbered about three million miles shortly after World War I but grew little for the next two decades. Miles of farm-to-market roads needed to be improved in order to drag rural America out of the mud.

One result of ongoing work during the interwar years was what an enthusiast described as "the poetry of road-building. The boon of year 'round church attendance to a devout woman, release from lonely mid-winter isolation, frequent family reunions, dances and social gatherings for the pretty daughters of a farm family, regular school stance for eager bright youngsters, the doctor's nick-of-time arrival—these are the stories hidden within the statistics."[29]

The road landscape, too, was ever changing during the interwar years. The average paved road of 1920 was a mere sixteen feet wide (automobiles were narrower then, too); and fence lines, telephone poles, bridge abutments, and other roadside hazards were potentially lethal to any inattentive motorist crowded close to the edges of the pavement. During the first two decades of the twentieth century most Americans had not fully made the mental transition from horse-and-buggy days to the automobile age, so they did not object, at least initially, to driving along narrow country roads that routinely detoured around natural obstacles or traced meandering and leisurely paths between towns. "It was not long after the World War, however, that we began to see the error of our ways," wrote Harry Byron Jay in 1929.[30]

By 1940 the typical American road was twenty-two to twenty-four feet wide, up from fourteen to sixteen feet in the early days; and no longer did it follow the line of least resistance or give the appearance of having been built originally along a meandering cow path. Increasingly, safety-minded highway departments pushed ditches and other hazards to motorists well back from the flow of traffic and spent money on massive cuts and fills that enabled the newest roads to bypass narrow, dipping, and zigzagging sections of the old highways. "Instead of going around a house near a village, they would move it out of the way. Instead of going through a village, they would avoid it entirely if possible," Jay wrote. A few years earlier, "towns and villages fought hard to have the trunk lines go down their main streets, figuring, perhaps, that Zeke's place would sell a few more sodas and cigars if it did."[31]

Highway departments crowned road surfaces for better drainage, and they began to regularly remove snow from main corridors to permit wintertime motor travel. They improved railway grade crossings to reduce the number of fatal crashes between trains and highway traffic. The modern generation of highway builders worked to smooth and bank curves, "making it safe to negotiate them at 40 miles per hour." They constructed gentler grades and passing lanes, which benefited motorists accustomed to following growing numbers of over-the-road trucks as they ground slowly up steep and winding mountain roads. The under-powered cars of the pre–World War II era invariably caused a hot and frustrated driver to tempt fate and attempt to pass on a blind curve. For all motorists, "hills that only a few years ago were gear-shifting steep now are gentle slopes, easy to take in high."[32]

Before the beginning of the 1930s, highway development in the United States was "largely *extensive*" as the nation rushed to build a comprehensive network of roads, "whereas now [1940] it is *intensive*—particularly as applied to through highways," noted the editor of *Highway Magazine.* "Two noteworthy 'errors' were made in the early work—if we may call them errors—although they are excusable on the ground of

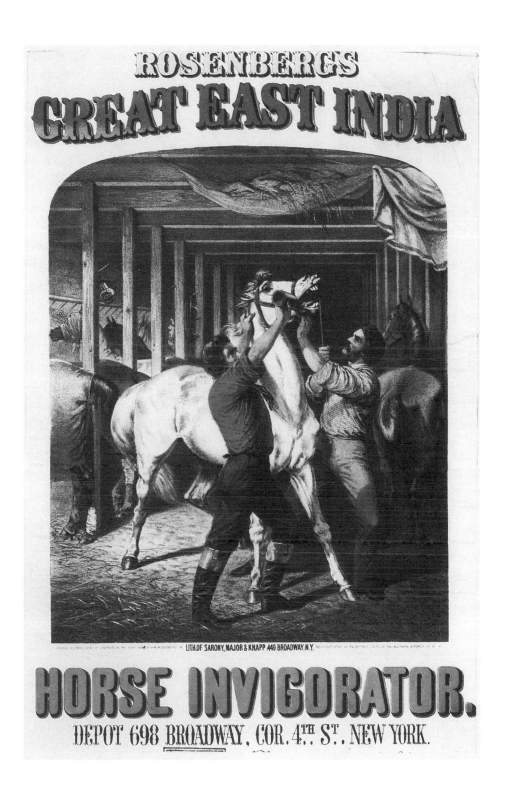

By the 1920s no "horse invigorator" could revive an historic mainstay of western land transportation. The population of draft animals declined rapidly after 1929. Courtesy Library of Congress.

The Emergence of New Corridors of Power • 159

insufficient engineering development and available experience." Those two errors were that the "phenomenal growth" of the automotive industry "made many of our roads obsolete—pavement and shoulder widths became too narrow as cars speeded up. Sight distance on vertical and horizontal curves became too short for safety." Second, "too many of the roads did not stay put, either because of erosion, slips and slides, or uneven settlement." All of this was a lesson for highway engineers, who "should keep in mind the constancy of change and then build for adaptability to future needs."[33]

Highway paving materials improved, as did methods of construction. Early-twentieth-century contractors undertaking a major road project commonly first laid down narrow-gauge railway tracks similar to those found in mines and gravel pits. Along those tracks they ran smoke-belching steam shovels and other heavy construction equipment, and they used diminutive railroad dump cars to move earth and bring in the necessary construction materials.

One common piece of early road equipment was the Fresno, invented in 1885 in its namesake city in California. Drawn by mules, this scraper could move up to a hundred cubic yards of earth a day. Though tractors often pulled a later-model Fresno, it became a museum piece after better earth-moving equipment appeared. In 1904 Benjamin Holt of Stockton, California, invented the first of a line of powerful tractors that crawled along on a chain of metal plates that it laid down and picked up again ad infinitum. As one writer described it, "These plates, corresponding to the cross-ties of the railroad, support inner rails, which in turn support the motor's revolving wheels."[34]

Holt's ingenuity, originally directed to solving the problem of how best to farm sprawling expanses of ranchland that typified California agriculture, eventually resulted in the Caterpillar line of heavy construction equipment—the large-scale, self-propelled, diesel-powered earth-moving and road-building machinery that did away with the need for special railroad tracks at highway construction sites. It took brawny machines of many types, along with a steady flow of tax dollars, to fashion roads and highways into the West's newest corridors of power.

Perhaps it was portentous, in an oddly mundane way, that in 1918, the year the Great War ended after forever altering the course of world history, the horse and mule population of the United States peaked at 26,723,000 animals. Thereafter, in response to the swelling ranks and growing efficiency of automobiles, trucks, buses, and tractors, the once-ubiquitous horse and mule joined the retreat led earlier by the stagecoach and buggy manufacturers. As a consequence of the transportation revolution of the 1920s, many a local passenger train soon followed Old Dobbin to the boneyard.

Six

The Twentieth-Century Transportation Revolution

General Motors was formed in 1908. Despite its impressive name, it was a weak and struggling enterprise, not the automotive giant that emerged in the 1920s. Its birth in 1908 nonetheless heralded the transportation revolution soon to sweep across the United States and leave no corner unchanged. That same year a young mechanical genius named Walter P. Chrysler used his railroad pass to attend an auto show in Chicago. Nurtured in a Union Pacific household in Ellis, Kansas, and later employed as a locomotive mechanic by several different railroads across the West, Chrysler was working in Olwein, Iowa, in 1908. In that bustling rail junction amid the cornfields, he was a superintendent of motive power on Samuel M. Felton's Chicago Great Western Railway.

Chrysler, a dedicated railroader, did not even know how to drive an automobile when he fell hopelessly in love with a Locomobile touring car. He borrowed most of its $5,000 selling price (on a monthly salary of $350) and had the Great Western ship it back to Iowa. For the next three months, Chrysler tinkered compulsively with his captivating new possession. Every night and all through each weekend, he disassembled it bolt by bolt, carefully studied each part, and then put it back together with the same passion for detail. His long-suffering wife finally asserted that if the Chrysler family truly owned the Locomobile, then its members must have a ride in it.

After a clash with Felton, Chrysler quit the Chicago Great Western and moved to Pittsburgh, where he became works manager of the American Locomotive Company. He truly loved building the big steam engines that powered the nation's railroads: "There is in manufacturing a creative joy that only poets are supposed to know," he observed in his autobiogra-

In small and relatively isolated settlements like the coastal lumber town of Garibaldi, Oregon, local passenger trains remained a prominent part of everyday life as late as the 1920s. Courtesy Oregon Historical Society.

NO 288. SCENE AT GA

ILDI ORE,

phy. "Some day I'd like to show a poet how it feels to design and build a railroad locomotive."[1]

Or an automobile, apparently, because in 1911 Chrysler accepted a job offer to be plant superintendent at the Buick Motor Company in Flint, Michigan, one part of General Motors' rapidly expanding landscape of production. Nine years later, when he was forty-five, Chrysler quit the giant enterprise to strike out on his own as the rescuer of faltering automobile firms. Three years later, in 1923, he quietly established his own Chrysler Motor Corporation in Michigan. In later decades the Chrysler firm emerged as one of the nation's Big Three automakers.

A key to success was that Walter P. Chrysler, the former railroader, understood clearly how well-engineered and stylishly crafted automobiles had energized the stodgy business of transportation. "As I visualized its future," he observed of the automobile in 1925, "it far outran railway development, which in a sense had reached its zenith, because the automobile provided flexible, economic, individual transportation which could be utilized for either business or pleasure. It knew no limits except a right of way, it was bounded by no greater restrictions than individual effort and will."[2] Acting on that belief, Chrysler amassed a personal fortune and a business empire that included one of the tallest and most striking skyscrapers in New York, the Chrysler Building, and the only such structure that featured oversize hood ornaments and hubcaps as part of its Art Deco styling. Carrying his name into the twenty-first century was a business colossus called DaimlerChrysler.

In the 1920s railroads noticed for the first time that the number of Americans riding their passenger trains had leveled off. In some regions, most notably the West, it was actually declining and had been for some time. The American passenger train was in serious trouble in the 1920s, and none more so than the ubiquitous local. Automobile competition was the main culprit. But why should passengers abandon a tried-and-true railway service for their sputtering and often-fickle automobiles and the nation's safety-deficient roadways?

As John Stilgoe astutely observed in *Metropolitan Corridor: Railroads and the American Scene,* "American travelers knew two landscapes, the one beyond the train windows and the one comprised only of the train itself."[3] For first class passengers, the train was a synonym for luxury only found in a fine hotel today. Stilgoe noted that "between 1890 and 1940, boarding a first class train meant entering a fantastical world." However, most passengers did not enter that world. There was nothing "fantastical" about the hand-me-down and often grimy, noisy, crowded, and pokey day coaches that typified local train service.[4]

Given the challenges faced by motorists brave enough to cross the

West by automobile during the initial years of the twentieth century, it is easy to understand why railroad executives as late as 1914 or 1915 failed to perceive that long-distance highway competition might someday pose a serious threat to their passenger and freight revenues. Nor were they alone in their dismissive belief that automobiles were essentially frivolous possessions and perhaps even only a passing fad. The historian Allan Nevins, in his study of Henry Ford and the business enterprise that bore his name, noted that as late as 1909–10 several financial institutions in the East "declined to bid on offerings of municipal bonds by western cities, explaining that these municipalities had 'too many automobiles in proportion to population' and were therefore unsafe credit risks."[5]

Like underground miners with their proverbial canary, which when it dropped dead from poisonous fumes warned them of eminent danger, railroad executives during the fifteen years from 1914 through 1929 had several indications of danger ahead if only they had interpreted the warning signs correctly. Unfortunately, their industry had no commonly agreed upon equivalent to the miner's canary, and the crushing passenger loads of World War I temporarily pumped new vigor into the faltering bird, thus giving railroad leaders the misleading impression that Americans were still committed to riding passenger trains of all types. Many rail executives first recognized that a transportation revolution of monumental proportions had overtaken their industry only after it suffered debilitating and permanent loses of patronage.

An event that should have greatly troubled perceptive railroaders originated on the streets of downtown Los Angeles in 1914, a benchmark year that also witnessed the outbreak of war in Europe, the opening of the Panama Canal, and Ford's record production of half a million automobiles by the new moving assembly line method. This was the birth of the "jitney craze." Within a matter of weeks it had spread from southern California to the far corners of the nation.

Ostensibly this odd social phenomenon began as a small-scale clash between city streetcar companies and automobile owners of modest means who discovered they could subsidize the cost of owning a car by offering rides to streetcar patrons at a nickel a head. Many veteran straphangers, instead of waiting patiently for the familiar trolley to come clanging slowly down the street, eagerly crowded aboard a jitney to experience, often for the first time, the thrill of riding on "rubber and air." One nickel (the usual trolley fare) seemed a small price to pay for an automobile ride, though the jitneys and their drivers were wholly unregulated. One jitney driver might offer courteous, safe, and reliable transportation in his late-model automobile, while another zigzagged through traffic in his overloaded rattletrap and possessed not a dollar's worth of insurance and possibly not even a valid driver's license. Many jitney patrons seemed not to care, and perhaps facing the unknown was part of the thrill. Curiously, many of these commuters had complained for years about the dangers and discomforts of overcrowded streetcars during rush hours.

By the time the "jitney craze" peaked in mid-1915, the strange new mode of urban transport had spread from coast to coast. An estimated 62,000 jitneys, all of them individually owned, competed with streetcar companies in metropolitan areas as diverse as San Francisco, Los Angeles, Seattle, and Denver. Perhaps never before in the history of the United States had any form of transportation grown so prominent so quickly. The once invincible "trolley trust," an enterprise that city dwellers loved to hate, faced its first significant rival as well as a sudden and stunning loss of passenger revenue.

The sheer number of jitneys darting along city streets momentarily staggered street railway companies, but after recovering from the initial shock they battled back by adopting cost-saving measures and promoting a tangle of municipal regulations intended to ensnare their brash and freewheeling competitors and force them off city streets. In what became their landmark struggle for survival, the jitney drivers of Seattle organized themselves and waged a seven-year legal fight against ordinances intended to curb their cars. Only after the United States Supreme Court rejected their appeal in 1921 did they surrender.

By then the number of jitneys had already plummeted, though they never entirely disappeared from city streets in some parts of the West. Moreover, a few diehard drivers ventured off city streets and onto rural roadways where they entered the promising new business of long-distance motor transportation. High-powered elongated touring cars—often labeled "super jitneys" and "fast-flying super stages"—especially turned heads in California, a state that pioneered a network of paved highways and was blessed with a mild climate that encouraged year-round operation of automobiles and intercity jitneys.

Before long it was the Southern Pacific and the Santa Fe, two of the West's most financially robust steam railroads, and not just the marginal trolley and electric interurban lines that lost dollars to intercity jitney operators. An unpaved road that opened in 1915 over Tejon Pass and greatly shortened the distance between Los Angeles and Bakersfield actually gave a competitive advantage to jitneys and buses over steam trains that operated between those two communities. Continuing north from Bakersfield, a drive up the level Central Valley to San Francisco and Oakland was easy. In fact, by 1916 it was possible for drivers of high-powered automobiles to speed along the new motor links between Los Angeles and San Francisco in a time equal to, if not faster than, the Southern Pacific's fastest passenger trains.

Because of increasing competition from jitney operators as well as from private automobiles, the Southern Pacific ended several money-losing locals in southern California. Passenger trains once deemed indispensable to rural or suburban communities had now become superfluous. A respected industry observer, *Electric Traction*, reported to its readers in July 1916 that "all sections of the country are coping with the jitney situation quite successfully, except on the Pacific Coast, where the jitneys are now affecting the interurban steam line traffic to as great an extent as they have the electric lines."[6]

That assessment proved far too optimistic. By 1916 a rising tide of automobile traffic, and not just in southern California, had begun to undermine the foundations of the railroad industry. That same year Samuel M. Felton, the highly respected president of the Chicago Great Western Railway, spoke to members of the Nebraska Bankers Association and warned the money men of changes already overtaking his industry, specifically that the combined capacity of 2,445,644 automobiles then registered in the United States had climbed to more than three times that of the nation's full fleet of railroad passenger cars. He further observed that in Nebraska alone there were at least 81,000 automobiles for which the state's railways had paid $2.6 million in taxes to build roadways.

Felton was an astute observer of trends affecting American railroad companies. Years earlier he had been a friend of Edward H. Harriman, the man who had rebuilt the Union Pacific into a giant of the West; and Felton himself was widely esteemed for his considerable talent as a "doctor of sick railroads." Thus, far earlier than most of his industry colleagues, he realized that the local passenger train was an institution in trouble, at least in parts of the West.[7]

Every additional mile of highway and every additional automobile would almost certainly have an impact on passenger trains, at least the local ones, though no one at the time fully understood how serious that impact would be or how to combat it. Would it be possible for railroads to retain their loyal riders in the long run, or would the newfound romance of the road permanently lure them away from trains and into automobiles or aboard the growing fleet of intercity buses? Hindsight suggests that the local passenger train never had a chance during the 1920s. It was the first significant victim of the twentieth-century transportation revolution.

At the end of the decade in 1929, the *Railway Age* assessed the dizzying pace of change during the past ten years and concluded that there had "indeed been a revolution in the transportation service" of the United States.[8]

⚙ ⚙ ⚙

As the "jitney craze" back in 1914 illustrated all too vividly, motorized competition with long-established streetcar and railroad companies had a way of arising suddenly from the least-expected quarters. Where might it arise next, and what forms might it take? Many clues provided answers to Americans who took time to ponder the mounting evidence.

For instance, in the unsettling aftermath of World War I, popular fears of a Communist-inspired revolution swept across the United States. After all, something equally unthinkable had occurred recently in Russia, where revolutionaries had grabbed power and proclaimed the existence of the Soviet Union, which Communists asserted was a harbinger of worldwide revolution. In this context, one event that frightened Americans was an unprecedented general strike that brought Seattle, Washington, to a standstill in early February 1919 and captured newspaper headlines across the United States.

Commentators inclined to believe the worst about the latest episode of unrest needed to search no farther than the front pages of the *Union Record,* Seattle's daily labor newspaper and a mouthpiece for the strikers. However, if readers cared to look beyond the often-incendiary rhetoric of the lead articles, they discovered feature stories devoted to another revolution taking place on the streets of Seattle, one that rode through town in the guise of an ordinary automobile. From hindsight it can be seen that the real revolution that changed forever the lives of Seattle workers as well as of all other Americans was the transportation revolution that swept across the nation during the 1920s.

Never mind that a Ford Model T was itself the product of big business—the kind of larger-than-life capitalism that labor agitators caricatured as the vested interests—and never mind that the model and year of an automobile likely reflected its driver's income level and social status. Along the roadways of the West, an automobile driver was his or her own boss; and whether the automobile was a humble Ford or a luxury Cord, it was a great democratizer. Any driver had the power to set the timetable and the destination as well as to change either one along the way. That kind of self-determination brought the most meaningful form of "power to the people," a goal the era's political revolutionaries mistakenly claimed as their own.

As had been true in earlier years, improvements in highways and automobiles during the 1920s continued forward as if the two technologies were joined at the hip, first one taking the lead and then the other, but always they made progress together. "Clearly, the automobile is responsible for the most outstanding highway development from 1910 to 1935, the greatest era of road building that the world has ever known," asserted one commentator in a mid-1930s issue of *Highway Magazine*. "This progress might have come in time, but would have been immeasurably delayed without the impetus of motor vehicles."[9] Then again, what progress would automobiles have made during that span of time without better roads?

The story of improvements both to highways and to automobiles is filled with unintended consequences. Where local government officials had originally fostered better roads in order to link farmers to railroad lines, which in turn united both the producers and consumers within a nationwide market, they also opened the countryside to early automobiles. Rutted dirt roads challenged drivers and their machines, but those same challenges spurred calls for still better roads, which influenced the evolving designs of automobiles. Where once it had been necessary for cars to fea-

One unsung reminder of the transportation revolution of the 1920s
was this crowded automobile junkyard near Spokane, Washington, in
1931. Courtesy Eastern Washington State Historical Society.

(NEXT SPREAD) Oklahoma's Garber-Covington oil field in 1926. This view,
showing a forest of derricks, is one section of a panoramic photograph
taken by E. J. Banks. Courtesy Oklahoma Historical Society.

The Twentieth-Century Transportation Revolution • 169

PHOTO FROM TOP OF A DERRICK
GARBER COVINGTON
OIL FIELD JUNE 12/26

ture large diameter but narrow wheels in order for drivers to cope success-fully with the occasional high spots and mud holes, expanding miles of smooth-surfaced highways encouraged designers to lower car bodies and their center of gravity and use smaller but wider tires that permitted faster speeds with greater safety.[10]

Automobile manufacturing, even in its rambunctious youth, never amounted to much of an enterprise west of the Mississippi River, apart from a modest mixed bag of local manufacturers. The industry's Big Three —Ford, Chrysler, and General Motors—later located major assembly plants in cities as diverse as Saint Louis, Kansas City, and Los Angeles, yet the auto industry's inevitable ups and downs affected the West's biggest commodity producers, notably those in copper and oil.

"Black gold" was pumped from beneath southern California long be-fore automobiles became mass-consumption items, and therein lies an-other unintended consequence of the transportation revolution. After the turn of the century, heavy grades of oil increasingly replaced coal for fuel in the modern steam locomotives that ruled the railroads of the West. A potent symbol of further changes overtaking the oil industry of the West was the gusher that erupted near Beaumont, Texas, in 1901. The black geyser of oil focused world attention on the hitherto unsung Spindletop field and energized the youthful petroleum industry of Texas and other parts of the Southwest, just as discovery of gold in the Mother Lode of California in 1848 had done earlier for the West's metals industry.

The West's oil industry, based on production from wells located main-ly in California, Texas, Oklahoma, Kansas, Wyoming, and Montana, had not loomed large in the regional economy or exerted inordinately great power in state legislative halls until growing numbers of automobiles caused demand for gasoline and other petroleum-based products to soar. Likewise, copper for automobile wiring and radiators caused mine pro-duction to soar in Arizona, Utah, Montana, and other metal producing states. Each cylinder of a Ford Model T required a separate ignition coil densely packed with copper wires to provide the high-voltage spark need-ed to energize it. In remote parts of the West, local jobs depended on the health of the automobile industry, though originally hardrock miners or oilfield roustabouts could seldom afford cars of their own. Conversely, today's cowboy and his pickup truck (often a "Montana" or "Durango" or some other brand name evocative of the frontier) is part of the popular perception of the modern western landscape.

✤ ✤ ✤

To place the automobile, its colorful history, and its widespread impact —all elements of the transportation revolution of the twentieth century— in proper perspective, it should be noted that as late as 1910 railroads shouldered responsibility for 95 percent of all intercity transportation in the United States. No wonder their dominance made the railroads supremely confident. Yet only a quarter of a century later, America's automobiles accounted for fully 90 percent of the nation's intercity travel. By 1933 railroad passenger revenues had dropped to only 25 percent of the high-water mark the industry attained in 1920. Railroads still hauled most of the nation's freight in the early 1930s, but who could say with any confidence how long that would last?

The vehicles that collectively wrought this revolution in transportation had themselves undergone profound changes during the years. During the span of just one decade, from 1916 to 1926, the number of enclosed cars increased from 2 percent to more than 72 percent of the total annual output of American manufacturers. Americans clearly intended to use their vehicles throughout the year. No longer was the automobile merely a seasonal convenience or plaything to be enjoyed during the good months but carefully stored for the winter in a commercial garage designed specifically for that purpose—like a yacht stored at a marina during the winter months today.

A writer in 1928 observed that "one of the great changes that has crept over American life during the past 10 years, indeed one of the most astonishing changes which has ever come over any people in the history of the world," has been that "we require food, clothing, shelter—*and mobility.*" He noted that "mobility—personal mobility—the motor car—has actually become part of our houses."[11]

He likened the family automobile to "a sheltered room on wheels in which they do much of their traveling, a great deal of their visiting, a large part of their recreating, and even some part of their eating." (He might have added that automobiles functioned as bedrooms on wheels, too.) When automobiles became integral members of most western households, they also gained special status and honored spaces of their own—commonly called garages and carports. Hence the automobile changed the architecture of American homes every bit as much as they altered whole neighborhoods and other commonplace spatial arrangements Americans had developed earlier for living, working, and recreating in an age dominated by railroads.

No state was more in love with its automobiles than California. Consider only that when the United States in 1930 recorded 214 motor vehicles per 1,000 residents, the state of California led the nation with 356 for each 1,000 residents. Put another way, Californians alone owned 2,041,356 motor vehicles, or nearly one-tenth of all 26,523,799 motor vehicles recorded that year in the United States. Moreover, between 1914 and 1920, before the transportation revolution was noticeable in most places, Californians had spent $42.2 million for state roads and another $104.2 million for county roads. To place those sums in perspective, it might be recalled that Congress in the Highway Act of 1916 had appropriated $75 million to be spent by all forty-eight states during the next five years.

Not surprisingly, the railroads of California experienced the impact of highway competition far earlier than did most other parts of the United States, and the automobile redefined everyday life earlier and more aggressively there too. The state's car culture encouraged the unprecedented growth of the suburbs of Los Angeles. During the 1920s alone, Beverly Hills grew by an astounding 2,485 percent, Glendale by 364 percent, and Huntington Park by 445 percent.

In all parts of the West, the automobile influenced the prevailing hierarchy of regional cities, towns, and villages. The extension of all-weather roads through rural areas lengthened the commercial reach of medium and large-size trading centers, often at the expense of small towns and villages, some of which quietly vanished from highway maps. Motorized buses enabled small rural schools to consolidate, and this caused the once-familiar one-room schoolhouse nearly to disappear. A list of all the social changes attributed to automobile ownership would be lengthy indeed.

Clothiers and haberdashers complained that automobile owners, "finding it impossible to keep grease spots from their clothing, are now buying an inferior grade and losing the art of good dressing." Still other observers claimed that the auto-infatuated generation of Americans was reading fewer books and newspapers, "and there is less attention paid to the cultural niceties of life. People go riding in the evening, so the Sunday evening church service is not attended." Some people even noted that as the automobile supplanted the horse along country roads it lessened the number of summer houseflies![12]

For the growing number of westerners who could afford one, an automobile combined the speed of a trolley or steam locomotive with the personal mobility of a horse. For westerners, as for Americans elsewhere, that alone constituted a modern declaration of independence. The exhilarating feeling of being in total control was "one of the greatest charms of country travel by automobile. That horrible fiend, the railroad time-table, is banished to the far woods; no longer does the early morning 'tramp, tramp' and sharp 'tap, tap' of the hotel bellboy rudely disturb one's quiet sleeping with the peremptory summons, as articulate as if spoken in words, to get up or miss the train; no longer does the perspiring traveler on the slow-moving local hurl anathemas at unseen and unknown foes because of interminable delays, soft-coal dust, soot and a long absence of ice water from the receptacle that tantalizingly bears those words."[13]

In a single day a traveling salesman could drive through sparsely settled territory and call on more customers than he had been able to do in a week when traveling by local trains. Not surprisingly, during the decade of the 1920s a majority of salesmen, those "commercial travelers" who once had formed the backbone of railroad passenger service, abandoned the trains and took to the roadways in their own automobiles because of the greater flexibility they offered; and following not far behind traveling salesmen came many other categories of former train travelers.

In short, the motor age transformed the West during the 1920s and 1930s as dramatically as the railway age had transformed the region during the 1880s and 1890s. And just as railroads had run freight wagons and stagecoaches out of business or consigned them to remote and lightly populated margins of the region, highway transportation threatened to do likewise to railroads, at least with their local passenger service, the sector of the railroad business that felt the impact of the new competition first.

※ ※ ※

It is not easy to pinpoint just when American railroads lost their competitive advantage to automobiles and other forms of highway transportation. It happened in different areas of the West at different times, and always it occurred so incrementally that it attracted little notice at first. Consider again the case of California. As Gregory Lee Thompson notes in *The Passenger Train in the Motor Age,* a superb case study for the Golden State, the number of Californians who rode passenger trains increased steadily during the first ten years of the twentieth century. At that time the railroad industry had only to accommodate an ever-growing passenger loads. However, the year 1910 proved a high-water mark for the amount of money a typical Californian spent to ride passenger trains. This expenditure declined noticeably in the coming years, and especially dollars spent for local train service. The state's demand for railroad freight service moderated too in 1910. At the same time, Californians increased their spending for automobiles and for improved roads and highways.[14]

As the trend grew increasingly noticeable nationwide, the *Railway Age,* one of the industry's most authoritative voices, sounded the alarm in 1919. The publication estimated that during that year alone the American public spent at least $5.5 billion to purchase and operate their automobiles (this figure did not include what the public paid for highway construction and maintenance). The total was $300 million more than the public paid for railroad transportation. *Railway Age* estimated that by 1919 Americans had, over the years, collectively invested $9 billion in their automobiles, a sum that was even more impressive when compared to the $19 billion value of all property owned by American railroads, a considerably older industry.[15]

Railroad executives annually assessed the impact of the transportation revolution with mounting frustration and alarm. The drop in passenger traffic during the 1920s was especially precipitous on branch lines, and for good reason. In *Main Street,* the popular novel of small-town life published in 1920, Sinclair Lewis observed that passenger trains serving rural America were plain and unadorned, "with no smug Pullman attached."[16] The hand-me-down wooden coaches featured rows of stiff-backed seats. The nameless but still numerous local trains offered none of the glamour of the luxury limited, and none of the speed and comfort.

Even worse, as one industry critic grumbled, "the rural steam railroad in many instances is an anachronism in communities of homes equipped with steam heating plants, radios, modern plumbing conveniences and telephones, the owners of which have their own automobiles. It is 1875 set down in the midst of 1925."[17] Not surprisingly, the trains that suffered the most dramatic loss of passengers were the locals most vulnerable to automobile competition. As a result, railroads began to operate them less frequently or stopped service entirely.

Likewise, the 85,000 rural depots that defined railroad lines across much of America had little of the glamour of a big city station, though even modest ones had served as important public gathering places. In isolated towns and villages across the West the arrival and departure of a community's daily passenger train had once been of collective interest, but during the 1920s that changed. Townsfolk came and went more or less as they pleased in their own automobiles. The road map, not the railroad timetable, became everybody's window on a larger world.

Some of the stations, though constructed relatively recently, were boarded up or converted to other uses. Many were torn down. When the Northern Pacific opened its impressive Union Station in Tacoma, Washington, in 1911, observers lauded the building for it architectural appeal and many public conveniences. "The Tacoma terminal is built for the future as well as the present. It has the room and substance to accommodate the great influx of people into the Pacific Northwest for years to come." Alas for railroads, the great influx of newcomers increasingly arrived in their own automobiles.[18]

⚜ ⚜ ⚜

During the first half of the 1920s, railroad passenger departments appeared too stunned or uncomprehending to fight back in a meaningful way. Some of the nation's largest railroads knew surprisingly little about marketing passenger service apart from encouraging summer or winter tourism. Passenger officers before 1920 had tended to devote most of their time to perfecting methods of handling a steadily growing load of traffic.

The prevailing assumption was that as prosperity increased the take-home pay of American workers, their ability and desire to travel by train grew along with that of more affluent citizens—and that meant increased passenger business, at least in the long run. It is true that railroad passenger traffic dipped dramatically following the Panic of 1893, but after that bout of hard times it did not slip even once between 1899 and 1920. By the eve of American entry into World War I, there was evidence that the passenger business as a whole was no longer growing; but a traffic boom that resulted from troop movements and the general business prosperity masked evidence of a long-term trend at least until 1920. After reaching an historic high that year, when the nation's railroads carried nearly 1.3 billion revenue passengers, the numbers diminished noticeably.

Railroaders at first thought the decline was only temporary. When statistics indicated an upturn in passenger revenues in the last four months of 1925, many optimists in the industry hailed the glimmer of hope as showing the true direction. Rail passenger traffic continued to rebound through May 1926, but then it dropped sharply again and continued in a downward direction for the rest of the decade. The industry's journals contained numerous hand-wringing articles about the "passenger traffic problem," but no messiah stepped forward to present a compelling or comprehensive solution.

During the decade of the 1920s, the population of the United States grew by 13.5 percent, while rail passenger traffic continued to shrink noticeably, especially on railroad lines located west of the Mississippi River. In was in the West that the full impact of the transportation revolution of the 1920s was felt first. Travel by rail there had declined by a whopping 40 percent during the 1920s, compared to an equally worrisome 32 percent decline in the South. However, in the East the decline amounted to only 18 percent, and because that region contained the nation's greatest concentration of rail passengers, those statistics helped mask (at least temporarily) the seriousness of the decline elsewhere.

For a short time the industry took comfort from the fact that despite the serious impact of automobile travel on their coach business, the number of patrons using sleeper and parlor cars actually increased. Moreover, commercial aviation posed no threat, or so it seemed in the 1920s. Many executives within the railroad industry remained optimistic about the overall health of their long-distance passenger service even as late as the 1940s, although as early as 1929 it was already obvious to some observers that motor buses had become a formidable long-haul competitor and that the recently established airlines were persistently pecking away at the fringes of railroad sleeping and parlor car business. The young airline industry's best planes remained clunky, slow, and even dangerous—the term "airliner" seemed clearly a misnomer in the 1920s—and its business practices and daily operations were sometimes erratic; but life for airline passengers would improve greatly during the 1930s.

※ ※ ※

In addition to traveling salesmen and local residents who rode the secondary trains, another type of passenger lured away in increasing numbers by automobiles during the 1920s was the tourist who wanted adventure in the great outdoors—in a national park, perhaps, or just along the roadway itself. A primary attraction of touring the West by automobile was the palpable sense of freedom that a road trip conferred on motorists, both to residents of the region and to visitors from distant places.

Elliott W. Hunter photographed the wreck of a Northern Pacific freight train on Montana's Bozeman Hill in May 1904. Courtesy Montana Historical Society.

All good highways entailed motion and the excitement that comes from following an open road. First, there was the highway itself, its concrete or asphalt or gravel surface shimmering in the sun. Often when ribbons of dark asphalt filled the cracks of a concrete section, it created an unintended but abstract work of art, a new Jackson Pollock perhaps. The highway corridor might also become an unsightly dump. Because of the clutter, *Life* magazine once described the three million miles of highways across the United States as the "supreme Honky-Tonk of all time." Supreme Honky-Tonk or not, the nation's roads and highways in the decades after World War I became true democratizers because they tended to erase, at least temporarily, boundaries that existed between country and city, between penthouse and slum.[19]

The pavement itself conveyed distinctive sounds. Tires often transmitted a high-pitched whine when running on smooth concrete, or a steady thump-thump when running over a much-patched section. Highway engineers in recent years have learned to use auditory cues conveyed by rumble strips to alert motorists to impending danger.

When travelers steered their automobiles off the paved highways and onto the dirt-and-gravel back roads, it often signaled the start of a journey of exploration. By contrast, when a long-distance passenger train abruptly deviated from the straight and narrow way defined by the twin ribbons of steel, the result was a wreck. Even if a derailment did not end in disaster, it inconvenienced passengers and caused cleanup headaches for railroad officials. Wrecks, moreover, were an embarrassment to railroads because they signified some kind of a breakdown—of carefully engineered equipment or tracks, or industrial discipline, or good management.

In all things, railroads prized regularity; conversely, automobile travel, while governed by traffic rules and regulations of its own, nonetheless offered an invitation to personal innovation and experimentation. Along the open road, possibilities undreamed at the start of each day's journey might create magical moments—though admittedly a day's unforeseen events were not uniformly pleasant, as in the case of a flat tire or a broken valve-stem or crankshaft.

Despite any mechanical shortcomings, a long drive across the West was a romantic adventure, the equivalent in the 1920s perhaps to a big game safari in Amazon jungles of earlier years. Originally, though, it was mainly rich people who could afford such adventures. Unlike many middle-class Americans in those early days, the rich had both the money and the time required to undertake a cross-country automobile trip. They knew how to dress properly for their great adventure too. The most stylish motoring attire for men included a pair of expensive leather driving gloves and a heavy overcoat, while women wore chic linen dusters. Until the closed car became common, everyone donned goggles to keep their eyes free from road dust. They chose their heavy, luxurious, and very expensive cars to showcase their wealth.

Gradually, a few adventuresome members of the middle class ventured well beyond familiar hometown streets and rural roads of the nearby countryside to challenge more distant mountains and deserts of the West, perhaps to visit faraway relatives or to vacation in remote national parks. Officials first admitted private automobiles to Mount Rainier National Park in 1908, to Crater Lake in 1911, to Glacier in 1912, and to Yellowstone in 1915. The nation's "wonderlands" would never be the same.

On the other hand, automobiles and all-weather roads enabled tourists to reach some new national monuments and parks that developed after World War I. One such place was Carlsbad Caverns in southeast New Mexico, which was originally considered little more than a subterra-

At the rustic Gardiner Station entrance to Yellowstone National Park in 1935. Courtesy Montana Historical Society.

nean network rich in guano deposits useful for fertilizer on the nearby farms. In 1924 a total of 1,876 people visited Carlsbad Caverns, the ruggedness of which made no concessions to city dudes. Four years later that number had climbed to nearly 80,000 visitors, and because of extensive underground lighting they no longer had to carry their own lanterns. It was much the same story in another remote part of New Mexico, where automobiles opened up the ruins of Chaco Canyon to tourists, and further north in Colorado at Mesa Verde.

Westerners themselves drove some of the first automobiles into the national parks, but as the years passed, vacation-minded motorists from more distant regions braved the dirt and gravel roads that extended hesitantly west across the United States from the East Coast and Midwest. At the beginning of the twentieth century, a two-week trip to savor the scenic splendors of Montana or Arizona was simply beyond the budgets of most Americans, especially when railroad fares and hotels bills had to be paid for four or more family members. Initially that complication was of no concern to most travelers because even the word "vacation" had not yet become part of the working vocabulary of westerners. Paid vacations for the mass of Americans remained unknown at the dawn of the new century. In 1900 vacations were still mainly for the wives and children of well-to-do businessmen—a summer at Cape Cod or Bar Harbor, perhaps, to escape the heat of city streets.

Later, when a growing number of Americans did get time and money enough to escape to the great outdoors, not everyone headed to national parks. "Autocamping" as an end in itself emerged as a new national pastime in the 1920s; and for the many tourists, it was far cheaper and easier than trying to use trains to reach nature's ubiquitous western playgrounds. "It makes one quite independent of time and itinerary, and it can be utilized by every member of the family. America has thousands of vacation playgrounds ranging all the way from the wilderness spots near home to the vast national park, and forest reservations containing much of the finest scenery in the world" *Highway Magazine* proclaimed. Published advice for "autocampers" in 1925 included these friendly warnings: "Don't try to cover too much territory each day." "Stop early, make camp and enjoy yourself." And, "do not attempt to travel 'dressed up'—you will have lots of company in khaki. Knickers no longer cause 'snickers.'"[20]

Economy-minded tourists often carried their own canned goods and a collapsible tent, either free-standing or one that easily attached to a side of a car. However, because they preferred to camp out at night and prepare their own meals over an open campfire to trim travel expenses, observers often ridiculed them as "tin-can tourists." It was common for "tin-can tourists" to heat a can of beans en route on their car's radiator or hot exhaust manifold. One organization of auto-camping enthusiasts turned the popular sneer inside out by calling themselves "Tin Can Tourists of the World."

Some automobile tourists simply wandered about the West in search of various forms of personal renewal. The ever-changing landscapes through which they passed offered their own special rewards. Motorists never knew what interesting people they might encounter next or what stunning scenery or fascinating sights might lie just beyond a rise only a few miles ahead. The first glimpse of the distant peaks of the Rockies never failed to delight automobile tourists from the East. Motorists might find the remains of a ghost town or a long-abandoned stagecoach station on the Overland Trail across Wyoming, or a set of wagon ruts left by pioneers. Perhaps the appeal was the local cuisine (though that was often more a disappointment than a delightful surprise). In any case, in this way the modern road trip was born.

❀ ❀ ❀

The improved thoroughfares that radiated from metropolitan areas of the West during the 1920s paved the way not only for tourists but also for numerous bus and truck lines, many of which had originated only recently as mom and pop outfits. Because of their humble and often obscure origins, no one can say when and where America's first intercity bus line originated. Certainly the jitney craze of 1914 gave the nascent industry a boost. Yet as early as 1912, and fully two years before the first jitney, a transportation pioneer used automobiles to haul passengers along a 125-mile route linking San Diego and El Centro, an agricultural town in California's Imperial Valley. Patrons waited on the curb outside the Pickwick Theater in San Diego. From this inauspicious beginning evolved Pickwick Stages, a California company that gained fame in the mid-1920s for running the longest bus line in the United States.

Another bus line antedating the jitney era used touring cars to link Oakland, San Jose, and Santa Cruz. Finally, a good claim can be made for Hibbing, Minnesota, and the surrounding Iron Range country, where in 1914 local operators planted an inconspicuous seed that later flourished as the modern Greyhound Lines, the sole nationwide bus system surviving in the twenty-first century. The fast-flying "super-jitneys" that sped along highways between Los Angeles and San Francisco after 1915 soon failed, but long-distance bus lines had clearly come to California and the West to stay. During the 1920s the new intercity bus and truck industry expanded as rapidly as the region's spreading network of all-weather roads permitted.

Early buses were exceedingly primitive conveyances, at least when compared to the finest railroad passenger cars. Some were little more than rebuilt and elongated automobile bodies attached to a heavy-duty chassis and provided with canvas curtains to keep the rain off any passengers. In winter weather warm bricks supplied enough heat to keep a passenger's feet from freezing. Fortunately, technological improvement fast became a keynote of early bus travel.

Bus operators of the 1920s were members of an aggressively innovative fraternity. The mechanics at the Pacific Northwest Traction Company of Everett developed double-decked parlor-observation coaches for service between Seattle and Vancouver, British Columbia. By the mid-1920s restrooms appeared on a few western buses, and some routes offered sleeper and buffet services. Pickwick Stages in 1928 introduced 26-passenger sleeper buses, or "Nite Coaches," along the highways linking California and the Pacific Northwest. During the previous year, Pickwick had amassed 5,000 miles of route stretching from Los Angeles north to Portland and east to El Paso.

Rail executives in the 1920s came to appreciate the advantages that buses offered, especially on relatively short runs never adequately or profitably served by steam trains or even by the internal combustion and self-propelled (or "doodlebug") rail cars that were briefly popular in the early twentieth century. One of the nation's first steam railroads to form a highway subsidiary was the Spokane, Portland & Seattle Railway, which began bus service in 1924 to replace several money-losing steam trains that linked Portland with Astoria and Oregon's north coast. By the end of the decade, nearly every major railroad of the West had done something similar on its lightly patronized branch lines, though a few railroads established bus service in a "rather gingerly fashion, as one picks up a strange object the strength of which has not been demonstrated." By 1929 approximately eighty railroads operated 2,389 motor coaches nationwide.[21]

One typical operation was the Southern Pacific Motor Transport Company incorporated on April 29, 1927. Its first bus puttered along sixteen winding miles of highway that connected Santa Cruz and Boulder Creek, California. Soon the Southern Pacific began wholesale substitution of buses for its faltering local train service. By late summer the company's rapidly growing fleet of buses replaced all streetcar service the railroad had formerly operated in Salem and Eugene, Oregon.

Reaching out from those and other population centers, the Southern Pacific launched over-the-road bus service between Portland and Ashland and many intermediate points to replace unprofitable steam and electric trains. By the end of 1927, interstate bus service linked together Southern Pacific communities in Oregon, California, and Nevada. Its buses reached north from Los Angeles to Portland in November 1928, and east from Los Angeles to El Paso. Some through buses offered long-distance railroad passengers the option of a side trip between Phoenix and Lordsburg, New Mexico, along the famous "Apache Trail." After only two years of operation, the Southern Pacific Motor Transport Company had amassed a fleet of 200 motor coaches operating over some 3,800 miles of route.

With or without railroad affiliations, by the late 1920s bus companies connected all major cities of the West and a good many smaller ones too. The highly flexible mode of transportation seemed tailor-made to meet the needs of oil boomtowns that sprang up seemingly overnight in areas of Oklahoma and Texas poorly served by existing railroads and their local

A Columbia Pacific "Nite Coach" pauses at a Texaco station in Salt Lake City in late 1932. Sleeper coaches disappeared during the Great Depression when bus passengers carefully watched every penny. Courtesy Utah State Historical Society.

passenger trains. One 1930s traveler in a small Oklahoma town recalled a timeless expression of optimism commonly heard in the oil patch: "Oh! Haven't you heard? Oil. About twelve or fourteen miles down south from here. It may turn out to be the richest field in the mid-continent area."[22] The problem for any responsible railroad company was that it could not hope to build a profitable branch on the strength of such daydreams. To be sure, in the opening years of the twentieth century when frequent oil strikes made people giddy, railroads might spike ties and rails together across a stretch of promising territory and dispatch freight trains over the temporary tracks, but the coming of all-weather highways made such construction heroics unnecessary.

Extending transcontinental bus service from the West Coast to cities of the East represented yet another facet of the transportation revolution of the 1920s, and it would not have been possible without the improved roads the decade brought to sparsely settled interior portions of the West. Even so, when a determined passenger became one of the first people to ride by common carrier bus from New York to Los Angeles in mid-decade, he found that the journey required at least a month and thirty-five separate buses operated by nearly that many companies. At a remote location in the desert Southwest, passengers reenacted a familiar ritual from stagecoach days when they climbed out to help the driver push the bus over a bad section of road. No wonder railroad executives dismissed long-distance bus travel as no serious competitive threat.[23]

Starting in 1927 a period of rapid consolidation reshaped the intercity bus network, even as railroads became more prominent in the industry. During one buying spree that lasted through the first nine months of 1929, several steam railroads engaged in the wholesale accumulation of numerous small and once independently owned bus lines. As the *Railway Age* observed in April 1929, "The last twelve months have seen a truly remarkable change in the attitude of the steam railways toward the motor coach." The publication noted that the change had "some of the aspects of an industrial revolution." Indeed, by 1930 almost one-fifth of all intercity commercial travel in the United States was by bus.[24]

That same year the pioneer phase of the intercity bus industry effectively ended when Greyhound Lines—the company name derived from motor coaches that sprinted "like greyhounds"—emerged as the nation's dominant carrier. This holding company, formed in the mid-1920s and initially dominated by railroads, absorbed numerous bus lines, including the California-based Pickwick Stages and their innovative sleeper buses, though such luxury soon disappeared from the highways.

By the early 1930s the basic pattern of competition between intercity trains and buses was well established. As a rule, trains attracted well-to-do passengers, who preferred the amenities of sleeping, parlor, and dining cars, while buses catered to less affluent and hence more budget-conscious riders. Middle-class travelers might go either way, depending on their personal preferences or destinations.

There was one conspicuous exception, and that was a special form of rail and bus co-ordination that continued to be popular in the West for many years to come.[25] These were the "detours," or alternate excursions by highway that railroads offered their long-distance passengers. Southern Pacific operated a Redwood Empire tour through the lofty trees of northern California and southern Oregon, and the Union Pacific operated a Utah Parks and Boulder Dam alternative. When the spectacular Going-to-the-Sun Highway opened in 1933, it allowed the Great Northern Railway to advertise a detour by bus or private automobile through the mountainous heart of Glacier National Park.

The most famous train-bus coordination was the "Indian Detour" through northern New Mexico that began in 1926 as a result of long-term cooperation between the Santa Fe Railway and the trackside restaurants and upscale hotels operated by the Fred Harvey company. R. Hunter Clarkson, an executive with the Harvey organization and the primary originator of the detour idea, described the experience as a "three-day, three hundred-mile motor tour to be furnished Santa Fe railroad tourists on an all-expense, bother-eliminated basis." Transcontinental travelers could leave main-line trains and board Harvey's well-designed touring cars (soon to be labeled "Harveycars") to get a more intimate look at Indian country than train windows alone provided.[26]

As for the intercity bus industry, Congressional passage of the Motor Carrier Act in 1935 extended the regulatory powers of the Interstate Commerce Commission to cover interstate motor carriers. The new law brought sobering change to a large segment of the once-freewheeling long-distance bus and truck industry. Furthermore, by making it difficult for newcomers to launch bus lines, Uncle Sam reduced competitive pressure on carriers already in operation and benefited passengers by eliminating fly-by-night outfits with their rickety, often wired-together coaches and honky-tonk station stops.

In response to restrictions imposed by the Motor Carrier Act of 1935, three big western railroads the following year chose to coordinate bus operations with carriers east of Chicago and Saint Louis by organizing an alliance of independent operators called the National Trailways Bus System. Missouri Pacific Trailways operated through a portion of the West defined by the cities of Saint Louis, Kansas City, Little Rock, and Houston, or roughly the service area of its parent Missouri Pacific Railroad. Burlington Trailways, which dated back to a bus subsidiary the Chicago, Burlington & Quincy Railroad had organized in early 1929, extended from Chicago to Los Angeles and San Francisco via Denver. It also operated extensive local routes in Iowa and Nebraska, an area served by its parent railroad.

For years the largest and most important member of the alliance was Santa Fe Trailways, controlled by a subsidiary of the Atchison, Topeka & Santa Fe Railway. In large part this system paralleled the Santa Fe's rail lines from Chicago to Los Angeles. It had originated in the early 1930s as the Southern Kansas Stage Lines, its name being an appropriate reference to the once-extensive system of stagecoaches that served the West.

As intercity buses grew longer and wider, they bore less and less resemblance to their stagecoach forebears. During the 1930s a modern bus typically featured amenities such as comfortable reclining seats, large overhead luggage racks, and individual reading lights. However, when engines were located at the front of the coach and open windows offered the only "air conditioning," hot weather and road dust remained just as irritating to passengers as they had been in stagecoach days.

In their struggle with competing modes of commercial transportation during the 1920s, railroads retained their all-important freight business and held firm to an upscale clientele that rode long-distance passenger trains and was willing to pay for luxuries that made such journeys pleasant. On the other hand, the local passenger train was clearly a lost cause, a victim of a far-reaching technological revolution. What rail executives did not know was that the modern transportation revolution had by no means run its course by 1929.

The next phase of the competitive assault came from growing fleets of long-haul trucks on the nation's highways and from airliners taking to the skies in ever-increasing numbers. Like the traditionalists who sneered, "Get a horse, mister!" when automobiles first sputtered through the countryside, or dismissed the "jitney craze" as nothing more than a passing fad, or belittled the emerging bus industry because early drivers handed out hot bricks to warm their passengers' feet, it was hard for most observers in the late 1920s to foresee that the youthful airline industry might one day offer real competition to railroads, much less contribute to a transportation revolution.

Seven

The New Overland Route

Aviation is a small but remarkable industry. Less important—in dollars or volume or men employed—than the five-cent candy bar business, it had nevertheless been a nation's darling for ten years, had grown into a sort of psychological escape for 120,000,000 air-minded Americans.

—*Fortune,*
May 1934

Precisely at 4:30 on the afternoon of January 25, 1915, with President Woodrow Wilson listening in from the White House, Alexander Graham Bell in New York called to his one-time assistant, "Mr. Watson, come here; I need you." The response of Thomas A. Watson was, "It would take a week for me to get to you this time." Watson, you see, was located in San Francisco. Thirty-nine years earlier, when the two men made history with the world's first conversation by telephone, he had been in the adjacent office when Bell uttered his now historic command.[1] This time Bell and Watson spoke to one another from opposite ends of a 4,300-mile long circuit formed by telephone wire attached to 130,000 poles that stretched from New York and San Francisco. January 25, 1915, thus qualifies as the birthday of the nation's first transcontinental telephone conversation.

Being first to cross the continent in a new way always ranked as a noteworthy achievement. When the explorers Lewis and Clark finally reached the mouth of the Columbia River in late 1805, they became the first of their countrymen to complete the long trek overland. Their journey from Saint Louis to the Pacific required twenty months. Slightly more than half a century later, the first scheduled transportation across the trans-Mississippi West dates from semi-weekly stagecoach service between Saint Louis and San Francisco. That was in 1858, when the Butterfield Overland Mail Company commenced service over a 2,795-mile route through the desert Southwest by way of El Paso, Tucson, and Los Angeles, all of which were only villages. A transcontinental stagecoach journey required almost a month of hard traveling. The Butterfield enterprise, it should be noted, was the first purveyor of

The photographer Charles Libby immortalized the day in 1933 when Nick Mamer's Ford Trimotor rushed a load of beer from Spokane to the flood-stranded mining town of Wallace, Idaho. Courtesy Eastern Washington State Historical Society.

commercial transport across the West to popularize the concept of a trans-continental or "overland" route in its official title.

In 1861, following the secession of Texas from the Union and the threatened outbreak of the Civil War, the transcontinental stage line moved north and out of harm's way to establish a new "central overland route" that stretched west across the future states of Wyoming, Utah, and Nevada. Initially, the stagecoaches followed the familiar Oregon and California trails through the valleys of the North Platte and Sweetwater rivers and across the Continental Divide at historic South Pass. However, because Indian troubles occasionally disrupted service, the transcontinental stage line relocated again, this time south to a more direct route that roughly anticipated the location of the tracks laid by the Union Pacific Railroad in the late 1860s. The most up-to-date transcontinental corridor became familiarly known as the Overland Route.

The Overland stage still required at least three weeks to convey passengers between Saint Louis and San Francisco in the 1860s, but Pony Express riders needed little more than ten days to sprint across the West bearing important letters and news during the eighteen months in 1861–62 that this unusual form of communication remained in business. However, the fastest horse and rider could not compete with the lightning speed of America's first transcontinental telegraph after its wires met in Salt Lake City in late October 1861 to complete a new circuit. For practical purposes, it delivered overland communication nearly as fast as the telephone and Internet do today.

Transporting people across the continent quickly was a different matter. For the remainder of the nineteenth century, even after completion of the first transcontinental railroad, travelers still needed about five days to cross the United States. The speediest passenger trains before 1900 decreased that seemingly immutable benchmark only by a matter of a few hours. That was insignificant compared to the monumental reduction that took place between the twenty-month westward trek of Lewis and Clark in 1804–05 and the twenty-eight day schedule of John Butterfield's Overland stagecoaches in 1858.

Fully half a century after Promontory, in 1919, it still required five days to cross the continent by rail. In fact, in terms of time, the earliest crossings by automobile and by airplane were both retrograde steps. As we have seen, when Dr. Horatio Nelson Jackson motored across the United States in 1903, it took him sixty-three days. His aviation counterpart was young and debonair Calbraith P. Rodgers, who in 1911 sought to become the first person to fly from New York to California in less than thirty days and thereby claim a tantalizing prize of $50,000 offered by the San Francisco publisher William Randolph Hearst.

On November 5, 1911, forty-nine days after he lifted off from a flying field at Sheepshead Bay, New York, Rodgers and what was left of his original Wright biplane, the "Vin Fiz Flyer," touched down in Pasadena, California. Twenty thousand onlookers waited to greet him. Unfortunately, the dashing young aviator with his trademark cigar clinched in his teeth arrived too late to claim Hearst's prize, but he enjoyed the personal satisfaction of being first to fly across the continent, more or less.

During his lengthy trek he had somehow survived a dozen crashes and an exploding engine that peppered his arm with jagged fragments of steel. He followed a 4,300-mile course that zigzagged along the major rail lines of the United States by way of Chicago, Saint Louis, and El Paso. From there Rodgers and his "Vin Fiz Flyer" roughly paralleled the original overland route pioneered by John Butterfield's stage company in 1858. A special supply train remained close at hand to help him make numerous repairs to his frail aircraft. In fact, when he reached Pasadena, fully 98 percent of his original wood, wire, and fabric plane had been replaced along the way!

Only five months later, as Rodgers flew low over the Pacific at Long Beach, his fragile plane abruptly plunged into the knee-deep surf. One account claims that he hit a flock of seagulls and spun out of control; another says that as he skimmed low over the waves he removed both hands from the controls to show onlookers how fully he had mastered his craft. Either way, America's first transcontinental aviator was dead.[2]

For aviators who followed Rodgers, an enduring quest was to shorten the time it took to cross the continent. In that way they pioneered the newest overland route, one that broke free from the constraints imposed by topography on earlier trails and rails, including the recently designated Lincoln Highway, the most modern transportation corridor to affirm the historic overland route across Wyoming. An overland route through the sky would also form an entirely new type of transportation corridor.

Or would it? Initially it was superimposed atop Union Pacific and Southern Pacific tracks, and thus the well-known railroad landscape determined the overland route followed by transcontinental airmail pilots no less than that of the familiar freight and passenger trains.

Commercialization of officially designated airways followed much the same pattern as that of the nation's highways. Early airplanes, looking much like oversized box kites fashioned from spruce wood, cotton cloth, and wire, were machines just as primitive and unreliable as the early motor vehicles, and their support system of airports and navigation aids, again like the earliest highways, ranged from very poor to nonexistent. There was one obvious difference. When those first buses or trucks stalled and sputtered to a stop, they did not fall from the sky and result in dramatic death, as was the fate of many aviation pioneers.

Consider the poor luck of nineteen-year-old Cromwell Dixon Jr., who touched down briefly at Spokane's Interstate Fairgrounds on October 2, 1911, after becoming the first person to fly across the Continental Divide.

That feat won him a $10,000 prize and a modest niche in aviation history. Young Dixon, alas, never had time to spend his dollars. Only minutes after being hailed a modern hero before a large crowd of Spokane admirers, he took off again, only to have his frail biplane whacked by crosswinds and plummet back to earth within sight of the runway. Onlookers rushed to snatch ghoulish souvenirs from the tangled mass. After rescuers recovered Dixon's body, they set fire to the debris to discourage further souvenir taking. The teenager was among the first air fatalities in the Pacific Northwest.[3]

Another early aviator was Nicholas Bernard Mamer, who pioneered commercial flight across the rugged backbone of the continent that Dixon conquered in 1911. Young Mamer was a quite a daredevil, as were many early pilots determined to challenge the limits of flight. They needed to be daring to conquer the mountain West. Mamer was one of approximately twenty thousand young Americans who joined the Army in hopes of carrying the fight to the skies over Europe during World War I. Like many other aviators of the era, he became a "barnstormer" after the war ended, putting bread on his table by thrilling passengers with brief plane rides at county fairs and similar events, and by his stunt flying. He typically charged $5 for a twenty-minute ride, sometimes taking off from a cow pasture and doing easygoing aerial maneuvers.

After relocating to Spokane in 1919 he set up Mamer Flying Service, which during the next few years acquired a modest fleet of transports it used to haul goods and people wherever they needed to go. During 1927 Mamer Flying Service logged a total of 64,000 miles, though it did not yet operate scheduled flights. Mamer simply charged his customers a fee of thirty-five cents a mile for longer flights, or a flat five dollars for short hops. Many passengers were local businessmen who needed to attend meetings at widely separated locations on the same day.

For all his serious business pursuits, Mamer never entirely forsook his early barnstorming antics. In a 1925 stunt he "bombed" the University of Idaho's homecoming bonfire the night before that school and nearby Washington State College squared off for their annual football contest. Freshmen at the University of Idaho traditionally stacked a huge pile of wood to set afire during a pre-game rally, but two Washington State College students who joined Mamer on his mischief flight hoped to ignite the stack prematurely and spoil their rival's fun.

Mamer swooped down low over the field, and as his plane sped about ten feet above the woodpile someone dropped a cake of phosphorous. The "bomb" easily hit its mark, but University of Idaho students pulled it away. Mamer completed two additional "bombing" runs, but each time the result was the same. By the time he prepared for a fourth run, a Latah County deputy sheriff had had enough of Mamer's aerial tomfoolery and let fly a volley of birdshot. Neither the plane nor pilot suffered any damage from the pellets, but Mamer wisely decided to withdraw from the contest.

One of Mamer's most famous deliveries—and one that showcased what aviation could accomplish in the rugged Bitterroot Mountains east of Spokane—took place in late 1933 when a severe flood isolated the town of Wallace, the trade center of a rough-and-tumble silver mining district in northern Idaho. When their booze supply ran low, hard-drinking men turned in desperation to Mamer Air Transport. Their angel of mercy was a Ford Trimotor named "Westwind II" that delivered a liquid cargo consisting primarily of barrels and bottles of beer.

In the landmark year 1927, Charles Lindbergh gained worldwide fame for his solo flight across the North Atlantic from New York to Paris. During that same freewheeling era, Nick Mamer also won his share of aviation accolades, such as in 1929 when he set a record by flying a plane called the "Spokane Sun God" back and forth across the United States nonstop. The feat required five days and at least forty-nine midair refuelings, a very dangerous practice at the time. During one such transfer in the skies over Wyoming, the plane's whirling propeller sliced the dangling fuel hose and doused the "Spokane Sun God" with highly flammable gasoline. It was the pilot's good fortune that nothing caught fire. When he landed, an exhausted Mamer claimed title to the longest nonstop flight (in terms of distance) made to that time.

Mamer's luck ran out in the skies over Montana in the late 1930s, however. Well behind him were his happy-go-lucky years of barnstorming and aviation record-setting. He now worked as a regular pilot for Northwest Airlines. A few years earlier he had pioneered commercial air transportation between Saint Paul and Spokane, using a six-passenger plane; but after five or six months he had switched to connecting Spokane, Seattle, and Portland with Ford Trimotors. He sold his fledgling company to Minneapolis-based Northwest in 1933 after it extended its first route across the plains and mountains separating the Twin Cities and the Pacific Coast. Mamer knew his tiny fleet could not compete successfully with the much larger carrier, so he joined Northwest as a pilot.

An industry observer noted in 1930 that "in the old days—for even aviation now has its 'old days'—the pilot was president, vice president, general manager, operations manager, and maintenance and repair department, and accounting staff." [4] That certainly described Nick Mamer until he became a Northwest employee and enjoyed regular hours and far more job security than he could have imagined possible in the 1920s.

On the afternoon of January 10, 1938, Mamer sat at the controls of a ten-seat Sky Zephyr, a name borrowed from streamlined trains introduced by the Burlington Route in the 1930s and favored by Northwest to suggest how fast its Lockheed planes flew. The twin-engined, all-metal monoplane represented the most modern addition to Northwest's growing fleet. It had been in service less than two months. When the company assigned Mamer to fly the best of Northwest, that was a sure sign of his seniority.

A blizzard in Butte briefly delayed what was otherwise a routine flight from Seattle to Chicago via the Twin Cities. A short time after leaving the

Montana mining city, Mamer radioed back that he was experiencing some unusual vibrations in his plane. The problem apparently disappeared, however, because he and his copilot continued on. Attaining a cruising altitude of nine thousand feet, the men in the cockpit radioed back to Butte that everything was now fine.

Speeding over the ground at approximately 225 miles per hour, a speed that pushed the envelope for commercial aircraft at the time, the veteran pilot felt the rudder control pedals under his feet begin to vibrate again—this time vigorously. This was probably Mamer's first intimation of truly serious trouble. Such vibration was curious, but perhaps he had no time to ponder how grave the problem was before the pedals abruptly went limp. Mamer was no stranger to trouble. There were few emergency landing strips in the Pacific Northwest that he had not used at one time or another. But this time his situation was hopeless. With no way to control his rudder, he could not steer the plane toward an emergency landing strip. He could only await certain death—and mercifully the wait was short.

Without warning, the tail section containing the all-important twin stabilizers had wrenched itself off Mamer's plane. The doomed airliner spun out of control and plunged through a cold Montana sky toward the snow-covered Bridger Mountains near Bozeman. Smashing nose first into a frozen meadow, the craft crumpled like a tin can, exploded, and burned fiercely until nothing remained but an ugly tangle of metal. The impact and intense fire killed everyone on board. The coroner identified Mamer's body only by the chevrons he wore on the sleeves of his pilot's uniform. He was forty years old.

Northwest's young president Croil Hunter announced that his rapidly growing fleet of eight Zephyrs would not return to the sky until investigators figured out why one of them had crashed in Montana. During the previous year Hunter and Northwest Airlines had collaborated with Lockheed engineers in Burbank, California, to design and produce a plane that flew significantly faster than the latest generation of aircraft used by its competitors—such as United and its fleet of Boeing 247s (which attained a top speed of approximately 185 miles per hour), TWA and its Douglas DC-2s (with a top speed of 210), and American and its DC-3s (which carried more payload but flew no faster than the DC-2s). However, Lockheed's model 14H streaked through the sky at an impressive 260 miles per hour when pilots opened its throttles all the way. Just five years earlier the top speed for commercial aircraft in the United States had been a lumbering 120 miles per hour.

Passengers aboard Lockheed's speed demon could for the first time cross the United States from coast to coast in 15 hours and 10 minutes. Northwest intended to use its Sky Zephyrs to grab the speed laurels (and hence advertising glamour) from its three big competitors—United, TWA, and American. In fact, the Lockheed plane enabled Northwest to trim flying time along its bread-and-butter route between Chicago and the Twin Cities to a mere one hour and forty-five minutes in the year 1937. Curiously, and by way of comparison, sixty-five years later, in 2001, Northwest's nonstop flights between those cities were scheduled for one hour and thirty minutes using late-model commercial jets! The figures suggest how much more time is consumed today in takeoffs and landings and how airline schedules are liberally padded to address frequent air traffic delays.

When investigators from the Bureau of Air Commerce reached the site of Northwest's January 1938 crash, they were startled to discover the twin fins and rudders missing from the wreckage. A structural failure that momentous was rare for airliners even in those early years. Without delay the federal agency charged with insuring safe operations of the nation's airlines prohibited Northwest from flying any of its Sky Zephyr fleet, which, in any case, the company president had already grounded. In the history of American aviation, this was the first time federal officials grounded a modern all-metal class of airliners until engineers found and fixed its fatal flaw. At the same time, they exonerated pilot Nick Mamer.[5]

Aviation experts needed little time to discover a design flaw that under certain conditions could result in "rudder flutter." The wrenching vibrations could destroy an airplane, yet all it required to prevent another disaster was for Northwest mechanics to place a small weight in the tail of each plane. The federal agency lifted its ban on Sky Zephyrs only to lob another bombshell into Northwest operations that same day. Taking an almost unheard of step, the Bureau of Air Commerce immediately grounded all of its Electras, Lockheed planes that Northwest used in addition to the Zephyrs. It cited the airline's failure "to maintain its aircraft in an airworthy condition." Service abruptly halted until the beleaguered carrier could requalify its Sky Zephyrs as airworthy or bring maintenance of its Electras up to federal standards.

The plane lost in the Bridger Mountains was Northwest's first fatal crash involving paying passengers (and the first crash of a commercial airliner in Montana). Airlines in the United States had to learn to bounce back quickly from such disasters, or few of them would have remained in the air in the 1930s. Accidents were frequent, and commercial flying was far more dangerous then than at any time in history. In 1932, for instance, the fatality rate for scheduled airlines in the United States was 1,200 times higher than for railroads and 900 times higher than for intercity bus lines.

Thus, just seven months after its Montana crash, Northwest bravely advertised in the August 1938 issue of the *Official Aviation Guide* that a dashing young aviator and Hollywood producer named Howard Hughes had flown around the world in a Lockheed Zephyr to set a speed record. "We, too make records with Lockheed Sky Zephyrs, sister ships of Howard Hughes' Record-Breaking Plane." Northwest boasted that every day during the summer of 1938 its own fleet of planes flew the equivalent of Hughes's globe-girdling journey.[6]

Commercial aviation in the West, as in the United States as a whole, evolved through several distinct phases, beginning with the circus-like displays and antics of early-day "birdmen"—and a few bird-women too. After the Wright brothers' epochal flight in December 1903 on a sandy hill in North Carolina, not even those two pioneer aviators understood the full potential of their machine. For another decade—at least until World War I—the airplane remained primarily a mode of entertainment because it appeared so aptly suited to stunt artists and a daring new breed of circus performer, the aviators who demonstrated their flying skills before crowds assembled at county fairs and other special expositions.

One such "circus" was the Los Angeles International Air Meet held in January 1910 at the Dominguez Ranch near San Pedro. This was America's first international air show, and as such it had a serious side. But for the reporter from *Sunset* magazine, the most noteworthy aspect of the eleven-day event was its raucous atmosphere. Apparently most of its spectators only wanted to be amused. "Have you seen Trixie?" The question boomed out from a large megaphone positioned at the entry gates. She is "the fattest girl in the world," boasted the announcer. Also on public display for the historic occasion were a brood of rattlesnakes, a fortune teller ("Tell me your birthday and I'll tell you your horrorscope"), and Cora-Etta, Siamese twins "now, in the light of present-day marvels, fitly termed the Human Biplane."[7]

At one end of the field stood a large grandstand closely packed with several thousand spectators. Nearby stood large circus tents used as temporary hangers by Louis Paulhan, a French aviator whose presence was the only reason the Los Angeles Air Meet could legitimately be billed as "international," and by several renowned American flyers of the day, most notably Glenn H. Curtiss, along with his southern California imitators. Of the latter group, one cynic quipped, "The local aviators were early on the ground—and never left it."[8]

Among the odd assemblage of local aircraft was "Prof. Zerbe's multiplane," a bulky five-winged creation "that looked like a ship under full sail, or a flock of great white geese, or a stand for potted plants, or some fossil vertebrate out of the enormous past, according to one's point of view. There was a noble spurt along the ground, some steam, and then the great creature with a laborious sigh lay over upon its side." The audience only laughed at the hapless Zerbe—"a cruel thumbs-down laugh."[9]

Reflecting on the serious side of the Los Angeles air meet, *Sunset* magazine described Glenn Curtiss as "a slender, sober-faced man—a blending of the practical engineer and the young college professor. He appears to have been born deaf and blind to the grandstand. His performance has about as much sensational atmosphere to it as that of a busy man leaving home in his auto for his office. He has an air of quiet authority, of intimate knowledge of his machine, a serious intentness upon the business in hand." Curtiss, observed *Sunset* magazine, was primarily interested in selling "flying-machines" and other motor vehicles, and though he gained considerable fame for setting aviation speed records, he did so primarily to advertise his businesses.[10]

Seen in historical perspective, the Los Angeles International Air Meet was a bit like the famed "philosopher's stone" of medieval alchemy that transformed all it touched. Consider, for instance, that among the onlookers wowed by Curtiss's "quiet authority" and "intimate knowledge" of aviation was William Randolph Hearst, the wealthy San Francisco newspaper publisher. Paulhan, the famed French aviator who only months earlier had earned his living as a tightrope walker, carried Hearst aloft for his first flight, an event exceedingly well publicized by Hearst's photographers and writers. It was only a short time later that he announced the $50,000 prize that lured Calbraith P. Rodgers west in late 1911 to become the first person to cross the continent by air.

Besides Hearst, another interested spectator at the original Los Angeles International Air Meet, but one who attracted no public notice, was a wealthy Seattle lumberman named William E. Boeing. A tall and mustached man wearing thin-rimmed glasses that made him the look more like an academic than a business executive, he had moved west to seek his fortune in the state of Washington in 1903, the same year the Wright brothers made history with their first flight.

Boeing, alas, was unable to wrangle even a short a ride with Curtiss in 1910. However, four years later, after his first plane ride above the Seattle area, Boeing was so smitten by the pleasures of winged flight that he soon attended the Santa Ana, California, aviation school run by a contemporary of Curtiss, Glenn Martin, who was apparently the first person to fly a plane in California. Close to home in Seattle, the lumberman-aviator founded a new enterprise in 1916 called Pacific Aero Products, which became Boeing Airplane Company the following year. It had eight employees. At a time when airframes were crafted from spruce and other strong wood, it was logical for Boeing to establish his airplane company in a Pacific Northwest community still surrounded by magnificent and seemingly endless stands of virgin spruce and fir.

In time, Boeing ranked among the most familiar names in aviation history. The Curtiss name lives on in the modern Curtiss-Wright Corporation, which supplies many components vital to Boeing jetliners; and Martin's name is part of the Lockheed Martin Corporation, one of Boeing's fiercest competitors for aerospace dollars.

There is far more to the Boeing story than aircraft and aerospace, however. The company also helped to launch one of America's pioneer air carriers, the enterprise today known as United Air Lines. That happened after Congress passed the Kelly Act in 1925 to privatize the transport of airmail and thereby give wings to commercial aviation in the United States.

Since 1918, the year regular airmail flights between Washington and New York began, Uncle Sam had relied on the United States Air Mail Service, a division of the Post Office Department.[11]

On Washington's Birthday, February 22, 1921, a group of brave pilots launched transcontinental airmail. Following the historic Overland Route defined by Union Pacific, they flew their fragile biplanes through all kinds of weather. With no aids to navigation other than the railroad landscape, that was no easy task. The Cheyenne airport, for instance, was 6,000 feet high, and from there pilots had to top the 9,000-foot-high Laramie Range only twelve miles farther west. Parachutes only became standard equipment for transcontinental airmail pilots in 1922, though in parts of the high country they did not clear the ground by enough altitude to make such emergency gear either safe or practical.

Charles A. Lindbergh recalled that when he flew airmail between Chicago and Saint Louis, a pilot's best aid to navigation was a Rand McNally railroad map. In the early 1920s Rand McNally became the first company to make air navigation maps, all of which were adapted from existing railroad maps. The navigation bible for pioneer postal airmen flying across the United States was a pocket-sized guide called *Pilots' Directions: New York–San Francisco Route*. Issued by the U. S. Post Office when its first transcontinental route opened in early 1921, it provided pilots a detailed description of the rail landscape they must follow. For example, the entry for Wahoo, Nebraska, "a fair-sized town" located thirty-three miles west of Omaha, advised pilots to note that six railroad lines radiated out from that location. For Rock River, Wyoming, it advised that the "double-tracked Union Pacific passes through 2 miles of snow sheds at this point," no small consideration when bad weather forced mail pilots to fly low to the ground. So it went, all along the Overland Route to the Golden Gate.[12]

To further aid airmail pilots, on August 21, 1923, federal officials inaugurated the world's first airway equipped for night flying. Along an 885-mile route across relatively level terrain between Chicago and Cheyenne thirty-four emergency airfields where lights outlined the runways were located in addition to the regular airfields that featured tall towers capped with rotating thirty-six-inch arc beacons that pierced the darkness with the most powerful light beams yet devised by humans. In the best weather, pilots could see the beams from a hundred miles away. Also across the Great Plains were acetylene beacons spaced at three-mile intervals to visually mark the first transcontinental airway. At the time it took regularly scheduled trains approximately ninety-one hours to cross the continent, but the Air Mail Service, by flying around the clock, trimmed that span of time by two-thirds.

The miles of lighted airway grew steadily, and beginning in the late 1920s, audible radio beams further aided pilots on some airways, as did two-way radio communication and hourly weather broadcasts. "Radio is eventually going to give to commercial air transportation just that added degree of positive safety and regularity of service which characterizes well

An historic stagecoach saluted one of Walter Varney's single-engine planes when it inaugurated airmail service between Pasco, Washington, and Elko, Nevada, in 1926. Courtesy Washington State University Library.

operated railroads," observed Herbert Hoover Jr., a radio technician employed by Harris Hanshue's Western Air Express in 1930.[13] The official airways of the United States, which at the time were defined pathways not unlike railroad right-of-ways, expanded from 2,000 miles in 1926 to 23,000 miles in 1938, all of them funded and maintained by a generous Uncle Sam. Cockpit instruments improved too, though they remained far from foolproof.

No one could anticipate all the improvements yet to come, yet the legislators who backed the Kelly Act and its privatization of airmail transport still needed a large amount of faith because in 1925 there were no commercial airlines in the United States—at least none of real consequence

—to fly the mail. Perhaps for that reason, Uncle Sam initially retained the transcontinental, or "Columbia" route linking New York, Chicago, and San Francisco as the nation's sole cross-continent airmail connection. To feed additional airmail to the trunk line, the government contracted out several north-to-south branches to private carriers, most of them aviation upstarts that took to the sky only after submitting a winning bid to federal officials.[14]

Walter Varney of Oakland, California, organized one such enterprise with help from his father, who headed a billboard company. The younger Varney won the Post Office contract to fly mail along a 460-mile desert route linking Elko, Nevada, and Pasco, Washington, by way of Boise, Idaho. On April 6, 1926, one of his single-engined planes inaugurated the new mail route. Boise citizens celebrated the occasion by mailing a sack of Idaho potatoes to President Calvin Coolidge; while in Pasco, a traditional stagecoach met the flight and offered observers historical perspective on mail delivery. It was not long afterward that influential Spokane residents lobbied successfully to extend airmail service from Pasco to their city.

When that day came, it was a festive occasion. A crowd of five thousand onlookers gathered to watch as two planes of Varney Airlines flew out of Spokane with more than 75,000 pieces of mail. To make the most of the celebration, local boosters had mailed ten thousand wooden postcards proclaiming Spokane the "Lumber Capital of the Inland Empire." No wonder it required two planes to handle the mail on that inaugural flight.

Wooden postcards notwithstanding, it could be said that the West's early airlines, like its railroads, depended on paper—in this case the paper represented by airmail. Just as dollars from federal contracts had underwritten early modes of long-distance transport—beginning in the late 1840s with steamships carrying the mail between California and the East Coast of the United States (via a steamy fifty-mile portage across Panama), and continuing with Butterfield's Overland stagecoaches in 1858—so Uncle Sam, during the second half of the 1920s, used dollars from mail contracts to keep the first airlines of the West aloft.

In many parts of the West, mail flights branching from the transcontinental trunk route helped to encourage passenger service by a variety of local carriers, including some that did not have mail contracts themselves. In Los Angeles, the city's ongoing envy of San Francisco, its older and more self-satisfied sibling to the north, resulted in the birth of an important new airline. After Uncle Sam chose San Francisco as the Pacific terminus of his east-west airmail route in 1920, Angelinos refused to take a back seat when it came to aviation. Sensing that civic pride was at stake, Harry Chandler, publisher of the *Los Angeles Times* and a sponsor of the city's international air show back in 1910, and other wealthy citizens backed a former racecar driver named Harris Hanshue when he proposed to launch a new airline. On April 17, 1926, Western Air Express inaugurated service between Los Angeles and Salt Lake City, soon to become the most important hub in the West along the transcontinental airmail route. In Salt Lake City, incidentally, Hanshue's backers included the Mormon Church and its head, Heber J. Grant.

The date of its first flight, which predated Lindbergh's landmark transatlantic flight of May 1927 by more than a year, gave Western Air Express a legitimate claim to be the nation's oldest airline. During the remainder of 1926 it carried 267 passengers. In those days, people at way stations like Las Vegas greeted Western's flights much as their forebears had done half a century earlier when a mail-carrying stagecoach rolled into a frontier town and attracted a crowd of onlookers.

Western Air Express rapidly expanded service throughout the Southwest as defined by Los Angeles, San Francisco, Denver, and Kansas City. During 1927 it carried a total of 400 passengers. That may not seem impressive, but by the end of 1929 when the total had climbed to more than 25,000 a year, Western Air Express handled 20 percent of all air passenger traffic in the United States. Moreover, under "Pop" Hanshue's no-nonsense style of management, it became the "world's first financially successful airline and the first air transport company in the United States to pay dividends." The secret: "One policy . . . and one only . . . *nothing but the best* . . . has built this system and maintained its unbroken record of passenger safety for more than four million miles," Western Air Express advertised in 1930.[15]

Western at one time flew Fokker trimotors, large, lumbering, low-flying planes with windows that opened to enable passengers to deal with their airsickness, but not always successfully. According to Robert J. Serling, leading chronicler of Western's colorful history, airsickness over the mountains of California, Nevada, and Utah was so common that crewmembers frequently had to hose out their plane at the end of a flight.

Last to be privatized was the transcontinental route. The mail contract for the western two-thirds between Chicago and San Francisco went to Boeing Air Transport in 1927, a recently organized affiliate of Boeing Airplane Company, which outbid Hanshue and Western Air Express. The main reason Boeing sought an airmail contract was to win a new market for its planes. Initially, those had space for mail only, but the Model 40–A that Boeing introduced a few months later featured a cabin spacious enough to carry two passengers and such travel amenities as blankets, cotton wads for the ears, and large jugs of strong coffee. Any passengers, however, might be obliged to carry excess airmail on their laps.

A one-way ticket from Chicago to San Francisco cost $200. Airmail still paid the bills, and the onboard crew consisted of a pilot who worked in an open cockpit outside the tiny enclosed passenger cabin. As if to underscore that airmail was more important than passengers, until the early 1930s the typical uniform of commercial airline pilots remained a leather cap and jacket, a style derived from aerial combat during World War I. As for Boeing Air Transport, it joined Varney Airlines and several other carriers to form a commercial aviation giant called United Air Lines. By flying the 2,760-mile corridor linking New York and San Francisco, it became the air industry's first coast-to-coast carrier

Among United's original components was Pacific Air Transport, organized on a shoestring budget by Vern Gorst, a former jitney driver from Oregon. He had to peddle common stock from door to door to raise enough money to get his airline off the ground, and he had to persuade Standard Oil Company officials to paint town names on the roofs of fuel storage depots so his pilots would know where they were as they winged along the West Coast. At one point a group of executives representing the Southern Pacific System briefly considered bidding for a mail contract that Gorst won to keep his airline aloft, but President William Sproul, a veteran railroad executive, dampened their enthusiasm when he proclaimed that commercial aviation would never amount to much.

In 1926 and 1927 the airlines of America were still operating in what might be called their tentative or experimental phase. The year 1927 was important not only because Uncle Sam privatized the transcontinental airmail route but also because the unprecedented publicity generated by Lindbergh's flight did more than anything before, including the first flight of the Wright brothers in 1903, to make the United States fully "air-minded." The young industry passed another milestone in 1928 when it introduced multiengine aircraft on domestic passenger flights, and with bigger and faster planes it became easier to attract more customers.

During the first half of 1929, the *Official Guide of the Railways* took notice of passenger travel by air, and Northwest became the first carrier to publish its schedules more or less regularly in its monthly issues. It also assigned passenger train-like names to its three flights: "The Gray Eagle," "The Black Bird," and "The Silver Streak." The Kansas City Southern, by the way, once operated a passenger train officially named "The Flying Crow," and the Chicago Great Western ran another called "The Blue Bird." In addition, to salute the growing contribution of aviation to the Wichita economy, the St. Louis–San Francisco Railroad launched the "Air Capital Limited," an overnight train between Saint Louis and Wichita, in the fall of 1929.

Rail executives at the time were not at all worried by airline competition—they were still crafting responses to automobile and bus competition—but they were intrigued by commercial aviation's potential to boost ridership on their passenger trains. When W. W. Atterbury, the respected president of the Pennsylvania Railroad (the self-proclaimed "Standard

Railroad of the World"), stated that his company was no longer a "rail-way" but a comprehensive "transportation" provider, he signaled that major railroads in the United States stood ready to embrace the air age. Atterbury's railroad launched a new passenger connection between New York and Los Angeles that promised to combine the comfort of luxury trains with the speed of modern planes.[16]

The *Official Guide* for July 1929 revealed what the Pennsylvania Railroad and a new carrier called Transcontinental Air Transport had in mind. Early pilots joked that its initials T. A. T. stood for "take a train," and in a literal sense that was correct: the new airline was a key link in an innovative plan to connect "New York to California by Plane and Train in 48 hours." The airline and railroad partners spent millions of dollars to ensure that their unusual combination would be first class in every sense.

Precisely at 6:05 on the afternoon of July 7, the inaugural "Airway Limited" glided out of New York's Pennsylvania Station as a band played "California, Here I Come." Slipping through the tunnel beneath the Hudson River, it soon emerged in the sunlight and hurried west across the meadowlands of northern New Jersey. At 7:55 the following morning it reached Port Columbus. From the new airport located seven miles east of Ohio's capital city, one of Transcontinental Air Transport's all-metal Ford Trimotor planes lifted off at 8:15 and reached Waynoka, Oklahoma, at 6:24 that evening after intermediate stops in Indianapolis, Saint Louis, Kansas City, and Wichita.

In Oklahoma the through passengers boarded a Santa Fe train called "The Missionary" and sped through the night to Clovis, New Mexico. Another plane of Transcontinental Air Transport departed Clovis at 8:10 that morning and reached Los Angeles at 5:25 that evening after making intermediate stops in Albuquerque, Winslow, and Kingman. Passengers continuing north to the Golden Gate were "given the option of using overnight trains between Los Angeles and San Francisco, or taking the airplanes of the Maddux Air Line."[17]

During the initial three weeks of operation a total of 150 passengers crossed the continent between New York and Los Angeles, while another 283 passengers used some portion of the joint air-rail service. Among them was a dentist from Long Beach who boarded the inaugural eastbound flight because he was in a hurry to reach Chicago, where he planned to elope with his girlfriend. Speed sold tickets.

Forty-eight hours, not five days, became the new benchmark for coast-to-coast travel. Curiously, a month earlier the Pennsylvania's arch rival New York Central had teamed up with Universal Air Lines System, Western Air Express, and Santa Fe to offer the first air-rail service between New York and Los Angeles, starting on June 14, 1929. The earlier feat notwithstanding, the air-rail service of the Pennsylvania, Santa Fe, and Transcontinental Air Transport won far more public attention because of their relentless campaign of publicity. The partners never let the traveling public forget that they, and they alone, formed the "Lindbergh Line."[18]

A Ford Trimotor at Glendale's Grand Central Air Terminal, which served as a primary airport for Los Angeles during the 1930s. Courtesy TWA Collection, St. Louis Mercantile Library.

TWA
TRI-MOTOR FORD
1930

"Experts headed by Colonel Lindbergh have invested over a year's time and millions of dollars in planning and construction (before operation) to insure the utmost of reliability, comfort and speed to T. A. T. travelers." The "Lindbergh Line" grabbed still more headlines when it arranged for movie star Mary Pickford to stand before a crowd of 20,000 onlookers at Glendale to christen a Ford Trimotor called "The City of Los Angeles" before that plane lifted off on its first eastbound trip from California. The pilot for the first leg of the trip was none other than Colonel Charles A. Lindbergh Jr., at that time the most popular person in America.[19]

Time magazine named Lindbergh its first "Man of the Year" in 1927 and described him as the nation's "most cherished citizen since Theodore Roosevelt." With youth combined with modesty that inspired confidence in Americans, Lindbergh became the one aviator above all others who conferred much-needed legitimacy on a struggling new mode of passenger transportation. The "Lone Eagle," as historian Joseph Corn observed, could lay claim to the mantle once worn by American folk heroes Daniel Boone and Davy Crockett—only Lindbergh conquered a new frontier with the "Spirit of St. Louis," and they did it with axe and muscle.[20]

One airline listing that appeared intermittently in the *Official Guide of the Railways* in early 1929 was for Universal Aviation Corporation. Holding companies such as Universal, thanks in part to Lindbergh having made the United States air-minded as never before, quickly became the darlings of Wall Street. Some big aviation combines managed to amass considerable financial muscle in a matter of months. "Aviation is no longer a small or untried business," wrote one industry observer in early 1930. "Prominent bankers" were backing large aviation companies. When the auto giants Ford and General Motors grew interested in commercial aviation, it was a sure sign that the "'swaddling clothes' stage has gone. The era of skepticism is past. Aviation is on the ascendancy, and will go far and reach unthought of heights in a few years. It is truly a big business."[21]

Universal Aviation Corporation, as listed in the June 1929 issue of the *Official Guide of the Railways,* consisted of the Robertson Aircraft Corporation, Continental Air Lines, Northern Air Lines, and Paul R. Braniff, Inc., four carriers serving major cities of the Midwest. Within a few months an even larger holding company called the Aviation Corporation (of Delaware) gobbled up Universal Aviation Corporation. The newcomer was incorporated in March 1929 and backed by several prestigious New York investment banking firms, including Lehman Brothers and W. A. Harriman & Company—Harriman as in Union Pacific Railroad.

Robertson Aircraft Corporation, "Lucky Lindy's" one-time employer in Saint Louis, formed a key component of the budding aviation empire that gave rise to the carrier now known as American Airlines. As for the transcontinental air-rail partnership that proudly billed itself as the "Lindbergh Line," not even the glamour of his name helped it to turn a profit, especially after the Wall Street crash on October 4, 1929. "Black Friday" sent an economy on the brink of a stall into a disastrous tailspin.

Even if railroads truly believed that they gained valuable publicity when they embraced commercial aviation, they quietly grounded all their air-rail alliances because of the grim economic outlook. Coast-to-coast travel by commercial airline continued to consume at least two full days until the mid-1930s; and given the pioneering nature both of the airplanes and aids to navigation, it could be quite an adventure.

One author who left an exceptionally fine account of early commercial flight across the United States from Los Angeles to New York entitled her article in *Good Housekeeping* magazine "Covered Wagon—1932." Marcia Davenport wrote, "I wanted adventure, or whatever semblance of it could be had in the year 1932. So, of course, I flew." She felt that to cross the continent "prosaically by rail was to be cheated. It made no sense for me to sit for days in big plush armchairs, tended by troops of expert servitors, eating and drinking delicacies, looking for ways to consume one's ennui." Instead of the steady "hum of the safe steel rails," she desired a trip that invoked the romance of "Oh, Susanna!" gone to Oregon by covered wagon "with a banjo on my knee."

Davenport flew first aboard a swift monoplane from Los Angeles to Salt Lake City, the junction where United collected eastbound passengers from San Francisco and the Pacific Northwest. It forwarded them along the Overland route "made dear by song, verse, and story, the route of the ox trains, the Forty-niners, the stagecoaches, the pony express." A total of eight passengers rode aboard a trimotored biplane that lumbered up and over the Rocky Mountains separating Salt Lake City and Cheyenne. From there they continued aboard an identical biplane to Chicago, where a fourth craft, one of United's trimotored monoplanes, helped them complete a transcontinental odyssey to New York.

Bad weather forced Davenport's plane to land at a U.S. government airmail emergency field at Parco, Wyoming, which she noted was located close to the site of Teapot Dome, the source of a major scandal that dogged the administration of President Warren G. Harding in the early 1920s. "There was here a beacon tended by a man and his wife and his daughter who lived in a little woolly-western shack on the edge of the field." In this isolated place the passengers waited out the storm.

In all directions stretch the vast Wyoming plateau, and Davenport's mind wandered back to the time of the pioneers. Describing her surroundings and her fellow passengers, she seemed to anticipate the motley travelers trying to reach Lordsburg, New Mexico, in John Ford's 1939 classic movie *Stagecoach*. Davenport observed that a "young divorcée fretted because she had wired she would be at Newark airport the next afternoon, and it was obvious that someone she was madly impatient to see was to have met her there." A quiet man from Portland was trying to get to Pittsburgh before Mother's Day. It was already Friday night. A stubborn old man from Los Angeles only complained that he "had started out to fly from coast to coast in a day and a half, and he was going to!"

After a fretful night with little sleep, they flew east the next day only to be forced by thick fog to make another emergency landing, this time in Laramie. Continuing on, they dropped down in the Wyoming capital about ten hours late. After pausing briefly in Cheyenne for breakfast, the passengers flew on to Chicago at about 160 miles per hour, making scheduled stops in North Platte and Omaha, Nebraska. United served them a lunch en route that consisted of tomato juice and two sweet buns. "It was all they could scrape together for us in Omaha—we were so late that our purveying had been forgotten."

Of meal service, Davenport observed: "Air lines feed you, en route, as steamships do. That's one reason why a long flight is comparatively so inexpensive. You have a day and a half in planes with all your meals for nothing as compared with five days in the train with a dozen or more meals to pay for. To be sure, you get your food regularly, and of luxurious variety, on the railroad; in the air—you wait and see!"[22]

✿ ✿ ✿

Service improved each year, and airlines (and aviation generally) matured as a business enterprise. Among the several holding companies that appeared in the United States was a particularly impressive aviation empire called United Aircraft and Transport Company that William E. Boeing and several colleagues assembled in 1929. It included commercial airlines and the manufacturers Pratt & Whitney, Sikorsky Aviation, Chance Vought, Hamilton Standard Propeller, and Boeing Airplane Company—all in addition to flying schools and even airports. At the time, the Boeing manufacturing plant in Seattle gained the distinction of being the largest in the United States devoted entirely to aircraft. Boeing himself served as chairman of the big holding company, a position he held for the next four years.

"And what [W. E. Boeing] doesn't know about flying," gushed *Aero Digest*, "could be written on an air mail stamp with a shaving brush." Observed Boeing in a 1930 interview with the magazine, "Happily the public is rapidly ridding itself of the impression that flying is romantic, spectacular, or heroic." It was, he emphasized, a business, pure and simple. In addition, "business men have been the first patrons of each new form of transportation, and history is now repeating itself."[23]

If airlines had indeed become bona fide business enterprises by 1930, it was thanks in large measure to continuous support from Uncle Sam. Just as land grants and loans had helped to underwrite the cost of building transcontinental railroads across the West in the 1860s and 1870s, so generous airmail contracts aided airlines struggling to stay aloft in the 1920s and 1930s.

Because dollars from federal mail contracts were so important, the postmaster general of the United States held the power of a czar over the nation's adolescent airline industry. Depending how he exercised that power, he alone could determine if an airline thrived and evolved into a major carrier or was grounded and forgotten. The official who most effectively used (or abused) his power in order to forge a modern airline industry for the United States was Walter Folger Brown, a dapper Harvard-educated attorney from Toledo, Ohio, who served as Herbert Hoover's postmaster general.

Basing his considerable clout on the McNary-Watres Act, which became law in May 1930 and amended the earlier Kelly Air Mail Act, Brown believed he now had the power to redraw the airline map of the United States. Untroubled by the technicalities of a federal law that required competitive bidding, he relentlessly pursued his personal goal by inviting executives of the largest airlines to attend a special gathering in Washington. The get-together was hush-hush and highly productive—that is, if you were among the winning carriers. A tiny outfit called Delta Air Service wasn't even invited to the conclave, and that snub later came back to haunt Brown.

Picking from among the odd assortment of forty-four airlines then in operation across the United States, he intended to create three transcontinental carriers big enough to weather financial storms and efficient enough to gain a growing number of passengers. Brown favored neither an airline monopoly consisting of one carrier flying the overland route nor a poorly integrated grab bag of regional airlines, many of them marginal outfits and thus likely to have little long-term staying power. That, unfortunately, described the situation across the United States. Brown intended to cajole existing mail carriers into swapping routes where necessary in order to forge major airlines. By means of such arm-twisting, he became the true godfather of the soon-to-be-familiar trio of United, TWA, and American.

Brown arranged for United to fly the central route between Chicago and San Francisco by way of Omaha, Cheyenne, and Salt Lake City, as its forebear Boeing Air Transport had done successfully since 1927; and for American to fly the southern route between Dallas and Los Angeles. More awkward was the shotgun marriage Brown forced on financially ailing Transcontinental Air Transport, the proud "Lindbergh Line" that would lose $2.7 million in eighteen months of air-rail operation, and Pop Hanshue's Western Air Express to form a new carrier called Transcontinental & Western Airlines, or TWA. It flew a route across the West linking Chicago, Kansas City, Albuquerque, and Los Angeles.

The full-bodied Hanshue was a one-time football player for the University of Michigan who attended Brown's conference only to protect his vital interests. Once described by *Fortune* magazine as "profane," "rough-edged," and "one of the very few legendary figures among airline chiefs," he let fly volley after volley of expletives as he voiced his bitter opposition to the forced merger. At one point the ever-volatile Hanshue paused to survey his fellow airline executives and then let loose with "I think you're all crazy as hell."[24]

Finally, Hanshue realized that further opposition was futile and surrendered to Brown. He reluctantly agreed to serve as president of TWA, much to the happiness of Wall Street investors. But his heart was never into running TWA, and through no fault of his own, the company lost an average of $200,000 a month during the worsening economic crisis of the early 1930s and suffered a crash in Kansas that killed Knute Rockne, the popular football coach of Notre Dame University. Hanshue quit after less than a year on the job to concentrate on rehabilitating what remained of Western Air Express, a mere shadow of a once-great enterprise that as recently as early 1930 flew forty planes along a 4,700 mile system that stretched across nine southwestern states and thereby ranked it as the largest airline in the United States.[25] With its best routes stripped away and made part of TWA, Hanshue struggled to keep his beloved Western Air Express aloft during the grim days of the Great Depression, yet the worst was yet to come. Its total fleet consisted of only four planes in 1934.

That was the year when word of Brown's clandestine meeting in 1930 finally leaked out. Postmaster General James Farley and President Franklin D. Roosevelt happily seized upon the "Airmail Scandal" to pillory their Republican predecessors. Following a predictable explosion of public outrage voiced by Roosevelt's Democratic allies on Capitol Hill, the political theatrics climaxed when Farley summarily cancelled all existing contracts in early 1934 and had pilots of the Army Air Corps take over the job of flying the nation's mail on February 2. The ten carriers that until that date had flown Uncle Sam's mail along 27,062 miles of airways now had to survive on passengers alone or simply shut down.

Passenger traffic fell dramatically. "Since cancellation of the airmail contracts, the air transport industry has been literally haywire. The substantial, well-organized lines have been losing money. Uncertainty of the future has created a very sad state of mind among the directorate and heavy stock-holders," complained one industry executive.[26]

Furthermore, the Army Air Corps was unprepared for the size of the job. The forced handoff soon produced such disastrous results that Eddie Rickenbacker, a World War I ace and the popular chief of Eastern Air Lines, decried Farley's hasty action as "legalized murder." The military pilots were ill-equipped and overconfident, and as they sought to fly the mail through inclement weather on a regular basis, they suffered fatal crashes. In a single day three young airmen died. The public outcry embarrassed Farley and Roosevelt and forced them to end their bungled experiment on May 8.

That summer a Democratic-dominated Capitol Hill passed the Air

*A United Air Lines stewardess welcomes passengers aboard
one of its new Boeing 247s at Salt Lake City in late 1935. Among
her stated duties, besides serving hot coffee, were to clean and
polish passengers' shoes en route and swat flies and other insect pests
that sneaked aboard during a transcontinental flight's many ground
stops. On the older model planes, stewardesses warned smokers
not to dispose of their smoldering cigars and cigarette butts out
an open window. Courtesy Utah State Historical Society.*

Mail Act of 1934, a piece of highly vindictive legislation that mandated the breakup of all aviation holding companies that combined engine and plane manufactures with airlines under their massive corporate umbrellas. Thus, Boeing Airplane Company was a stand-alone business once again. But William E. Boeing, disgusted by this turn of affairs, sold his stake and never again involved himself in aviation.

Uncle Sam also punished airline executives connected in any way with Brown's infamous "spoils conference" in 1930. Among those forced out was Phil Johnson, head of United Air Lines; and replacing him was 34-year-old W. A. "Pat" Patterson, a former Wells Fargo banker in San Francisco. Patterson had entered the airline business in 1929 when the managers at Boeing and United Aircraft invited him to take charge of Vern Gorst's Pacific Air Transport, a West Coast carrier that Boeing had purchased the previous year. It was Patterson, going against the counsel of his bank superiors, who advanced Gorst a much-needed loan, and with them looking over his shoulder, he decided to keep a very close watch on what happened to Wells Fargo's dollars. Who knows, perhaps some of the wealth that helped bankroll Pacific Air Transport came from money Wells Fargo & Company originally earned in the 1860s by operating the western end of the Overland stage line.

Patterson remained head of United until the late 1960s, and it was he who hired the first airline stewardesses in 1930, eight "Sky Girls" in all. Initially, he refused to allow them to serve liquor; he did not want them to become aerial cocktail waitresses, an unseemly thought. United hired only women who were graduate nurses and were less than twenty-five years old; stood at most five feet, four inches tall; and weighed no more than one hundred fifteen pounds—and it mandated that its "Sky Girls" all retire by age thirty-two.

When it came to forced retirement, no one got a worse deal than Harris Hanshue, one of the chief victims of 1934's political theatrics. It made not one bit of difference to New Dealers that he had attended the "Spoils Conference" only under duress to defend the interests of Western Air Express. Uncle Sam had spoken, and Hanshue, like all other airline executives who broke the law by meeting secretly with Brown, had to be punished. Injustice must be served. Eddie Rickenbacker hired him for a brief while at Eastern, but he gave Hanshue no official title. Rapidly becoming bored, Hanshue returned to California where he became involved in a gold-dredging project in the northern part of the state. He was finished as an airline president, though. Hanshue died in 1937 ostensibly of a cerebral hemorrhage, but as the aviation writer Robert Serling observed, "At least that was what the death certificate listed as cause of death, inasmuch as there is no such official medical ailment as a broken heart."[27]

Western Air Express, though, managed to hang on and even to enlarge itself in 1937 by acquiring National Parks Airways, which connected several Montana stops with Salt Lake City. The company changed in other ways as well. As Western, like all other commercial airlines, adopted more formal and bureaucratic ways of conducting business in response to increased government regulation imposed in the late 1930s, one outspoken pilot recalled the freewheeling ways of former days and protested to his president that he was running the airline "like a goddamned railroad."[28]

Western Air Lines, the new name dating from 1941, became part of Delta. That carrier, incidentally, though not one of the nation's original major airlines, did originate west of the Mississippi River as a crop dusting service based in Monroe, Louisiana. The first commercial flights of Delta Air Service connected several cities of the Mississippi River delta country and hence its name. After being left out of Brown's "cabal" in 1930, Delta voiced the complaints that thundered onto the public stage four years later as the "airmail scandal."

Once calm had returned to Capitol Hill, the major carriers implicated in the uproar changed their names slightly to appease federal officials; for example, former American Airways became American Airlines. The majors bid successfully for new contracts and took to the skies one again with loads of airmail, but joining them were Delta and Braniff, two newcomers that won their first airmail routes. Delta at the time extended from Fort Worth to Charleston, South Carolina, by way of Dallas, Birmingham, and Atlanta. It was on this unimpressive foundation that one of the nation's current big three carriers was built.

In truth, if one can look past the finger pointing, Brown's forced creation of three major transcontinental carriers plus Eastern to serve cities along the Atlantic seaboard stood the test of time, providing the basic configuration that prevailed until deregulation of the industry in 1978, the histories of Braniff and Delta notwithstanding. Moreover, by modernizing the funding formula for airmail, the McNary-Watres Act encouraged more night flights, greater use of two-way radio communication, and more spacious accommodations for passengers.

In other words, instead of paying to transport airmail by how much a load weighed, Uncle Sam now compensated carriers on the basis of how much space was available on board their planes—not just for mail alone but also for passengers. In days when weight determined how much Uncle Sam compensated carriers, some aviators had succumbed to the temptation to wrap heavy bricks in paper and dispatch them via airmail to boost revenues. The 10,000 wooden postcards once used to inaugurate Spokane service by Varney Air Lines were probably more than a publicity stunt because they added extra weight and extra airmail pay.

Aircraft manufacturers responded to the new space-based incentives by designing the kind of aircraft the industry now needed. As trunk carriers phased out their single-engined Boeing Monomails and their Ford and Fokker trimotors, they replaced them with more commodious aircraft,

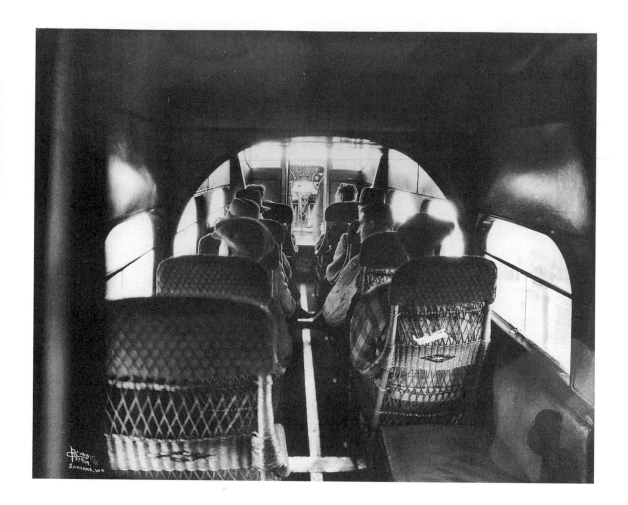

This Charles Libby photograph shows the interior of a Spokane Airways plane in 1928. Note the lightweight rattan seats and the absence of overhead luggage racks. Courtesy Eastern Washington State Historical Society.

including the all-metal Boeing 247, in production from 1932 to 1935 and often called the first modern airliner. Even more significant was the Douglas DC-3, popularly acclaimed as the first plane to enable airlines to earn a respectable profit carrying passengers without additional dollars generated by airmail contracts.

Douglas manufactured a total of 10,629 DC-3s. Never was a more popular airliner built when measured by its dominance of the market. By the late 1930s, Douglas DC-2s and DC-3s carried fully 90 percent of commercial airline passengers in the United States. Even so, it still took from 1926 to 1941 before revenue from passengers overtook that from carrying the mail.

Only along the Pacific Coast of the United States in the late 1920s did airlines carry enough passengers to adversely affect railroad revenues. Elsewhere, the planes flying overhead seemed to make little difference in the number of people who still rode the trains. That was why *Railway Age* in 1929 dismissed claims by would-be prophets that airlines of the United States "will ultimately carry all of the long-distance passenger traffic."[29] Railroads at the time provided passenger service over a quarter-million miles of lines serving all parts of the country. How insignificant airline passenger service seemed by comparison!

Yet in a single landmark year, 1936, the airlines of the United States sold more than a million airline tickets. Maybe it was time for railroads to start worrying. The era of air-rail cooperation was long over. The nation's newest overland route had come of age, and unlike the original overland route extending across the West, it was not limited by geography to one portion of the United States.

Eight

Hard Choices for Hard Times

"The public be damned" is the most legendary utterance in the history of American railroads. W. H. Vanderbilt, heir to the New York Central fortune, allegedly spoke those infamous words in 1882. In truth, a dishonest newspaper correspondent put them in Vanderbilt's mouth—invented the whole interview, in fact—after porters barred him from entering Vanderbilt's sleeping quarters late one night to interrogate him as his private railroad car passed through Chicago on its way to Denver. The writer, claiming the interview actually took place in Chicago's Grand Pacific Hotel, purportedly asked the rail baron if one of his premier passenger trains paid its way. "If not will you abandon it, or are you running it for the benefit of the dear public?"

Vanderbilt was supposed to have snarled, "Look here, young man, do you know me? The public be damned. I don't take any stock in that twaddle about working for the good of anybody but ourselves. I continue to run the 'Limited Express' because—well, because I want to." The Vanderbilt quotation was reported as fact in newspapers around the United States and even the world. Though his words were a total fabrication, they expressed what many Americans wanted to believe about railroad leaders of Vanderbilt's stature—that they were all callous and arrogant men.[1]

By the 1920s, unlike in Vanderbilt's day, railroads of the United States were thoroughly regulated. However, if industry leaders dared to protest that the heavy hand of regulation kept them from responding effectively to competitive threats posed by buses and automobiles, both of which benefited from publicly funded roads and highways, few Americans cared to listen. Few people could shed tears for the industry, for Ameri-

Western railroads were by no means unique when they issued brochures depicting the attractive scenery through which their trains passed. The cover image from a New York Central brochure of the 1920s highlights its four-track main line and the Hudson River Valley, which seasoned travelers often compared favorably with the Columbia River Gorge on the opposite side of the continent. Author's collection.

cans were certain that, after swaggering confidently through years of monopoly power, railroads had at long last gotten the vigorous competition they deserved.

Buses, as well as a small but rapidly growing fleet of over-the-road trucks, still operated largely unregulated in the 1920s, apart from state motor vehicle licensing and safety laws; and thus they were incredibly agile compared to heavily regulated railroads. In many states the newcomers could add or drop service almost overnight and could raise and lower their fares equally fast. If, on the other hand, a railroad wanted to drop a money-losing passenger train, even if its crewmembers outnumbered paying passengers, it often faced a complex and time-consuming set of public hurdles. Meanwhile, the nearly empty train rattled along as usual. Government regulators sometimes forced a big railroad to continue operating dozens of these money losers.

Furthermore, the newest modes of transportation seldom had to wrestle with problems caused by overcapitalization and related financial laxity. They usually employed low-cost, non-union labor; and they had few if any high-priced executives. The railroads—highly organized, wholly unionized, and fully regulated—had trouble raising the capital they so desperately needed to modernize tracks and equipment. The smart money shied away from businesses that offered them such poor returns on their investment. Railroads, to be sure, had allies on Capitol Hill and in state legislatures, but they had many sworn political enemies too.

Until the Federal Motor Carrier Act of 1935 regulated intercity bus and truck operators, the swift-footed newcomers ran their businesses wholly unfettered by Uncle Sam. Railroads appeared slow and plodding by comparison. Indeed, in terms of any significant innovation, the railroad industry by the 1920s had little incentive or ability to take action to fend off the pack of aggressive competitors. One writer in the influential *Atlantic Monthly* probably spoke for many Americans when he griped in 1925 that railroads of the United States were showing "many signs of decaying old age. There has been no substantial improvement in railroad equipment or management in twenty years or more."[2]

Criticizing railroads had long been a popular pastime. Railroads presented an attractive target to muckraking journalists in the early twentieth century, "and it has been popular to attack them," sighed Howard Elliott, the able president of the Northern Pacific Railway, in a speech in 1911. The industry remained a tempting target through the first half of the twentieth century. "Bull baiting has long ago been stopped by penal laws; bear baiting is not allowed, but railroad baiting survives," President William Sproule of the Southern Pacific Company responded in a public speech in January 1924. "In the public interest," he insisted, "it is time that railroad baiting cease to be a popular pastime."[3]

When railroad executives complained about unfair treatment, Americans typically responded that they were tired of hearing the "continued calamity howl of the railroads." The industry could have coexisted with unpopularity had it not continued to be translated into imposition of still more regulations and still greater trouble raising money on Wall Street. Within a brave new world defined by largely one-sided regulation drawn tight by popular opinion and widespread indifference or hostility to the industry's plight, rail executives struggled to find the right balance between business as usual, which only the most hidebound person believed was possible, and modernization, which cost money that railroads did not have.

There were some bright spots. Railroads remained the backbone of passenger and freight transportation across the American West during the 1920s and 1930s. Curious as it may seem, automobile manufacturing and widespread highway construction in the mid-1920s actually swelled railroad freight revenues. "The most gigantic single change in American industry" during the first three decades of the twentieth century, noted *Railway Age* in 1929, "has been the development of the automobile industry. This has affected the railways in two ways. It has given them a large amount of freight business, but it has caused them to lose a large amount of passenger business."[4]

Apart from automobile-related freight traffic, which rose for a time, it was sobering to think that opportunistic competitors could grab away almost any commodity that the railroads had once considered their exclusive traffic. More and more perishable foods went by truck from farm fields direct to processing plants and markets, completely bypassing the railroads. By 1932 the list of commodities hauled in sizeable amounts by the rapidly expanding intercity trucking industry included fruits, vegetables, grain, coal, automobiles, tires, cement, sand, gravel, canned goods, livestock, and lumber, all of them once part of the prized mix of railway traffic.

One thing that made it hard for rail leaders to accurately assess the changes overtaking their industry in the 1920s was that there were such pronounced regional variations. Though declining numbers of passengers were most noticeable on the local trains, the "passenger problem" was by far most acute in the West. In 1928 the railroads of the West suffered a net loss of more than $11 million on their passenger service, while railroads in the East had earnings of slightly more than $114 million on passenger service. Those in the South pretty much broke even. Even within the West there were regional variations. The railroads of the Pacific Northwest lost the most money on passengers, followed by those of the Southwest. Those railroads serving the central West actually made a little money on passengers. *Railway Age* took note of such variations in 1929 and asserted that "motor competition for passenger business has been much more effective in territories where population is sparse and highways not congested than

Luxury and elegance were the keynotes of this observation car introduced on the Spokane, Portland & Seattle Railway in 1930. Courtesy Oregon Historical Society.

in territories where population is dense and there is much highway congestion"—namely West versus East.[5]

As early as 1925 most rail leaders in the West seemed resigned to writing off the local passenger train as a lost cause. On the other hand, during the second half of the decade they worked hard to preserve their still-remunerative long-haul passenger service by refurbishing well-known luxury limiteds or by introducing whole new trains. All of the western transcontinental lines operated prestige limiteds (so called because flagship trains made few scheduled stops as they sped along the tracks)—the "Sunset Limited" of the Southern Pacific, the "Overland Limited" of the Union Pacific, the "North Coast Limited" of the Northern Pacific, the "California Limited" of the Santa Fe, and the "Great Northern Flyer," to name just of handful of the better trains. But more was required in the increasingly competitive 1920s.

One new train was the "San Francisco Overland Limited," a 63-hour express between Chicago and the West Coast that commenced service in 1926. It featured comforts such as on-board shower facilities, a luxury in the days when summer rail travel meant open windows and dust and cinders, and a spacious dressing room exclusively for women that included the services of a maid, manicurist, and hairdresser. Another premier train on the Overland Route, the "Los Angeles Limited," commenced 63-hour service between Chicago and southern California, a speedup that prompted the Rock Island and Southern Pacific to match the Union Pacific with their rival "Golden State Limited."

The "Panoramic Special" resumed service on April 24, 1925, on the Denver & Rio Grande Western between Denver and Salt Lake City. The all-Pullman train featured an open-end observation-compartment sleeping car to afford passengers sweeping views of the mountain scenery though which it passed, including the narrow canyon called the Royal Gorge. In late 1927 the Union Pacific added posh "limousine-lounge cars" to its "Columbine" between Chicago and Denver. "They will contain one drawing-room, one compartment, smoking-room, buffet, observation parlor, and a glassed-in 'Limousine' observation room or lounge, all being finished and decorated in the 'Adam' period."[6]

Though most advertising of through trains centered on their first-class amenities, American railroads during the latter half of the 1920s finally took a long and hard look at the humble day-coach, at least those they attached to their better trains. For years, coach riders had grumbled that railroads pampered their Pullman passengers with luxuries of all descriptions—"Milady may have a manicure in the boudoir, or enjoy a refreshing shower bath"—while coach passengers had often had been herded like cattle and expected to travel in grimy and over-crowded cars.[7]

Southern Pacific established a deluxe coach train on a weekly basis between Portland and San Francisco in 1927. By mid-year the service had become tri-weekly, with reduced fares. In late 1928 the Union Pacific introduced a new type of coach that featured individual seats, diffused lighting, and soft blue plush fabric with an accent on light browns and tans.

In the mid and late 1920s, American railroads for the first time turned to professional designers to help them create up-to-date interiors for their passenger cars, both coaches and Pullmans. One result was a bright and cheerful departure from the dark and ornate mahogany panels that had typified passenger train interiors since the Victorian era. Ironically, it was the modern motor coach that helped to inspire these much-needed im-

Great Northern in the mid-1920s advertised its posh "Oriental Limited" as a "Woman's Train," though many of its passengers were undoubtedly men. The train joined Chicago and Seattle by way of Minneapolis and Saint Paul, Minnesota. Courtesy Minnesota Historical Society.

provements, admitted the *Railway Age*. "There is nothing particularly inviting about even the cleanest, newest day coach of what is now standard design. There is something definitely inviting, however, about a parlor motor coach with its individual cushioned chairs and luxurious appointments."[8]

The Spokane, Portland & Seattle Railway, for instance, had seats on its buses upholstered in genuine leather. Private automobiles played a role too, because owners came to equate comfort with a seat with cushions and to concern themselves with aesthetics. It was during the 1920s when General Motors (with close financial ties to DuPont, a major paint maker) chose to make a fashion statement by the colors it used on the exteriors of its automobiles. Ford, who had worried little about aesthetics, for the first time produced fewer cars than General Motors' Chevrolet division because he stuck to basic black for too long.

It was a sign of the times that when Union Pacific introduced its new "Portland Rose" in 1930, it designed the train to be "not just a vehicle of transportation—not just iron, steel and wheels. It must tell a story—the story of Portland, the Pacific Northwest, and the scenic Columbia River along which it travels for 200 miles." It carried the rose motif throughout the train. It wove it into carpets and printed it on train stationery, bridge score pads, menus, and magazine binders. "The Portland Rose is truly a 'triumph of train comfort' . . . a comfort that is reflected in the equipment—the fine linens, coil spring mattresses, parchment-shaded lamps and commodious dressing rooms of the splendid modern Pullmans." The "Portland Club" observation car "is a masterpiece of the interior decorator's art." "Even the coaches are a delightful departure from the usual type. The interiors are tastefully decorated and the deep-seated individual seats are exceedingly restful."[9]

Regardless of the source of inspiration, railroads regarded the results of their increased attention to long-distance passenger service with satisfaction. "The increased patronage of long distance trains, particularly the Oriental Limited, has more than offset the loss in local passenger traffic," the Great Northern optimistically told stockholders in 1925. As long as premier trains like the Oriental Limited and the Empire Builder made money, revenue lost to automobiles and buses by local trains did not cause rail executives undue concern.[10]

But then came hard times. Only during the frightening days of the early 1930s did rail leaders fully realize how changing times demanded truly radical responses. Then, as in the 1920s, the passenger train dilemma occupied center stage as the railroads of the West reformulated responses to increased competition. Merely speeding up their premier trains or brightening car interiors, as they had done during the late 1920s, did nothing to win back motorists or the one-time rail travelers who had defected to buses or airlines. Only adding to the troubles of railroads, a growing number of shippers switched to long-haul trucking companies to carry their freight.

Commercial truck registration rose spectacularly during the 1920s, and the industry continued to expand rapidly even during the worst days of the Great Depression. During hard times, many an unemployed driver somehow managed to buy a modest truck of his own on credit and establish a "fly-by-night" local hauling business. In fact, nearly two-thirds of all commercial trucks at the time traveled less than a hundred miles per day.

Like bus operators, however, when the fledgling trucking companies expanded their geographical reach, they benefited from the concrete and asphalt right-of-ways that extended into all parts of the United States. More than three million miles of road and highway network (compared to 250,000 miles of railroad network at its peak) gave highway users a flexibility that railroads could not hope to achieve. Already by the eve of Pearl Harbor, over-the-road trucks carried 10 percent of all intercity freight, or a total of 62 billion ton-miles a year, though the massive tractor-trailer combinations so common on the highways today remained almost unknown at the time. It was less-than-carload shipments that initially proved most vulnerable to highway competition, though by World War II a rapidly growing number of long-haul trucks transported everything from California oranges to Idaho potatoes and Washington apples.[11]

The general prosperity of the late 1920s boosted freight traffic across the West, which helped railroads compensate for losses incurred in the passenger business, though the growth of freight traffic was far less than during the first two decades of the twentieth century. Because of how freight traffic helped lessen the "passenger problem" on steam railroads, the first and hardest hit carriers in the West were its electric interurban lines, which carried little freight. They felt the full impact of the motor age a full decade before most steam railroads did.

Already during the 1920s most interurban railroads of the West had trimmed service in response to increased automobile use along highways that paralleled their tracks. The Great Depression of the following decade pretty much killed off the industry. Only a few trolley and interurban lines survived into the 1940s. The Utah-Idaho Central Railroad served one of the least-populated areas of the United States until it quit running in 1947. In the final years more than 80 percent of its passenger revenues came from children, most of them transported under contract with local school boards.

At the opposite extreme was the Pacific Electric, which served the Los Angeles area. It saw its traffic rise sharply until 1923 because of a population boom in southern California, but then it dropped off because of growing automobile ownership. The onset of the Great Depression halved its revenues between 1929 and 1933. As the result of a stunning string of losses, Pacific Electric pruned large portions of its extensive passenger service between 1938 and 1941. A ridership surge during World War II proved to be only temporary, although several high-density lines continued to carry passengers until the early 1950s. Looking at the industry as a whole, railroad historian Albro Martin aptly described the interurban interlude as "one of the least edifying chapters in the history of American transportation and finance."[12]

During the Depression Decade even the strongest steam railroads suffered financial setbacks too, as when officials of the Great Northern reluctantly shaved the annual dividend on common stock from $5 to $4 a share in 1931. For a weak carrier like the Milwaukee Road, the hard times meant a second descent into bankruptcy in mid-1935.

American railroads had once hoped that their ailing passenger business would stabilize by 1929, but the onset of hard times only made a bad trend worse. "The condition of the passenger business of the railroads is nothing short of appalling," the *Railway Age* worried in 1933. "Since 1920 there has been a reduction of more than 70 percent in their passenger revenues, and the decline is continuing." Passenger traffic reached a low point in March 1933 during the frightening days of the national banking moratorium.[13]

The Great Depression forced railroads of the West to tackle the problem of ailing passenger service anew. One way was to trim costs. From 1930 to 1935 the railroads of America reduced expenditures for upkeep of passenger stations and office buildings by $100 million. During hard times many railroads lost interest in the direct operation of motor coach subsidiaries. Several major companies—notably the Burlington, Santa Fe, Missouri Pacific, and Rio Grande—placed their bus operations under the umbrella of the National Trailways system created in March 1936. Interestingly, the nation's intercity bus industry as a whole had matured and grown so large that by 1937 it could boast that with little more than 5 percent of the combined total plant and equipment investment of the steam railroads, electric railroads, airlines, and trolley buses, it carried 29 percent of the total passengers hauled by its competitors. At that time the future looked bright for the bus industry.

Even with the cutbacks, railroads sought to improve the equipment on their best trains and increase the pleasure of a long-distance journey. Perhaps nothing did more toward achieving that end in the early 1930s than air-conditioned cars, which culminated a quest for comfort that had begun some years earlier. In 1927 the Chicago, Rock Island & Pacific, for instance, had added special water sprinklers to the underside of its Rocky Mountain Limited (as it did earlier to its Golden State Limited) to "prevent dust and add to the comfort of Summer travel through the Rockies."[14]

Air conditioning became important as an amenity that added to passenger comfort as well as market appeal. The Santa Fe Railway "has been experimenting" for several years "on the problem of keeping the air cool in club, dining and sleeping cars during the Summer season," the *Official*

Guide reported. In 1930 the railroad was able to adapt a system already used successfully at one of its Fred Harvey station hotels to its premier trains. The innovation proved immensely popular with passengers, not just because of cool air across the miles of desert landscape that separated Los Angeles and Chicago but also because the closed windows sealed out the usual dust and grime of the journey.[15]

When the Union Pacific added air-conditioned cars to its best passenger trains serving the Pacific Northwest, the Great Northern was unhappy about having to spend precious dollars during hard times, but for competitive reasons it felt compelled to join the trend. In 1935 it advertised its refurbished Empire Builder as "the first completely air conditioned transcontinental train throughout the Northwest." However, when seen from trackside, the appearance of even the best and newest trains seemed to change little until railroads introduced a visually different passenger train called a streamliner.

❀ ❀ ❀

In the mid-1930s two western railroads introduced the first thoroughly modern generation of passenger trains. Nothing like these had appeared on the rails before. In fact, they were so different that the enhancements to passenger car interiors in the late 1920s, the most common form of rail modernization at the time, seemed little more than cosmetic by comparison. At the time the steel exteriors of passenger cars were still riveted together for great strength and usually painted dark and somber colors to hide the soot and grime they collected while riding behind steam locomotives that burned tons of coal or oil during a long journey. Thus, even with their fashionable interiors, passenger cars built in the late 1920s and early 1930s still added up to trains that on the outside had the stylistic elegance of a hulking battleship. In the eyes of modern young people, these trains often seemed little different from the old-fashioned ones their parents and grandparents rode.

The newest trains featured lightweight air-conditioned cars throughout and clean-burning internal combustion locomotives. More important in terms of design, they were streamlined, a visual concept that easily equated with modern. As such they owed a great deal to the newest generation of airliners. In fact, the 1930s were preeminently the age of the streamliner; and not just trains and planes but also buses, automobiles, and ferryboats—even skyscrapers, vacuum cleaners, and pencil sharpeners—were "streamlined." When Walter Dorwin Teague, an industrial designer, proposed a new style of gasoline station for Texaco that featured clean lines and aerodynamic pumps, that industry streamlined many of its outlets in the late 1930s.

Among the most enthusiastic proponents of the concept was Otto Kuhler, an industrial designer who insisted that streamlining made rail-

UNION PACIFIC SYSTEM

UNION PACIFIC
THE OVERLAND ROUTE

Time Tables

Union Pacific Railroad Co.

Oregon Short Line R. R. Co.

Oregon-Washington R. R. & Nav. Co.

Los Angeles & Salt Lake R. R. Co.

St. Joseph and Grand Island Ry. Co.

The July 1935 timetable of the Union Pacific System featured both traditional steam and modern streamlined trains. Courtesy William S. Greever.

road passenger trains appear up-to-date and fashionable—qualities that provided them much-needed sales appeal. It became an article of faith among railroad executives, too, that streamliners added prestige and advertising value to their industry. The public enthusiasm that welcomed both the "Zephyr" of the Chicago, Burlington & Quincy and the "M-10000" of the Union Pacific further bolstered their faith. "Stream-line trains with which the Union Pacific and Burlington have just recently astonished the world not only seem to be an answer to our necessities but are splendid advertisements for the railroad industry as a whole. They make the public conscious that the railroads are really doing something to meet the new conditions," observed the passenger traffic manager of the Chicago & North Western in 1934.[16]

When the Burlington's Zephyr made its historic dash from Chicago to Denver in the spring of 1934, "roads became parking lots as spectators gathered at every highway crossing to watch it go by—and not just at the crossings only, but also in the fields, among the embankments, behind ropes stretching along station platforms, on the tops of buildings—where ever the view was good. Women threw kisses, men tossed their hats in the air," wrote railroad historian Mark Reutter.[17]

Whether the Burlington or the Union Pacific ranked first in the streamliner derby depended on a number of technical points. The Union Pacific's M-10000 made its appearance in February 1934, but the Burlington's Zephyr began regular service between Lincoln, Omaha, and Kansas City in mid-November 1934, several weeks before the rival streamliner began serving neighboring Kansas on January 31, 1935, as the "City of Salina." Moreover, the diesel engine that powered the Burlington streamliner was a harbinger of things to come on American railroads; whereas the Union Pacific train used a distillate engine, similar to gasoline engines used in automobiles but dead-end technology for railroads. Regardless, there can be no doubt that in the mid-1930s these two railroads ushered in the age of the streamliner. By the end of 1935 no less than ten railroads in the United States had introduced fourteen streamlined trains of various configurations.

During the 1930s, however, not every railroad serving the West rushed to add fleets of streamliners. Some, like the Milwaukee Road, were so strapped financially that the best they could do was dress up their regular passenger cars and attach them behind a streamlined steam locomotive. Apart from Union Pacific, no railroad serving the Pacific Northwest introduced a streamlined train in the region until 1947. Most of the prewar transcontinental streamliners concentrated on linking Chicago with southern California, perhaps the most glamour-and-speed-conscious part of the United States. The two most vigorous rail competitors serving this important market were the Union Pacific and the Santa Fe.

Ranking not far behind was the highly competitive race between Chicago and Denver, which the Burlington commenced with its original Zephyr and the Union Pacific joined with its streamlined "City of Den-

Lettering the "City of Portland." External appearance grew increasingly important with the coming of brightly painted streamlined trains. Courtesy Union Pacific Museum.

ver." In late 1939, the Chicago, Rock Island & Pacific sprinted to catch its competitors when it debuted its "Rocky Mountain Rocket" on a fast overnight schedule between Chicago and Denver or Colorado Springs.

The new train consisted of seven lightweight stainless steel cars built by the Edward G. Budd Manufacturing Company and drawn by a General Motors diesel-electric locomotive. It was one of eight diesel-powered streamliners the Rock Island introduced in the late 1930s, and the first with sleeper accommodations. The Rocky Mountain Rocket was "completely streamlined of stainless steel, with the same flashing red color scheme on the power unit." The Rock Island teamed up with the Southern Pacific to run the "Arizona Limited," a streamlined train they inaugurated during the winter of 1940 to connect Chicago and Phoenix by way of Kansas City, El Paso, and Tucson. It was a "deluxe, all-room, extra-fast, extra-fare train that provides stewardess-nurse service and every other travel luxury and comfort, and is completely streamlined for its high-speed schedule."[18]

Wherever they ran, streamliners featured bright colors instead of the usual dull paint intended not to show dirt and grease. With diesel locomotives that was far less a concern than it had been in the time of soot and ashes. The cool blue and silver colors of the Missouri Pacific streamliners, for instance, were intended to make travelers think of "a summer resort on wheels." Even its name, the Eagle, "was intended to convey an impression of speed and strength."[19] Only Pearl Harbor and World War II brought a temporary halt to the railroads' annual debut of their flashy streamliners. When the first generation of postwar passenger trains appeared in 1947, streamlined diesel locomotives and lightweight cars had become standard equipment.

At about the same time that Union Pacific and Burlington officials introduced their first streamlined passenger trains, American railroads took another look at tourism and how it might be used to fill half-empty coaches and sleeping cars. That was a logical response to declining passenger revenues. Few if any regions of the United States were blessed with more spectacular scenery or a greater variety of outdoor activities than the West, but it drew few tourists from distant locations until the transcontinental railroads made the trip easy and comfortable—starting in 1869 across the central portion of the West and in the early 1880s across the Northwest and the Southwest. Especially from 1880 to 1915, regional boosters sought to lure wealthy tourists to the West along with homeseekers and investors. Like railroad passenger service in general, rail tourism changed noticeably during the post–World War I decade.

By 1923 it was possible to observe that "most of the world is a mammoth circus in summer time and thousands of men and women—publicity promoters, secretaries of civil bodies, steamship and railway passenger agents and Uncle Sam himself are competing as keenly as rival showmen on their respective ballyhoos for attention. The tourist crowd is moving. Someone is going to get 'em," enthused one booster. "The less fortunate of America's millions will be well satisfied with an evening on the beach within reach by trolley, or a steamboat ride on the river, down the coast or across the lake over the weekend." Nonetheless, "folks in 'the know' so far as America's vacation and recreational centers are concerned have broadened their vacation vision beyond the Sunday afternoon trolley ride to the city park to feed the animals or roll about on the grass; watch the baseball game between teams from rival department stores or rub elbows with their tradesmen and their tradesmen's children in the public swimming pool." Their attention increasingly centered on the national parks.[20]

Personally conducted summer vacation travel west from Chicago on the Union Pacific and Chicago & North Western lines dated from 1900. The two railroads had originally emphasized such California attractions as Yosemite National Park and Lake Tahoe but added Yellowstone National Park and the North Pacific region in 1905. So successful was their joint tour department that it handled 954 groups in 1917 and fully 5,600 in 1928, with many of them traveling by special trains. In 1900 most tour patrons came from the Chicago area, but by 1928 almost half came from the East Coast, and some came from as far as Germany and England. Their preferred destinations were Rocky Mountain, Zion, Grand Canyon, and Yosemite national parks; the Canadian Rockies; and Alaska.

Yellowstone National Park remained a perennial favorite. "Old Faithful Inn is a marvel of wooden construction—the most curious and successful combination of a log house and modern luxury," noted the editor of the *Official Guide* in 1905. One peculiar feature of the park's several hotels especially caught his eye, for he reported that "after the evening dinner a great number of the guests regularly visit the garbage piles, a custom which we venture to say does not exist elsewhere. The reason for this is that numerous bears come out of the woods at this hour to visit the piles for their evening meal, and the queer antics of the black, the brown and the grizzly varieties, with their cubs, add one more strange feature to the attractions of the Park."[21]

During the summer of 1925 the number of visitors to Yellowstone Park broke all previous records. Of the 154,282 people who entered the park that year, 44,786 came by rail, 106,329 by automobile, and the remainder by foot, horse, or motorcycle. During the Yellowstone Park season the dining car department of the Northern Pacific Railway made a special effort to tempt the appetites of the many children who traveled: "A set of six special menu cards has been designed, each illustrating in natural colors one of the animals which may be seen in a trip through the park. There is Peter Rabbit, Sammy Squirrel, the Hold-up Bear, Piggy Porcupine, Bill Beaver and Aunty Antelope. Descriptive rhymes on the reverse of these cards provide entertainment for the tiny tots (and incidentally for the grown up) and make the set an attractive souvenir of the trip over this line."[22]

Several less-known scenic and historical parks gained railroad sponsors during the 1920s and 1930s. For vacationers desiring to visit Carlsbad Cavern National Monument, the combined Missouri Pacific–Texas & Pacific Railways operated a through sleeping car twice a week to Van Horn, Texas. From this railroad station the trip to the caverns "is made in seven-passenger automobiles over a scenic and historic highway. Arrangements are made for the tourists to re-enter the car on return from the cavern on the evening of the same day."[23] Later in the 1930s it became common for Southern Pacific to offer two-day automobile tours from its trains at El Paso to Carlsbad Caverns. In addition, the second day's itinerary offered "a tour of the New Mexico Military Institute, Hondo Valley, Lincoln National Forest, Mescalero Apache Indian Reservation, and White Sands National Monument."[24]

In connection with its usual Yellowstone Park tours for the summer of 1941, Burlington offered "a dude ranch optional stop-over for the purpose of providing a 'taste' of this type of American-style vacation."[25] Just a few years earlier a Northern Pacific booklet entitled "National Forest Vacations in the American Rockies" had taken care to describe dude ranches as "real ranches, so titled because they are equipped with cabins, cottages, or ranch-house rooms enough to entertain Summer guests. The title 'dude' simply distinguished the welcome visitor from the seasoned old-timer. All newcomers from the city are 'dudes' to the Westerner."[26]

Each tourist season the railroads of the West competed vigorously with one another to develop and promote new destinations, most remarkably in the desert country of the Southwest that had both wearied and repelled passengers crossing it on hot summer days before railroads air-conditioned their transcontinental trains. Southern Pacific Lines in late 1928 issued booklets entitled "Guest Ranches in Southern Arizona" and "Southern California Desert Winter Resorts" to call attention to "the colorful desert and mountain regions of the Southwest, where Americans in increasing number are discovering a new Winter playground." The Union Pacific late that same year offered two-day side trips by motor coach through California's Death Valley, which its clever wordsmiths promoted as an area of "mystery, desolation, and grandeur."[27]

Motor detours of various types offered travelers to and from California a pleasant break in their long rail journeys. A perennial favorite were the Santa Fe's cruises through Indian pueblos, prehistoric cliff ruins, and old Spanish-American dwellings in the Sangre de Cristo Mountains. "Those desiring to spend the Christmas holidays at Santa Fe may enjoy the interesting ceremonials in the old Spanish churches and a succession of Indian dances in the near-by pueblos."[28]

Railroads regularly searched for new attractions to promote. During the summer travel season of 1930, Santa Fe arranged a highway detour through the Petrified Forest in Arizona, permitting passengers to detrain

The Great Northern Railway once arranged for members of the Blackfeet tribe to dance for passengers aboard its through trains as they paused at the east entrance to Glacier National Park. Courtesy John W. Barriger III Collection, St. Louis Mercantile Library.

in Holbrook, board coaches for a seventy-mile ride, and reboard the same train in Winslow, all with enough time for lunch in the dining car. The Chicago & North Western Railway offered a series of seven-day, all-expense tours of the Black Hills of South Dakota for the 1931 tourist season. Entertainment included "sightseeing, hiking, trout fishing, and golf."[29]

Indians presented a particularly compelling attraction. In mid-summer 1929 the passenger traffic department of the Santa Fe System issued leaflets telling the tourist where he might see "more Indians than he has ever seen anywhere—any time." It described the three big celebrations—

tives to do that. Only on airlines, in fact, did streamlining prove to be more than skin deep.

Observers had only to compare the clean lines of a DC-3 in 1936 with the ungainly trimotors that formed the backbone of transcontinental airline fleets only five years earlier to see how streamlining had forever changed the shape of commercial flight. For the generation of all-metal airliners that replaced the trimotors, some of which had wings crafted partially from wood and remained faithful to an increasingly antiquated biplane design, streamlining boosted speed as well as the industry's image.

The Boeing 247 may have ranked as the world's first streamlined airplane, but even more eye appealing as well as economical for airlines to operate were the Douglas Commercial series, notably the DC-3. But for the politics of commercial aviation in the 1930s, it might never have taken to the skies.

The Boeing 247 resulted from the close working relationship that existed between Boeing and United Air Lines, at one time two components of the same holding company. The plane carried ten passengers together with a flight attendant in a soundproofed and air-conditioned cabin. It even featured an onboard lavatory. The Boeing 247 began regular service on United during the spring of 1933 and positioned that company well ahead of its competitors. TWA at the time still flew slow and increasingly old-fashioned Ford Trimotors. The "Tin Goose," as the ungainly airship was commonly nicknamed, had briefly become a mainstay of carriers in the United States in the late 1920s and early 1930s. However, the Ford Trimotor required twenty-seven hours and fourteen refueling stops to fly from coast to coast. By contrast, the Boeing 247 trimmed that time to twenty hours and only seven refueling stops.

United's original order for sixty Model 247s was so large that it effectively tied up production lines at Boeing and froze out all competitors. That proved a costly mistake for both Boeing and United because miffed executives at Transcontinental & Western and American sought help instead from a bright young engineer named Donald Douglas. Educated at the Massachusetts Institute of Technology, he headed a small firm in Santa Monica, California, that manufactured airplanes.

What TWA originally wanted from Douglas (or any other willing manufacturer) in mid-1932 was to purchase ten or more trimotored aircraft. These, it specified, were to be of all-metal construction, capable of carrying twelve passengers in comfort, cruising at 145 miles per hour, attaining a ceiling of 21,000 feet, if needed, and covering 1,080 miles between refueling stops. The Douglas designers wisely chose to ignore the trimotored requirement and proposed instead a streamlined plane with retractable landing gear and newly available high-powered radial engines. TWA chose Douglas, and on July 1, 1933, the DC-1 flew for the first time.

The rounded edges and mirrored aluminum surface gave the Douglas plane a streamlined, almost futuristic look that made it seem a perfect centerpiece for the art deco style of those years. The word "streamlined," which originally meant to cut down wind resistance, applied equally well to the most impressive products of rail and air. In fact, as streamlined harbingers of transportation's future, both the Boeing 247 and the DC-1 beat the Union Pacific's M-10000 and the Burlington's Zephyr out of the starting gate; and in the end they proved far more significant machines.

The Douglas planes, beginning with its one-of-a-kind DC-1, was superior in terms of both comfort and speed to the Boeing 247s. Even better was the Douglas DC-2, which on February 18, 1934, set a coast-to-coast record of thirteen hours and four minutes. Next came the DC-3, longer and wider than its immediate predecessor though it cost about the same to operate and carried a significantly greater payload. Thoroughly impressed by the DC-3's potential to improve the bottom line of their financial statements during the aptly named Depression Decade, airlines clamored to buy DC-3s. Among those was United. Forced to swallow its pride, it dumped its Boeing 247s and purchased a fleet of DC-3s to catch its competitors. Incidentally, the DC-3s could fly coast to coast with three stops to refuel, compared to seven for Boeing 247s.

United sold all of its 247s to less well-endowed airlines, most of which served lightly populated areas of the West before World War II. Though Boeing built fine-quality military aircraft during World War II and after—notably the big B-29s that dropped the world's first atomic bombs—after the Model 247 disappointment it remained confined to the margins of commercial aircraft manufacture until in the late 1950s. That was when it staged a spectacular comeback with its Model-707, which ushered in the jet age for air travelers.

⚜ ⚜ ⚜

During the years from 1926 through 1933, which witnessed the birth of commercial aviation across the West, any airline's main selling point was speed. During 1934, when the debut of the nation's first two streamlined trains attracted widespread public attention, United Air Lines scheduled fourteen arrivals and departures a day from Portland's Swan Island airport, and local boosters could then claim, "Broadway of Portland is now only 21 hours from Broadway of New York, while Southern California may be reached by air without the loss of daytime business hours." Passengers willingly sacrificed comfort for speed, and it was the speed of a modern airplane that neither the Union Pacific's soon-to-be introduced City of Portland nor any other streamlined train could hope to match.

On May 18, 1934, TWA placed the first DC-2s into regular commercial operation along its Columbus-Pittsburgh-Newark route. Two years later American Airlines scored a world first when one of its new DC-3s lifted off on June 25, 1936, to launch "Flagship" service between Newark and Chicago. In addition, the plane was part of an order for ninety-four DC-3s that by the end of the decade helped to make American the nation's

The unusual floating bridge that stretched east across Lake Washington from Seattle opened to motorists in mid-1940. The inaugural enthusiasm recorded by the camera of Asahel Curtis was repeated frequently on highways across the West during the post–World War II decades. Courtesy Washington State Historical Society.

number one domestic airline. Only recently that title had belonged to United, which in December 1936 used one of its new DC-3s to inaugurate coast-to-coast service by offering a scheduled time of fifteen hours and fifty-seven minutes.

That same month in Oakland, California, United opened the first airline flight kitchen. "A few years ago an aerial meal service consisted of sandwiches and coffee in paper cups, with apples, oranges and candy bars for dessert," recalled the head of the food service department of United Air Lines. "Today a choice of entrée and full course dinners are served." Furthermore, "each passenger has an individual table, or swivel chairs can be turned around so that two or four people may dine together."[37]

The DC-3 itself made it possible to cross the United States with both speed and comfort. One version, called the Douglas Sleeper, featured interiors designed much like railroad Pullman cars in that sectional seats could be easily reconfigured as berths for night travel by fourteen passengers.

By mid-1936 it was possible for a Transcontinental & Western flight called the "Sky Chief" to leave New York at 5 o'clock each evening and touch down in Los Angeles (Burbank) at 8 o'clock the following morning. It was no red-eye flight, either. While the passengers dozed in their beds, the plane made brief stops in Columbus, Kansas City, and Albuquerque. The fare for a one-way trip was $149.95. The *Aero Digest* advertised this flight as "one of six fast transcontinental schedules operated daily out of New York by 'the Lindbergh Line.'"[38] One problem with sleeper planes was that DC-3s were unpressurized, so before descending at each stop through the night, a cabin attendant had to awaken passengers to have them swallow and clear their ears, otherwise they experienced a painful buildup of pressure.

⚜ ⚜ ⚜

During these same years, the speed of the nation's premier passenger trains increased noticeably, as did that of its freight trains. "Since 1920 there has been an almost constant increase in the average speed of freight trains in this country," observed the president of the Association of American Railroads in late 1939. For perishable commodities running from the West Coast to markets in the East, "as much as four days have been clipped off the schedule."[39]

Despite such achievements, the speed laurels belonged to the airlines. Airlines taught Americans to think of distances in a whole new way, to see landscapes from a fresh perspective, and to adapt to a new travel habitat defined by airplanes and airports. World War II postponed some basic changes in the travel habits of Americans, but only until the fighting ended.

Nine

Is This Trip Necessary?
The Impact of World War II

In no other corner of the earth have people been so heavily dependent on the use of the automobile as in the United States. Nowhere else has "my car" become so much a part of the average citizen, for business or pleasure.

—Leon S. Wellstone, *Highway Magazine*, October 1942

Television newscaster Tom Brokaw calls them "the Greatest Generation."[1] For their many sacrifices during World War II they certainly merit the praise. However, not all of the Americans who struggled to cope with challenges posed by the global conflict have recollections that focus on combat, distant battlefields, or the stress of personal privation. My mother will probably take to her grave simple memories of trying to travel during the greatest crush of passengers ever recorded on American railroads.

In 1943 she had been married less than a year and was traveling by train from her parents' home in North Carolina to see her soldier husband stationed at Camp Grant, near Rockford, Illinois. The Chesapeake & Ohio train from Richmond, Virginia, pulled into the Cincinnati Union Station late. When Mom got through the crush of people to reach the tracks of New York Central Lines, she found the train for Chicago already moving. The lower halves of the Dutch doors of its vestibules were all closed. Uniformed soldiers crowded every car and spilled out into the vestibules. Overwhelmed by the stress of the journey, she burst into tears. She was nineteen years old.

Suddenly she felt someone grab her by the shoulders and lift her onto the rear platform of the slowly moving train. She recalls that seats, aisles, bathrooms, and even the luggage racks were awash in a sea of olive drab uniforms. She had either to share an already crowded seat or sit in the vestibule on her upended suitcase. She was grateful for the crowded seat. At least she was headed to Chicago. "Is this Trip Necessary?" signs conspicuously posted by the Office of Defense Transportation asked. Yes, she remembers, indeed it was.

Pacific Intermountain Express posed one of its over-the-road trucks in front of the Utah Capitol to promote patriotism during World War II. Courtesy Utah State Historical Society.

On another occasion, Mom recalls, the coach she rode was fresh from the rail yards where it had been stored for a long time—a very long time. It may have been from the railroad's boneyard, awaiting the scrap heap because it was too old and broken down to use in regular service. But this was wartime, so it was put to work. The inside of the car was cold, and frost covered its ceiling. Someone kindled a fire in the potbellied stove, for which shivering passengers were grateful, but the hot air also melted the frost. Down with dripping water came a generation's worth of soot. The passengers looked like face-blackened minstrels ready to perform in the next show.

Meals were on the minds of wartime Americans, whether they traveled aboard crowded trains or stood at trackside to watch as countless freight cars loaded with grain passed by. Courtesy William S. Greever.

My retired history colleague from the University of Idaho, William S. Greever, recalled that as a young soldier he rode aboard one of Southern Pacific's new streamliners from Los Angeles to San Francisco. As usual the cars were packed. Space for meals was limited, and long hours of work made the servers stressed and gruff. The railroad limited passengers to a single cup of coffee, a common practice at the time. When an older man seated at Greever's table dared to ask for a second cup, the server indignantly snapped, "Don't you know there's a war on?"

"Yes, I know," the stranger quietly replied. "I've already lost two sons."

The server said not a word but turned on his heels and disappeared into the busy galley. A few minutes later he returned with a full pot of coffee. Without a word he set it down by the older man. No words were needed.

All such recollections speak to the importance of transportation in winning World War II and also to the difficulties of wartime travel. Trains were crowded and passenger cars so well used that their seats grew threadbare and their windows dirty. Travel by train became an ordeal, but everyone accepted the inconveniences because winning the war demanded sacrifice from all. Americans learned to forego comfort for victory. It was the least civilians could do.

Conditions aboard city buses and streetcars were no better; many of them were ancient vehicles that creaked and groaned under a staggering load of passengers. But travel by personal car was equally difficult. Uncle Sam strictly rationed all gasoline and tires and set a national speed limit at 35 miles per hour, which was appropriate because of the dangerous condition of many oft-repaired tires. Some of them bore so many patches that they literally thumped along the highways. Most civilians remained close to home, if at all possible, and worked hard to win the war of production. They dutifully saved dollars, bought war bonds, and dreamed of peacetime when they could use their accumulated savings to pay for needed vacations, new cars, or modern homes—preferably all three.

No event of the twentieth century, neither the Great Depression nor the activism of the New Deal, brought more fundamental economic change to the American West than did World War II. The pressures of wartime life left scarcely any part of it untouched. In what soon proved to be a classic of understatement, the Portland *Oregonian* observed in early April 1941, eight months before Pearl Harbor and the formal entry of the United States into the conflict already raging elsewhere: "Few persons realize the magnitude of the national defense efforts in the Pacific Northwest."[2]

Even before the United States declared war on its Axis enemies, oil production boomed in California, Texas, and other parts of the West; and railroads hauled more of the black gold than ever before. By the fall of

1942, some 70 percent of the crude oil that reached East Coast refineries arrived aboard long trains of tank cars that originated in the Gulf Coast states of Louisiana, Mississippi, and Texas as well as farther inland in Kansas and Oklahoma. These were the first prosperous years in two decades for the region's many metal mines. The war also boosted the West's timber industry.

As part of a government effort to decentralize production of vital war materials, the western cities of Tucson, Phoenix, Albuquerque, and Denver became sites of defense-related industries. Billions of federal dollars flooded the West to fund war industries and the construction of numerous military training facilities. California alone received 10 percent of all federal spending during World War II. Some of those dollars took the form of huge aircraft factories arising from the former pea fields and orange groves of southern California. Located in the Golden State was the nation's greatest concentration of aircraft factories, and airplane manufacturing ranked among southern California's most important industries.

In April 1930 an advertisement had appeared in *Aero Digest* touting the advantages of "Air-Minded Los Angeles County." Among its boasts: "No snow, no sleet, no ice, no winter blizzards to interrupt flying or slow down production." "55 airports and landing fields." "More licensed pilots than in any other county of the United States." "Adequate supply of skilled expert labor." "25, or more, aviation schools now training over 2500 students." "Ideal labor and living conditions." Perhaps the last phrase alluded to the fact that aircraft workers in southern California, at least initially, were not members of labor unions. "Leading manufacturers of aircraft, airplane motors, parts, and equipment, who are making history in the aviation industry today, now have either major or branch plants in Los Angeles County," the advertisement claimed.[3]

The benign climate and an abundance of millionaire venture capitalists helped to make southern California attractive to early airplane builders, yet even with these several advantages it was tough for the industry to survive there or anywhere else during the lean years that followed World War I. One company cking out a modest living was T. Claude Ryan's San Diego firm that achieved fame in 1927 by building Lindbergh's "Spirit of St. Louis."

An even more significant turning point occurred when Donald Douglas, an engineer for the Glenn Martin Company based in Cleveland, formed an enterprise of his own in 1920 and relocated from Ohio to southern California, where he had temporarily worked earlier. With a few hundred dollars of his own and a $15,000 loan from Harry Chandler and associates, the Douglas Aircraft Company launched production in a former movie studio, a large and drafty building not unlike a typical hanger. Building planes for the Army, Douglas succeeded in California, but only barely.

During the depression days of 1932 Douglas struggled through four months without a single order, while his Burbank neighbor and competi-

Production for victory: Boeing B-17s being assembled in the Seattle area. Courtesy Library of Congress.

tor, Lockheed, went bankrupt. From 1927 to 1937 military purchases accounted for fully 91 percent of all Douglas sales. That changed with the phenomenal success of the Douglas Commercial series. The big Douglas factory in Santa Monica (the former movie studio) gained fame as the home of the DC-3 and its military counterpart, the C-47 of World War II fame. Because of his firm's impressive production figures, Douglas himself was widely hailed as "the Ford of the aviation industry."

Unlike Henry Ford, Douglas was a professionally trained engineer. That was not true for most of his competitors. The legendary Glenn Martin, as well as John K. Northrop and the two Loughead brothers, all prominent in aviation manufacturing, were, like many of the backyard auto mechanics of that era, essentially self-taught men—tinkerers really. In fact, Malcolm Loughead gave up the aviation business and made his fortune as the inventor of an improved type of automobile brake. His Lockheed Hydraulic Brake Company adopted a phonetic spelling of the family name that his brother Allan later used for the airplane manufacturing company he incorporated late in 1926.

To compete with the DC-3, Lockheed pinned its hopes on a speedy twelve-passenger plane called the Super Electra. The DC-3 carried twice as many passengers, but Lockheed's small plane flew significantly faster. Northwest bought Super Electras even before the Department of Commerce approved them for passenger service, but then in early 1938 it lost three of its original fleet of eleven as the result of a series of alarming accidents. In early 1939 Lockheed made good on a promise to repurchase Northwest's remaining Super Electras, and the Minnesota-based carrier turned instead to DC-3s. As a domestic passenger plane, Lockheed's once-promising Super Electra was finished. That was a big blow to the struggling firm.

Though Lockheed constructed only thirty-seven planes in 1937, it bounced back dramatically during World War II when it built approximately eighteen thousand between 1941 and 1945. In January 1946 *Time* magazine featured Robert Gross, head of Lockheed, on its cover. His company had recently delivered its first postwar Constellation to Pan American, the premier international airline of the United States. Lockheed's Constellation was a big, beautiful plane that had been in development since 1938.

In 1935, the birth year of the DC-3, another manufacturer, Consolidated Aircraft, relocated from Buffalo, New York, to San Diego; and the following year North American relocated to Los Angeles. By 1939 southern California was home to more than half of all aircraft-manufacturing workers in the United States. Another great concentration on the West Coast was in western Washington.

While many of America's aircraft manufacturers gravitated to sunny southern California, Boeing chose to cluster its assembly plants in Seattle and nearby Renton and scattered its subassembly and parts factories throughout the Pacific Northwest. Before war erupted in Europe in September 1939, Boeing had employed about four thousand people to produce military planes for the Army Air Corps as well as a handful of commercial aircraft. One of Boeing's best-known models from the 1930s was the B-17, or Flying Fortress, which Britain's Royal Air Force purchased to strike back at the Germany. By mid-1941, at least five months before Pearl Harbor, nearly ten thousand people worked for Boeing, a number that doubled to twenty thousand in September and jumped to thirty thousand when the United States officially entered the war after Japan's sneak attack on December 7. At the peak of B-17 production, Boeing's Seattle plant rolled out sixteen B-17s every twenty-four hours.

A much larger and longer-range Boeing plane, the B-29 Super Fortress, became operational in 1943. On each of several assembly lines in Renton, Boeing workers were capable of constructing a B-29 bomber in only five days. By mid-1945 six new planes rolled out of the plant each day, for a wartime total of 1,119 Renton-built B-29s. Boeing built another 1,644 B-29s in Wichita, Kansas, in addition to the nearly 7,000 Boeing B-17s. At its peak of production in 1944, Boeing employed nearly fifty thousand people in the Seattle area and amassed total sales in excess of $600 million, an impressive sum, considering that in 1939 the value of all Seattle manufacturing totaled only $70 million.[4]

⚜ ⚜ ⚜

Uncle Sam spent still more dollars on shipbuilding on the West Coast, some $5 billion in California alone. Employment in shipyards on San Francisco Bay mushroomed from four thousand to two hundred sixty thousand jobs during the war. One noted industrialist, Henry J. Kaiser, assembled an unprecedented shipbuilding empire that included yards on San Francisco Bay and the Willamette and Columbia rivers in the Pacific Northwest. At the peak of production, the yards launched a new ship every ten hours and earned Kaiser the popular sobriquet of "Sir Launchalot."

During the early years of the war, new production techniques transformed both aircraft and shipbuilding from craft to mass production industries. This decreased the necessity of hiring skilled labor and opened the doors to people who had never before been inside the gates of a shipyard or aircraft factory. Filling thousands of the new jobs created at Lockheed, Douglas, and other aircraft manufacturers were many one-time refugees from Oklahoma who just a few years earlier had traveled to California along Route 66 and had worked first as harvest hands in the state's many orchards and fields.

Shipyards, aircraft factories, and other war industries paid such high wages that they created an almost unreal opportunity for westerners who remembered ten long years of economic struggle. Yet even as their standard of living rose, they, along with all other Americans, saw consumer goods and services grow increasingly high-priced, rationed, or simply un-available. During the war many staples of life, including meat, milk, sugar, and clothing, were in short supply. Even if a prized item were available, everyday shopping required standing in long checkout lines or doing without. The discomforts endured by shift workers may have been responsible for the unusually high absentee rates recorded in manufacturing centers on the West Coast, where the annual rate of labor turnover reached 150 percent in some areas in 1943. It grew so noticeable at Boeing that observers began to describe the company as a "giant turnstile."

Getting to work became a daily ordeal too. Along some Seattle streets, the amount of traffic nearly doubled by late 1941; and when gasoline and tire rationing restricted automobile use in mid-1942, it only increased the need for personal sacrifice. "Millions of workers in war production plants throughout the United States have been mobilized by private automobiles," reported the American Automobile Association. In December 1942 some 92 percent of the 50,000 workers in aircraft plants rode to work in private automobiles. Buses and streetcars, overcrowded though they were, still carried only 3.4 percent of the total. For that reason, the nation's "Rubber Czar," William M. Jeffers, observed, "You can't take America off wheels. You can lose the war doing that, because of the disruption it would cause in our economy. . . . But you can reduce the use of rubber to the irreducible minimum"—and gasoline, too, from which synthetic rubber was made.[5]

Because of the gasoline rationing that began on May 15, 1942, Idaho's Sun Valley converted from a posh resort into a Navy convalescent center. American resorts in general, wrote one observer, "have been hard hit" and were "gloomy over their prospects. They were caught between shorter vacations on the one side, and no gasoline on the other." Gas rationing put many small highway and automobile-dependent businesses out of business because the number of Americans traveling to golf courses and out-of-town parks, beaches, and mountain retreats declined dramatically. Gasoline rationing, in addition, "created problems for real-estate men handling suburban property. Houses which can be reached mainly by private transportation, or by that means alone, are hard to sell or rent."[6]

As travel of all types grew more difficult, business and professional organizations found it easy to forego their annual conferences and conventions, symphony orchestras cancelled their annual tours, and intercollegiate football teams shuffled their schedules to minimize the time they spent aboard crowded trains. More than offsetting any noticeable decrease in civilian travel, however, was a huge jump in military traffic.

⚜ ⚜ ⚜

The typical American soldier in World War II made eight moves by train from induction to embarkation, compared with only three in World

War I. Solid troop trains and special troop cars became a common sight along the railroad landscape. Sometimes a single troop train consisted of as many as twenty-five cars, though in winter weather it was nearly impossible to adequately heat more than fourteen or fifteen. At one time the Northern Pacific placed extra locomotives in the middle of long trains to supply enough steam to heat the rear cars. Army officials soon permitted the railroads to operate several sections of shorter trains, which were easier to keep warm. In the early months of the war, troop trains carried an average of fifty thousand soldiers a day. Some dining cars served seven hundred meals a day; and with every bunk full, well-worked Pullman porters grew exhausted and unable to get needed rest on many long runs.

In November 1942 the Office of Defense Transportation eliminated high-speed competitive freight schedules and lengthened the run times for through passenger trains between Chicago and the West Coast to accommodate an ever-growing volume of mail and express. On Midwest-to-California trains operated by the Rock Island & Southern Pacific, that meant slowing the Golden State Limited by three hours between Chicago and Los Angeles. During the following summer, railroads dropped their resort trains in order to free up passenger equipment for use elsewhere, and they even sold seats in their lounge and club cars, an unheard of practice.

For years travelers had avoided the cramped upper berths of Pullman sleeping cars, but now the Army assigned three men to each section, two in the lower berth and one in the upper. Curiously, the Navy assigned only one man to each berth. Regardless of the arrangements, military personnel from all branches filled to capacity all available sleeper accommodations.

Unlike World War I, this was a two-ocean war. That placed especially heavy burdens on the Southern Pacific and the Southern Railway, which on the Pacific and Atlantic coasts respectively connected more military camps and bases than any other railroads in the United States. Those two companies often had to borrow needed passenger cars from other railroads. Southern Pacific hauled an especially heavy volume of freight over its sprawling system, and keeping all the trains moving safely and efficiently was no simple feat for a railroad that for the most part had few miles of double track. Even before Pearl Harbor, during the months from September 1, 1939, and December 7, 1941, when freight traffic had unexpectedly surged on the Southern Pacific, the carrier ordered an additional 110 steam locomotives and 72 diesel switchers. After Pearl Harbor it reactivated dozens of steam locomotives recently destined for scrap yards, and it borrowed many more from other railroads. When many of its regular employees went off to war, Southern Pacific managers hired women to clean passenger cars, wipe dirty locomotives, and do numerous other tasks formerly done exclusively by men.

The flow of military traffic composed of personnel traveling on furlough and under orders became so great that patriotic exhortations urged

Jack Delano photographed the busy icing platform of the Indiana Harbor Belt Railroad near Chicago in January 1943. Ice maintained a safe temperature for perishable commodities, notably fruits and vegetables from California, as they traveled across the United States. As many as four thousand passenger and freight trains entered or departed Chicago each day. No wonder the Midwest metropolis ranked as the world's greatest railroad center. Courtesy Library of Congress.

civilians to "give your seat to a serviceman." Better yet, avoid unnecessary trips. "Don't Plan a Trip This Christmas," Northern Pacific recommended. And Southern Pacific advertised throughout its sprawling West Coast domain: "Next Time—Don't Take the Train." Such advice would have been unthinkable during the lean years of the 1930s.[7]

By late 1943 Southern Pacific had spent $75,000 on advertising designed to *discourage* passenger travel. At various points along its tracks, it erected billboards urging, "Don't Travel Unless You Have To: Our Locomotives and Cars Are Needed More by Uncle Sam and His Men." Southern Pacific officials warned Americans, "If gasoline rationing causes many more people to travel by train, we may have to hang out the 'Standing Room Only' sign." Another Southern Pacific slogan intended to shame civilians into avoiding any unnecessary travel was, "How's Your Conscience Today?"[8]

Despite the impressive parade of more than 143 new streamlined passenger trains on twenty-nine different railroads by 1942, it took the massive troop movement of World War II and civilian rationing of gasoline and rubber to push passenger train ridership to all-time highs. Revenue passenger miles on American railroads climbed from a Great Depression low of 16.3 million in 1933 to 87.8 million in 1944, almost twice the total of the nation's previous high-water mark set in 1920.

❊ ❊ ❊

Wartime increases in freight tonnage were equally staggering. Train crews worked around the clock to keep traffic moving and prevent car shortages. When war broke out in Europe in September 1939, the railroads of the United States had 1,737,000 freight cars. By the time of Pearl Harbor a little more than two years later, the size of the fleet had grown by a mere 2.7 percent, yet railroads hauled 43 percent more ton-miles of freight than they had as recently as 1939. The key to their success was greater efficiency, and they achieved it none too soon.

After Pearl Harbor, the flow of ship traffic through the Panama Canal abruptly dried up, and American railroads almost immediately assumed the additional burden this created. Because enemy submarines lurked along the East Coast, railroads carried oil and other valuable commodities that formerly would have traveled by coastal steamer. All the while, the rail industry worked hard to prevent car shortages and other transportation snarls that had resulted in a federal takeover during the previous world war, and they succeeded. Though American railroads moved an unprecedented volume of freight, no one during World War II saw miles of loaded cars hopelessly clogging marshalling yards and export terminals.

In 1944 railroads handled a record 740 billion ton-miles of freight traffic in addition to a record 96 billion passenger-miles. At year's end, when the war load peaked, the nation's railroads possessed only 6.6 percent more freight cars than when the conflict began, but the ton-miles that fleet generated had fully doubled since 1939. "Keeping 'em rolling for Victory" became the slogan of railroads in World War II, and it proved to be an apt description of what took place day after day for three busy years. Given the vital nature of their assignment, it should not be surprising that the West's railroads once again occupied a prominent place in public life.

Ironically, making the railroads' freight-handling job easier were the nation's many trucks. "While the railroads have done well," noted Joseph Eastman, director of the Office of Defense Transportation, in 1942, "they would have been in a sorry plight if they had not had the help of their erstwhile foes, the trucks and buses."[9]

Only half a million trucks hauled freight along the streets and highways of the United States in 1917, compared to nearly five million trucks in use at the time of Pearl Harbor. Truck owners and operators purchased 700,000 new trucks during 1941 alone, and during the war they kept their freight fleets on the move, using gasoline and rubber that was denied civilian motorists. Railroads themselves operated at least 94,000 trucks in 1942, of which 14,000 belonged to the Railway Express Agency. It used them mainly to make local deliveries.

⚙ ⚙ ⚙

On the eve of World War II railroads had owned 1,759 buses traveling along 44,700 miles of route, but many companies left the business even as the nation's bus lines expanded rapidly to handle wartime and postwar traffic. In February 1942, for the first time in American history, more passengers rode motor coaches than rail coaches—and that remained true for years to come. Six billion passengers rode motor coaches in 1942 alone. The handful of surviving electric interurban lines shouldered a staggering load of passengers too.

The good news for American railroads was that for the nation as a whole their passenger service operated in the black in 1942 for the first time since 1929. This was despite the fact that overcrowded passenger trains discouraged vacation travel or even short pleasure trips. "Increases in travel by railway are occurring so fast that the railways apparently will be called upon to handle more passenger traffic in 1942 than in any previous year in history," noted *Railway Age*. "If they satisfactorily succeed, it will be in spite of difficulties."[10] One of these difficulties was that the shift from travel by train to automobile during the interwar years had caused a sharp decrease in the number of rail passenger cars available to handle the wartime loads.

American railroads operated fewer passenger cars than at any time during the previous forty years, but like their freight cars, they ran them much more efficiently. They had no choice. In 1944 only one-seventh of the nation's wartime fleet of 37,940 passenger cars had been constructed

As during World War I, women temporarily filled many railroad jobs during World War II. This crew composed of women of Mexican heritage worked for the Southern Pacific in Tucson, Arizona. Courtesy Arizona Historical Society.

during the previous ten years, while half of the cars were more than twenty-five years old, a full lifetime and more for all such conveyances. In 1942 Uncle Sam permitted the Pullman Company to build 157 much-needed sleeping cars to meet the increased demand. Federal authorities assigned them to the important transcontinental trains, such as the Golden State Limited and the Overland Limited, both of which ran between Chicago and southern California with its heavy concentration of war industries and military bases. Except for a fleet of 1,900 boxcar-like triple-deck troop sleepers, 400 troop kitchen cars, and 200 hospital cars, railroads acquired no more new passenger cars until after World War II had ended. Until then, numerous antiquated wooden cars destined for scrap remained on active duty.

Because of gasoline and rubber rationing imposed in 1942, many would-be motorists ignored the warnings and flocked back to passenger trains in unprecedented numbers. Long lines, congested terminals, and interminable waits for crowded trains became the stuff of nightmares. Once on board a train, a traveler often found standing room only, with people crowding the aisles and overflowing into restrooms, vestibules, and even into the overhead luggage racks. Car cleaners did their best, but their task was hopeless when eight hundred people were crammed aboard a train designed to accommodate only five hundred.

When many Americans continued to ride trains despite an obvious lack of space, federal officials took formal steps to further discourage civilian rail travel. A federal ban on conventions reduced civilian travel by 6 percent in 1944, yet that same year during the Christmas season American railroads handled more passengers than ever in their history.

Earlier, in late 1942, Uncle Sam had curtailed excursion train travel and also seasonal passenger trains to resort areas in order to save coal. "Vacation at home," federal officials urged. "The vacation season coincides with the peak of the military movement." The Office of Defense Transportation further urged motorists to keep their cars "in good running condition" and to "observe wartime speed limits. Tires, batteries, parts and mechanics continue in critically short supply. It will be years before the average motorist can buy a new car. With local transit facilities already overloaded, they cannot carry careless, carless motorists."[11]

Apart from crowded trains and buses, and the gasoline and rubber rationing imposed on private automobiles, there were other matters to worry wartime motorists. The American Automobile Association published a twelve-step guide explaining how to drive in a blackout. Among its suggestions were to make temporary masks for headlights and to "drive very slowly, always on the alert." If driving is impossible, the AAA advised, "Turn out all lights, lock car securely to prevent possible use of car by saboteurs or parachutists. Then seek place of refuge." A final suggestion was: "Stay sober. Do not drink."[12] Sobriety and efficiency were important. In the interest of encouraging greater efficiency and thereby bolstering national security, President Roosevelt on January 20, 1942, signed into law a bill passed by Congress to promote daylight-saving time.

On its Pacific Coast line, where tracks paralleled the sandy beaches of southern California in several locations, Southern Pacific shop workers fitted locomotives with specially shielded headlights and marker lamps to conceal them from the eyes of enemy submariners who might be lurking beyond the surf. The railroad carefully curtained every passenger car window or painted it black. Likewise, it hooded trackside signal lamps.

In July 1945 Colonel J. Monroe Johnson, director of the Office of Defense Transportation, held a special press conference to warn civilians of the tremendous increase in military traffic expected as the United States redeployed its military might from Europe to pursue final victory over Japan. Immense tonnages of military freight were likewise headed to the Pacific. The bright spot was that people on the West Coast would have no trouble getting reservations on eastbound trains, all of which would return west with military personnel headed to the Pacific. "The possibility of Easterners getting west of the Mississippi is almost nil, or, properly, it will be impossible," he asserted. If vacationers did succeed in reaching their destinations, there was a good chance that they would be stranded for a long time. Johnson warned that in mid-1945 there were still many travelers in Florida who had journeyed there originally for short vacations the previous fall.[13]

❧ ❧ ❧

Railroad executives gave generously to aid the war effort, in some cases literally cannibalizing their track and equipment. They sent nearly a thousand miles of abandoned track, including switches, spikes, and related equipment to the Army and Navy to use in its existing form, or they consigned it to steel mills as scrap metal. In that way they provided some 200,000 tons of iron and steel products to support the war effort. Near the site of the Golden Spike in 1869, Southern Pacific workmen tore up the historic line north of the Great Salt Lake and consigned its rails to scrap metal. Likewise, the Union Pacific reduced its first streamliner, the acclaimed M-10000, to scrap metal during 1942 to provide aluminum for the war. These patriotic gestures were symbolic of how railroads were using their property to help win the global fight—though in a real way that property included the hard-won public favor of the prewar years.

From the perspective of their 1930s efforts to lure Americans onto streamlined passenger trains, travel conditions during World War II were nothing less than a public relations nightmare. Little things like the military's need for Freon to propel the mosquito sprays it used in the tropics meant that none of the gas was available to cool the latest generation of railroad passenger cars. Without air-conditioning and with car windows permanently sealed shut, the interiors became unbearably hot and stuffy in warm weather. Dining cars grew so packed that Union Pacific and Southern Pacific lines inaugurated the practice of serving civilian travelers only two meals a day, breakfast and dinner, and they removed items like pancakes and poached eggs from the menu to save preparation time. Because of federal rationing, the Southern Pacific permitted only a single cup of coffee to be served at breakfast and none at dinner. In its timetables it advised dining car patrons, "Please don't dally."[14]

The Southern Pacific apologized to passengers in mid-1942 for the slipping quality of its dining car service, noting that while its cooks and waiters were doing their best, they often had to work double shifts. "But sometimes there isn't as much spring in your step when you're tired."[15]

Many travelers later described the experience of riding aboard a crowded passenger train in wartime as horrible. Patriotism aside, many Americans remembered only the crush of travelers, antiquated equipment, a general lack of courtesy on the part of harried railway employees, dirty washrooms on trains and in stations, grimy coaches, and unsatisfactory dining car prices and service. Rail leaders were too busy moving people and goods to contemplate seriously how the unfavorable impressions created by wartime conditions might affect their passenger business after the conflict ended. In the end, the greatest beneficiaries of wartime travel conditions on the railroads were the airlines.

As the grim news of Pearl Harbor flashed across America, the nation's airlines responded immediately. Some turned flights around in midair, put their passengers off at the nearest airport, and flew off to serve the needs of the military. War was a totally new experience for the youthful industry. Unlike the railroads, it had no precedents to follow because not a single carrier had been in business during the previous world conflict.

After the airlines flew off to war, the size of the nation's commercial fleet dropped from 359 planes to 176 because Uncle Sam drafted a number of airliners for military service. The standard airliner at the time was the DC-3. Of the three hundred aircraft available for commercial use at the end of 1944, all but twenty-five of them were DC-3s. A typical plane contained twenty-one passenger seats, and military personnel were likely to fill nearly all of them on any scheduled flight. The remaining seats went first to civilians hurrying to visit sick or dying relatives. Vacation travelers ranked very low on the list of airline priorities.

Fortunately, all major airlines had modernized and enlarged their fleets during the previous six years of peace when manufactures introduced the first generation of planes likely to supersede the DC-3. The Boeing Stratoliner, which took to the air in late 1938, featured a comfortable and fully pressurized cabin that could accommodate as many as thirty-three passengers. The plane attracted few purchasers, and Boeing built only ten of the four-engined Stratoliners. The plane nonetheless encouraged Douglas to respond to Boeing's incipient competition with its new DC-4. Another major contender was the big Lockheed Constellation, featuring a pressurized cabin that allowed it to cruise easily at twenty thousand feet, well above the dips and bumps likely to cause airsickness. Though the industry had not yet adopted the newest generation of airliners at the time of Pearl Harbor, these planes anticipated the high-flying, long-range bombers that later flew above Europe and Japan.

An unusual view of one of TWA's majestic Lockheed Constellations. The plane, distinguished by three tails and a sleek "Dolphin"-shaped fuselage, ranked as aviation's fastest and largest passenger transport immediately after World War II. Courtesy TWA Collection, St. Louis Mercantile Library.

Because Northwest pilots had gained plenty of experience flying through stormy weather between Chicago and Seattle, the federal government assigned that carrier to fly north to Alaska to meet military needs along a front line that ran through the Aleutian Islands, where Japanese invaders had established bases. Before Pearl Harbor, Northwest had sought permission from federal authorities to fly the North Pacific route from Seattle to Japan. The experience it gained flying north to Alaska during World War II helped it win concessions for postwar routes to Japan and China, which transformed it in 1946 into a carrier of international stature then officially known as Northwest Orient Airlines. The Minnesota-based carrier originally flew to Asia via Alaska and along what was called the "top-of-the-world" route.

Air express, commencing in 1927 with a modest 17,000 shipments, evolved into big business during World War II, when airlines handled some two million shipments in 1942 alone. United Airlines inaugurated all-cargo flights in November 1942 with service between New York, Chicago, Salt Lake City, and the West Coast.

* * *

When the war ended in August 1945, the demands placed on American railroads did not immediately return to normal. They still had to accommodate staggering numbers of military personnel returning home. During December 1945, said one railroad official, it almost seemed that "a good broad-jumper could have hopped from boat to boat all the way from San Francisco Bay to Hawaii during that fantastic demonstration. And it may be that there were those who thought that this would be the deluge that would force the railroads to cry, 'Hold, enough!' If there were any with that belief, they were disappointed."[16]

As 1945 drew to a close, the nation's railroads handled a heavier volume of military passenger traffic than at any comparable period during the year. "The peak of this military movement, coinciding with the heavy holiday travel at Christmas and New Year, created for the railroads the most difficult passenger-handling problem they have ever faced."[17] They did it with virtually the same passenger equipment they had at the start of the war.

"Getting the boys back home" represented the biggest passenger load in the history of Southern Pacific, where traffic was about six times the prewar level, reported the railroad's president A. T. Mercer in his late-1945 report on the company's activity. "The railroads still have a war job to finish," he emphasized, "and until the homecoming movement of veterans is completed, this will continue to have my first attention."[18]

Military movements, both of personnel and prisoners of war, dropped rapidly after December 1945. The Office of Defense Transportation announced that restrictions placed on the operation of through sleeping cars would end on March 15, 1946. Since July 15, 1945, federal officials had forbade railroads to operate sleeping cars on runs of 450 miles or less.

When peacetime conditions at last prevailed, the railroad industry had reason to congratulate itself. During World War II it had handled double the load of World War I, but with one-quarter fewer passenger and freight cars and a third fewer locomotives than were available in 1917. The skill and dedication of railroaders in keeping traffic moving day and night, month after month had staved off a feared government takeover. The rail industry had done its patriotic duty. No one could ask for more.

Meanwhile, toward the end of World War II many westerners feared that a return to peace would likely mean a return to the hard times that prevailed during prewar years. That did not happen because their savings during the war enabled a record number of Americans to purchase dream cars, vacations, homes, and a comfortable middle-class life in the suburbs, all of which buoyed construction as well as the forest products and metal mining industries. An inadequate number of new houses built during the war years, coupled with the unprecedented relocation of Americans to the suburbs and an increase in new families, kept the West's major commodity producers running at record levels for two full decades following the war. As early as 1946, logging and sawmilling regained their prewar status as Oregon's number one industry. There and elsewhere, tourism boomed too.

In one sense, wartime production did not end until several decades after 1945. That is, the infusion of federal dollars into the western economy that had become so noticeable during the New Deal and World War years continued unabated when Cold War fears of the Soviet Union (ironically, one of America's allies in World War II) prolonged life indefinitely for many industries nurtured to maturity by World War II. "Air power is peace power," declared William Allen, president of Seattle's Boeing Aircraft, which prospered from defense orders after suffering a brief postwar slump. Cold War fears kept many of the West's defense plants in full operation, most notably those of the aerospace giants that made jet aircraft, intercontinental ballistic missiles, and space equipment.

By 1958 Boeing alone employed seventy-three thousand people and added thousands more to assemble its Model 707, the world's first successful jet passenger airplane, as well as to build many different types of military hardware. Defense-based industries became a major employer in postwar Utah, too, where as recently as 1941 the economy had been almost entirely dependent on agriculture and mining. Utah's biggest aerospace industry became the Thiokol Chemical Company west of Brigham City, which produced solid fuel for rockets and later, as Morton-Thiokol, built booster rockets for the ill-fated space shuttle "Challenger." It is worth noting that this facility, which may well portend the future of passenger transportation in space, was located in a remote corner of the Great Basin desert only a few miles from where rail barons drove the golden spike at Promontory in 1869 to complete the first transcontinental railroad. This was the line torn up for scrap metal needed to produce armaments to win World War II.

Because of a rapid decline in military traffic after December 1945, railroad passenger miles dropped about 30 percent during the first full year after the end of the war. Railroad executives did not view the decline with alarm, but rather it confirmed what they needed to do now to remain competitive: "Railroads have much deferred maintenance work to be done, although they are not undermaintained in the sense that they cannot perform freight and passenger services safely and efficiently. There is also a considerable amount of deferred improvements in roadway and equipment which could not be carried out during the war, but which will now be undertaken to the extent required for better service and more efficient operation in the future."[19]

The industry had not entered the war in great physical shape, but it had labored so hard during the conflict that the return to peace left it nearly exhausted. Even its newest and finest prewar equipment was worn out. Railroads now required thousands of new cars and locomotives to handle the anticipated postwar traffic. The industry remained optimistic about the future of long-distance passenger train travel too.

As part of an ongoing modernization process that World War II had interrupted, railroad officials eagerly anticipated introducing additional streamlined trains to the lure the traveling public. Leading the postwar parade were the "Pere Marquette" streamliners that entered service between Detroit and Grand Rapids, Michigan, on August 10, 1946. An even more impressive demonstration of faith in the future of railroad travel was the modern "Empire Builder" that Great Northern inaugurated between Chicago and Seattle and Portland on February 23, 1947.

The first of the postwar generation of transcontinental streamliners, the Empire Builder consisted of five sets of twelve-car trains representing an investment of $7 million. In anticipation of increased postwar patronage, Great Northern had ordered the equipment in late 1943 to be built when steel and other scarce materials became available again for civilian use. Swept along by the optimism of the time, other transcontinental railroads rushed to buy new streamliners of their own. During just the first two years after the war, the Union Pacific alone spent some $20 million on new passenger cars and diesel passenger locomotives.

Sun Valley reopened before the winter of 1946 after four years as a rehabilitation and recreation center for naval personnel. Early the following year, Southern Pacific advertised that space was once again available on most of its passenger trains. Two years later, on July 10, 1949, that railroad introduced a handsome streamliner called the "Shasta Daylight" and placed its "Luxury Train That Everyone Can Afford" on a record-breaking fifteen-and-a-half-hour daytime schedule between Portland and Oakland. Among the train's distinctive features were extra spacious windows to give travelers better views of scenic attractions and a special device to broadcast music when radio reception was poor.

Many features of the postwar parade of streamliners represented refinements of earlier technology, such as improved air-conditioning and modified color schemes and interior design. It was the General Motors' "Train of Tomorrow" that caught the public fancy with a series of innovations that appeared truly new. When unveiled in late May 1947, it drew crowds much like the first streamliners had done in the mid 1930s. During

The brochure cover for General Motors' "Train of Tomorrow."
Author's collection.

its tour of the United States, large and curious crowds marveled at its "Astra-Dome" cars and numerous other refinements.

Even with additional streamliners, passengers during the first five years after the war did not always find train travel pleasant. A common complaint was that too many railroad employees lacked courtesy. The Union Pacific, in fact, pointedly reminded its personnel to listen when passengers protested callous attitudes dating from the wartime crush. During these same years, as the railroad industry knew all too well, airlines leaned over backward to impress their passengers with courteous treatment—a practice derived in part from days when the airlines actively pampered travelers, including serving them free hot meals as a psychological sedative to reduce the fear of flying.

World War II had witnessed a noticeable falloff in civilian air travel, but after the conflict ended, the number of passengers climbed again, from 6.7 million in 1945 to 12.5 in 1946. The airlines of America stood ready to accommodate them. As a result of rapid conversion from military to commercial use, domestic airlines in the United States in late 1945 had more than five hundred planes on hand, with predictions that they would have a total of 1,200 in the air by the end of the following year. Many young military aviation veterans were eager to take the controls of civilian aircraft, and a few even wanted to start feeder airlines.

The term "feeder" was gradually replaced by "regional" as the new breed of carriers grew in size and complexity. By whatever name, this segment of the industry had been cautiously sanctioned by federal officials toward the end of World War II in order to link small cities previously unserved by the major carriers. That would not be easy. Even with federal subsidies, seven of the thirteen new feeder lines operated at a loss in 1948. At the height of the movement in the 1950s, fourteen feeder lines provided service to 413 communities in 44 states. This group of airlines obtained hand-me-down DC-3s from major carriers determined to acquire the next generation of propeller-driven aircraft, such as the graceful Lockheed Constellations that became a hallmark of TWA during the years before the introduction of jetliners in 1959.

When the Douglas plants were slow to convert production from military to civilian aircraft at the end of World War II, Lockheed jumped to the fore by selling ten of its Constellations to TWA in late 1945. Compared to its utilitarian competitor, the DC-7, the Constellation's sleek and gracefully curving appearance not only made it an object of unusual beauty but also implied both speed and comfort. TWA placed its Constellations in coast-to-coast service in March 1946 with an intermediate stop in Chicago or Kansas City. For the first time, passengers could fly from the West Coast to the East in slightly less than ten hours, and in eleven in the opposite direction against the prevailing winds. Until United received the first of its fleet of DC-6s in the spring of 1947, it suffered a three-and-a-half-hour competitive disadvantage against TWA's Constellations.

All the major air carriers upgraded their fleets during the years immediately after World War II. Many new planes were civilian versions of four-engined aircraft that had served the military well during four years of fighting. An airliner derived from Boeing's B-29 Superfortress bombers was the 377 Stratocruiser, a luxurious twin-decked giant that was larger than either the Constellation or the DC-6. Stratocruisers were so big, in fact, that the Boeing plane significantly raised the competitive stakes for size and luxury by seating eighty passengers on its upper deck and adding a fourteen-seat bar and lounge to its lower deck. Some models even included a honeymoon suite in the tail section.

As might be expected for so massive a plane at the time, Stratocruisers were mechanically complex beasts that pushed piston-engine technology to the brink—and perhaps beyond, because engine failures were common. It is the "best three-engined plane flying," joked its critics. In the wry words of Croil Hunter, president of Northwest, which flew Boeing 377s between the Pacific Northwest and Hawaii, "You're safer flying than on the ground around that plane" because you were so liable to be hit by falling parts from one of its engines. Northwest, which had become America's fourth transcontinental carrier in 1945, also used them on its new coast-to-coast routes.[20]

Its complex engines notwithstanding, the Stratocruiser remained in production from 1945 to 1950, during which time Boeing constructed fifty-six of the big planes. It delivered its last one to British Overseas Airways Corporation, which was then poised to enter the jet age with the first of its sleek Comets.

After years of deprivation, Americans took to the skies in record numbers after the war ended, though the late 1940s, paradoxically, were difficult years for the airlines as they worked feverishly to adjust to new passenger loads, new routes, and new aircraft. It might be said that the nation's airline industry emerged from World War II a far more mature enterprise than it had been at the time of Pearl Harbor, but that would not portend smooth flying in the immediate postwar years. Fortunately for commercial aviators, the railroad industry faced even greater problems.

A Gallup Poll published in mid-January 1946 noted that 46 percent of Americans preferred planes for commercial travel, although respondents over age fifty continued to strongly favor trains. Those under thirty strongly preferred planes. That statistic did not bode well for railroads. Postwar commercial aviation reaped the benefit of aerodynamic, mechanical, and structural advances of the war years. Two wartime technologies, radar and jet propulsion, promised a bright future for airlines but spelled troubled ahead for the railroads.

Clearly, by 1949 the railroad industry's wartime enthusiasm for recapturing lost passenger business was waning. For all their efforts, including the vast sums of money spent on advertising and modern equipment, railroads realized that rapidly rising labor costs and high price tags for streamliners made the break-even point for passenger trains in the late 1940s almost double that in 1939. In other words, they needed either a hundred passengers where fifty had previously supplied sufficient revenue to break even, or fifty passengers had to ride twice as far.

The passenger train's most formidable competitor during the postwar years, in reality, was the personal automobile. By the mid-1950s, when interstate highways first took shape, almost 90 percent of passenger traffic in the United States was by private automobile. Superhighways benefited the ever-growing numbers of over-the-road trucks too. Those were the real challenges American railroads had to meet.

The Santa Fe issued this brochure in 1947 to salute its many
accomplishments "despite economic depression and war."
Author's collection.

Ten

Auto Euphoria and Other Postwar Enthusiasms

Corporal Arnaldo Schwantes was among the American soldiers who returned home to the United States only three months after Japan surrendered in mid-August 1945. That was ahead of many other GI's, and I think it had something to do with the stunning green and gold medal he received from the Brazilian army while serving in the Fifth U.S. Army in Italy. His special award was apparently worth several points, and the Army discharged its soldiers on the basis of the total points they had amassed in service.

My father sailed home from Naples to Norfolk in November aboard the USS *Lake Champlain*. Despite stormy seas, the prow of the big aircraft carrier sliced through the waves of the North Atlantic in record time: four days, eight hours, and fifty-one minutes. Many of the soldiers on board grew seasick, but that hardly mattered as long as they were headed home to their sweethearts, wives, and children. The "Champ's" record remained unbroken until 1952, and then only by the SS *United States*, a luxury liner built for speed.

I think Dad liked to tell this story because he liked speed. After our family moved to Indiana in 1947, he bought his first car, a well-used Hudson, from an officemate at Eli Lilly & Company, the pharmaceutical giant where he worked as translator of Portuguese and Spanish for nearly forty years. I don't recall that it was a particularly fast car, but a few years later Dad bought a new Hudson that, despite its hulking dimensions, zoomed along the highways fast enough to earn him several speeding tickets.

The Indiana capital is home to the famed Indianapolis 500. Dad took me to see the 1963 race as a high school gradu-

Capturing the postwar enthusiasm of motorists is the cover image from a map of toll roads that Standard Oil of Indiana offered free to travelers. West of Illinois the modern motorist seldom encountered a toll road. Author's collection.

ation present. That was a rite of passage in Indianapolis at the time, but again I think he liked the speed. Dad's all-time favorite driver, I am certain, was the Brazilian speed-demon Emerson Fittipaldi, who won the Indy classic in 1989. I think he saw a kindred spirit in Fittipaldi because in his heyday Dad liked to drive fast too, only he did it on roads and highways. Not recklessly fast, mind you, but he did earn two speeding tickets during a trip from Indianapolis to Miami, from where we flew to Brazil in 1952. To his credit, Dad never had a serious motor accident.

For him the highway was always a means to an end. Once, back in the carefree 1950s when gasoline was cheap, he drove more than two hundred miles north from Indianapolis to near Toledo just to access the Ohio Turnpike so he could drive fast and steady across Ohio and Pennsylvania on his way from Indianapolis to Washington, D.C. The way east via U.S. 40 was much shorter, and despite its numerous stoplights and two-lane sections the older highway may have gotten us there just as fast, but Dad wanted the freedom of the expressway.

To Dad's can-do-anything generation, the modern superhighways must have symbolized the promise of a bright technological future. Their "auto euphoria" was a perfectly understandable response to the new world of highway travel that they saw taking shape in the 1950s and 1960s. I, on the other hand, have already been there and am not so impressed.

I much prefer to amble along the old highways. I revel in a curving and idiosyncratic roadway alongside which I am able to pause to sample sun-ripened tomatoes or sip fresh cherry cider at a farmer's stand instead of following a visually boring strip of concrete and asphalt confined by seemingly endless miles of fence wire. Along the fast-flowing interstates I observe at almost every interchange the same array of fast-food outlets and service stations. John Steinbeck perhaps expressed it best in *Travels with Charley* (1961) when he prophesied that when the expressways were completed, "It will be possible to drive from New York to California without seeing a thing."[1]

⚜ ⚜ ⚜

During the decade that followed the end of World War II, most roadways of the United States remained basically the same as they had been in the late 1930s, only more worn and more crowded. The main corridors remained the U.S. routes first numbered in 1926, but there were conspicuous exceptions. The Pennsylvania Turnpike, all 160 miles between Pittsburgh and Harrisburg, opened to traffic on October 1, 1940. It was four lanes, in most places, and limited access, much of it superimposed on an old right-of-way graded for the never-completed South Pennsylvania Railroad line of the 1880s. Odd narrow sections of the turnpike, long since removed, occurred where the expressway had to squeeze through old railroad tunnels. Originally the Pennsylvania Turnpike imposed no speed limits, but even at a more ordinary pace it was possible to drive from downtown Harrisburg to Pittsburgh in less than four hours, and it carefully controlled all eating and service areas within its corridor.[2]

On the West Coast the first section of the modern Los Angeles freeway to be constructed was the Arroyo Seco Parkway, a six-mile divided roadway that opened to great fanfare through a park between Los Angeles and Pasadena in December 1940. It offered a glimpse of the future network of superhighways that effectively redefined the Los Angeles area. Indeed, by the end of World War II the Arroyo Seco Parkway had evolved into the Pasadena Freeway, the new name connoting speed over beauty and thus being oddly prophetic of future developments.

Before the Pennsylvania Turnpike or the Arroyo Seco Parkway could inspire motorists and highway planners elsewhere, however, World War II intervened. When the conflict ended, transportation across the West would never be the same. Rail and air corridors had changed along with highway habitats—and not always for the better. One harbinger of future trouble that illustrated how highway habits might encompass far more than the roadway itself was the smog that blanketed Los Angeles on July 26, 1943, and sufficiently alarmed county supervisors that they appointed a Smoke and Fumes Commission to study the problem. In the mid-1920s the environmentalist Aldo Leopold had worried about how roads and automobiles might physically impact his beloved forests. Half a century later the pollutants released by internal combustion engines combined with those from factories, backyard incinerators, and numerous other sources to threaten the health of *both* the forest and the city. At first that was of little or no concern to most Americans. When the war ended, they simply wanted to enjoy the freedom of the open road once again.

Tourists had spent about five billion dollars in the United States during the twelve months preceding Pearl Harbor, and there was every reason to anticipate that they would spend that amount and much more when peace returned. Indeed, after gasoline rationing ended and rubber tires again became available, Americans withdrew money from their bulging savings accounts, cashed in their war bonds and stamps, and motored along the highways in record numbers. "Although the cars were older, on the average, and tires poorer than in pre-war years, people insisted on going places and seeing things," *Highway Magazine* reported. Neither crowded hotels, motels, and tourist camps nor inflated meal prices "put a damper on the determination to travel."[3] One big motivator was the trend to vacations with pay for those who worked with their hands, and not just for office workers.

After more than fifteen years of privation, during both the Great Depression and World War II, more Americans than ever before had money to spend and a pent-up desire to spend it on travel. Or maybe just pent-up desire, for 1946 was the beginning of the greatest baby boom in modern history. It became commonplace in the late 1940s and 1950s for young families to travel together for pleasure. Tourism became big business in

Not just automobiles but heavy industry, including this oil refinery in Richmond (near Oakland), contributed to air quality issues that grew important in California during and after World War II. Courtesy Library of Congress.

the West. In California it ranked second only to the state's vital petroleum industry, and soon it gained first place.

The "Golden West" beckoned to vacationers again, and not just to the tourists traveling by automobile. Long-distance passenger trains carried heavy loads too, though railroad ridership in the late 1940s dropped substantially from the peak years of World War II. That trend did little to discourage American railroads from rolling out a parade of postwar streamliners. If they built them, the prevailing wisdom seemed to say, crowds of passengers would surely fill the glitzy new trains. And they did—at least until they could once again purchase the latest-model automobiles. The popular passion excited by new cars recalls the quip of a southern California dealer in 1921 when he observed that an automobile "is 10 percent pleasure, 90 percent utility and 100 percent necessity."[4]

Unfortunately for railroads, the passions stirred by thoughts of passenger train travel for many Americans were highly negative, because they were based on unpleasant memories of crowded and dirty trains all too common during the crush of World War II traffic. Some travelers neither forgave the railroads, which were not really at fault, nor rode their passenger trains any longer than it took to buy a decent car and have a smartly dressed service station attendant fill its tank with gas: "Regular or Ethyl?"

That was a primary reason why buying power created by enforced saving during the war contributed to a feeding frenzy in automobile dealers' showrooms when the first postwar models went on display in 1946. The emerging baby boom further encouraged family travel by private automobile, as did the trend toward suburban living, which made the downtown railroad station an anachronism. Unlike the Joads, most Americans in the postwar era motored across the nation, not in search of a promised land, but rather to "See the U.S.A. in your Chevrolet"—or in our family's case, to see it in our tough-as-a-tank Hudson.

Among the first postwar tourist primers was *A Guide Book to Highway 66* by Jack D. Rittenhouse. Today his slim volume provides a fascinating snapshot of long-distance motoring across the West at that time, and not just along Route 66. Rittenhouse offered practical advice to any motorist determined to sample the pleasures of the open road once again: "In spite of the housing shortage, there are still accommodations for tourists—if you do not wait until too late in the day to secure lodgings. The best idea is to plan to stop before 6:00 P.M., earlier if possible, and locate lodgings promptly. Don't wait until after the evening meal—get your cabin or hotel room first, then eat."[5]

Of road food Rittenhouse observed, "East of the Mississippi there are many excellent cafes, even in the small towns. This is not the general rule along western cross-country highways, although occasionally very excellent food is obtainable. Many roadside 'cafes' serve only chili, sandwiches, pie, coffee, etc. Other establishments bearing a 'cafe' sign may be chiefly devoted to the sale of beer or liquor."

Concerning road conditions on Route 66, Rittenhouse advised prospective motorists that the "entire highway from Chicago to Los Angeles is well paved and passable. War-worn stretches of pavement are being repaired wherever pitted. Snow comes early and lingers late in stretches between Amarillo, Texas, and Kingman, Arizona, so inquire about road conditions ahead at gas stations when driving during November through March. In case of snow, plows clear the road quickly, but ice on mountain grades is a problem at night."

Among his "few small tips which mean big comforts" was Rittenhouse's admonition: "DON'T WORRY! A trip is no fun if worry sits at the wheel, even if this worry is not voiced to others in the car. So—first of all—rest assured that you're not going to be 'hung up' in some forsaken spot. You'll never be more than a score of miles from gas, even in the most desolate areas. There are no impossible grades." Any hint of temporary hardship or danger may have only added to the thrill of a road trip along Route 66 in 1946. "Well, you're on your way—over two thousand miles of fascinating highway ahead of you," Rittenhouse encouraged his readers. "One of life's biggest thrills is the realization that 'we're on the way,' which the motorist feels as he eases the car away from the curb and heads out of town."

There was a reason that Route 66 became known as the "most magical road in all the world." Any motorists who headed west from Chicago to Los Angeles in 1946 had only to think about how the highway had changed since 1926, the year of its birth just two decades earlier. "In those days, even Lindbergh's solo flight over the Atlantic was easier than a cross-country trek by automobile in the same year," writes Tom Snyder in *The Route 66 Traveler's Guide and Roadside Companion* (1990). "Travelers who made it as far as the Great Mojave paid dearly to load their vehicles onto railroad flatcars rather than risk a breakdown out on the vast desert."[6]

By the mid-1930s, Snyder continued, "the highway had begun to create its own myth; it grew larger than life. It became the way west." Over the years, Route 66 "became much more than a highway. For the millions who traveled her (and the millions more who still want to), the road was transformed from a concrete thoroughfare into a national symbol: a vital life-sign for us all. A pathway to better times—seldom found, but no less hoped for. Route 66 came to represent not only who we were as a people, but who we knew we could be. Not a bad thing to find in a road."[7]

Even in early 2001, though Route 66 had been officially decommissioned back in 1984, the powerful memories it still evoked generated an editorial in the *St. Louis Post-Dispatch* titled "No-tell motel no way." It seems that Route 66 buffs wanted to erect a six-foot-high obelisk in a Saint Louis suburb to commemorate the one-time site of the Coral Court Motel, which had been demolished in 1995. In later years, the seventy mustard-colored, art deco units comprising the 54-year-old landmark had suffered hard times, surviving as "St. Louis' most notorious hot-sheets motel." Trustees of the Village of Marlborough deferred to homeowners, who gave the proposal their collective thumbs down. "Because for all the talk about the Coral Court's architecture, for all the nostalgia about Route 66, it is the motel's legacy as a lovers' hideaway that is best remembered—rooms by the hour, individual garages to maintain privacy, and bumper stickers that read, 'Your place, my place or the Coral Court?'" The editorial writer, speaking for Joseph Pulitzer's hometown paper, concluded with this sentence: "That's one historical marker we'd rather not have to explain to the kids."[8]

An equally curious commentary on changing times is Route 66 State Park that the Missouri Department of Natural Resources opened west of Saint Louis in 1999. This is the original site of Times Beach, a town that government officials rooted up completely after the waste oil used to control dust on its streets was found to contain highly toxic dioxin. In this case, an environmental nightmare had a positive outcome, something that could not be claimed for automobile smog in Los Angeles and elsewhere.

Despite the nostalgia (and controversy) that still attends it, for most long-distance motorists Route 66 was only a means to an end, not an end in itself. That was true for all the lesser-known highways of the West too. Often a motorist's goal was to reach one of the region's several national parks. The number of visitors entering Washington's Mount Rainier National Park in 1946, for instance, broke all previous records.

National parks of the West had long been recognized as major tourist draws, and especially so after the network of all-weather roads expanded in the 1920s and 1930s and as more Americans than ever acquired automobiles, money, and the leisure time required to explore remote corners of the West. One of its best-known attractions was Yellowstone, the nation's oldest national park, which during summer seasons in the mid-1950s lured four times as many people through its gates as then lived in the entire state of Wyoming. Glacier National Park likewise attracted more visitors each season than lived in Montana. Roosevelt's Interior Secretary, Harold Ickes, correctly prophesied of Olympic National Park, which was established in 1938, that "in the long run it will mean more for the State of Washington to have a real national park on the Olympic Peninsula than it will be to log this area, either selectively or otherwise."

Intercity bus ridership soared during the war years, and that lured a host of new operators onto the highways when peace returned. The size of *Russell's Guide,* the bus industry's counterpart to the *Official Guide of the Railways,* increased to reflect postwar expansion. Among the new carriers was the Kansas Central Lines, which according to its map and timetable published in the December 1946 *Russell's Guide* operated buses north from Wichita to serve farm communities between there and Emporia. Its president was H. F. Lehrer. What the formal listing did not reveal was the human drama behind Kansas Central Lines.

Those details come from James Lehrer, co-anchor of the *MacNeil/Lehrer Newshour* on Public Television, who composed a warmhearted memoir of a boyhood with buses. His book *We Were Dreamers* recalls how his father aspired to own and operate a bus line of his own. He used $3,500 in cash to purchase three road-weary vehicles and thereby launched an all-consuming family adventure. Indeed, for everyone connected with the intercity bus industry, those heady days encouraged big dreams.[9]

Lehrer's Kansas Central Lines folded, alas, after a financial struggle that lasted a year and ten days, but the good times lasted well into the 1950s for some of the West's largest intercity bus operators. Along two popular routes—from Los Angeles to San Francisco and Seattle, and from Hollywood and Los Angeles to Las Vegas—Continental Trailways offered five-star "Luxury Service" on coaches that featured on-board hostesses, light refreshments, restrooms, and "restful music."

Intercity bus operators benefited from miles of superhighway opened to traffic after Congress passed the Interstate Highway Act in 1956. Just the next year (and well before construction of the new network was well underway), express buses needed only fifteen minutes more than the fastest trains to complete a highway trip between Seattle and Portland. Between Seattle and Spokane the swiftest intercity buses beat the Empire Builder by a full forty-five minutes and the North Coast Limited by almost two hours.

Total intercity bus traffic in the United States (in terms of passenger miles) exceeded the volume of rail passenger business for the first time in 1962, but that proved an empty victory because the number of railroad passengers had fallen off so much since the late 1940s. Ironically, the interstate highway system that enabled intercity buses like Greyhound's big double-deck Scenicruisers to clip along at express-train speeds increased the number of automobiles on the road, and the swelling ranks of motorists meant fewer people to ride on buses and trains. As ridership continued to decline in the 1960s and 1970s, the monthly issues of both *Russell's Guide* and the *Official Railway Guide* grew steadily thinner.

Greyhound relocated its corporate headquarters from Chicago to Phoenix. Not many months after the Bus Deregulation Act of 1982 dramatically changed the industry, a crippling strike halted Greyhound operations for forty-seven days. It acquired its one-time competitor Continental Trailways in 1987, which at the time was by far the largest component of the Trailways System. But after suffering another strike in 1990 and 1991, Greyhound filed for Chapter 11 bankruptcy. Nothing, however, arrested the downward trend in bus ridership; and as result, Greyhound followed the lead of railroads by pruning money-losing lines and scaling back service on even its most popular routes. Thus, at the start of the twenty-first century, the United States had only one continent-spanning bus system left, though Greyhound was a mere shadow of its former self.

Railroads followed a different path with the creation of Amtrak in 1971, but the result for passenger train travelers was much the same as for intercity bus riders. That is, only a skeletal network of intercity operations remained in place at the start of the new millennium. With encouragement from Uncle Sam (in the person of Richard Nixon), most U.S. railroads combined their long-distance (as distinct from commuter) trains into a quasi-government operation called Amtrak. During a single day, May 1, 1971, the number of intercity passenger routes and trains dropped dramatically when Amtrak shouldered responsibility for the little that was left of a once-extensive network of passenger trains.

Though intercity buses and passenger trains were ostensibly competitors, by the 1970s and 1980s it was clear that both modes of transportation suffered from some of the same inherent limitations. That is, they had neither the flexibility of private automobiles nor the speed of commercial aviation. Thus, while the nation's network of intercity buses and trains shrank, long-distance travel by automobile and airliners broke all records. In that way, Americans extended and enlarged the impact of a transportation revolution that began after World War I. Giving automobile travel its biggest boost since the 1920s was the Interstate Highway System launched in 1956. And helping to shift highway building into high gear during the 1950s and 1960s was America's Cold War anxiety.

⚜ ⚜ ⚜

Ideas that culminated in the passage of the Interstate Highway Act had been around for a long time. The pattern leading to the launch of construction is comparable to that resulting in the first transcontinental railroad or the Erie Canal many years earlier. First came the idea, often controversial, then a gradual marshalling of public support, and then legislative action. The final step in a process that might extend over years and decades was implementation.

Regardless of where it ran, the highway habitat of the West developed mainly through accretion. It represented an accumulation of personal aspirations, and as such it appeared unsightly, messy, and maybe even dangerous to the engineers who aspired to design controlled-access highways built according to rational and uniform standards—highways designed from the ground up for speed and safety.

"High-speed motorways" had been discussed as early as the mid-1920s as a way to relieve traffic bottlenecks increasingly common in California. "Congestion outside San Francisco and Los Angeles is now so great, particularly in the morning and late in the afternoon, that motorists can move at only eight to ten miles an hour, for fifteen to twenty miles outside these cities," one commentator wrote in 1925.[10] In time a favored West Coast highway extended from the Canadian to Mexican borders along a corridor defined today by Interstate 5, but original U.S. Route 99 had so many limitations that it left motorists dreaming of an even better road—a superhighway.

"Engineers who have devoted some time to the study of the plan have decided that the speed limit on the trunkline motorway should be not less than 50 miles an hour, with a minimum speed of 30 miles, so as to eliminate the slow driver." Such a road "will be fenced, permitting no access to or exit from the motor way within the towns." Furthermore, the motorway first proposed in the mid-1920s would have "no projecting buildings, no signs except those of direction and information for the motorists and all danger from obstruction to vision along the line of travel will be eliminated."[11] A highway built to such radically high standards remained at best a dream in most of the West when Pearl Harbor plunged the United States into war.

During World War II, economic planners worried that a big road-building program was needed to put men to work when the conflict ended and to avoid the kind of depression that had followed World War I. To that end, President Franklin Roosevelt presented to Congress on January 12, 1944, the report of the National Interregional Highway Committee, which was based in part on earlier studies made in 1939 and on the popular enthusiasm that greeted the Pennsylvania Turnpike after it opened in mid-1940. The study recommended construction of a 40,000-mile expressway system designed to interconnect all cities of 300,000 or more population. These superhighways would consist of four lanes of limited access roadway designed to eliminate stop lights, cross traffic, headlight glare, constricting roadside development, and all steep hills and sharp curves.[12]

The nation had long hesitated to take that bold step, especially now that it was preoccupied with winning the war. Nonetheless, when Roosevelt signed the Federal Aid Highway Act on December 20, 1944, he added an important new category, interstate, to existing primary or trunk roads, farm-to-market roads, and urban roads as part of a long-range coordinated program. The 1944 act was based on the report Roosevelt presented to Congress and provided for an extensive network of interstate highways to aid national defense, though the funds needed to build it were not actually forthcoming until 1956 because parsimonious legislators long prevented Congress from appropriating enough money to do the job. They were happy with the existing network of roads and highways—and so too, apparently, were most Americans, until traffic jams and motor accidents became intolerable.

By 1947 it could be claimed that a motorist could reach any destination in the continental United States during a two-week vacation. At the time, Americans bragged that their nation had 3,250,000 miles of roads and streets used by 34 million passenger cars, trucks, and buses, a figure that represented 80 percent of all the motor vehicles in the world. But some drivers at the time complained: "We'll drive our 1947 cars over 1928 roads that are full of curves, hills, and dangerous intersections that lead through the hearts of cities—large and small, two-lane highways carrying-four-lane traffic."[13]

Back in the 1920s, when the nation's motorists first took to the highways en masse, everyone seemed impatient. With a nightmarish horde of honking motorists uppermost in their minds, road builders worked as quickly as possible with little thought to planning to accommodate future population growth or improved technology. But by the early 1950s, growing traffic congestion threatened to choke the existing system of highways. The most obvious solution was to emulate the Pennsylvania Turnpike and other pre–World War II superhighways. That is, the United States needed now to implement the system of defense highways approved by Congress late in 1944 but never funded.

⚜ ⚜ ⚜

Defense became a key concern of Americans during the frightening days of the Cold War in the early 1950s, and helping to marshal public opinion in favor of funding and building a system of superhighways was "the bomb." Ostensibly, highways and atomic bombs had nothing in common, but the dreaded mushroom cloud that hung over the newfound automobility of post–World War II America provided a grim counterpoint to the open road as an invitation to national giddiness. The modern Interstate Highway System ranks as one of the greatest and most enduring legacies of the Cold War.

In 1949 the Soviet Union exploded its first atomic bomb, ending America's five-year monopoly of the most horrifying weapon of mass destruction ever known. To make matters worse, in living rooms across the nation a new medium called television provided black and white images of American troops shipping out from West Coast ports to fight a grim new hot war with Communism in Korea. Equally disturbing and far closer to home was talk of Communist conspiracy within America itself. Would war in Korea lead to an all-out atomic war with the Soviet Union and with Communists elsewhere?

No one knew. But that was why schools staged atomic bomb drills along with fire drills, and a Boy Scout "Family Be Prepared Plan" of 1951 admonished Americans to stockpile food and keep doors and windows shut during an atomic attack, advice better suited to World War II than to the unpleasant new realities of the 1950s. When it seemed that national anxiety could rise no higher, the Soviet Union tested its first hydrogen bomb less than twelve months after the United States did so. Hydrogen bombs packed far more destructive clout than the first generation of atomic bombs—enough to obliterate major cities.

In October 1953, *Newsweek* quoted President Dwight Eisenhower's civil defense chief gloomily predicting that "atomic warfare is inevitable and the United States faces the possibility of destruction by bombs, disease carriers, sabotage, and possibly gas." When asked what Americans could do to protect themselves, he lamely advised, "go underground."

Come away with me in my 1962 Buick Special. This photograph from September 1961 captured the allure both of the modern automobile and the open road, which is implied but not pictured here. Courtesy Oregon Historical Society.

No wonder that when the first issue of *Playboy* magazine appeared two months later, it promoted voyeurism as "a little diversion from the anxieties of the Atomic age."[14]

Even as Americans in the early 1950s faced possible conflict with the Soviet Union and the threat of atomic annihilation, the nation enjoyed unprecedented prosperity. Ironically, anxiety and affluence seemed inextricably linked. A list of leading growth industries during the years from 1950 through 1966—ammunition, television picture tubes, semiconductors, computing equipment, small arms, tufted carpets and rugs, primary nonferrous metals—clearly shows how production for defense kept pace with increased personal consumption. Perhaps the sense of uncertainty the Atomic Age created, especially its intimation of doom, caused Americans to seek maximum diversion by enjoying their newfound prosperity.

Whether westerners of the 1950s were fully conscious of it or not, their affluence empowered them to radically redefine the space around them. Indeed, their dollars could buy security, not just in the form of big, shiny cars and single family suburban dwellings that became the symbols of the decade, but also in terms of the larger economic and social environment. The shopping mall was one such secure place.

The multiplication of malls and suburban neighborhoods derived, in part, from powerful middle-class desires to redefine familiar space to reflect the hoped-for triumph of affluence over anxiety. That is, even if individuals could do nothing to deter Soviet bombers, they could find solace by moving to a quiet house in the suburbs and shopping in the friendly space of a shopping mall, all the while driving between such places in the enclosed space of a large and comfortable automobile. Enormous tail fins gave some automobiles the look of the space age, though such automobiles were often nicknamed "bombers," an unconscious reference, perhaps, to the Cold War. Not surprisingly, by the end of the 1950s nearly a third of all Americans lived in the suburbs. But with the diffusion of the urban population came worsening traffic problems.

One response was a superhighway era that peaked in the mid-1950s with the completion of a series of state toll roads connecting New York and Chicago. A driver could for the first time cruise between the nation's largest cities without encountering a stoplight. Toll roads never proved popular in the West, apart from short stretches built in Texas and Colorado and longer ones across Kansas and Oklahoma, and the idea was totally anathema in automobile-conscious California.

As a result of landmark state legislation passed there in 1947, California undertook a ten-year program to improve or expand a 14,000-mile system of highways, all the while managing to keep them free from tolls. At the time California first announced plans to upgrade its highway system that had become rickety and congested, its miles of superhighway totaled exactly nineteen. During the decade of the 1950s, it added numerous additional miles of freeway, especially in the Los Angeles and San Francisco areas. Even so, the pace of improvement remained far too slow for motor-minded Californians, so in 1959 the state legislature authorized a freeway system to interlace every major population center in the state. For a time the cloverleaf and the limited access highway symbolized a bright future. However, in many states the problem of antiquated highways only grew worse. And along the modern freeways of Los Angeles, exhaust fumes from an increasing number of automobiles only worsened the growing problem of smog.

President Dwight D. Eisenhower, perhaps more than any of his predecessors, recognized that something had to be done about the nation's increasingly antiquated infrastructure of highways—and sooner, rather than later. Young Eisenhower had traveled with the 1919 Army convoy across the United States, an experience that gave him firsthand exposure to the nation's then wretched roads. Certainly, its highway network had improved greatly during the interwar decades, but most of it remained primitive compared to the German superhighways built during the 1930s, all marvels of civil engineering that Eisenhower as supreme commander of the Allied Expeditionary Force in Europe clearly admired. As he later recalled in his memoirs, "I had seen the superlative system of German–Autobahnen—national highways crossing that country and offering the possibility, often lacking in the United States, to drive with speed and safety at the same time. I recognized then that the United States was behind in highway construction." Ike saw clearly that a "burgeoning automobile population" created an "acute" need for the nation to build a more efficient network of highway arteries, which he once described as "a true concrete and macadam lifeline"[15]

Eisenhower later observed: "Between 1952 and 1955 the total number of motor vehicles in use increased by 10 million—more than the aggregate owned in 1955 by the British and French together." One unhappy consequence of America's overcrowded and often inadequate highways was that "accidents were taking the lives of more than thirty-six thousand persons a year and injuring more than a million."[16]

President Eisenhower and his industry allies needed to persuade reluctant members of Congress to approve the greatest and most expensive highway-building program in all American history. They packaged it as a national defense measure, an argument that grew increasingly persuasive during the grimmest Cold War years of the 1950s. "Our roads ought to be avenues of escape for persons living in big cities threatened by aerial attack or natural disaster," he noted, "but I knew that if such a crisis ever occurred, our obsolescent highways, too small for the flood of traffic of an entire city's people going one way, would turn into traps of death and destruction. And though we were not planning highways for wartime exigencies, if peacetime prosperity kept on rising, the growing number of cars, used by the growing number of people, would slowly clog our road system and make the pace of today's traffic seem a rushing river by comparison."[17] Eisenhower might have noted that over-the-road trucks were growing wider and longer too, with more than ten million of the gigantic vehicles registered by the mid-1950s.

Building roads to aid national defense was nothing new. After Con-

Wars between service stations that drove down the price of a gallon of regular gas to twenty-nine cents or less were common throughout the United States during the affluent years that preceded the gasoline shortages of the 1970s. This example of the competitive rivalry that never failed to delight motorists took place in Portland in 1969. Courtesy Oregon Historical Society.

gress enacted the 1916 Federal Aid Good Roads Bill, proponents argued that the United States could now construct the highways it needed for military purposes. The first one, "naturally," would be the "Mexican frontier highway," which "parallels the boundary between the United States and Mexico, and traverses the states of Texas, New Mexico, Arizona and California." At the time Americans had good reason to believe that revolution in Mexico would spill over the border.[18]

Nearly forty years later, on February 22, 1955, Eisenhower sent members of Congress a special message urging them to take "comprehensive and quick and forward looking" action to improve the nation's highway system. He also provided them the text of a report by a special presidential commission headed by General Lucius Clay, which set the ten-year cost of this modernization job at $101 billion, the federal government putting up more than $31 billion. The highway bill passed the Senate in 1955 but died in the House, mainly because of differences over how to finance the new construction.

Eisenhower refused to give up. He placed superhighways at the top of his legislative agenda for the next year. The need, he pointed out to Congress, had only grown more pressing because automobile accidents during 1955 alone had claimed the lives of 38,000 Americans. With strong bipartisan support and a newly conceived way to fund it, the Interstate Highway Act moved quickly through both houses of Congress. "On June 29 I signed it into law," he wrote. In Eisenhower's self-congratulatory words, the result "was not only the most gigantic federal undertaking in road-building in the century and a half since the federal government got into this field by improving the National Pike between Cumberland, Maryland, and Wheeling, West Virginia—it was the biggest peacetime construction project of any description ever undertaken by the United States or any other country."[19]

To underwrite the cost of building a National System of Interstate and Defense Highways, Congress invented the Highway Trust Fund. This keystone of the 1956 law committed Uncle Sam to spend nearly $5 billion a year on improved roads and highways, though this originally left little, if any, money for other forms of transportation. Dollars for the Highway Trust Fund came from federal taxes imposed on motor fuels, tires, new buses, trucks, and trailers, plus a use tax on heavy trucks. At this time the highway lobby emerged as one of the most powerful groups on Capitol Hill.[20]

After Eisenhower signed the highway measure, two western states raced to the head of the line. Missouri began the nation's first interstate project in August 1956, but Kansas completed the first section of interstate highway the following November. In the end, as writer Tom Lewis notes, "the Great Wall of China and the Interstate Highway System are among the only human creations that can be seen by astronauts from an orbiting spacecraft." Because the superhighways were engineered for speed, builders tackled the Herculean task of constructing some 16,000 exits and nearly 55,000 bridges and overpasses. Making this challenge all the more formidable, when the state of Utah, for example, launched construction, it had virtually no expertise building limited-access divided highways.[21]

Eisenhower observed the expanding miles of interstate highway with paternal pride. He mused that "more than any single action by the government since the end of the war, this one would change the face of America with straightaways, clover-leaf turns, bridges, and elongated parkways. Its impact on the American economy—the jobs it would produce in manufacturing and construction, the rural areas it would open up—was beyond calculation."[22]

Millions of motorists, it might be added, understood a primary purpose of the superhighway system because in the early years large signs were erected alongside the pavement to warn them that in the event of an enemy attack the road would be closed. That was because broad and straight sections of the superhighway might double as Air Force emergency landing strips. Overpass bridges were supposed to be at least sixteen feet high, not just to handle behemoth trucks expected in the future, but to accommodate the largest weaponry common in 1956, which America's military brass might be required to relocate on short notice by road.

Interstate highways formed the nation's newest "metropolitan corridor." Though most sections carried heavy volumes of traffic, the highway habitat itself appeared rather boring and sterile because the roadway was often more functional than beautiful, though some stretches, such as Interstate 84 through the scenic Columbia River Gorge, contradict that claim. Likewise, roadways of the twentieth century typically formed matter-of-fact landscapes rather than consciously attractive ones—though the original Columbia River Highway provides another exception. Scenic parkways were uncommon in cities of the West, and attempts to beautify the general highway habitat date mainly from the 1930s, only after many miles of good roadways had already been extended across the United States.

Initially, few Americans gave the subject much thought, though by the late 1930s the Garden Club of America emerged as one of several organizations promoting beautiful as well as efficient roads. "More flowers than ever before will flame along American highways this summer," one commentator wrote in 1938. "More trees will be planted or selected from woodlands where new roads are cut through. Vines and shrubs will cover unsightly cut slopes, and a lot of ugly billboards, filling stations and rubbish dumps will be eliminated. A great deal of rawness and disfiguration will remain, but enough has been accomplished to suggest further beautification which may take place in the near future." In the late 1930s, the state of Texas took the national lead in planting roadside trees, shrubs, and vines. It collected tons of flower seeds for roadside beautification.[23]

Oregon, which often ranked as the nation's top timber producer in the 1920s and 1930s, began to fret about the loss of stately old growth forests that once lined roads and highways on the rainy west side of the state. Tourists were not impressed by a landscape that consisted only of blackened stumps left by loggers. Thus, as early as 1925 Oregon sought to preserve tracts of standing timber alongside its highway corridors. "In some instances private holdings have been purchased by public spirited citizens and presented to the state as park sites. In others a strip of timber on each side of the highways has been acquired by the state and held for future development."[24]

Ironically, juxtaposing highway corridors and preserved timberland to preserve natural beauty might backfire and endanger the forest itself because thoughtless travelers sometimes left campfires burning or tossed lit cigars or cigarettes from car windows. At a time when the almighty timber industry paid nearly two-thirds of all wages in Oregon and Washington, fire prevention was literally everyone's business. One fire prevention slogan dating from the 1920s was called "What the Trees Sang." It stated, "Ashes to ashes, and dust to dust, if the loggers don't get us, the cigarette must." Smokey Bear and the popular slogan "Remember . . . Only YOU Can Prevent Forest Fires" date from 1944 and 1947 respectively.[25]

For good or ill, the typical highway, at least during the time that antedated limited-access superhighways and modern toll roads, was accessible to all motorists and even to hitchhikers who did not possess automobiles of their own. The boundaries of the highway allowed immediate interchange with the passing countryside. Roadside trees shaded the road and cooled the pavement on hot summer days. Any farm wife could set her fruit stand alongside the roadway, and passing motorists could just as easily turn off to purchase fresh cherries or peaches.

The pre-interstate highway habitat included individually owned service stations, auto courts, and roadside diners and cafes that simply sprang up alongside the pavement. Many featured distinctive, even idiosyncratic architecture to attract the eyes of passing motorists. These places often embodied a rough democracy. Remarkable too, when you think about the kaleidoscopic mixture of good and bad that defined Route 66 and similar federal highways across the West, was that the roads themselves were free to all users. They still are for motorists who prefer to leave the pulsing interstates, slow down, and drive the roads less traveled, the "Blue Highways," in the evocative words of William Least Heat Moon. It is along such routes that a motorist can still catch glimpses of the old landscape that predates the scenery-crunching interstate highways and look-alike chains of fast food restaurants and motels.[26]

Highway travel itself had evolved into big business by the late 1930s. This had a noticeable, though not always negative, impact on the general landscape. As one writer described it, "Shabby, tumbledown farm houses scarcely are recognizable in modern trim and fresh paint. Main street has blossomed with traffic lights. Mud and dust have been eliminated by improved highways. The general store is now an emporium, with bustling clerks carrying armfuls of bags to waiting motor cars."[27] Likewise, increased automobile usage rearranged the streets of many a country town, orienting local traffic away from the railroad station and to the flow of the main highway corridors.

The need of motorists to purchase oil and gasoline or to repair rock-punctured radiators, flat tires, and motor malfunctions of various types gave rise to the highway garage, some of them attached to new service stations erected by national corporations, but some being stand alone shops set up by local tinkerers. Formerly, a curbside pump in town had been a common way to dispense gasoline, but service stations became more common in the 1920s.

The Great Depression and the general business slowdown spurred oil companies to compete ever more vigorously for customers. The number of service station nearly doubled from 121,513 in 1929 to 241,358 only a decade later, and service stations in those days did truly emphasize service. Uniformed attendants gladly checked your oil and cleaned your windshield at no extra charge, offering free air for your tires and a free map to guide you down the road as well.

As country roads improved and farmers purchased automobiles, an increasing number of rural consumers motored past the nearby crossroads villages where they had formerly done business and continued to more distant market towns. An impressive array of merchandise lined the shelves of their biggest emporiums, including the same stylish clothing that many urban dwellers wore. Likewise, it now became easy for farm families to skip church, if they were so inclined, and take a short holiday trip on Sunday, or motor to another community where the minister and worship services were more to their liking. In time, many a once-lively country church, like the one-room schoolhouse, stood empty and abandoned along the nation's increasingly busy roadways.

One big factor in the transformation of the highway landscape was what became popularly known as the "tourist business." Before the coming of the automobile, tourists ignored many a small town because they had no reason to go there. "But today the motor car goes everywhere, and so the small town is on the through route at last—the through route which means business the year-around," proclaimed a writer in *Highway Magazine*. No one planned what happened next. "Pretty soon the brief pause in the tour changed to an overnight stop, with more 'foreign' money left in town. Then the idea of coming for the summer developed. And that led to brief winter visits for sports or rest."[28]

By 1939 vacation motor travel expenditures constituted a $5 billion a year business. That figure encompassed everything from money spent on postcards and souvenirs to meals, gasoline, and sleeping accommodations. During the years between the wars, it was a common belief that the most luxurious overnight facilities for motorists were generally located west of the Mississippi River—luxury at one time being defined by such amenities as tiled shower stalls, innerspring mattresses, and individual garages for automobiles.

If the hotel was a product of the railway age, early tourist cabins and later the motel belonged to the automobile age; yet even in the late 1930s and early 1940s, few Americans had ever stayed overnight in one. The experience was novel enough that in 1941 the American Automobile Association offered this advice to motorists under the heading: "To Smooth Your Travel Way." Curiously, it did so by using terms familiar to travelers still accustomed to going by rail: "One makes Pullman reservations as a matter of course. The railroad can add extra sleepers, Pullman cars or coaches when travel is heavy. The hotel cannot add extra rooms. When, therefore, you don't engage your accommodations in advance, don't be offended if you cannot get what you want. Occasionally, when you do make reservations, you may not get just what you want at the particular time you want it. There may be prior reservations, or perhaps the room you want is not vacated. The hotel cannot throw the other fellow out— you have to wait until he departs."[29]

A good many motorists had grown accustomed to staying overnight in tourist cabins along the roads of the nation. After World War II these numbered about 13,521, with a combined capacity for accommodating about 160,000 families. More tourists stopped overnight in private homes, trailer camps, dude ranches, and private vacation cabins. There was no standard design for tourist camps. Some had only a bed and a washbasin; others were as luxuriously equipped as a modern hotel, except that they lacked bellboys and in-room telephones. Many featured steam heat, Venetian blinds, and fluorescent lighting. "Together with innerspring mattresses, tile baths, luxuriously thick rugs and maple furnishings, chenille bedspreads, the setting is not only one of comfort but splendor as well." The most luxurious courts, most motorists agreed, were typically located in Texas and California.[30]

Roadside iconography changed visibly in 1952 when Charles Kemmons Wilson opened his new motel along a busy stretch of suburban highway leading into Memphis, Tennessee. He named his three single-story buildings clustered around a swimming pool after a Bing Crosby movie called "Holiday Inn." In 1955 Raymond Albert Kroc, a fifty-three-year-old milkshake machine salesman, launched the now-familiar McDonald's fast-food restaurants in the Chicago suburb of Des Plaines. He purchased rights to franchise the hamburger business from the McDonald brothers, Dick and Mac, who operated a popular stand in San Bernardino, California. By the late 1960s these two businesses—and their many copycats— had forever changed the face of roadside America: Holiday Inn opened one new lodge every three business days, while McDonald's opened one new restaurant every business day.[31]

By 1980 tourism had become California's largest industry. What was actually a very old business in the Golden State had evolved in a dramatic new direction after 1955, the year Walt Disney opened his namesake amusement park amid fragrant orange groves in Anaheim. Before that, amusement parks had catered mainly to local populations, but Disneyland became a national attraction. It lured an impressive four million visitors

Countless brochures were issued to lure tourists to California, including this one from 1948 that highlighted the state's "Redwood Empire." Its southern gateway was San Francisco's Golden Gate Bridge. Author's collection.

that first year and soon became one of the top tourist draws in the West. The great economic impact of Disneyland helped transform the Anaheim-Santa Ana area into a regional rival to downtown Los Angeles.

One of Disneyland's popular sections was a fantasy frontier complete with Mark Twain-era steamboat and runaway mine train. Located well outside Disneyland, vestiges of the West's real frontier—places like Virginia City, both in Montana and Nevada—discovered how to lure tourists by refurbishing and emphasizing the look of mining boom days, perhaps borrowing consciously from Disney's impressive magic. In dozens of one-time mining communities across the West from Tombstone, Arizona, to Jacksonville, Oregon, look-alike shops sold wide-eyed tourists much the same assortment of trinkets, tee shirts, and taffy. Many such businesses grew adept at commodifying local scenery, culture, and history and selling it to passing motorists.

Ranking high among the West's increasingly popular tourist draws was skiing, which essentially dates from the mid-1930s when the Union Pacific Railroad opened the region's first major ski resort in Sun Valley, Idaho. When World War II ended, just two ski areas in Colorado were operating, with business limited mainly to the weekends. But Sun Valley began a trend in vacations that after the war resulted in the development of new winter vacation facilities throughout the West. In Colorado, the pacesetter for winter sports activity, some popular facilities were located in refurbished mining towns like Aspen and Telluride. Still others were in Vail, a planned community of post–World War II vintage and easily accessibly from Interstate 70 that connected it to Denver.

For Route 66, the new Interstate Highway System meant slow death. The old route was "abandoned in many places, reduced to the homely duties of 'frontage road' in others, her magic double digits were given away, her job taken over by a homogenized, fast-food freeway," observed Tom Snyder. But, he continued, "there ought to be a saying that you can't keep a good road down. You may take away her destination, even steal her magic numbers. But you can't keep old Route 66 out of the hearts and thoughts of three generations of road-borne Americans." Snyder noted that "all across the country and even beyond, there's a groundswell of popular interest in old Route 66."[32]

Likewise, nostalgia has helped to preserve sections of what is now called the Columbia Gorge Historic Scenic Highway. While heavy traffic crowds Interstate 84, travelers along the old Oregon road can pause to sample the scenic splendors of Oneonta Gorge or Horsetail Falls, or park their cars and hike along a series of moss-draped trails. Some of the same nostalgia has attached itself to long-vanished passenger trains and stretches of long-abandoned railroad right-of-way. Following the banks of the

Missouri River across its namesake state is the Katy Trail, so named because it once was the main line of the Missouri-Kansas-Texas Railroad. Now a state park, it is popular with hikers and bicyclists. One published guide suggests how to vacation along the old right-of-way.

As for the interstate highways responsible for such changes, the network was originally scheduled to take thirteen years to complete and cost the taxpayers $27 billion. By 1970, when Congress stretched the network by another 2,500 miles, its completion seemed likely to require another quarter-century at a cost of approximately $70 billion. In all, it took fully forty years to get the basic network in place. It seems unlikely now that the job will ever really be finished. In numerous places it has become necessary to raise the height of the original overpasses or add more lanes for traffic or improve some of the now antiquated interchanges.

Fundamental changes took place in the skies overhead and on the railroads that ran through America's collective backyard too. As automobile use increased, ridership on railroad passenger trains and intercity buses dropped noticeably in the late 1940s and early 1950s. Only further adding to postwar passenger train blues were growing numbers of Americans riding aboard commercial airliners. But that is another chapter.

Eleven

The Sky's the Limit

In 1952 when my parents took me to Brazil to visit my paternal grandparents, we flew from Miami to Rio de Janeiro aboard one of Aerovias Brasil's DC-4s. Apparently the company had only that one plane suitable for international travel, and Aerovias Brasil itself did not seem to amount to much of an airline. Serious engine trouble delayed us in Miami and again for several more hours in Trinidad. Still, the flight along the bulge of South America and across the mouth of the Amazon River was exciting. Perhaps it seemed so because I was so young, but commercial aviation itself was also very young. Western, the oldest airline in the United States in 1952, was a mere twenty-six years old.

Because in those innocent days no one had yet heard the word "skyjacking," pilots and co-pilots regularly welcomed children, even seven-year-olds, into their cockpits to help them "fly the plane." It mattered not to me that we reached Rio twenty-four hours late: I had helped fly our plane. Though we were a full day behind schedule, the pilot still insisted on giving us an aerial tour of city sights. He was proud of the beach at Ipanema, Sugar Loaf Peak, and other famous Rio attractions; and he especially wanted to share them with his several passengers from the United States. I cannot imagine the pilots of United or Delta taking time to do that today—or the companies or federal authorities allowing them to do so. Commercial flight is now so standardized that it is almost mind numbing. ("Hours of boredom and moments of stark terror" is how a commercial pilot friend for U.S. Airways once described it to me. I can gladly skip the "stark terror" part.)

On our return flight from Brazil to Miami, we plunged headlong into a tropical storm over Cuba. It was dark, and

> When aerial transportation comes into its own, the airport terminus will be a magnificent plant which will make the best of present day landing fields look like the lonely way station along the railroad track. Numberless airliners will arrive and depart according to precise schedules, linking with bus and train services, coördinated for rapid distribution of passengers and freight.
>
> —Edgar H. Felix in *Aero Digest,* December 1928

A portion of the airport landscape as seen from inside one of American Airlines' Flagships. A stewardess welcomes aboard smiling passengers in 1960. At the time, most airports had not yet installed jetways to link the terminal gates and the airplanes. Author's collection.

lightning flashed all around the struggling DC-4. The plane seemed almost to lurch through the air as powerful winds lashed it from side to side and simultaneously bounced it up and down. Special effects artists in Hollywood could not have outdone Mother Nature that night. The pilot's voice came over the loudspeaker. He was excited, but he spoke only in Portuguese. Dad turned white. The three English-only members of his family said nothing. Some situations don't require words.

After we were finally back on terra firma in Miami, I asked him what the pilot had said. Dad carefully translated his words: "I hope you are all good Catholics because we may be going to crash." I cannot imagine the pilots of United or Delta saying that either, even if they were experiencing one of those "moments of stark terror." Too much stiff-upper-lip professionalism, I suppose. Memories of our flight to Brazil in 1952 serve to remind me how much commercial flying has changed just in my lifetime.

When I lived in central Indiana in the 1950s, Indianapolis claimed to be the largest city in the United States not located along a navigable waterway (Phoenix, in the Sonoran Desert, now has a far better claim to that dubious distinction). But Indianapolis did have a port of another sort, and the maritime analogy was appropriate to describe air service even in that landlocked metropolis. Early navigation beacons, after all, served as the lighthouses, buoys, and other channel markers that guided ships of the sky along the designated airways of the United States. Appropriately enough, back in the 1920s the Airways Division of the Department of Commerce was housed in the Lighthouse Bureau.

At Weir Cook Airport, now called Indianapolis International Airport, I recall how anyone could stand outside a modest chain-link fence and watch Lake Central DC-3s crank up their big radial engines with an impressive display of noise and smoke. It only seemed natural that a ground employee stood by with a tall red fire extinguisher. The regional carriers Lake Central and Ozark Air Lines were for me both puddle jumpers. On the other hand, TWA with its Constellations had international connections and elegance.

To my youthful mind, both TWA and the Pennsylvania Railroad, which ran near our Indiana home, were synonymous with glamour—and inordinately great power. The Pennsylvania Railroad was by far the mightiest thing I knew. The federal government, I was told at school, was much bigger, but as far as I could see, it ran only a post office in Greenfield. Any one of the Pennsylvania's many streamlined passenger trains rushing to Saint Louis or New York was far more impressive than the Greenfield post office. Alas, as I type these words in 2001, those once-busy mainline tracks are long gone, and TWA will be gone by the end of this year. The decline and fall of TWA, a company synonymous with the golden age of commercial aviation, is an especially painful story to tell, yet it speaks volumes about the tumult through which the industry flew during the past quarter-century.

One of Pan American's Clippers moored at Treasure Island, near San Francisco in 1939. The flying boats spanned the Pacific to link the West Coast with Manila and Hong Kong. Courtesy Oregon Historical Society.

On March 12, 2001, a bankruptcy judge in Delaware approved the purchase of Trans World Airlines by American Airlines, a deal formally consummated a month later on April 9. The *Post-Dispatch* of Saint Louis devoted most of the top half of its front page to the story, while two full pages inside provided particulars of the historic deal. Its lead editorial for March 12, titled "Greasing a Landing," addressed concerns of Saint Louisans who feared losing a hometown carrier and possibly their city's status as a major airline hub. It noted that American's own corporate roots reached back to Robertson Aircraft Corporation, a 1920s carrier based at Lambert Field. Its first flight had been in 1926, "a mail run from Chicago to St. Louis flown by its chief pilot. A skinny kid named Lindbergh."[1]

Adjacent to the editorial was a large cartoon showing a jetliner labeled "TWA Acquisition" and plastered on its nose wheel was the figure of a businessman labeled "Icahn." In the recent gloomy history of TWA, Carl Icahn was the one person airline personnel most loved to hate. A corporate raider and throwback to railroad barons of the nineteenth century who milked corporate cash cows for personal gain and then left them half-dead and struggling, Icahn was widely blamed for TWA's current malaise because of what he did after he gained control of the carrier in 1985. He took the airline private three years later through a leveraged buyout deal that put $469 million in Icahn's own pockets and weighted TWA down with a massive $1.2 billion in debt. That was the last year it made any money.

The load of debt and sharply rising fuel prices caused TWA to file for chapter 11 bankruptcy in 1992. To make loan payments to Icahn, the ailing carrier sold several of its most lucrative routes, such as to London's Heathrow airport, and its most valuable airport gates. Icahn refused to upgrade TWA's airline fleet, saddling it with the oldest and least fuel-efficient planes in the industry.

A color photo on the front page of the *Post-Dispatch* showed airline employees in a break room at Lambert Field rejoicing "while watching a TV interview with TWA president and CEO William Compton about the end of Carl Icahn's association with the airline." The scene brought back personal memories of December 4, 1991, the day I witnessed one of the last, if not the last, Pan American World Airways flights land at Los Angeles International Airport. By coincidence I was aboard an Alaska Airlines flight between Tucson and Seattle as it pushed back from the gate following its scheduled stop in Los Angeles.

The Pan Am shutdown was both historic and very sad. Air travel across the Pacific Ocean dates from November 22, 1935, when Pan American's first China Clipper, a Martin M-130 flying boat, hopped from island to island on a lengthy journey from San Francisco to Manila. At the time that feat pushed the envelope of aviation technology to its limits. Earlier, Pan American planes flying down from Miami to Rio made the carrier synonymous with South American adventure and glamour. After December 4, 1991, all that remained of original Pan American were memories. At least employees of TWA had something to celebrate after their merger in 2001, because ongoing jobs with American promised to keep hard times at arm's length—that is, until air terrorists on September 11, 2001, wreaked havoc for carriers as large as American, United, and Delta and threatened their financial futures.

⚜ ⚜ ⚜

In shaping the often-turbulent course of commercial aviation in the United States, the American West and westerners played inordinately great roles, especially since World War II—far greater than was true for railroads, bus lines, highways, and waterways of the United States. That applies to major manufacturers like Boeing and Douglas, to federal regulation of the airline industry in the 1920s and 1930s, and to deregulation forty years later. The West played a major role in defining federal control over navigation across the nation's aviation landscapes too.

To understand how this happened, let us start with a mystery. How was it that Trans World Airlines and Pan American, at one time the premier carriers of the United States, disappeared from the skies—along with Eastern, Braniff, and numerous additional airlines both major and minor? Our explanation begins with the retelling of a forgotten incident that took place on May 6, 1935, near a village in central Missouri called Atlanta. In a farmer's field near there, a Transcontinental & Western DC-2 Sky Chief ran out of fuel and crashed as its pilot attempted unsuccessfully to maneuver through thick fog. It was only one of a string of fatal air crashes in the mid-1930s, including Nick Mamer and his Northwest Sky Zephyr in Montana, which greatly alarmed the industry and threatened to frighten away passengers.

What set the Missouri crash of TWA Flight 6 apart from others and increased demands by Congress for stricter federal regulation was that among the five passenger fatalities was one of their own, Senator Bronson Cutting of New Mexico. Some of his Capitol Hill colleagues wept openly when news of his untimely death reached the Senate chamber. Federal investigators of the Cutting crash turned up procedural irregularities and broken rules by the pilot, TWA, and the Bureau of Air Commerce. Even as scrutiny of the Cutting crash continued, the newspapers carried word of additional air disasters.

A little more than three months after Cutting's death, famed aviator Wiley Post and popular actor Will Rogers died in a crash in Alaska caused by suspected icing of the plane's carburetor. That fall a United Air Lines Boeing 247–D crashed near Cheyenne, Wyoming, killing all twelve people aboard when it undershot the field by a thousand feet of altitude. Eight more fatal crashes followed in 1936—including five just between late December 1936 and the end of January 1937—and five more in 1937. One was a Western Air Express flight that disappeared over the rugged mountains of southern Utah; another was a United flight that plunged into a mountainside near Los Angeles. Only a short time later one of United's new DC-3s crashed into San Francisco Bay on its final approach to the airport and drowned all its passengers. Investigators soon discovered that the pilot had dropped his microphone and inadvertently jammed his flight controls. The nation's press reported each lurid incident, and not without reason did the American public lose confidence in its airlines. Their passenger revenues fell sharply.

Eddie Rickenbacker, the World War I ace and legendary head of Eastern (at one time the nation's most profitable airline), once groused that if something can move, it can crash. "The only time man is safe is when he is completely static, in a box underground." [2] He ought to know because in early 1941 he had almost died aboard an Eastern flight that crashed outside Atlanta. Many less-fatalistic Americans believed the nation's skies could be made far safer for passengers. Among those were Senator Cutting's colleagues on Capitol Hill. Shocked by his death and those of passengers and crewmembers in the several other crashes of the mid and late 1930s, they wanted to do something to ensure greater safety along the airways—a timely movement of interest to passengers and the struggling airline industry alike.

At this time, the Air Commerce of Act of 1926 provided for the Department of Commerce to set rules of flight, license pilots, and produce maps and charts as well as build more lighted airways. What Congress did when it enacted the Civil Aeronautics Act of 1938 was to establish a new cadre of federal regulators to bring additional order and stability to the nation's airline industry. It consciously modeled the new bureaucracy after the venerable Interstate Commerce Commission.

For commercial airlines, regulation meant that federal overseers of the Civil Aeronautics Authority gained power to limit entry into the business as well as control expansion of airline routes. Bureaucrats in this way more or less insured that established carriers enjoyed the steady flow of profits required to purchase expensive new planes like the DC-3. No longer could commercial airlines recklessly underbid one another to win a federal airmail contract. They henceforth operated in the old school manner comparable to any regulated utility. The Civil Aeronautics Board, as the regulatory body became known in 1940, oversaw any expansion or contraction of airline route structures as well as the fares they charged their customers, much like Interstate Commerce Commission officials did for the nation's railroads, buses, and over-the-road trucks.

In the waning months of World War II, the Civil Aeronautics Board fostered the creation of a whole new group of regional or feeder airlines. The idea was to fill gaps left by major carriers as well as feed more passen-

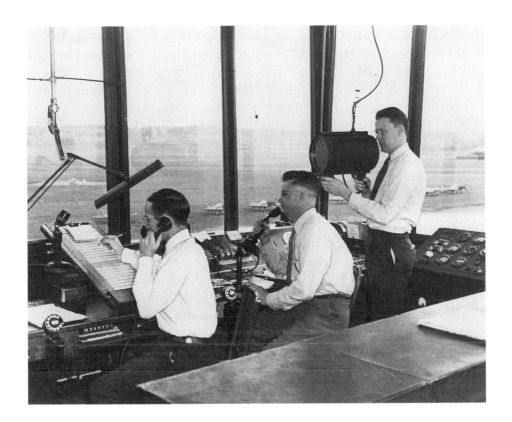

Control of the airways took many new forms in the 1930s and 1940s. Herb Allen, an Oregon Journal *photographer, recorded a group of ground traffic controllers at work at Portland main airport. The date was 1948 and well before computers and other electronic aids became part of their workaday tools. Courtesy Oregon Historical Society.*

gers to them. In this way a new tier of commercial aviation sputtered to life, literally, with many regionals using hand-me-down DC-3s and similar aircraft. The oldest of the nation's feeder airlines was Pioneer, the self-proclaimed "Gateway to the Southwest," which launched service in West Texas and New Mexico in mid-1944.

Four-engine DC-4s, a North Atlantic workhorse during World War II, briefly became the peacetime mainstays of United and American transcontinental routes. In April 1945, United placed its first DC-6 into transcontinental service. Larger and more powerful than the DC-4, it made it possible for United to offer coast-to-coast service in ten hours, including a refueling stop in Lincoln, Nebraska. At first all went well, but in October 1947 a United DC-6 burst into flames over Utah's Bryce Canyon and crashed, killing all fifty-two people aboard. A few days later an eerily similar fire forced an American flight to make an emergency landing in Gallup, New Mexico. All DC-6s were grounded until the cause (a faulty air intake the could suck fuel into the heating system) was found and corrected.

On TWA, the Lockheed Constellation with its gracefully contoured lines carried its first commercial passengers after the war ended, including on the airline's new routes across the North Atlantic. These pressurized planes carried sixty-four travelers, could climb easily to 25,000 feet, zip along at 280 miles per hour, and outdistance any previous airliner. The wingspan of a Constellation was greater than the distance the Wright's first successful plane covered at Kitty Hawk some forty years earlier. Like the Douglas DC-6, the early Constellations suffered from serious technical problems that had to be corrected, but in time the big plane became a staple of TWA's postwar fleet.

After years of deprivation, Americans took to the skies in record numbers after World War II. In 1947 commercial airlines of the United States carried more than three times the record of 3.6 million passengers set in 1941. However, these were difficult years as airlines adapted to new aircraft, expanded routes, and increased passenger loads. Unfortunately, few airport terminals were built to handle so many travelers. They often became dirty and chaotic places. *Fortune* magazine described Chicago's Midway, then the city's main commercial airport, as "a slum." The terminal was dingy and dirty, its floors littered with chewing gum, paper, orange peels, and cigar butts. So bad were the jostling crowds, the "unintelligible squawk of the loudspeaker," and the flight delays that Midway made "bus terminals look like luxury."[3]

In addition, a new type of carrier, the irregular or nonscheduled airline, sought to lure still more passengers into the skies over America. These carriers advertised vacation travel at bargain-basement prices, and they made economics work in their favor by flying at off-peak hours and only when their seats were full. For their passengers, that frequently meant flying a day later than originally planned. It was inconvenient, to be sure, but "nonskeds" appealed to travelers determined to save money. Further encouraging the first generation of low-fare airlines was the ready availability of inexpensive military surplus transports along with many ex-military pilots to fly them.

In some cases these were literally fly-by-night operations. One nonsked ran so short of cash that passengers had to "pass the hat" at an intermediate stop to buy enough fuel to get them to their destination. On another occasion a transcontinental flight from Burbank to Newark hopped around the United States from airport to airport until it finally reached the

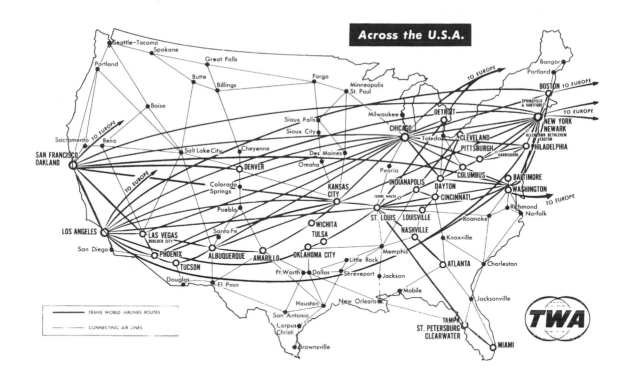

Airline route systems across the United States in the 1960s and 1970s still tended to be linear. The hub-and-spoke pattern grew increasingly popular with all major carriers except Southwest after Congress deregulated airlines in 1978. Courtesy TWA Collection, St. Louis Mercantile Library.

East Coast at Philadelphia three days late, where the nonsked carrier simply left its passengers stranded. These were the exceptions, however, because passengers continued to flock to the nonskeds for the bargains they offered.

Capital Airlines was the first major carrier to copy nonskeds by offering coach-class service between New York and Chicago in 1948. TWA and American joined the growing trend at the end of 1949 by offering coach-class flights between New York and Los Angeles. In mid-1950 TWA inaugurated a transcontinental service called "Sky Coach" in Lockheed Constellations. It set the fare at $110 coast to coast versus $157.85 on regular flights, and it configured planes to hold eighty-one seats versus only fifty-seven on regular flights. "Sky Coach" service featured only one hostess instead of the usual two, and it required passengers to buy box lunches rather than be served complimentary hot meals and snacks.

The popularity of coach class continued to climb during the early 1950s with the blessing of the Civil Aeronautics Board. Prior to the trend to coach-class service, travel aboard major airlines was all first class and commanded a high price. Passengers dressed in their Sunday best for flights and expected full meals served on quality china. Flying was altogether a chic travel experience.

Nonstop flights between New York and California began in late 1953 with the latest generation TWA Super Constellations and United DC-7s. Moreover, expansion of air-coach service attracted more passengers than before, and by 1955 they had a choice of coach or first-class seats on most flights. Travelers by air first surpassed the number by Pullman sleeper in 1951, by bus in 1956, and by all other classes of train service in 1957. That same year Northwest Orient Airlines offered through air coach service across the continent between New York City and Seattle for $99. Because of such low rates it was not surprising that within ten years commercial flights carried seven times the passenger-miles of trains.

The 1950s were the golden age of propeller-driven airliners, but it did not last long. The industry passed a milestone in 1958 when it entered the jet age, thunderously taking to the sky in the first-generation Boeing 707 and DC-8 four-engine planes. The jet age had experienced an embarrassing false start in 1952 when British Overseas Airways Corporation launched De Havilland Comets, the pioneer passenger jets, on its far-flung routes linking Europe with Africa and Asia. For comparison, the DC-3s cruised at 180 miles per hour, while Comets streaked through the sky at 480 miles per hour. But the proud British carrier grounded all of its Comets after two of them mysteriously exploded in midair in early 1954, killing all on board. Investigators blamed tiny stress fractures in the jet's skin caused by compression and decompression at takeoff and landing, but the ill-fated plane never flew again.

The same year that the last Comet flew, Boeing rolled out a prototype of the 707 on May 15, 1954. William E. Boeing himself, by then 72 years old and long departed from the aviation industry after New Deal zealots forced a breakup of big holding companies, had a chance to compare it to the early aircraft his company had manufactured. Two months later, on July 15, Boeing test pilot A. M. "Tex" Johnson piloted the first 707 through the skies above Seattle.

Perhaps even more memorable was what happened on August 7, 1955, when Boeing asked Johnson to put its brand-new 707 prototype through its paces at the Seattle Seafair festival. Following the precision aerobatics of the Blue Angels, the flamboyant forty-year-old Johnson casually put his 707 through a couple of barrel rolls above Lake Washington, to the shock of Boeing executives and the delight of 250,000 fair goers. As spectators cheered, the company's stunned president, William M. Allen, was said to have gulped a handful of pills for his ailing heart.

One of Western Airlines' new Boeing 707s as photographed at Portland's International Airport. Had Harris Hanshue, the airline's founder, lived long enough to see this sight, he doubtless would have been thrilled. Courtesy Oregon Historical Society.

Boeing first manufactured a military version of the 707 to serve the Cold War needs of the Strategic Air Command. The best known of the military 707s was Air Force One. Then Boeing turned to civilian aviation, and on the drizzly evening of October 26, 1958, a Pan American 707 made aviation history when it lifted off on the first scheduled United States jet flight from New York to Paris. It paused for fuel in Newfoundland, but the transatlantic flight was still an impressive feat.

This time it was no false start for the jet age. Boeing worked hard to make sure its new 707s would not meet the same fate as the British Comets. At one point as they probed and tested for any signs of weakness, engineers fired frozen chickens against the fuselage to make absolutely certain the thin metal skin was tough enough to withstand the rigors of flight, including a collision with large birds.

Domestic airlines launched scheduled jet service between New York and Miami and across the United States in December 1958 and January 1959 respectively. That was when American Airlines 707s reduced coast-to-coast travel time to just four and a half hours. For the traveling public, America's jet age truly arrived in 1959.

Soon nonstop jet service linked cities of the West Coast to cities of the Far East, thus helping the West to play a pivotal role in expanding trade with nations of the Pacific Rim. Already by September 1959 it was possible to circle the globe aboard pure jets, not just jet props, operated by commercial airlines. Soon thereafter, the term "jet lag" became part of the vocabulary of every weary traveler. Quieter and more fuel efficient jets came later, along with somewhat smaller and nimbler planes like the Boeing 737 and DC-9, two models that especially appealed to regional airlines. A total of 4,100 Boeing 737s had been sold by 1998, making it the world's best-selling jetliner.

The Boeing 707 was the first jetliner to find favor with U.S. airlines. The Douglas DC-8 followed a short time later but never overtook its competitor. In the end, Boeing sold nearly a thousand of its 707s to Douglas's 556 DC-8s. Convair, a third entrant, with encouragement from Howard Hughes, sought to play catch up with jetliners it called the 880 and the 990. By most measures, these were inferior planes. They never appealed to air carriers and thus lost Convair a whopping $450 million by 1962, a sum that represented the largest single financial loss of a U.S. corporation at the time. Douglas, in like fashion, failed to regain the glory of former years, such as 1954, when its aircraft of various types accounted for half of the 164 million passenger miles flown each day by scheduled airlines around the globe. In 1997 Boeing acquired its once-proud rival when it took over the ailing plane maker then known as McDonnell Douglas.

The dawn of the jet age, despite its undeniable promise of greater speeds, caused the airline industry major financial headaches. In the mid-1950s, United alone had $175 million invested in its fleet of 160 propeller-driven Mainliners. "The first airline to order a jet fleet will either revolutionize the industry, or go broke," its president quipped.[4] Yet when United learned that TWA and American had ordered fleets of Boeing 707s for their transcontinental service, it had no choice but to replace relatively new but suddenly obsolescent piston-driven 357-mile-per-hour craft with jetliners that cruised 575 miles per hour from one coast to the other. Fortunately for United and its rivals during this time of financial uncertainty, in 1954 the rate of airline fatalities in the United States dropped to a level comparable to that for railroad travel. At last it was just about as safe to fly as take a train.

Airline executives cautiously optimistic about the future of their industry were pleased when jet travel soared. For a time the sky alone must have appeared to be the limit to their hopes. In practice, rigid restrictions continued to define commercial airline service, at least when service was measured by price and route structure, because officials of the Civil Aeronautics Board determined both of those. Typically, only after months of exhaustive hearings by federal examiners could airlines add even a short segment to their route maps. All major carriers charged the same price for service between the same two cities, though they could compete in terms of amenities they offered passengers.

Within their heavily regulated environment, the big airlines of America grew comfortable—and perhaps a bit complacent. There were occasional upstarts that worked within the federal rules to expand service as regulators permitted. One such airline was Continental, which originated as one of several small carriers started in various parts of the West by Walter Varney. His first airline, as we have seen, delivered mail between Salt Lake City and Spokane in the late 1920s and become a pioneer component of United Air Lines.

Another of Varney's air ventures held the mail contract for settlements along the sparsely settled Front Range of the Rockies between Pueblo and El Paso. Robert Six, a one-time bill collector for San Francisco's Pacific Gas and Electric Company, took the controls of tiny Varney Speed Lines in 1936 and carefully piloted it into the ranks of the major carriers by modernizing and expanding its fleet of aircraft. By the early 1950s Continental (as it had been named in 1938) served thirty-six cities with a fleet of twenty-one planes. At one time it advertised itself as "The Route of the Conquistadors" and urged people to "Fly the Old Santa Fe Trail." Also known for years as "The Proud Bird with the Golden Tail," Continental held its own on the highly competitive Los Angeles-Denver-Chicago routes against United and American by offering the first jet service, and it trailed only United on the busy Los Angeles-Honolulu route. In the late 1950s Six boldly extended his airline's route system across the South Pacific to Australia.

Something of an aviation playboy, Six at one time was married to actress Audrey Meadows (known as Alice on the popular Jackie Gleason television show *The Honeymooners*). Six's handpicked successor in 1979 was Alvin Feldman, president of Denver-based Frontier Airlines. Continental's energetic new executive developed hubs in Denver and Houston before becoming a tragic figure in a post-deregulation power play that shocked the industry in 1981. I will explain those tumultuous times later.

Flying almost unnoticed by most people in aviation was a peculiar

Postwar elegance, when airlines offered one class of service and passengers dressed up to fly. Courtesy TWA Collection, St. Louis Mercantile Library.

class of carriers that thrived only in the western states of California and Texas. These were the *intrastate* airlines, which flew completely unregulated by the Civil Aeronautics Board because their planes did not cross state lines. Perhaps only in Texas and California were local markets large or distant enough to permit profitable intrastate flying. The first of the post–World War II era intrastate airlines in California dates from 1949 and prospered by offering frequent, low-fare service between cities such as Los Angeles, San Francisco, and San Diego.

The *Official Airline Guide* for December 1954 shows that Pacific Southwest Airlines, an intrastate carrier that took to the skies in 1949 with a single DC-3, offered $5.45 flights between San Diego and Los Angeles and $9.99 flights between Los Angeles and San Francisco. Not surprisingly, by the early 1960s those low fares enabled Pacific Southwest to carry more than one quarter of all air passengers between Los Angeles and San Francisco. Another intrastate carrier of note was Air California, which took to the skies in mid-January 1967 to serve the fast-growing Los Angeles-San Francisco market.

Success in California inspired a Texas upstart in 1971 to offer the same kind of frequent, low-fare service along a triangular route defined by Dallas, San Antonio, and Houston, the three largest cities of the Lone Star state. Passengers unhappy with high fares charged by Braniff and American, two major carriers closely regulated by Uncle Sam, flocked aboard the Boeing 737s operated by Southwest Airlines. Many of them were first-time flyers.

The quiet revolution based in California and Texas inspired academics and politicians interested in American air commerce in the 1970s to propose deregulation of the industry nationwide. Why not? The business itself had changed dramatically since 1938, the first year that Uncle Sam regulated the airlines. That same year, 1.1 million passengers flew aboard commercial flights; by the 1970s that many people flew in just one day. All planes owned by U.S. carriers in 1938 could not carry as many passengers as a single stretch DC-8 could in a year in the early 1970s.

Even so, at that time the industry could not avoid flying through troubled skies once again. The problem this time was that a new generation of airliners—the jumbo Boeing 747s, DC-10s, and Lockheed L-1011s—initially caused such over-capacity that the industry believed its key to survival was to fill every available seat. That was not easy when the Civil Aeronautics Board controlled the airlines. "The price of every drink, the rental cost of every movie headset, the number of seats installed abreast, the square footage of the lounges—every last detail required the approval of the CAB," observes Thomas Petzinger Jr. in his book *Hard Landing*.[5] The industry of the United States saw its losses climb sharply in 1970 to $150 million, by far the worst year yet in its relatively short history.

After nearly four decades of federal control, the time seem right to kindle a competitive spirit that would fill empty seats and make the industry profitable once again. The expectation was that unfettered competition would give rise to new and aggressive carriers that would invigorate the industry and benefit passengers with lower fares and more frequent service. To achieve that goal, two senior Senators, Edward Kennedy of Massachusetts and Howard Cannon of Nevada, both Democrats, held public hearings and pushed the deregulatory legislation through Congress that President Jimmy Carter signed into law in late October 1978. Cornell University economics professor Alfred Kahn, selected by Carter the previous year to head the Civil Aeronautics Board, was a strong proponent of deregulation. He was eager to relax federal control of the industry well before the regulatory body officially ceased operation on the last day of 1984. That in itself was a landmark, because it was the first time a federal regulatory agency had ever shut its doors.

Looking back, the Kennedy-Cannon deregulation bill represented a radical departure for Democrats, who in modern times have often been tagged the party of big government. But if deregulation represented a brave new world for Democrats, it was doubly so for airlines. The legislation was supposed to spur startups, which it did for a time; but after a chaotic period of readjustment, which saw bankruptcy after bankruptcy ground several long-established carriers as well as most newcomers, it seemed clear that a handful of megacarriers—United, American, Delta, Northwest, and Continental—were likely to dominate the industry in the United States as it flew into the twenty-first century. That was precisely the opposite of what proponents of deregulation sought. Senator Ted Kennedy grew increasingly unhappy with the unintended consequences of what he and his Capitol Hill colleagues had wrought.

❧ ❧ ❧

The big shakeout began in the West. Braniff Airways, a Texas-based carrier, went bankrupt in May 1982. Like Pan American and Eastern, two additional casualties of deregulation, this was no upstart. Never before during the forty-year stewardship of the Civil Aeronautics Board had a major airline of the United States gone bankrupt. This was a disturbing development for an industry that had witnessed more than its share of troubles since the late 1920s.

It was back in mid-1928 that the brothers Paul and Tom Braniff, a World War I flier and an insurance executive respectively, organized their namesake airline to fly a five-passenger Stinson Detroiter between Tulsa and their hometown of Oklahoma City. Over the years, Braniff had distinguished itself by expanding service along a Great Plains corridor effectively defined by the cities of Dallas, Oklahoma City, Kansas City, and Minneapolis. It further expanded service in the Heartland in the 1960s and 1970s before it extended an ambitious reach to Miami, a city that served as its gateway to Latin America. By the time of deregulation, Braniff was the nation's tenth largest airline.

The troubles that grounded Braniff—too rapid expansion accompanied by rising fuel costs, staggering inflation, and a recession—were symptomatic of the times. Only a day after President Carter signed the deregulation bill, Braniff staked claims to 626 of the approximately 1,300 new routes that federal regulators made available to airlines. By contrast, United asked the Civil Aeronautics Board for only one new route. During the following year, Braniff actually commenced service on more than fifty of its new routes. In fact, in a single day it commenced service to sixteen new cities, a feat no other airline had before attempted.

Harding Lawrence and his wife, advertising executive Mary Wells, rapidly transformed Braniff into the most flamboyant carrier in the industry in the late 1970s. Scorning what the company called the "plain plane," Braniff repainted its aircraft in a rainbow of bright colors. In fact, it hired Alexander Calder to hand paint one of its jets with an original work of art. Furthermore, it sought to transform its flight attendants into fashion models, who changed their flashy outfits during flights in what the company dubbed its "air strip." Such gimmicks helped attract public attention to Braniff, but not necessarily travel dollars.

A string of losses soon humbled its brash and overconfident executives. New management only made a bad situation worse by ripping out first-class seats in favor of all-coach cabins (at a time when Braniff was the leading carrier of business flyers who enjoyed and paid for first-class seating), trimming operations and personnel, and realigning its route structure to converge at a Dallas-Fort Worth hub. Nothing worked, and Braniff simply ran out of cash on the evening of May 13, 1982. Nearly two years later, in March 1984, a slimmed-down version of Braniff took to the skies again, but it was unsuccessful too and quit flying in 1989.

Feeder airlines, their routes once heavily subsidized by the Civil Aeronautics Board, survived deregulation by combining into multiregional carriers, which in turn were acquired by major airlines. One western carrier, Hughes Airwest, itself a union of three small feeders, consolidated with North Central and Southern to form a new national carrier, Republic Airlines, which struggled to remain aloft despite a heavy load of debt before Northwest acquired it for nearly a billion dollars. The same clumsy multiregional amalgam arose in the East after Pittsburgh-based Allegheny Airlines gobbled up Mohawk and Piedmont to become today's U.S. Airways. In 1988, along the way to becoming a national carrier of sorts, it acquired Pacific Southwest Airlines, one of the two California intrastate carriers that had helped to spark the deregulation revolution.

As the regional carriers disappeared, so did the once-familiar forty-seat Convair-240s and Martin-202s that had formed the backbones of their fleets. Commercial service to many small airports ceased too, or it was transformed by a new generation of commuter airlines that allied with majors to funnel local traffic through their hubs. Horizon Air did that with Alaska Airlines in Portland and Seattle, and Skywest did likewise with Delta in Salt Lake City. Commuter airlines existed before deregulation, but the 1978 legislation greatly boosted their fortunes by encouraging them to expand and join forces with major carriers. Unlike the former regionals, commuter airlines had been exempt from federal regulation of fares and route structures. Flying small planes (their seating capacity kept low by regulators), they could enter or leave local markets with a minimum of oversight.

Taking full advantage of this freedom were entrepreneurs like Milton G. Kuolt II, a logger, tree surgeon, and later a college-trained accountant who worked for Boeing in Seattle. He launched Horizon Air on September 1, 1981, on a route between Seattle and Yakima, a city of 50,000 residents. That was only the beginning of a route structure that eventually blanketed the Pacific Northwest. Late in 1986 Horizon sold out to the Alaska Air Group for $70 million, of which Kuolt personally received a large portion. "Milton Kuolt's ability to build a single route into a company worth $70 million over a period of less than six years is unprecedented in the world of modern airline business," noted the authors of the definitive history of commuter airlines.[6]

⚜ ⚜ ⚜

The problems that grounded Pan American were in many ways unique to that carrier. For fifty years it had reigned as a premier international airline of the United States, extending routes first to South America in the late 1920s, then to Asia, and finally to Europe. Its reach west across the Pacific from San Francisco to Asia in the mid-1930s was typical of its boldness.

By the 1970s Pan Am suffered from a glaring omission that deregulation helped turn into a fatal flaw: the airline operated no routes of its own within the United States to funnel passengers onto its international flights. To remedy that predicament, it acquired National Airlines, but their merger was made in hell. The corporate cultures of the two carriers were so vastly different that the infighting only weakened Pan Am. It sold off real estate and valuable routes—the lucrative transpacific ones going to United—in an effort to raise the cash it needed just to survive. In the end, a terrorist bomb destroyed one of its Boeing 747s high above the quiet Scottish town of Lockerbie and generated the appalling kind of publicity that frightened away passengers and helped destroy the once-proud carrier. Like Eastern, it liquidated its remaining assets.

At the time Pan Am shut down in December 1991, the American airline industry was in turmoil once again, having lost a staggering $4 billion in 1990. It lost another $2 billion in 1991. During those two years alone, the nation's airlines lost more money than they had earned in total profits since the industry began in the 1920s. That was not how deregulation was supposed to work. Corporate corpses lay piled everywhere, and that did not even include earlier casualties like Braniff.

Following World War II, TWA joined Pan American as a major overseas carrier when it received permission to bridge the North Atlantic between the United State and Europe—but unlike Pan American it operated a good system of domestic routes as well. In 1950 it formally acknowledged its enlarged ambitions by changing its corporate name from Transcontinental & Western to Trans World Airlines, thus keeping familiar initials even as it expanded its reach.

During the depression days of 1931, TWA had moved its headquarters from New York City to relatively provincial Kansas City; but in keeping with its plans for global expansion, it moved them back to the Big Apple in the late 1950s. During that decade, its big Lockheed Constellations helped to burnish TWA's image as an airline of substantial financial clout. Eventually, in August 1969, it successfully reached completely around the globe, one hand clasping the other when its routes stretching

*Howard Hughes as a handsome young aviator, business mogul,
and Hollywood producer. Courtesy TWA Collection,
St. Louis Mercantile Library.*

across the Atlantic and Pacific Oceans joined in Asia. The carrier probably reached the pinnacle of power and prestige just prior to deregulation of America's airline industry in 1978.

For about twenty-five years, from 1939 until 1965, the legendary tycoon Howard R. Hughes tightly controlled TWA through Hughes Tool

Company, though he never held an official position with the airline or attended its board meetings. Hughes Tool was the source of his original fortune. His father had started this lucrative business after the Texas oil boom in 1901. Hughes manufactured a drill bit that could bore easily through solid rock in search of black gold. It quickly became an industry favorite.

In 1926, having recently inherited the family's fortune, Hughes moved to Hollywood where he directed and produced feature films—successfully too. He was just twenty years old. During his career in California he made movie stars out of both Jean Harlow and Jane Russell. One of the Hughes films, called *Hell's Angels,* featured aerial combat in World War I. This, the first multimillion-dollar picture of the Hollywood's talking era, inspired Hughes to learn to fly in 1927. As was typical of all he did, he took up flying with great gusto. For a period of three months in 1932, Hughes even worked as the copilot of a Ford Trimotor for American Airlines under the assumed name Charles Howard. Later in the 1930s, flanked by a bevy of his Hollywood starlets, he won newspaper headlines as an aviation playboy.

In July 1938 Hughes piloted a Lockheed plane around the world in less than four days to set a new aviation record. That same year Jack Frye, president of TWA, turned to Hughes for money to help wrest control of the carrier from its conservative owners, who refused to back investments in state-of-the-art planes like Boeing's Stratoliner. By 1940 Hughes effectively controlled TWA. During the next fifteen years he enlarged his stake until it totaled a whopping 78 percent of the airline. When Hughes became a major proponent of Lockheed's Constellations, he used Hughes Tool Company money to help TWA finance purchases of the big planes costing $450,000 apiece. Thanks to his ability to persuade Hollywood stars to fly TWA, that airline more than any other became synonymous with travel glamour.

Hughes himself, alas, suffered the first of several nervous breakdowns in late 1944, probably as a result of incessant wartime pressures on him and his enterprises. He grew increasingly erratic and mentally unstable. Deathly afraid of germs, he developed a host of eccentric ways to ward off the invisible invaders. He might at times wash himself again and again yet paradoxically remain unwashed for months and allow his hair to grow stringy and long down his shoulders and back. His uncut toenails might grow so long that they curved around and dug into his skin.

Because of his mental instability and increasingly erratic behavior, Hughes stubbornly refused to support TWA's bid to acquire the new jetliners that were soon to revolutionize the industry. That, and growing concern that the once-proud airline was lurching from prosperity to near bankruptcy, was why the airline's board forced Hughes out in 1960. TWA was last among the nation's Big Four airlines to enter the jet age. Then, briefly, it was "Up, Up, and Away," in the words of one of its popular commercials. It was "Up, Up, and Away" for Hughes, too, because TWA shares that were worth only $7 when he first took control of the carrier were worth $86 in the mid-1960s when he sold them for a total of $547 million. That money, noted *Fortune* magazine, was the "largest sum to come into the hands of one man at one time."[7]

Hughes went on to invest in Las Vegas hotels and casinos, but he was not yet finished with commercial aviation. In August 1968 he gained control of Air West, a new company formed six weeks earlier from a three-way union of the regional carriers West Coast, Pacific, and Bonanza. The new airline looked impressive on paper and had routes that blanketed much of the Far West, but from day one its component parts meshed poorly or not at all. Its managers on occasion lost track of their assortment of planes, and no one could say with assurance whether they flew full or empty. To its many critics, the carrier became known as "Air Worst." Its reclusive owner renamed it Hughes Airwest in July 1970. Hughes himself died in Las Vegas on April 5, 1976—his final years marked by the physical and mental deterioration that left him a disheveled hermit living at one of his posh Las Vegas hotels.

As for TWA, twenty years after Hughes, corporate raider Carl Icahn won control of the airline and occasionally sold off lucrative routes for immediate gain. In January 1992 the struggling carrier had to file for reorganization under Chapter 11 of the federal bankruptcy code. It survived with a shrunken route system and a domestic market share that was approximately 5 percent. Icahn remained in charge, though he resigned twelve months later. The carrier relocated its headquarters from a building Icahn owned in Mt. Kisco, New York, to Saint Louis in 1994. The following year it completed a second financial reorganization.

For the second quarter of 1996, TWA publicly announced a substantial profit for the first time in almost seven years. Only hours later, July 17, 1996, Flight 800 exploded over Long Island Sound and killed all 230 passengers and crew. That catastrophe may have been triggered by a tiny spark from a frayed wire feeding to a sensor in the 747's cavernous fuel tanks. Concern naturally focused on the condition of TWA's aging fleet of aircraft, which it had not upgraded since the pinchpenny Icahn era.

TWA responded in late 1998 with the biggest order for new aircraft in its history, a total of 125 state-of-the-art jetliners from Boeing and Airbus with options to buy 125 more. However, the airline only continued to lose money, and in early 2001 it declared bankruptcy for a third and final time before American acquired it.

By 2001 at least 130 U.S. airlines had filed for bankruptcy since deregulation of the industry nearly a quarter-century earlier. Among them were several components of what was briefly the nation's largest airline empire, the one assembled by young Francisco A. Lorenzo after he became president of ailing Trans-Texas Airlines in 1972. The son of Spanish immigrants, Lorenzo grew up in a blue-collar neighborhood of Queens before working his way through Columbia University and Harvard Business School. He was an unlikely airline mogul, but like Walter Varney, Harris Hanshue, and other airline pioneers of the 1920s, he was determined to succeed.

To that end Lorenzo extended his reach beyond the Southwest by forming a holding company called Texas Air Corporation, which in turn launched a new low-cost carrier called Air New York, and gained control of Continental Airlines, into which he folded Texas International in 1981. Along the way, his bold maneuvering engendered considerable criticism. After Lorenzo bested Al Feldman in a bitter struggle for control of Continental, the beleaguered chief executive quietly retreated to his airline offices at Los Angeles International Airport on the night of August 9, 1981, stretched out on a couch, and placed a pillow under his head and a handgun to his temple. It could have been that Feldman was simply overwhelmed by Continental's record losses that year, but given the acrimony of the time, a growing legion of enemies was quick to blame Lorenzo for his suicide.

Lorenzo achieved his ambition to become a major player, but he pursued cost-cutting measures, no matter how justified, in such a ruthless and heavy-handed manner that it made him anathema to members of organized labor. At one point in 1983, Lorenzo and his business allies had Continental declare bankruptcy in order to void its union contracts and then take to the skies again a few days later as a low-cost carrier. When a strike threatened to ground Eastern in March 1989, Lorenzo tried to repeat his previous success at Continental by using bankruptcy law and crews of nonunion workers to keep that property aloft. This time the old trick did not work. The end for Eastern came in January 1991, after which the venerable airline liquidated its assets. Like George Gould, who sought but failed to assemble the first viable transcontinental railroad empire, Lorenzo's ambition exceeded his grasp, and he became an industry pariah.

Despite the downward spirals and corporate crash landings, there was one conspicuous success story: Southwest. Its remarkable story begins with Herbert Kelleher, a lawyer from New Jersey, and some business allies who decided to launch a Texas carrier modeled after successful intrastate airlines in California. Before Southwest Airlines' three Boeing 737s took to the skies in June 1971, much legal maneuvering was needed to break a hammerlock on the Lone Star State by Braniff and a fumbling regional carrier called Trans-Texas Airlines, which critics disparaged as "Tree Top" or "Tinker Toy Airlines." It was still a formidable opponent in court, and it is fortunate that the feisty Kelleher was a skilled lawyer able to fight Southwest's many legal battles at no cost to his not-yet-airborne company.

Legal challenges dragged on and on. "What do I do if the sheriff shows up tomorrow with another restraining order?" a worried executive asked Kelleher as Southwest prepared for its first flight with paying passengers.

"Leave tire marks on his back," Kelleher shot back. That was typical of Kelleher, a super-confident, high-energy executive who smoked his way through several packs of cigarettes a day. One way or another he was determined to make flying on Southwest distinctly different—and fun.

For years the unconventional and unabashed showoff Kelleher personified the company. Flight attendants occasionally sang their in-flight announcements. Southwest further defied industry convention by flying only Boeing 737s, thus enabling mechanics to become experts on one plane and eliminating the need to stock parts for many different models. It refused to pre-assign seats in an effort to return planes quickly to the air, and it served only peanuts and pretzels, not full meals, to passengers. Among the large airlines only Southwest remained committed to point-to-point routes, often with several stops in between, while its competitors embraced the hub-and-spoke arrangement.

Southwest established a nationwide network, first reaching east of the Mississippi River to serve Chicago's underutilized Midway Airport in 1985, and then flew still farther east to Baltimore in 1993. That was only a good beginning for the nationwide carrier that had clearly outgrown its regional name.[8]

Southwest under Kelleher liked to cultivate the image of a scrappy underdog taking on a host of big-league competitors. "Southwest has been kind of like a little puppy that gets fat off the table scraps of other airlines," noted Kelleher, the airline's founder and chief executive officer until he stepped down in 2001. Kelleher's puppy was, in truth, rapidly becoming a mighty big dog—a Saint Bernard at least. By the year 2000 it had become the nation's second biggest passenger carrier behind Delta. Moreover, and most incredibly, Southwest's market capitalization of about $13 billion was greater than the value of United, American, and Delta combined.[9]

These three and other survivors among the major airlines had themselves only grown bigger since 1978. During the first eight years of deregulation there were no fewer than twenty major airline mergers, eleven in 1986 alone. American and United expanded by picking up choice pieces of Pan American, Braniff, Continental, and other struggling carriers. American acquired intrastate carrier Air California in 1987, and Reno Air, one of the startups, a decade later.

Delta, which had no major presence west of Dallas and Kansas City before deregulation, acquired Western, the nation's oldest airline, for $860 million in 1986 and thereby transformed itself into a respected nationwide powerhouse with an important hub in Salt Lake City to match those in Atlanta and Cincinnati. At the time it ranked as the nation's fourth-largest airline, no small accomplishment for the one-time crop duster from the Mississippi delta. By the turn of the new century it would reign briefly as the nation's largest airline.

Always the most conservative of the big carriers, Delta gradually extended a blanket of routes across the North Atlantic as well as service to

South America—not wholesale like its one-time competitor Braniff, but by very carefully adding a stop in Santiago, Chile, and months later another in Buenos Aires, Argentina. It followed the same pattern across the Pacific. Delta was at all times cautious, as befits the image of an Atlanta-based carrier that once agonized over whether to serve liquor on board its planes for fear of offending its Bible Belt constituency, which had long provided a valuable core of support.

Northwest expanded following deregulation by gobbling up Republic Airlines, a union of several regional carriers that included Hughes Airwest. One problem Northwest faced was its record for perhaps the worst labor relations of all major airlines. As a result of its employees' willingness to strike for long periods of time—thus giving a new twist to the old phrase "the public be damned"—some uncharitable observers labeled it "Cobra Airlines" because "Northworst" employees were willing to "strike at anything." Most recently, in September 1998 its pilot strikers shut down Northwest for two weeks.[10]

By the beginning of the twenty-first century, only one major airline remained in business serving primarily the West. That was Alaska, which together with Horizon, served cities of the West Coast from Alaska to Mexico. Alaska Airlines established a reputation for exemplary service until a disastrous loop-the-loop crash off the coast of southern California in early 2000—a crash apparently caused by a worn jack-screw that adjusted vital control surfaces in the tail of the MD-83—raised serious questions about the airline's maintenance practices and tarnished its image.

Finally, there was America West, a carrier with hubs in Phoenix and Las Vegas but with routes extending across the United States. This airline grew rapidly in the late 1980s—too rapidly, as it turned out. Hammered by rising fuel costs, debt, and slumping passenger loads, America West went bankrupt in 1991. It survived to continue flying as a somewhat smaller and (one hopes) smarter carrier, though in the year 2000 it gained an unenviable reputation for shoddy maintenance that gave its fleet one of the worst on-time records in the industry.

Western Airlines in the mid-1950s bragged of its "Californian," a nonstop flight that featured "champagne and all-luxury service" between Seattle and Los Angeles. At no extra fare it offered "sparkling vintage champagne, filet mignon dinner or sirloin de Lesseps luncheon, reserved seats, super-pressurized DC-6Bs, and an orchid for the ladies!"[11] Other airlines of the time provided equally classy touches of their own. Alas, such amenities are gone today, at least for economy-class passengers, and not even in first class do ladies get a complimentary orchid. Such service was another casualty of deregulation.

Though lower prices tended to prevail on major routes after 1978, for most flyers the service standards of major airlines became comparable to those on long-distance buses. And as flight delays became common, Americans were increasingly likely to revile and scorn the airlines. On any given day at the start of the twenty-first century, a mass of travelers crowded into terminals and onto planes, and pushed the limits of civilized behavior—or went beyond, as violent incidents of "air rage" attested. Long-distance bus travel that I experienced in years gone by was far better than this.

It might be worth recalling the words of the *Seattle Times* when Boeing Field was dedicated in 1929, that "the future of aviation rests upon the ground. It is on the ground that every device of aeronautics must be planned and perfected." The newspaper noted that "aviation cannot be sustained by air alone."[12] Indeed, the miserably overcrowded airport facilities in so many places at the start of the new millennium make that observation the essence of wisdom.

Just as events in the West played a major role in regulation of the airlines in 1937 and in their deregulation forty years later, so it did in defining the nation's aviation landscape. On the ground in the late 1920s was the Grand Central Air Terminal built in Glendale, once the main airport for Los Angeles. Its Mediterranean-style architecture illustrated how such structures could be beautiful as well as functional. (Alas, suburban housing covers the site of the classy Glendale terminal today.)

All airports of the West had in common that they homogenized the landscape surrounding their terminals. Of course, they had to remove obstructions to safe flight, and that generally meant leveling acres of land that they then interlaced with runways. However, the earliest airports typically consisted of little more than a grassy field and a few hangers, all located close to the heart of the city. Waiting travelers assembled in the lobby of a downtown hotel or ticket office, and airlines would drive them to the flying field—in many cases to the door of their waiting plane. They walked across a short section of turf and shook hands with the pilot before climbing aboard and taking a seat, often a lightweight wicker chair.

With the arrival in the mid-1930s of the DC-3, which required long and hard-surfaced runways for takeoff and landing, the 1,500-foot strips of cinders or gravel that typified flying fields of old were no longer adequate. Like the well-known relationship between modern computer hardware and software, as planes grew bigger and their flights more frequent, airports struggled to became more capacious to handle the load. They had to level more acres of ground and build larger terminals. But can any post–World War II airport landscapes, as distinct from the streamlined planes that use them, ever be made visually appealing? Certainly the terminals are functional, but they are seldom really eye-catching—though the newly opened one at the Denver International Airport is a striking exception.

Designers of the Denver terminal wanted to create a landmark as distinctive as Golden Gate Bridge of San Francisco or the Gateway Arch of Saint Louis. To achieve that goal, architect Curt Fentress created a structure defined by thirty-four white Teflon-coated fabric peaks that mimicked Colorado's dramatic mountain landscape visible in the distance on a clear day. It certainly made a dramatic entrance to the Mile-High City. The Denver International Airport opened on February 28, 1995, after a two-year delay caused in part by a balky automatic baggage system. Covering an impressive fifty-three square miles, it was at the time the largest airport on earth. Also among the ranks of the nation's "jumbo" airports was the Dallas–Fort Worth facility dedicated in September 1973: it covered an area nearly the size of Manhattan Island.

Apart from Denver, Dallas-Fort Worth, and Kansas City International, only a handful of wholly new airports were built after World War II to serve cities of the West. Until Los Angeles International Airport opened in December 1946, several different airports, including Grand Central at Glendale and United Airport at Burbank, met the city's needs. The new Seattle-Tacoma International Airport was officially dedicated July 9, 1949. Until then, close-in Boeing Field served the Emerald City. In many other cases, existing flying fields, some of which originated as military facilities, expanded after they became public airfields during the years since 1945.

Another ground-based necessity that made air travel possible was the evolving system of navigation (at least it was ground-based until satellites offered a new way to navigate), and once again the West led the way. The nation's first lighted airway opened in 1923 across the relatively level terrain separating Chicago and Cheyenne. Ultimately some 900 "air lighthouses" defined a 2,700-mile airway that extended across the continent from Newark to Oakland. Air corridors defined by visual contact with beacons and other landmarks gave way in the late 1920s and early 1930s to electronic ones defined by electronic signals beamed from ground stations; and the newest corridors, unlike the original ones, were usable in all weather.

Instruments for night flying were soon perfected, as were safer ways to land planes in foggy conditions. "Even today the air transport plane is in closer touch with its ground terminals and stations through the use of radio than is the railroad train," one observer noted in 1930.[13] At the airports, signal lights replaced hand signals and flags used to guide traffic along runways.

Control of air traffic, originally an airline responsibility, gravitated to federal officials beginning at the Newark, Chicago, and Cleveland airports in 1936. But once planes left their defined airspace, the pilots controlled navigation. Starting in 1941, the Civil Aeronautics Authority set up an Air Traffic Control Division to make the invisible skyways safer; but across most parts of the United States, the pilots themselves remained in control of where they flew. By the 1950s if they flew south of Washington, D.C., or west of Chicago, modern radio signals permitted them to deviate from established airways to find better flying weather or take aerial shortcuts if visibility permitted.

As long as the nation's skies remained uncrowded, the loose system of visual rules worked well. It was over the Grand Canyon on June 30, 1956, that it resulted in disaster. The pilots of a United Air Lines DC-7 and a TWA Super Constellation both spied a large hole in the clouds and maneuvered their planes to give passengers on the transcontinental flights a better look at one of the West's best-known natural wonders (TWA once billed itself as "The Scenic Transcontinental Route" and bragged that only its planes flew over Grand Canyon, the Painted Desert, and Boulder Dam). What the pilots did not see was one another, and 128 passengers and crew died in the resulting midair collision.

Federal officials hastened to install more long-range radar, and Congress passed the Federation Aviation Act of 1958, which transferred responsibility for air safety from the Commerce Department to the Federal Aviation Administration. Later the National Transportation Safety Board gained responsibility for investigating air accidents. Prior to the 1958 legislation, Uncle Sam assumed control only of flights above 9,500 feet within a triangle defined by Washington, New York, and Chicago.

Another horrific midair collision between a United DC-8 and a TWA Super Constellation on December 16, 1960, rained debris and 139 bodies into the streets of Brooklyn and prompted federal officials to implement additional regulations to ensure the safety of the skies. Uncle Sam had long been responsible for making sure that airliners were airworthy, but now his ground controllers insisted on policing all airspace from takeoff to landing, with another set of controllers directing airplanes on the ground at main airports. Airline pilots were now required to fly by instrument flight rules even across clear skies.

Federal officials mandated additional safety measures as the need arose. On May 7, 1964, a crazed passenger shot the cockpit crew of a Pacific Air Lines, which until then had never suffered a fatal accident, causing the F-27 to crash near San Francisco and kill all forty-four people aboard. At that time the Federal Aviation Administration ordered all cockpit doors locked during flight. No longer would pilots invite children to help them "fly the plane."

✤ ✤ ✤

The defining event in the history of commercial aviation across the West since World War II has been deregulation and its unintended consequences. For railroads, that same span of time was marked by the unpleasant consequences of continued regulation in an ever more competitive environment, followed by deregulation and all the challenges that posed. The continued decline of passenger traffic and the mergers that resulted in industry-wide consolidation into a handful of mega-railroad systems form a large part of the story too.

Twelve

Reinventing the Railroads

In the Indiana town our family called home in the 1950s, I enjoyed a front row seat alongside several evolving transportation landscapes of the postwar era. At the far edge of our backyard ran the twin tracks of the Pennsylvania Railroad, which formed my personal "metropolitan corridor." Every day passenger trains sprinted past my bedroom window on their way to New York or Saint Louis and also to Washington, Pittsburgh, and Columbus. One favorite was "The Jeffersonian." The name of the all-coach, reserved-seat streamliner sounded impressive, although only many years later did I fully appreciate the word play between the surname of the third president and a train intended to cater to the financial prudence of the common man (and woman). Another posh train was the all-Pullman "Spirit of St. Louis."

Every evening around dinnertime, a long mail train lumbered past. It bore no name, and few riders peered out of the windows of the ancient coach that brought up the rear. But the Railway Post Office never failed to impress me, and on a ledge above the computer where now I type these words sits a model of that type of car. Its dark Tuscan red paint and the word "Pennsylvania" lettered in gold evoke pleasant memories of those Indiana evenings at trackside.

On my tenth birthday in March 1955, at least seven passenger trains were scheduled to pass through Greenfield in each direction. Preserved copies of the *Official Guide* list "The Indianapolis Limited," pulling a heavy string of sleeping cars between New York, Washington, and the Hoosier State capital, in addition to "The Allegheny," "The St. Louisan," "The American," and, of course, the flagship Spirit of St. Louis. The cars on most trains wore the railroad's familiar maroon paint,

but one speedster called the "Penn Texas" carried in addition several sleeping cars of the Missouri Pacific, Missouri-Kansas-Texas, and Frisco lines. These had originated in New York City and would continue beyond Saint Louis to San Antonio, Houston, or El Paso aboard the "Texas Special" or the "Texas Eagle." Those three Texas destinations, together with New York City, effectively defined the extreme geographical limits of my boyhood dreams.[1]

One block north of our Greenfield home ran U.S. Route 40, which, as I recall from a sixth-grade class in Indiana history, had many years earlier been the way west for travelers using this portion of the original National Road from Cumberland, Maryland, to Vandalia, Illinois (and on to Saint Louis). In the opening years of the twentieth century, Greenfield's main street carried the newly laid tracks of an interurban railroad reaching east

The Indianapolis bus station that I remember as a child.
Photographer Esther Bubly recorded one of the old-style buses that
drivers called a "dive bomber." This one belonged to Pennsylvania
Greyhound, a carrier partially owned by the Pennsylvania Railroad.
Clearly visible in the asphalt pavement are short sections of the
former electric interurban railway tracks. Courtesy
Library of Congress.

from the center of the state at Indianapolis. At one time it was possible to board the electric cars of the Terre Haute, Indianapolis & Eastern Traction Company and ride them all the way to Dayton, Ohio. They sparked through Greenfield and along that portion of the old National Road for a final time in early January 1932, shortly after the company merged with a mixed bag of struggling interurban lines that grandiloquently called itself the Indiana Railroad System.

On Terre Haute, Indianapolis & Eastern tracks, it had once been possible to make the twenty-mile trip from Greenfield to Indianapolis in 54 minutes. I walked past what remained of the one-time interurban depot every school day, and we lived only a couple of blocks from the former car shops, though I did not recognize either place for what it originally was until many years later.

The Pennsylvania's passenger trains no longer stopped regularly in Greenfield after the summer of 1951. When my mother wanted to take me shopping at one of the big department stores in Indianapolis, which was always an important occasion for both of us, we boarded the motor coaches of Central Swallow Lines. The Indianapolis bus station seemed cavernous because an arched roof more massive than any I had ever seen spanned the boarding area. Another source of youthful wonderment in that place were the rails that shone through worn areas of the asphalt. Later I learned that these were the remnants of a network of interurban lines that fanned out from Indianapolis, the onetime hub of the most extensive traction system in the United States. The Indianapolis Traction and Terminal Company in 1904 erected a tall office building and an adjoining train shed covering nine tracks. It hardly seemed possible, in the 1950s, that just a few years earlier four hundred interurban cars had arrived and departed from the facility each day.

A highway habitat called Route 40 connected Greenfield with Indianapolis. It was a busy corridor in pre-Interstate days. Every day I walked parallel to it through the center of Greenfield on my way to and from school. Along Route 40 a couple of blocks from our house stood a small brick Standard Oil (of Indiana) gas station, complete with outdoor grease pit. On the other side of town was a glitzy station that belonged to the Hoosier Pete chain. Gradually I came to understand that the architecture and function of gas stations, motels, and restaurants, three prime components of the highway landscape, were always in flux—just like that of bus and train stations and airports.

Then there was the road itself. Running north from Greenfield at a right angle to Route 40 was Indiana Highway 9. Compared to the three and four lanes of the federal highway that were always crowded with traffic, the state road was unimpressive. It was a run-of-the-mill two-lane highway—except now I realize there is no such thing as a "run-of-the-mill" highway. The physical appearance of a road or highway reflects the civil engineering know-how at a particular time, and not just its surfacing materials but also the width of its right-of-way; style of guardrails and bridge abutments; and location of ditches, telephone poles, fences, and even signage. Roadside landscaping became more important during the 1920s and 1930s, and unsightly billboards were a big concern in the 1960s, though in some states new ones keep accreting all the time. Signs put up in the 1920s and 1930s by the Burma-Vita Company of Minneapolis invariably included bits of folksy verse spaced at close intervals along the road with the tagline "Burma-Shave," but these odd missives disappeared because modern automobiles traveled much too fast to permit motorists to read them. It is too bad the same cannot be said for the obtrusive billboards today.

Along Indiana 9 my parents referred to one crossroads location as "Deadman's Corner." It conjured up terror for a youngster. I almost expected to see a skeleton come dancing into our headlights; and the memory of a driver, probably drunk, sideswiping our big Hudson near there one night only added to my motoring malaise at the time. Later I realized how the ongoing task of removing dangerous intersections and curves helped to reshape the highway landscape. It was along Indiana 9 that I first saw Highway Post Office buses whoosh through the night, their interior lights blazing like those of the nocturnal mail trains that thundered past our house. After discontinuance of the railway and highway post offices in the 1970s, mail delivery seemed far more prosaic.

All in all, central Indiana in the 1950s was a good place to nurture a fascination for various modes of transportation and how they affected the surrounding landscape—and people's travel habits and pocketbooks. But how could I know in the mid-1950s that my favorite railroad already suffered from an insidious form of corporate dry rot? I was not alone in my overestimation of the once-great Pennsy. I later learned that when a kindly Greenfield banker wanted to reward his housekeeper for years of faithful service, he set aside shares of Pennsylvania common stock for her retirement. It was a good investment for widows and orphans, people said in those days, because by the 1950s the railroad had paid regular dividends for more than a century. Alas, that changed.

The Pennsylvania Railroad merged with long-time rival New York Central in the late 1960s, but a few months later their ungainly union known as Penn Central declared bankruptcy, an unthinkable event that shocked corporate America—and the widows and orphans especially. All along the former main line through Greenfield, weeds sprouted between the rails and ties rotted from lack of maintenance. Tracks grew so rough and uneven that Amtrak gave up running a passenger train on them in 1979. They are completely gone today.

I mention these personal recollections because they invariably shape how I think about transportation landscapes of the twentieth century. Perhaps the subject fascinates me so much because it embodies elements of a good morality tale.[2] That is, because of changing technology no less than management miscalculation, proud and mighty carriers of one era may be mendicants in another, if they survive at all. The transportation landscape is forever in flux, as rails shining through worn spots in the blacktop at the old Indianapolis bus station ("Traction Terminal") reminded me as a child.

There is one constant, however, and that is mobility. Commentators have often noted how restless we Americans are, both individually and collectively. Our love of mobility is a manifestation of national restlessness as is our enduring love affair with the automobile, the true techno-logical embodiment of that national character trait. In the post–World War II era, the quest for personal mobility led more Americans than ever to switch from passenger trains, even the fastest and most luxurious ones, to automobiles for their great flexibility, and to airplanes for their great speed.

By 1950 the passenger train was already in serious trouble. Like a tree disease that began innocently enough with a few dead leaves but ulti-mately killed the elms and chestnuts that once shaded the nation's main streets, this trend was noted first in remote corners of the United States and Canada in the 1920s. Three decades later, after a period of dormancy during the bustling days of World War II, the malaise spread to the largest cities and the busiest stations.

During the twentieth century, few if any organizations had more at stake in the future prosperity of passenger trains than the American Asso-ciation of Passenger Traffic Officers. That organization in the 1950s could legitimately claim to rank as one of the oldest business associations in the United States, if not the oldest. It traced its lineage back to the Convention of General Ticket Agents held in Pittsburgh on March 13, 1855, for the purpose of "agreeing upon a uniform system of adjusting all matters con-nected with through ticketing."[3]

Outsiders would likely consider "ticketing" to be a mind-numbing subject. For the rest of the nineteenth century, their annual meetings dealt mainly with arcane matters relating to issuing and collecting tickets—such as how to keep cheaters, both passengers and a few sticky-fingered ticket agents and conductors, from stealing money rightfully belonging to a railroad. The gathering held in Louisville, Kentucky, in 1874 was typi-cal. The ticket experts discussed "rates, rates, and nothing but rates." However, at their 1901 gathering in Asheville, North Carolina, the orga-nization did an uncharacteristic thing by seeking to predict the future of the American passenger train in 1955, the year the group expected to celebrate its golden anniversary.

Their anointed prophet was General Passenger Agent John Francis of the Chicago, Burlington & Quincy. Standing before his colleagues, he began by observing that the number of railroad passengers in the United States had climbed from 37 million in 1859 to 537 million in 1899. Given that the number of railroad passengers was likely to march in lockstep with the expanding population of the nation, his prognostications re-flected the rosy outlook of the industry at the start of the new century.

For the coming years, Francis envisioned good highways and "com-paratively noiseless, smooth running" motor vehicles, but for them to compete successfully with railroads for long-distance travel "is too fanciful to prophesy." On the other hand, he continued, it did not require "a wild flight of imagination to see that the motor and the improvement of American roads may bring about a change in the manner of travel for short distances—and may it not be that when we arrive at our one hundredth anniversary we shall find motor carriages competing with the railroads in local passenger business." As for airplanes posing a competitive threat in 1955, Francis (two years before the first successful flight of the Wright brothers) asserted that "the flying machine will probably have made but little more progress than (it has) in the last fifty years, and we need have no fear of competition from airlines."[4]

How ironic that 1955, the golden anniversary of the American Association of Passenger Traffic Officers, saw the emergence of a trio of newcomers as the nation's top passenger carriers. In descending order, the nation's Big Three were American Airlines, United Airlines, and Eastern Airlines. During the decade that followed World War II, the traditional Big Three had been the Pennsylvania, the New York Central, and the Santa Fe railroads, followed in descending order by the Southern Pacific and the Union Pacific. By 1955 the Pennsylvania and New York Central railroads had slipped to the fourth and fifth rungs respectively, and it was up, up, and away for the airlines.[5]

The ranking of the nation's top passenger carriers was only one measure of the tidal wave of change that washed over the railroad industry during the 1950s. It might be argued that two decades, the 1950s and the 1920s, witnessed the most far-reaching changes in the twentieth century in terms of transportation. Maybe the impact was not as great as the revolution wrought by motor vehicles and improved roads during the 1920s, but events during the 1950s permanently reshaped the railroad industry across the West. Apart from longsuffering passengers and crew who sensed that "this train's got the disappearing railroad blues"—an apt description used in Steve Goodman's popular song "The City of New Orleans"—a sense of malaise also prevailed in the nation's rail freight yards, where the impact of intercity trucks was felt keenly. The recession of 1957–58 showed just how grim life had become for American railroads.

Perhaps the main bright spot at the time was the industry's nearly complete transition from steam to diesel locomotives, with the internal combustion technology offering much greater operating efficiency and much-needed trimming of costs. Even so, it was sad to watch steam engines, many still in their prime, shuffle off by the thousands to scrap yards. The railroad landscape minus hissing steam, billowing clouds of smoke, and massive drivewheels and clanking siderods never looked, sounded, or smelled the same. Even now the acrid-sweet smell of coal smoke transports me back to trackside in Greenfield, where as a boy in the 1950s I witnessed the passing parade of the Pennsylvania Railroad's finest steam locomotives.

★ ★ ★

American railroads ended World War II with high hopes for the future of long-distance passenger service. The millions of dollars they invested in streamlined trains during the late 1940s testify to their postwar optimism. However, with the advantage that hindsight confers, we can now see that during the ten years from 1947 to 1957 the railroads of the United States were locked in a struggle they could not possibly win. In later years critics accused rail executives of trying to exit the passenger business, but that was an unfair assessment of their renewed commitment during the decade after 1945.

Railroads of the West worked hard to lure a new generation of travelers aboard their best streamliners with clever innovations. Among these were dome cars, nicknamed "penthouses on wheels," from which passengers could survey the passing landscape from a new perspective. First introduced in regular train service by the Chicago, Burlington & Quincy in the late 1940s, dome cars won extensive positive publicity after the California Zephyr commenced service in late March 1949 between Chicago, Denver, Salt Lake City and Oakland (San Francisco via ferry) along 2,532 miles of track owned by three railroad companies: the Burlington; the Denver & Rio Grande Western; and the Western Pacific.

The luxury train carried more than 82,000 passengers during the first six months of operation. Observers uniformly attributed its great popularity to Vista-Dome cars that afforded passengers unobstructed views of the West. From their "grandstand seat" in the Vista-Domes, Zephyr passengers could observe the scenic wonders of their curving route through the canyon of the Feather River, a distance of 120 miles through the Sierras of California. In addition, through passengers enjoyed viewing the multicolored canyons of the Colorado Rockies by daylight.

Dome cars really came into their own in the mid-1950s when it could be said that "the handful of 'dome' passenger cars in service on American railroads can no longer be brushed off as fads."[6] Rail executives firmly believed that dome cars increased passenger business. Every western transcontinental railroad had several such cars in operation on its premier trains by 1955. Northern Pacific added domes to its North Coast Limited in 1954 and to the popular "Traveler's Rest" lounge car the following year.

Another innovation of that era was the economy sleeper that the Pullman and Budd companies introduced to solve the dilemma of sparsely occupied coach and sleeper space. "Slumbercoaches" appeared on the Burlington's Denver Zephyr in the fall of 1955 and the North Coast Limited in 1959. By paying a modest supplement to coach fares, their passengers could travel in a private room that featured both bed and bathroom facilities. The economy rooms were tiny, to be sure, but they were comfortable. And at a time when passengers still lit up cigarettes freely in

The cover of a Great Northern Railway brochure issued in the early 1960s served to highlight passenger amenities, including the full-length domes of the "Empire Builder." Author's collection.

coaches, economy bedrooms offered a pleasant haven from second-hand smoke.

In addition to dome cars and economy sleepers, American railroads in the mid-1950s experimented with several entirely new breeds of trains. For a time there was something truly new under the sun for railroad passengers. Among the unconventional conveyances was "Train X," one-third lighter than conventional trains; the "Talgo Train," a Spanish design; and General Motors' "Aerotrain," an ultra-lightweight contender using coach bodies that closely resembled intercity buses, and that for a brief time showed the most promise. Union Pacific experimented with "Aerotrain" in 1956–57, operating it between Los Angeles and Las Vegas as the City of Las Vegas. Rail officials awaited public response with an air of expectancy, but this time neither new equipment nor new trains lured many passengers back for the long term. The problems confronting the rail industry were both specific and systemic: while many passengers complained about the bumpy and noisy ride aboard the lightweight cars of "Aerotrain," many more quit riding trains altogether.

Many young Americans never started riding trains. Ever since the early 1930s, railroad passenger officers had warned that the younger generation did not have "the same degree of fear that some of the rest of us have or have had as to traveling in an airplane."[7] Nor did most of them have any love for trains. Many younger Americans had never ridden a passenger train. It simply did not appeal to them, much as travel by horse and buggy did not appeal to modern motorists.

When the respected editor of *Trains* magazine, David P. Morgan, spoke to the 1958 interim conference of the American Association of Passenger Traffic Officers, he amplified the generational theme: "I am disturbed by my observation that elderly people ride your Pullmans, that the rank and file are surprised if one does not arrive by car or plane, and that a generation of Americans is—for the first time in railroad history—totally unfamiliar with the passenger train." Morgan suggested, perhaps half in jest, that the century-old group should rename itself "The Society for the Preservation of the Passenger Train"; and he chided them by observing that "too many railroads, echoing a monopoly that died with the pneumatic tire, would rather squabble with each other over a dime's worth of rail-bound business than unite in a bid for the deluge of travel dollars that never come to Union Station."[8]

Morgan urged American railroads to make the passenger train a popular topic of conversation once again, as happened in the 1930s when people flocked to depots and grade crossing to catch a glimpse of the Zephyr or the M-10000 as they flashed by—something that late model DC-7s and Constellations did in subsequent years—and also the Scenicruisers, the streamlined double-deck buses Greyhound introduced in the 1950s. To be blunt about it, American passenger trains by the mid-1950s lacked "sex appeal." In the words of Pierre Martineau, director of research for the *Chicago Tribune,* who spoke to the 1955 gathering of the

Railroads may have advertised less than the airline industry in the 1960s, but many of their promotional brochures were still quite attractive. The Atchison, Topeka & Santa Fe Railway System issued this one in 1963 to highlight travel aboard a fleet of streamliners that included "The Chief," "Super Chief," "San Francisco Chief," "Texas Chief," and "Kansas City Chief." Author's collection.

American Association of Passenger Traffic Officers, "Your biggest competition comes from the auto industry and the airlines. Both are very active in creating color and buying excitement."[9]

Survey research revealed that practically all travelers responded favorably to "airline hostesses," added Martineau. But with regard to railroad conductors, over half of all people polled were neutral or negative in their responses. "Grumpy conductors in contrast to airline hostesses are a distinct liability," he warned. With the exception of a few outstanding streamliners, he asserted, the aura of romance and glamour had passed from railroad to the airlines.[10]

Among the improvements that Pullman introduced in the latest generation of sleeping cars it delivered to railroads in the mid-1950s was a new type of roomette that featured a cutaway bed. This permitted any passengers needing to use their in-room toilet in the middle of the night to lower or raise the bed without having to stand outside in a public walkway in their pajamas or underwear (perish the thought). Its most modern open-section sleepers featured handy folding ladders that permitted passengers to reach or leave upper berths without ringing for a porter. Still other Pullman improvements included vitreous china washbowls, circulating ice water, ceramic tile floors, and "rubber topped mattresses developed by The Pullman Company after many years of tests."[11] But did railroaders seriously believe that rubber-topped mattresses or any other of Pullman's modest enhancements really generated new business? To repeat what outside speakers tried to explain to the American Association of Passenger Traffic Officers in the 1950s, modern passenger trains lacked "sex appeal."

Railroads suffered from lack of a positive image in the eyes of most Americans in part because they no longer had a great desire to reach out to the traveling public in a highly visible way. The rail industry in 1968 purchased a mere 20 pages of advertising space in the *New York Times,* for example, compared to 791 pages purchased by the airlines.

⚜ ⚜ ⚜

During the nationwide recession of 1957–58, freight car loadings and revenues dwindled too, and employment in the industry shrank to the lowest level yet recorded in the twentieth century. What made the latest bad news especially disheartening was that between the end of 1945 and the end of 1951 the largest (Class I) railroads had spent $1.4 billion, an all-time record, to buy new equipment, including 84,000 freight cars and 3,500 locomotives, nearly all of them of the diesel type, and to modernize their physical plants. That bundle of money enabled them to increase carrying capacity and improve operating efficiency, despite a skimpy return on invested capital. They raised many of their improvement dollars through borrowing or by using working capital piled up during the wartime crush, though their cash reserves were now running dangerously low.

The volume of freight traffic dropped sharply in the late 1950s and remained down for another decade. While trains carried almost half of the nation's freight in 1955 (49.5 percent), fifteen years later they hauled a little more than one third (37.5 percent). The decline was worse for railroads of the Northeast than for those of the South and West. In fact, total rail traffic across the West more than doubled between 1955 and 1980, in large measure due to movement of commodities, though it remained depressed in the Northeast, where industrial decline resulted in a number of closed factories.

The recession of 1957–58 was partially to blame for rail industry woes, but at much the same time, the nation's growing fleet of over-the-road trucks gained a major advantage with the expanding superhighway system. World War I has been described as the cradle from which the intercity trucking industry sprang in the 1920s. During that formative decade over-the-road trucks only got bigger and longer. Pneumatic tires, first offered as optional equipment on trailers in the mid-1920s, further encouraged intercity expansion. But it was World War II that gave the industry its biggest boost, particularly when it encouraged use of large tractor-trailer combinations that eventually came to rule the interstates. As recently as 1929, America's railroads accounted for nearly 75 percent of all intercity ton-miles of freight.

In addition, the problems created by falling numbers of passengers only went from bad to worse as the railroad industry's deficit climbed to an alarming $723 million a year in 1957. For financially ailing railroads, the passenger losses became an intolerable burden, and especially so when freight revenues no longer covered them. For railroads, the one bright spot amidst the gloom was a surge in piggyback freight service.

During the recession of 1958 it was not just passenger trains but entire railroads that were at risk. Some of them were in worse financial shape even than at the depths of the Great Depression. By February 1958, 45 of 114 Class I railroads operated in the red and thus failed to earn enough money even to cover the interest on their debts. Industry giants like Pennsylvania and New York Central struggled to remain solvent. The 1950s turned out to be one of the most traumatic decades in the history of American railroads. But worse was yet to come.

❧ ❧ ❧

With the exception of four war years—1942 to 1945—the ratio of passenger-train revenues to expenses had recorded an industry-wide loss every year since 1930, although no one could say with confidence just how many dollars were draining away annually. In the late 1940s or early 1950s, railroad executives grew increasingly aware that something had blighted the industry's dreams for postwar passenger train travel. Did the millions of dollars they spent for flashy streamliners and speedy diesel

locomotives really win the traveling public back to the trains? It was not easy to tell, nor was it easy to tell whether passenger trains made money or lost it.

Beginning January 1, 1936, the Interstate Commerce Commission required railroads to separate passenger and freight revenues according to a complex accounting formula that made industry executives increasingly aware of how little passenger service contributed to total corporate income. The Milwaukee Road, for example, reported in 1938 that freight accounted for 83 cents of every income dollar and passenger service for a mere 8 cents. The problem with the ICC accounting formula was that few people in the rail industry really trusted the numbers it generated. The problem even for rail industry veterans was much like standing in a hall filled with smoke and mirrors and trying to make some sense of what you perceived.

Trains magazine argued as early as 1946 that the passenger deficit that year of approximately $140 million was merely "bookkeeping slight of hand," and it repeated the claim over the years. Many people in the industry agreed. Because of apparent flaws in the accounting formula—disparaged by some as nothing but accounting "black magic"—some executives during the years after World War II remained certain that streamliners more than covered their direct costs of operation.

Though the accounting formula suggested that in the aggregate the passenger trains of the United States lost money, some railroaders voiced skepticism. It was true, they conceded, that most local trains lost money, but certainly not streamliners, or at least not the best of them. And even if it could be proved that the finest passenger trains lost money, industry executives remained certain that streamliners had prestige value and that an El Capitan, Empire Builder, or Olympian Hiawatha justified ongoing operation because it generated freight business as well as passenger dollars. That was why it paid to modernize popular long-distance trains.

Alas, confessed the long-time editor of *Trains,* David P. Morgan, at a 1968 meeting of the American Association of Passenger Traffic Officers: "Our dreams came apart, of course, when that deficit shot up over 700 million dollars a year by 1953 and thereafter couldn't be throttled to within much less than 400 million dollars a year; and it is now once again approaching the 500-million-dollar mark. I was once again a poor prophet—along with a few other people—when I concluded the problem, all the problem, was hardware. Briefly, I thought that if we could somehow lower the train's center of gravity, we could also proportionately lower the train's deficit. And so we had Aerotrain, Talgo, Train X, Keystone, etc. et al, and the deficits went right on eating us out of passenger house and home because a few inches of center of gravity more or less didn't affect World War I era work-rules, top heavy terminal costs, or any of the multitude of other non-hardware problems afflicting the passenger train business."[12]

After 1958 a steadily growing number of rail executives came to regard passenger service as an intolerable financial "millstone" about their corporate necks and determined to trim the losses as fast as state and federal regulators permitted. As recently as 1958 the railroads of the United States still operated passenger trains along routes totaling 107,000 miles. By 1970 they had trimmed such service to 49,000 miles of a national rail network that then totaled 206,000 miles. That year the number of intercity passenger trains in the United States had dwindled from a pre–World

War II high of some twenty thousand per day to fewer than four hundred, and many survivors were a disgrace to the industry.

John Stilgoe described travel aboard long distance trains in their heyday as a fantasy experience. By the late 1960s, on a good many trains the fantasy had turned into a nightmare. The once-grand Twentieth Century Limited had quit running altogether, and things got so bad on the Penn Central, the disastrous offspring of a merger made in hell, that thirty-five passengers on the once-deluxe Spirit of St. Louis sat down in front of the train in 1969 until officials made needed repairs to its single coach. The car lacked lighting, air conditioning, and drinking water despite the hundred-degree weather outside.

I myself took the Spirit of St. Louis from Indianapolis to New York in late December 1970 and saw firsthand how bad conditions were. When the train wheezed into Indianapolis Union Station, the decrepit relic of the once-glorious streamliner era consisted of a locomotive and a single coach. At each stop along the way through the night, the conductor or brakeman flipped on the car lights. Perhaps that was required for safety reasons, but it did nothing to aid sleep.

Only adding to the general malaise, a small child on the seat ahead of me wet her diaper and urine ran down into the hot coils of a baseboard steam heater. This added a pungent new aroma to the already stale and musty atmosphere in the car. Boarding a New Haven parlor car for the concluding leg of the trip from New York to Boston, I found it impossible to see out of the windows. Not only were they scratched and dirty, but the railroad had simply covered over several broken ones with sheets of plywood. When I reached Boston, I promptly cancelled the return portion of my rail ticket and booked a flight on American Airlines.

Such horror stories, both personal and those prominently featured in daily newspapers, caused observers to wonder whether the American passenger train was a victim of suicide or murder. Senator George Smathers of Florida pondered aloud during discussion of the abortive Passenger Train Act of 1960: "It's sort of a question which comes first, the chicken or the egg, and we are not quite certain whether some of the passenger loss results from bad service or whether the passenger loss then results in the deterioration of cars and so on."[13]

Evidence is mixed, but one thing is clear: the federal government must take partial responsibility for the near-death of the long-distance passenger train. During the crucial years from World War II to 1978, Congress provided $103 billion in subsidies to highway users, $31 billion to air, and only $6 billion to rail.

The future looked especially grim to assembled members of the American Association of Passenger Traffic Officers. "Fascinating though the

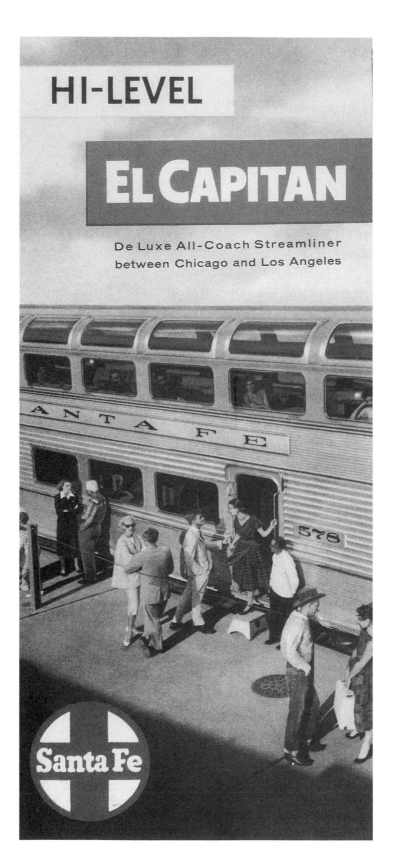

HI-LEVEL

EL CAPITAN

De Luxe All-Coach Streamliner
between Chicago and Los Angeles

Santa Fe

The Santa Fe, unlike the struggling Penn Central, maintained a fleet of high quality streamliners until the day Amtrak took over in 1971. For years a worthy companion train to its "Chief" streamliners was the all-coach "El Capitan," which, as depicted in this 1957 brochure, featured a set of deluxe and innovative "high-level" cars. The railroad advertised "dining penthouse style" and promised passengers "soft music, magnificent views, and of course, tempting Fred Harvey dishes—all high above the noise of the kitchen below." Author's collection.

INTERCITY RAILROAD PASSENGER ROUTES
National Railroad Passenger Corporation

The skeletal route Amtrak proposed to operate on May 1, 1971, the day it took over most intercity passenger train service across the United States. In the West, the Denver & Rio Grande Western declined to participate, and thus the map is incorrect for the line between Denver and Salt Lake City. For several years, the Amtrak trains followed the original Overland Route through southern Wyoming instead. Author's collection.

history of your organization is," remarked Eldon Martin, vice president and general counsel of the Burlington, "I cannot escape the strong feeling that a sense of destiny overshadows this 1968 meeting. I suspect that at few times in your 113 years—if, indeed, at any time—have so many members of our industry and of the public been so interested in what the future may hold for railroad passenger service." He warned: "Make no mistake about it, the passenger problem is one of the most troublesome our industry faces, or ever has faced."[14]

Long-distance passenger trains would probably have vanished along with the overland stagecoach but for creation of the National Railroad Passenger Corporation. Popularly known as Amtrak (from *Am*erican *tra*vel by trac*k*), the federally supported agency commenced operation in

1971 with $40 million in direct government grants, $100 million in government guaranteed loans, and another $200 million from railroads buying into the system. Twenty railroads turned over their passenger operations to Amtrak and paid fees over a three-year period equivalent to 50 percent of each company's 1969 passenger service deficit.

When its wheels began to turn at 12:01 a.m., May 1, 1971, Amtrak preserved fewer than two hundred daily trains on a nationwide passenger network that in a single day shriveled from 43,000 route miles to 16,000. Amtrak initially hauled an average of only 45,000 passengers a day, or approximately half of one percent of all intercity travelers in the United States. Apart from the well-trafficked Northeast Corridor running between Washington and Boston, the nation's long-distance passenger trains continued on life support after 1971, their heavy losses subsidized by American taxpayers, most of whom had never ridden a train.

❧ ❧ ❧

The disappearing passenger train during the second half of the twentieth century was but one act in an ongoing drama that saw railroads of the West essentially reinvent themselves. First, there came their dramatic conversion from steam to diesel power in the 1940s and 1950s. A big selling point for diesels was that they did not have to pause for water, in contrast to ever-thirsty steam locomotives; and unlike steamers, which lost efficiency in cold weather, they worked as well in winter as summer. Diesel locomotives, in addition, did not need to be changed frequently on long runs; they stopped and started more quickly, required less maintenance, and were far more reliable. Diesels could run five or six hundred miles between refueling, compared to only a hundred miles or so typical for steam locomotives. For these reasons they cost about a third less than steam power to operate.

The technological revolution had major social consequences both for train crews and for residents of trackside communities. Conversion to diesel power changed the railroad landscape as railroads trimmed expenses by abandoning hundreds of watering towers across the United States. Diesel locomotives decreased and then eliminated the need for thousands of firemen. The new technology and accompanying changes in union work rules not only reduced the number of rail employees, but the diesel's ability to make long runs without pausing for service or to change crews rendered many railroad towns of the West obsolete.

The physical appearance of long freight trains that rumbled across the West changed too, and not just on the head end. Cabooses became a rarity by the end of the 1980s. A modest-sized recording device and a flashing red light replaced most of them after a study in 1987 indicated that end-of-train devices were as safe as cabooses and could save railroads considerable money. Likewise gone were the once-familiar slat-sided stock cars

Salida, Colorado, when cattle still traveled to market by rail.
Courtesy Colorado Historical Society.

that hauled bawling herds of cattle to market. As late as 1969 the railroads of the United States still operated more than 15,000 stock cars, but only a decade later those were a rarity.

The old-fashioned boxcar seemed headed for the scrap yards too, as more and more freight rode in intermodal containers of various sizes and configurations, including semitrailers. Gone even earlier were crates of household goods and other kinds of less-than-carload freight, a category of cargo that decreased from 51 million tons in 1919 to 1.4 million in

1965 before disappearing entirely. Moving vans and the familiar United Parcel Service trucks offered the convenience of door-to-door service that railroads could not match.

In 1966 railroad freight traffic in the United States (in ton-miles) amounted to roughly twice that hauled in 1916, but it had dropped from 77 percent to less than 43 percent of the total intercity freight movement. Its competitors included river and canal barges, pipelines, and especially intercity trucks. Railroads battled back with unit trains that hauled nothing but grain or coal, and by 1980 an estimated 60 percent of all grain in the United States went by rail. Until the 1960s, the grain had typically been hauled in boxcars. Now it traveled in covered hoppers.

Most of what freight trains now carry across the West consists of new automobiles, merchandise in double-stacked containers, and bulky commodities like lumber, grain, and coal, much of it traveling in single-purpose unit trains. Ironically, an increasing volume of the railroads' transcontinental freight might once have gone via the Panama Canal, but it returned to the rails because the largest container ships could not fit through the locks. The "double stack" cars of the 1980s hauled containers lifted off ships at West Coast ports to inland centers for final distribution by truck.

The most dramatic development of recent times was the increased coal traffic handled by western railroads starting in the early 1970s. For both Union Pacific and Burlington Northern, the low-sulfur coal they hauled from Wyoming and Montana soon accounted for a bigger percentage of their annual incomes than any other commodity. As a result of the energy boom of the 1970s and 1980s, both Union Pacific and Burlington Northern laid hundreds of miles of new track across Wyoming's Powder River Basin. Not since before World War I had any area of the United States witnessed such a boom in rail construction.

Coal traffic boomed too. By the mid-1990s, eighteen Powder River Basin coal mines produced almost 300 million tons of black diamonds annually, a jump from just 3 million tons in 1970. In some places, recently built rail lines had to be expanded to three or four tracks to handle the swelling flow of coal headed to distant power plants and other markets. Much of the Wyoming and Montana coal traveled in unit trains owned by utility companies themselves that were shuttled back and forth between market and mine.

During the 1980s concrete crossties began to replace wooden ones on some heavily trafficked lines. Across the West, welded rails and concrete ties gave even the right-of-way a new look—and sound. Welded rails eliminated the "clickty-clack" of car wheels crossing numerous joints between short sections of rail. The heavier freight loads meant that track had to be redesigned to carry more weight at the expense of express-train speeds. One way to do that was to flatten the elevation of the outer rail on curves, though this forced many of Amtrak's long-distance passenger trains to operate at far slower speeds than was typical in earlier years.

Western Pacific
SUPPORTS
Santa Fe control

Western Pacific
OPPOSES
Southern Pacific control

Railroads of the West jockeyed for position as the merger game heated up and pitted one company against another. This brochure from 1960 makes the Western Pacific's preference unmistakably clear. Given the sentiments expressed here, it is ironic that the Western Pacific, once a key component of George Gould's dream of a transcontinental railroad, ended up as part of the Union Pacific, an empire that later included the Southern Pacific. Author's collection.

No less dramatic than the evolution of the rail landscape was the process of consolidation and pruning whereby strong railroads of the West grew stronger, and the weak ones withered and died or merged with larger ones. This process redefined the industry and redrew the rail map during three decades beginning in 1970. That year the first of the West's megamergers, the union of the historic "Hill Lines"—Great Northern, Northern Pacific, and Chicago, Burlington & Quincy—gave rise to Burlington

Northern, then the longest railroad in the United States. Also occurring in historic 1970 was the bankruptcy of Penn Central.

Burlington Northern was a strong railroad from the beginning, a combination greater than the sum of its parts; but after the shocking collapse of Penn Central in the biggest business failure in American history at that time, it became common to speak of railroads collectively—which in 1970 included seventy-six Class I railroads—as a "sick industry." Consider that the return on equity of Class I railroads in 1976 was a mere 2.3 percent compared with 13.1 percent for airlines and 14.8 for trucking.

For years the Milwaukee Road had struggled along as the nation's weakest transcontinental line. Its financial troubles, many of them self-inflicted, greatly increased after Burlington Northern emerged as a powerful competitor. The Milwaukee Road's third and final bout of bankruptcy years occurred on December 19, 1977, following three years of heavy losses. Bankruptcy was perhaps inevitable and would no doubt have come sooner had the Milwaukee Road not tapped the resources of its land company. In all, some seven thousand miles of Milwaukee track were pulled up, while many remaining portions of the line were parceled out to Union Pacific and Burlington Northern, or evolved into one of several new short-line railroads. On January 1, 1986, the remaining core mileage of the Milwaukee Road, all located in the Midwest, officially merged into the Canadian-owned Soo Line, and a venerable name in American railroading disappeared.

Events of the 1970s dealt an equally harsh blow to the fabled Chicago, Rock Island & Pacific, which filed for bankruptcy on March 17, 1975. Over the years this 7,000-mile railroad, chartered in 1847, had managed to extend a lightly trafficked network of tracks across fourteen Midwestern states. It was perhaps a miracle that it survived as long as it did. The words of one popular song celebrated the Rock Island Line as a "mighty good road," but in reality it was not and had not been for a good many years. In the public assessment of Transportation Secretary Brock Adams in 1978, the Rock Island was a "walking dead man."[15]

In August 1979, when unionized clerks, brakemen, and conductors demanded more pay from the cash-starved Rock Island, they walked off their jobs and shut down the carrier. That turned out to be forever, because the dead man no longer walked. As an emergency measure, the Interstate Commerce Commission ordered the Kansas City Terminal Railroad, a switching line jointly owned by twelve rail carriers, to take over Rock Island service and operate it on a temporary basis. A year later a federal judge ordered the railroad liquidated. Actually only about a thousand miles of track was pulled up at the time. The bulk of the old Rock Island went to other railroads. Never before in American history had so large a railroad simply gone bankrupt and disappeared. It was the most vivid example yet that the Uncle Sam's power to regulate had become the power to strangle weak members of an industry. The collapse of the Chicago, Rock Island & Pacific, like that of the Milwaukee Road at much the same time, pointed up the need for fundamental changes.

What happened to the Milwaukee Road and the Rock Island was symptomatic of a sick industry that continued to decline. On a good many other struggling railroads, tracks deteriorated because of deferred maintenance, and the number of serious accidents increased, many of them attributed to broken rails or wheels. Something dramatic had to be done to save the rail industry, and that something was deregulation.

A little history is in order here. The Interstate Commerce Law was enacted in 1887. During subsequent years "regulation of the railroads has been extended and broadened until to-day a dual control of the roads may be said to exist consisting of governmental representatives on the one hand and the corporate officers representing the owners of the properties on the other, but with much the greater power vested in the representatives of the Government," complained the *Official Guide of the Railways* in 1932.[16]

A nearly impenetrable mesh of red tape encumbered railroads. The Interstate Commerce Commission required carriers in the 1950s to keep 258 types of records, about five times more than federal regulators then demanded of the airlines. Regulation of the railroads perhaps made some sense in an era of monopoly, but that era was long past by the time World War II ended. After so many years of federal oversight, few people took the idea of rail deregulation seriously. It happened only incrementally. President Gerald Ford signed the Railroad Revitalization and Regulator Reform Act of 1976, which led to creation of the Consolidated Rail Corporation, or Conrail, which would successfully revitalize a collection of bankrupt Northeast railroads, including the old Penn Central.

Congress passed the Motor Carrier Act of 1980, signed into law by President Jimmy Carter. However else history may judge him, Carter should probably be remembered by textbook authors as the nation's deregulation president. The Motor Carrier Act of 1980 promised to phase out a fifty-five-year accretion of regulations and thereby spur greater competition within the intercity trucking industry.

As was true also for airline deregulation, some old-line trucking companies that had thrived in a comfortably regulated environment were forced to scramble for survival by battling a pack of aggressive newcomers. That was not easy. Of the top fifty less-than-truckload carriers operating in 1979, only eight survived fifteen years later. During that same time 11,500 trucking companies disappeared and another 30,000 arose to take their place. Major players included venerable Roadway, a survivor that dated back to 1930, as well as the newly emerged kings of the road J. B. Hunt and Schneider National.

In 1980, the same year Uncle Sam deregulated the trucking industry, Harley O. Staggers Sr., a congressman from Keyser, West Virginia, gave his name to the Staggers Rail Act of 1980, which began the process leading to federal deregulation of the nation's railroads. When President Carter signed that act into law on October 14, 1980, he hailed it effusively as "the capstone in my own efforts to get rid of needless and burdensome federal regulations." The Staggers Rail Act of 1980 loosened federal regulatory control over railroads, many of which had suffered through more than a decade of anemic earnings. For the first time in almost a century, railroads regained broad powers to set their own rates without prior approval from Uncle Sam. During these eventful years the nation's largest (or Class I) railroads halved the number of miles of track they owned, from 196,479 in 1970 to approximately 98,000 in 2000, but doubled their freight traffic to 1,456,000 revenue ton-miles at the start of the new millennium.[17]

The Interstate Commerce Commission retained a measure of power over railroad rates, mergers, and line and service abandonment, but the timetable for its decisions was greatly shortened—from a matter of years to months—and railroads regained some of the freedom to bid for business or raise rates that they had lost during the Progressive Era at the start of the century. This was a brave new world for railroad executives. As Harold H. Hall, president of the Southern Railway, observed: "No longer will we have the ICC to blame for our troubles. We will be masters of our own fate." Actually, because the inflation rate ran as high as 10 percent a year in the early 1980s, American railroads took a long time to realize significant financial prosperity as a result of deregulation, though by the end of the 1980s the future of the industry looked far brighter than it had been in many decades.[18]

Following passage of the Staggers Act, the pace of railroad mergers picked up, much as had happened earlier in the airline industry. Burlington Northern expanded to 27,000 miles with addition of the 4,700-mile Frisco in November 1980, which extended the railroad's reach diagonally across the continent from Vancouver, British Columbia, to gulf outlets at Mobile, Alabama, and Pensacola, Florida. In that oblique way Burlington Northern became the first modern railroad in the United States to link the Atlantic and Pacific oceans.

Two years later the Union Pacific won financial control of the 1,482-mile Western Pacific to gain access to central California and the San Francisco Bay area. That same year it added the 11,500-mile Missouri Pacific, which extended its reach across the Southwest and created a combined system of 21,000 miles. In 1988 it added the 3,100-mile Missouri-Kansas-Texas to provide it a shortcut from Kansas City to Texas.

Not until deregulation of the 1980s did railroads of the West (apart from the technologically obsolescent electric interurbans and logging lines) abandon lengthy sections of track. As late as 1960 the nation's rail network totaled 217,000 miles, or just 15 percent below the peak figure attained in 1916. By 1980, after dismemberment of both the Milwaukee and the Rock Island lines, it had dropped to 179,000, and it continued to drop as companies abandoned additional track. Even as Burlington Northern and Union Pacific acquired the railroads that made them the

West's dominant carriers, they also abandoned miles of lightly used line to improve the efficiency of their systems, or they spun off track to form new regional carriers. By the end of the century, the shakeout had resulted in the creation of a pair of industry giants and numerous local and regional carriers, most of which had not existed prior to 1980.

Railroad employment fell too, from an all-time high of two million workers in 1920 to less than one-quarter that number in 1980. All the while, efficiency also went up. After the administration of Ronald Reagan did not hesitate to fire airline controllers who staged an illegal walkout in 1981, railroad executives gained renewed courage to tackle troublesome labor problems of their own, including "featherbedding," the union practice of requiring larger operating crews than modern technology required. Smooth-running roller bearing cars and trackside and end-of-train safety detection equipment eliminated the need for rear brakemen—just as diesel locomotives had eliminated firemen. With the hard-won blessing of the United Transportation Union, railroads reduced the standard size of their train crews to an engineer, a brakeman, and a conductor.

In 1995 the Interstate Commerce Commission approved the merger of 22,000-mile Burlington Northern with 8,000-mile Santa Fe to create Burlington Northern Santa Fe. It was a good fit because a third of Burlington Northern revenues came from coal mined in Wyoming's Powder River Basin, while the largest source of Santa Fe revenues came from truck trailers and intermodal containers. Incidentally, approval of this merger was the last significant act of the 108-year-old Interstate Commerce Commission.[19]

In late 1995 President Bill Clinton signed legislation passed by both houses of Congress to eliminate the Interstate Commerce Commission. Replacing the nation's oldest federal regulatory body was the Surface Transportation Board housed within the Department of Transportation, but it held far less power over the nation's railroads than the ICC had in its heyday. Even so, it could be argued that the railroad business remained an uphill struggle. The industry's after-tax return on stockholders' equity in 1995 was an anemic 7.9 percent, up from 2.49 percent in 1978 when the nation's railroads ranked dead last among all major industries, but still not worth bragging about. The only major industry in the United States in 1995 to rank lower than railroads in the money they returned to stockholders was textiles.

Unlike Burlington Northern Santa Fe, which coined a new title for the enlarged company, Union Pacific retained the most venerable name in American railroad history. The 16,000-mile Union Pacific acquired the Chicago & North Western, long its strategic partner between Omaha and Chicago, in 1995. The takeover was not as easy as Union Pacific officials expected, and it resulted in snarled freight traffic and unhappy customers. Bad as that was, "Uncle Pete's" problems only grew much worse after it gained Southern Pacific in 1996 and forged a 36,000-mile system linking 26 states.[20]

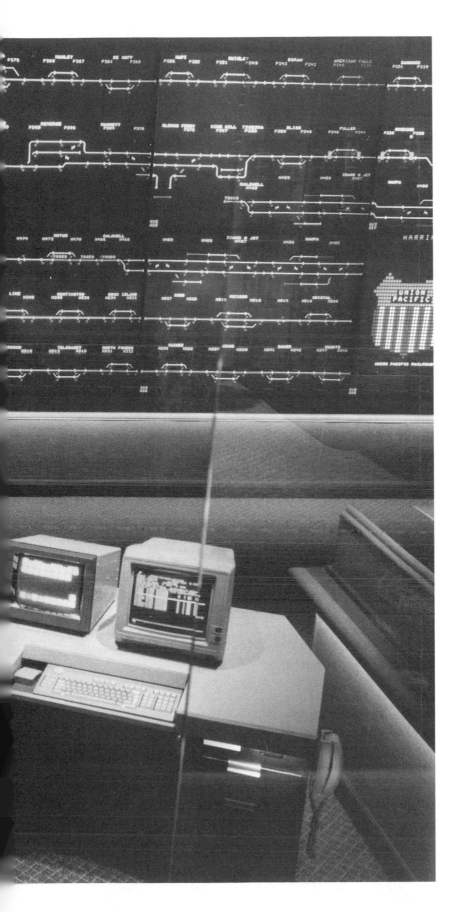

The Union Pacific's Harriman Dispatching Center in Omaha, Nebraska, at one time controlled traffic throughout the sprawling system. The Burlington Northern Santa Fe center in Fort Worth, Texas, did likewise for that big railroad. In recent years some decentralization of dispatching has taken place. Courtesy Union Pacific Railroad.

In this way it fulfilled Edward Harriman's one-time dream of a railroad empire blanketing much of the West. Alas, a traffic tangle even worse than that resulting from the Chicago & North Western acquisition gave Union Pacific a self-inflicted black eye and caused considerable freight traffic to migrate to trucks at a time when highways were already overcrowded. Some critics even called for federal reregulation of Union Pacific and other large carriers.

In the American West at the dawn of the new millennium, two great rail giants dominated the industry. Much more modest in stature were medium-sized and regional carriers like Kansas City Southern and Montana Rail Link. The former was an old-line company dating from the 1890s, while Montana Rail Link was one of the many smaller railroads that originated in the 1980s and 1990s as spin-offs from corporate giants created by the mega-mergers. Encouraging the new trend was the Staggers Act of 1980, which gave railroads unprecedented freedom to abandon unprofitable branch lines or to spin them off as regional and local carriers.

Burlington Northern in 1987 had parceled out much of the historic Northern Pacific mainline to Montana Rail Link, a 994-mile-long carrier running between Huntley, Montana (just east of Billings), and Sandpoint, Idaho. Between 1980 and 1987 alone, a total of 173 such railroads began serving different parts of the United States. Regional and local rail companies paid lower wages and enjoyed more flexible union work rules than did big railroads, which could never have operated the spun-off lines profitably.

☙☙☙

It was mainly competition, originally the struggle among individual railroads, or later among different modes of transportation, that gave us the transportation system we have today across the West. The theme that dominates the history of transportation in the twentieth-century West is the changing nature of that competition and the response—or lack thereof—from transportation providers. Every decade since the 1920s witnessed a dramatic development either in new modes and levels of competition, or in the amount of federal or state involvement with various competitors.

Over the years competition has taken such forms as increased use of private automobiles during the 1920s, air coach and interstate highways during the 1950s, and jumbo jets and commuter airlines during the 1970s and 1980s. A related development was growing government regulation, and then, starting with the airline industry in the late 1970s, dramatic deregulation of American transportation.

In response to nearly a century of change, railroads adopted new technology—perhaps the most important being streamlined passenger trains, diesel locomotives, and computerized dispatching systems—and these in turn affected work rules and jobs. There was the creation of mega-railroads through merger, and then shrinking systems through the formation of regional carriers. If anything, changes wrought by competition have only accelerated in recent decades.

None of this happened in an economic or social vacuum. Technological changes in transportation affected communities, indeed whole landscapes. Competition redefined the relationship between railroads and the development of the West. At least until the 1920s, railroads and regional development formed two sides of the same coin. During an era of growing competition, that relationship grew less obvious to most people, though the railroads of the West still played a vital role in hauling regional commodities to market and they remained its largest landholders. There is still abundant evidence of the railroad industry's historic role in shaping the modern West if one knows where to look.

Along the way there were both winners and losers. We see the winners about us today, for it is these modes of transportation that currently shape our everyday landscape. The losers left their marks too, but it is most likely the industrial archaeologists who can best discern bits and pieces of those often-lost landscapes. Likewise, the landscape is shaped by technological discards of the winners such as remained behind when transcontinental airlines outgrew the one-time marvel of the lighted airway. Collectively they define the space of place.

Conclusion

The Space of Place

In the 1920s and 1930s the nation's airways at night formed lighted corridors easily visible to observers both on the ground and in the air. One passenger on board a flight headed west through the dark from Chicago in 1932 penned these words: "Then, dead ahead, there is a brilliant flash. It is repeated. Every ten seconds the two-million-candlepower airway beacon beckons us along the course. Far beyond, we can see another and another; sometimes as many as five are in sight at one time, part of an unbroken chain leading us westward across the lonely prairies and over the towering Rockies."[1]

In mountainous areas the rotating beacons of the transcontinental airway were mounted atop the highest peaks to warn pilots of the minimum level at which they could safely fly. In these difficult locations the corridor of lights did not conform to the pattern of straight lines visible across the Great Plains. Because of powerful and dangerous wind currents that blew east across the mountaintops, pilots of westbound flights in the early 1930s frequently did not clear the Rockies and high Sierras by more than a thousand feet, and often even that was a generous margin of safety.

Late in 1926 the first lighted airway opened from coast to coast. Less than seventy years had passed since 1858, when horses of the Overland Stage Line had first traced a commercial corridor across the breadth of the West. It had not amounted to much, apart from the dirt ruts and lonely stage stations where drivers got fresh horses and travelers paused to eat their meals. During seven intervening decades, tracks, highways, and the wires carrying telegraph and telephone lines had defined more transcontinental corridors.

Comparisons between them were perhaps inevitable. "Imperceptibly, an age of specialization enters to mark the matu-

Addressing one aspect of the space of place is this Great Northern brochure from the 1950s or 1960s that urged travelers to "Go East via Glacier National Park to Chicago and the historic cities of Eastern United States." Author's collection.

rity of the aviation industry," noted one industry observer in 1928. "Aviation is no longer the exclusive business of pilots, any more than the automobile industry is one of chauffeurs, and railroading of locomotive engineers." Henceforth, he continued, the future of aviation rested with the auxiliary services, the support structure "backing the pilot and his ship of the air."[2]

"Aircraft must ultimately be guided from airport to airport by means of radio beacons which lay down an infallible path along completely equipped airways. Marker beacons must serve as block signals to warn unfailingly of dangers besetting the path of the air." He further predicted a future system to control airplanes in the air "much as the movement of trains in railroad yards is indicated in the signal control towers on a map of glass tubes, each of which becomes luminous as a train moves along the section of track which it represents."[3]

Over the years as technologies changed, older corridors simply faded away, physically if not in memory. A few modest stage stations are preserved today, as are remnants of the first lighted airway. The remaining segments of old Route 66 attract numerous devotees, though most motorists whiz along on the parallel interstate highway and give the historic route little thought. Radio signals complemented the lighted airway in the late 1920s and eventually supplanted it entirely. When invisible electronic beams defined airways, the concept of a visible corridor became almost meaningless apart from the jet contrails that occasionally mark busy sections.

Other corridors are more important today than when they were first conceived. Interstate highways are without doubt the most heavily used and most visible of all the nation's corridors. At nearly every interchange is clustered an array of fast-food restaurants, motels, and gas stations, all of them looking remarkably similar to the clusters at other interchanges. Driving only interstate highways from coast to coast would effectively insulate a motorist from the rest of America—or maybe busy interstate corridors *are* America today. Anyone who has ever motored along a secondary highway, firmly committed to the old road despite enticements to pull into the national mainstream, senses the vast differences that exist between the worlds those two highway systems define.

Truly, the interstate highways are America's modern metropolitan corridors, and the secondary ones are but its pleasant backwaters. To understand what I mean, you need only contrast the experience of talking by cell phone on an interstate, where connections are generally good, with that along a typical secondary road of the West, where electronic connections are intermittent at best and any cell phone conversation is always frustrating.

Furthermore, consider that within ten miles of either side of Interstate 5 reside perhaps half of all residents of the Far West. That corridor traces an artery of commerce extending from Canada to Mexico by way of Seattle, Portland, Sacramento, Los Angeles, and San Diego. Like all transportation corridors, it has given a new meaning to the space of place, not just along the highway itself but also within the urban sprawl it fostered. Highways and urban sprawl traveled hand in hand through the twentieth century, making the nation's retreat from its highway-based transportation network exceedingly difficult.

The preference of Americans for detached dwellings in suburban settings meant that more people must endure commutes that grow longer and more frustrating each year. *Fortune* magazine recalled wistfully in October 2000 that Lady Bird Johnson, the former First Lady who once was America's foremost advocate of roadway aesthetics, had forty years ago selected California Route 280 as the nation's most beautiful highway. But now, because of urban sprawl that mars Silicon Valley, it was clogged with bumper-to-bumper traffic.[4]

The worst traffic jam I ever experienced took place on Interstate 5 just south of Seattle in the mid-1990s, when a multi-vehicle accident snarled all southbound lanes and transformed an easy forty-five-minute drive to Tacoma into a five-hour ordeal that did not end until well into the evening. Motorists who somehow managed to reach one of the exits found the parallel routes hopelessly blocked as well. Drivers desperate to relieve their bladders left their cars in the middle of the interstate and headed for the bushes along its sides, and this further snarled traffic. I missed my appointment in Tacoma. Nonetheless, the day's frustrations helped me to understand for the first time why many urban dwellers consider a cell phone to be one of life's necessities. Here was another example of how effectively transportation and communication technology had complemented one another during the twentieth century to redefine the space of a place.

Likewise, transportation and communication redefined the place of the West within the framework of the larger nation. Foremost was their role in fostering the national economy that extends along the interstate corridors today. Yet all we can currently observe is the latest act of an ongoing drama, and it is by no means the final one. Writing in 1923, one commentator observed that advances in transportation and communication had "extended Broadway clear across the continent." He quoted a fellow writer who noted that as a result of a personal automobile tour, she "found the American world extends from ocean to ocean, that the hat she purchased in New York had its duplicate in every millinery window all the way across to Los Angeles. She further found that the people between were not all 'hicks,' and that farmers did not go around with alfalfa on their chins and straws in their mouths as shown in the cartoons of the funny section."[5]

Also redefining the place of the West within the nation was the shrinking size of the nation itself. Americans, it has often been noted, are a people in a hurry. During the course of the nineteenth century the time required to travel between New York and San Francisco dropped from a matter of months to mere days, but in the twentieth century that was not nearly good enough. Hours were what counted now. Railroads took inordinately great pride in trimming hours here and there from their transcontinental schedules, as did the airlines. One carrier or another frequently advertised a one-hour time advantage on board its flights between New York and San Francisco or Los Angeles in an effort to woo passengers from a rival airline—or from long-distance passenger trains.

"Breakfast in New York! Why exclaim over that? Luncheon in Kansas City! Worthy an exclamation. But wait . . . dinner in Los Angeles!!" That was how Harris Hanshue, head of Western Air Express, enthusiastically portrayed the aviation industry's quest for greater speed. His 1930 essay titled "Across the Continent in 12 Hours" seemed almost utopian at the time, but what made such speed worth attaining was how it lured a growing number of travelers by air.[6]

A New York businessman explained in the *Atlantic Monthly* in mid-1932 that he now flew regularly to San Francisco instead of traveling by train. Why? "*Speed.* I leave New York soon after nine o'clock on Monday morning and am in Oakland at two o'clock on Tuesday afternoon. By train, I should get there on Friday morning." He observed that by air a roundtrip ticket cost $228, and that sum included all meals; whereas by train a ticket cost $317, which included a lower berth. In addition, he had to pay for twenty-two meals in the dining car. Not to be ignored, he insisted, was the enjoyment of a flight. "To see America from the sky, unveiling her beauty, state after state, range after range, river after river is unforgettable—a gift of pride and wonder and delight." The plane followed the longest lighted airway in the world, 2,700 miles with 900 "air lighthouses" forming a chain from Newark to Chicago and Oakland. He acknowledged that the latest corridor was made possible by our "earlier speed crusades" of the pony express, the Overland Stage, and the railroads.[7]

High above the earth he observed: "We seem to be suspended in space while the country rolls slowly by far below. A toy earth is framed in our slightly quivering window. The big wing stretches out utterly motionless over hill and valley shrunk to the dimensions of a Lilliput. For a moment we are as gods, complacently surveying our world from a more splendid chariot than ever Phaëthon drove." In this case, though, the chariot of the gods was none other than a Ford Trimotor.[8]

As the plane droned along, the copilot methodically passed out pieces of chewing gum and cotton wads for the ears. "The co-pilot retires to the cockpit, leaving the door open, so that we can see both pilots sitting there, the big instrument panel before them, the dual controls, the telephone headsets clamped over their ears."[9]

Reflecting on the amount of time an airplane saved him in getting from coast to coast, the businessman mused that "the everlasting chorus in our world of noise and hustle" was "Save time! Save time!" But what, he wondered, "are we going to do with all this time?"[10]

Increasingly, time and place became intertwined. United advertised in the late 1930s that "two weeks is plenty of time for the vacation you've always dreamed of—if you fly United's Main Line." Its air map of the United States highlighted Yellowstone, Glacier, Yosemite, Zion, and Bryce as "vacation lands." TWA advertised itself as "The Lindbergh Line" that was "famous for scenery and service." Elsewhere it claimed that its planes followed "The Scenic Transcontinental Route."[11]

In the end, speed triumphed over place. That is, as newer airliners flew higher and faster, it became increasingly difficult for most passengers to make sense of what they saw below. Flying above layers of clouds instead of below or through them, one could often not see the ground at all. Pilots might still call the attention of passengers to the Grand Canyon, but the natural wonder is not really grand when viewed from 30,000 feet and above. Experienced flyers usually prefer an aisle seat because that location will offer greater personal freedom and more convenience, especially on long flights when a traveler can walk to the bathroom without disturbing one or two seatmates.

The quest for greater speed went on until only about four hours separated New York and San Francisco, but then the race stalled. Congestion on the ground and in the airways wreaked havoc with airline schedules and cost even the best carriers the goodwill of their passengers. The summers of 1999 and 2000 were two consecutive travel nightmares, marked by innumerable flight delays and cancellations—evidence that the air traffic system in the United States was as close to gridlock as some of the nation's well-traveled freeways. In fact, by the summer of 2000 flight delays had climbed 50 percent during just the past five years.

As recently as 1995 there were just 35 regional jets in the nation's commercial fleet. By 1999 there were 407, and more arrived daily. At Los Angeles International 60,000 people a day drive to the main terminal. During the summer of 2001 the number of delays at the nation's busiest airport dropped, and it dropped even further in September after terrorists used two airliners to destroy the World Trade Center. But when popular fears of flying diminish and the economy rebounds, delays will surely become common again.

I wrote an initial version of this text on a day in August 2001 when Midway Airlines announced that it had filed for bankruptcy protection. To survive, the North Carolina-based carrier announced plans to slash its flight schedule and lay off half of its employees, about seven hundred people. It cited a "calamitous drop in business traffic," low fares, and high-priced jet fuel as the causes of its troubles.[12] As a result of a slumping economy, all airlines experienced sharp declines in business travel as corporate America trimmed its costs. Businesses increasingly substituted communications for transportation—that is, they held videoconferences instead of sending employees to meet with one another in person or with clients. The fastest, most comfortable airline flight, even one aboard a plush corporate jet, could not compete with instant communication among several different offices or conference rooms, often located in different parts of the country or world.

This, of course, presumes that employees can easily commute from home to office—or maybe not, in the case of some headquarters cities. It is worth noting that in early 2001, when the Boeing Company announced plans to relocate its head offices from Seattle to Chicago, it cited traffic congestion in Seattle as a reason. At much the same time, it proposed to build a "Sonic Cruiser," a plane of radical design that would fly 20 percent faster than current jets, perhaps as fast as 648 miles per hour, or just under the speed of sound. No commercial plane except the Concorde flew significantly faster than 550 miles per hour, the original cruising speed of the Boeing 707. Thus a Sonic Cruiser would trim only 35 minutes off a Boston to Los Angeles flight, and less than that for flights between New York and San Francisco. All of this presumed that congestion at airports, both on the ground and in the air, did not grow worse. What would Boeing do about that?

Spatial relationships are important when I seek to answer the one question people most frequently asked me when they heard I was writing a book about transportation and the twentieth-century West. Given the congestion that clogs the highways and skyways, they often asked, will the long-distance passenger train ever make a comeback? I am convinced that most questioners really do not wish me to say no. After all, I myself enjoy riding passenger trains. Recently, I calculated that I had logged nearly 50,000 miles on board the American Orient Express since 1995, plus many more miles crisscrossing the United States and Canada by Amtrak and Via Rail. Before the advent of Amtrak in 1971, I had journeyed across the West aboard the flagship trains of the Union Pacific, Northern Pacific, Burlington, and Denver & Rio Grande Western lines.

Especially enjoyable was a White Pass & Yukon trip from Skagway, Alaska, to Whitehorse, Yukon Territory, in 1982, and two Alaska Railroad trips between Anchorage and Fairbanks, one in the dead of winter aboard a rail diesel car. In a place where drifts towered almost as high as the RDC, we paced a moose running ahead of us along the snow-packed tracks at fourteen miles per hour! Indeed, I do like trains.

That said, no one should expect to turn the clock back to 1900 when passenger trains ruled. Even then, the nation's most important mode of transportation poorly met the everyday travel needs of most westerners. Because of the region's low population density, train service in most areas was infrequent. Even between the two metropolitan centers of Los Angeles and San Francisco in 1900, only three trains a day ran each way, and the fastest of them took nearly fifteen hours to complete the journey of 480 miles.

Along the rail corridors that connected major population centers, it was easy for residents to travel by train from one town to a nearby one on the same line. But try going by train from Santa Barbara to Bakersfield, California, in 1900, for example. As the crow flies, that is a distance of about seventy miles, but a crow had better be prepared to cross a range of mountains. By rail it was 214 miles, and the journey took 11 hours, including a necessary wait to change trains at a country station north of Los Angeles. More extreme was the difficulty of travel by train between Santa Barbara and San Luis Obispo. Today the two communities are located a hundred miles apart via U.S. Highway 101 and only slightly more than that by rail, but back in January 1900 a traveler determined to journey from Santa Barbara to San Luis Obispo by rail had to ride four separate trains as well as a ferryboat across the bay separating Oakland and San Francisco. The distance totaled 795 miles, and the ordeal required nearly 26 hours to complete!

It was not uncommon in numerous other parts of the West for residents of towns close to one another but served by separate rail lines to spend several hours making the journey by train—but only as infrequently as possible. Not without reason were the rail travelers who were forced to endure such inconvenience (traveling salesmen, for instance) among the first converts to automobiles once they became practical for a journey of any distance. The automobile represented a perfectly rational response to the inconvenience of making certain journeys by rail: local ones at first, and regional and national ones later. When American travelers abandoned trains in favor of personal automobiles and airliners, it was only a commonsense approach to the alternatives.

Rail enthusiasts like to recall the civility and comfort that a long train journey supposedly entailed in 1900. Perhaps for travelers pampered by first-class service and luxury accommodations that was true—at least in part. But affluent Americans today would not likely part with good money for a berth in an open-section sleeping car, and most would discover even the standard rooms of more modern times to be claustrophobic and uncomfortable. The American Orient Express does a good job of recapturing the lavishness of first-class travel of bygone times, yet it must tactfully remind guests before boarding that they will find their standard rooms to be rather cozy. Private rooms of the same size were suitable for travelers aboard luxury trains as late as the 1940s and 1950s, but most well-to-do travelers today are used to far larger personal spaces.

The aspect of train travel in 1900 that is easiest to recreate today is a sumptuous dinner in the diner. Railroad diners were notable for good food then, and currently many different entrepreneurs across the United States attempt to capitalize on that tradition by operating a variety of dinner trains. The American Orient Express features two dining cars, plus

Several dome cars appeared on the Union Pacific's streamlined "City of Portland" in the 1950s and 1960s. This train is near the eastern end of the Columbia River Gorge, where wetness of the Cascade Mountains rapidly gives way to the dryness typical of the sparsely populated landscapes of eastern Oregon and Washington. Courtesy Union Pacific Museum.

A brochure cover for the Santa Fe's "San Francisco Chief" depicts a beautiful but sparsely populated landscape that could be seen from windows of its trains across northern New Mexico and Arizona. Author's collection.

I have in hand a copy of the *National Rail Timetable* for summer 2001. This massive volume sells for £10 in W. H. Smith stores found in all major stations in Great Britain. In a suitcase it looks like a brick—and it feels just about as heavy. Its 2,272 pages remind me of the bulky *Official Guide of the Railways* in its heyday in the late 1920s, except that the British guide is far more densely packed with train schedules. In total it includes listings for twenty-six separate passenger carrying companies, including Eurostar, which links London with Paris and Brussels via high-speed trains that zip along at one point beneath the English Channel.

Eurostar trains cruise through the French countryside at 180 miles per hour, but not faster than 100 through Britain, lending validity to the claim I overheard in Dover in southern England that its residents now live closer in terms of time to Paris than to London. That may change after a new high-speed link being built from the ground up between the coast and London is in operation. That will be the sole exception to the fact that English passenger trains, even the ones that regularly cruise along at 125 miles an hour between London and Edinburgh, follow a rail network spiked in place in the nineteenth century.

I mention this information simply to contrast how different the transportation situations in England and the American West are, and why the model of high-speed rail transportation will not work in the West—at least not in most places in the foreseeable future. Nonetheless, we will have to deal with the consequences of our enduring love affair with the automobile as compounded by the peculiarities of our regional geography that have caused us to spread our settlements across so much space, else our largest cities will eventually choke or atrophy as a result of their own transportation inadequacies.

The downtown retail area was once the true heart of any city, but now that area takes a back seat to the outlying shopping districts. And that is true not just in the large cities. In many smaller communities "sprawl malls" at the outskirts have severely mauled the downtown business centers. The result is greater congestion on the highways. Three of the nation's five most traffic-congested cities in the late 1990s were located in the West. Ranked first was Los Angeles, followed closely by San Francisco and Seattle. Rounding out the traffic dishonor role were Washington, D.C., and Chicago.

It might be tempting to ask why westerners grew so dependent on highway transportation; and some might answer by conjuring up a conspiracy of automobile, tire, and oil monopolists. More realistically, personal automobiles gained early and extensive use across the region because the technology was so well suited to meeting the needs of westerners for travel across areas containing vast spaces and few people, at least until the post–World War II population boom.

Perhaps the best we can hope for in a modern system of transportation is improvements that make our automobiles more efficient users of highway corridors already in place. Somewhat like electronic signals that control air traffic, an electronic guideway added to the centers of existing highway lanes could, with the aid of computer commands, more efficiently space and pace our cars—perhaps. Something so basic as visible time signals that count down the seconds until the next green light could reduce motorist frustration at heavily used intersections and lessen the stresses of driving—and these devices are already in place at a few busy junctions in the United States and Canada.

As for commuter train service, probably the most westerners can hope for are large parking lots where they can leave their precious cars and board the trains. Already, though, parking lots at some stops are large enough to land a small plane, and one only wonders how much larger they will get before lazy commuters refuse to walk from their cars to the trains. Another alternative is a system of light rails. Many of these are already in place in the largest cities of the West, often laid along corridors where the rails of former electric interurban lines were abandoned years ago. That is true for the light rail line east into the suburbs of Portland, Oregon. The city's MAX (Metropolitan Area Express) most recently built a line to the Portland International Airport, an arrangement that recognized the need to integrate more fully two major modes of transportation, rather than relying heavily on automobiles.

In April 1961, the last passenger interurban train on the Pacific Electric ceased running from downtown Los Angeles to Long Beach. But in 1983, after turning down the proposal three times, voters in southern California approved construction of a 150-mile network of light rails to be paid for by sales tax revenues. The first line connected Los Angeles and Long Beach once again. Light rail systems have also appeared in San Diego, Sacramento, Salt Lake City, and Denver.

❧ ❧ ❧

More than anything else, transportation technology has defined for westerners—both rural and urban—the space of place with which they must contend today. The most obvious problems, and thus those most likely to be widely discussed, involve urban space; yet those occurring in the rural West are no less real. These include the disappearance of any form of commercial transportation in many places and thus a heightened dependency on automobiles by an aging population. Apart from automobiles, many such areas are far worse off in terms of any long-distance transportation than they were in 1900 when the passenger trains ruled.

Another transportation-related phenomenon noticeable today in the rural West is the rise of noncontiguous urban settlements.[14] Many of these are affluent communities in a rural setting, yet they are just as dependent on automobile transportation as a down-at-the-heels farm town that years ago lost its last rail or bus service. Noncontiguous urban settlements, in fact, exist only because of the automobile. As such they serve to showcase its transforming power in the twentieth-century West and to show how that power will likely be projected into the future.

In any case, noncontiguous urban sprawl is most obvious when, for example, a motorist crests a hill or rounds a curve in some seemingly rural part of the Colorado Rockies and unexpectedly encounters an impressive array of "trophy homes" filling once-remote valleys or dotting hillsides that only recently were ranchland. Such settlements often seem to possess no discernible urban core, but instead they resemble a raft of extravagant suburban housing set adrift in the pristine high country landscape. "Plant your nest where the eagles rest," was the way one developer advertised his spread in a high mountain valley a few years ago. I haven't been back to see what happened, but I fully expect that the only eagles and elk resting there now are lodge brothers.

Colorado is not alone. The same transformation is occurring in the highlands of New Mexico and in scenic mountain meadows across Idaho and Montana. Interestingly, perhaps in a tip of the hat to rusticity, many such dwellings take the shape of enormous log cabins. In Montana the log home industry is actually growing, though the number of timber jobs is declining. One cannot help but wonder whether any remaining timber workers can afford to live in these upscale developments.

In the traditional model of urban expansion, suburban development occurred at or very close to the periphery of already-existing centers of population. The physical expansion of urban areas of the United States is a very old process, and it has been the subject of many notable books, including the one that first interested me in the topic: *Streetcar Suburbs* (1962) by the urban historian Sam Bass Warner Jr., one of my professors at the University of Michigan. Warner's book provided a model to explain how late-nineteenth-century cities expanded outward from core to periphery as a result of changing transportation technology. Warner was correct in identifying urban expansion as a product of technological innovation, such as when suburban towns and villages grew alongside the tracks of commuter railroads or new city neighborhoods took shape along streetcar lines powered first by horses and later by electricity.[15]

Even in the early years of the automobile era, there was no great departure from the pattern of urban expansion first encouraged by the steam railroads and streetcar lines. Moreover, when Westerners at that time undertook to develop a portion of the region's vast and seemingly empty rural landscapes, they typically did so for purely functional reasons, as the railroads had done before them. That is, most often they expected the land around them to yield a commodity such as cattle, grain, timber, or minerals—the rare dude ranch and mountain recreation cabin notwithstanding. A few areas were also set aside for their beauty or historical value as national and state parks.

The second half of the twentieth century witnessed an expansion of the West's network of all-weather roads, the standardization of the forty-hour work week (which enabled urban residents to spend weekends away from their city homes), the lengthening of annual vacations, the tendency for Americans to live longer and more productive post-retirement lives, and a continuing quest for a personal rural retreat. All of these have combined in recent years to spur noncontiguous urban sprawl—developments that seem to have no function other than to allow people to escape metropolitan areas, including the suburbs that were themselves originally intended to offer a pleasant alternative to big city life. Furthermore, many of the new settlements no longer serve merely as vacation getaways but have evolved into year-round communities. In addition, noncontiguous urban sprawl appears likely to flourish and spread farther as a result of the not-too-distant retirement of the oldest of the Baby Boomers, large numbers of whom will enjoy steady incomes from the savings, investments, and pensions that will permit them to settle anywhere they please.

Perhaps it is the sparseness of vegetation across the West that makes this new urban phenomenon so visible. Literally, you can see some of these developments from many miles down the road. Recently, while driving up the Hudson River Valley in New York, I was struck by how effectively the trees there camouflage urban growth, at least during the summer months. Many people live in the cities and towns along the river between New York and Albany, and yet for the most part their homes and businesses are hidden among the trees. Surveying the Connecticut landscape from a hilltop state park, I noticed the same thing. The valley before me was covered with a mantle of green that effectively concealed the built-up environment. That is not the case in much of the West. The aridity that contributes to the region's fabled blue skies and seemingly limitless vistas is no friend when it comes to hiding noncontiguous urban sprawl.

While it is easy to condemn this change and wring our hands about how settlement is marring the majesty of the mountains, it is undoubtedly here to stay—at least for as long as westerners can purchase enough gasoline to retreat periodically to getaway properties. Nonetheless, some of us are thankful that so much of the West is still "locked up" in lands controlled by the Forest Service or the Bureau of Land Management and thus remains off limits to the ravages of noncontiguous urban sprawl. I don't think any of us can hope to reverse the trend—unless, perhaps, the price of gasoline climbs to stratospheric levels.

Even amidst the farm and ranchland of the rolling Palouse country of northern Idaho and eastern Washington where I originally typed some of these thoughts before moving to Saint Louis in early 2001, people talk about county rezoning to permit recreation homes to be built along the high and presently empty bluffs overlooking the Snake River downstream from Lewiston and Clarkston. The result, of course, would be additional noncontiguous urban sprawl.

One concern I have as I drive and observe evidence of this phenomenon all over the West is what will happen to the vast open spaces that have historically done so much to define the western landscape. This much is already true: in a very real sense our expansive western landscape has shrunk noticeably because of the automobile, and it will continue to shrink. This visual tragedy, a process already occurring around my Idaho home, provides a powerful personal reminder of the how transportation continually redefines a landscape.

Noncontiguous urban sprawl represents only one recent example of how transportation continually redefines the space of place in the American West. In the interest of accuracy I should further note that whatever

The camera of Richard Steinheimer recorded a Northern Pacific passenger train about to depart Tacoma's Union Station on May 10, 1964. A similar photograph taken today would show that the Union Station building had been remodeled to serve as a federal district courthouse. To the left now sits the modern Washington State History Museum. It is designed to complement architecturally the former station building. Several Amtrak trains serve Tacoma from a modest new station located well behind the vantage point of the photographer. Courtesy DeGolyer Library.

A smiling uniformed service station attendant appeared on maps issued in the 1940s by the Standard Oil Company of Indiana. Author's collection.

the impact of transportation in the coming years, it will be people-caused but technology-enabled, as was always true in the twentieth century. Thus, *Going Places* offers an extended look at westerners and the different transportation technologies we embraced in hopes of improving our lives (or so they imagined) and how those same technologies reshaped for good or ill the space we inhabit. Westerners remain a restless people, but where we are going with our transportation technology is by no means clear. We can be certain, however, that transportation will continue to play an important role in our lives by redefining basic spatial relationships that make the West livable—or not, in the case of massive traffic jams, air pollution in urban areas, and unsightly sprawl. I'd like to believe that new or modified modes of transportation in the twenty-first century will help us untangle the spatial dilemmas we created for ourselves during the past century.

Preface and Acknowledgments

1. John R. Stilgoe, *Outside Lies Magic: Regaining History and Awareness in Everyday Places* (New York: Walker and Co., 1998).

Prologue

1. *Aero Digest* 16 (June 1930): 94.
2. Carlos A. Schwantes, "The Case of the Missing Century; or, Where Did the American West Go after 1900?" *Pacific Historical Review* 70 (February 2001): 1–20.
3. These issues are discussed in detail in Carlos A. Schwantes, *Long Day's Journey: The Steamboat and Stagecoach Era in the Northern West* (Seattle: University of Washington Press, 1999).
4. *Poor's Manual of Railroads of the United States, 1900* (New York: H. V. & H. W. Poor, 1900), xxvii.
5. Harris M. Hanshue, "Across the Continent in 12 Hours," *Aeronautics* 6 (June 1930): 463–64, 482.
6. *Travelers' Official Guide of the Railway and Steam Navigation Lines in the United States, Canada and Mexico* (New York: National Railway Publication Co., January 1900), 499.
7. Joel Garreau, *The Nine Nations of North America* (Boston: Houghton Mifflin, 1981), 287–337.
8. *Better Roads and Streets* 6 (September 1916): 32.
9. Emily Post, *By Motor to the Golden Gate* (New York: D. Appleton & Co., 1916), 3.

1. Transportation Corridors Transform the West

1. As quoted in Joseph R. Daughen and Peter Binzen, *The Wreck of the Penn Central: The Real Story behind the Largest Bankruptcy in American History* (Boston: Little, Brown, 1971), 36.
2. *Highway Magazine* 17 (May 1926): 112.
3. *Aero Digest* 16 (January 1930): 9.

4. The actual title varied over the years, but hereafter, for the sake of consistency and simplicity (and to distinguish it from the later *Official Airline Guide*), I will cite this publication in the notes as the *Official Guide of the Railways*. I cannot think of a better source to trace the month-by-month evolution of the railroad industry in North America. Undoubtedly the world's most complete set of *Official Guides* is preserved at the St. Louis Mercantile Library, which maintains a collection that encompasses virtually all issues published from July 1871 to the present.

Planning for a monthly reference work commenced at the October 1866 conference of the National General Ticket Agents' Association (which later became the American Association of Passenger Traffic Officers) held in Cleveland, Ohio. The first issue of the *Official Guide* appeared in June 1868. For further details, see Harold H. Baetjer, *A Book That Gathers No Dust* (New York: National Railway Publication Co., 1950).

5. *Official Guide of the Railways*, May 1918, xxiii.

6. Ibid.

7. *Proceedings of the Annual Conference of the American Association of Passenger Traffic Officers* (1948), 56. A virtually complete set of more than a century of convention proceedings is on file at the St. Louis Mercantile Library.

8. Those seventeen states comprising the West that are given the most in-depth treatment by this book are Arizona, California, Colorado, Idaho, Kansas, Montana, Nebraska, Nevada, New Mexico, North Dakota, Oklahoma, Oregon, South Dakota, Texas, Utah, Washington, and Wyoming.

9. *Official Guide of the Railways*, January 1900, 688.

10. *Official Guide of the Railways*, April 1901, xxv.

11. *Official Guide of the Railways*, June 1915, xxvii; *Official Guide of the Railways*, June 1917, xxv.

12. E. L. Bevington, Secretary of the Trans-Continental Passenger Association, *Proceedings of the Annual Conference of the American Association of General Passenger and Ticket Agents* (1912), 77.

2. When Railroads Ruled

1. *Official Guide of the Railways*, April 1916, xxiii.

2. *Official Guide of the Railways*, July 1916, xxv.

3. *Official Guide of the Railways*, November 1915, xxvi; *Official Guide of the Railways*, September 1917, xxiii.

4. *Official Guide of the Railways*, November 1916, xxv.

5. Robert M. Fogelson, *The Fragmented Metropolis: Los Angeles, 1850–1930* (Berkeley: University of California Press, 1967); Bradford Luckingham, *Phoenix: The History of a Southwestern Metropolis* (Tucson: University of Arizona Press, 1989); John R. Signor, *The Los Angeles and Salt Lake Railroad Company: The Union Pacific's Historic Salt Lake Route* (San Marino: Golden West Books, 1988), 7.

6. Carl Snyder, *American Railways as Investments* (New York: Moody, 1907), 220, 223.

7. *Official Guide of the Railways*, November 1915, xxvi.

8. John R. Stilgoe, *Metropolitan Corridor: Railroads and the American Scene* (New Haven, Conn.: Yale University Press, 1983).

9. *Official Guide of the Railways,* April 1915, xxv.

10. *Official Guide of the Railways,* June 1909, xxxi.

11. Colorado Midland Railway, *Public Timetable,* December 1902.

12. *Official Guide of the Railways,* January 1887, xvii; Ian R. Bartky, *Selling the True Time: Nineteenth-Century Timekeeping in America* (Stanford, Calif.: Stanford University Press, 2000), 2.

13. *Official Guide of the Railways,* September 1889, xvii.

14. Gregory Ames, "Fire and Frost: The Steam Locomotive in Winter," *Locomotive and Railway Preservation,* January–February 1991, 10–26.

15. *Official Guide of the Railways,* January 1900, iv; *Official Guide of the Railways,* July 1900, iv.

16. *Official Guide of the Railways,* April 1893, xxiii.

17. Arthur Edward Stilwell, *Cannibals of Finance: Fifteen Years' Contest with the Money Trust* (Chicago: Fairhaven Publishers, 1912).

18. As quoted in the *Official Guide of the Railways,* February 1888, xviii.

19. Gerrit Fort as quoted in the *Official Guide of the Railways,* September 1914, xxviii.

20. Ibid.

21. *Official Guide of the Railways,* October 1909, xxviii.

22. *Official Guide of the Railways,* May 1893, xxii; *Proceedings of the Twenty-First Annual Meeting of the American Railway Development Association* (1929), 121.

23. J. H. Jasberg, "Practical Colonization Work," *Proceedings of the Fourteenth Annual Meeting of the American Railway Development Association* (1922), 52–55.

24. Kansas City Southern Railway, *Public Timetable* (November 1911), 23. A copy is on file at the St. Louis Mercantile Library.

25. *Official Guide of the Railways,* October 1908, xxx.

26. *Official Guide of the Railways,* April 1916, xxv.

27. *Official Guide of the Railways,* August 1914, xxix; *Official Guide of the Railways,* June 1912, xxxii; *Official Guide of the Railways,* April 1900, xxvii.

28. *Official Guide of the Railways,* August 1912, xxix.

29. *Official Guide of the Railways,* June 1907, xxxii; *Official Guide of the Railways,* October 1890, xxi.

30. *Official Guide of the Railways,* June 1907, xxxii.

31. *Official Guide of the Railways,* August 1913, xxix.

32. *Official Guide of the Railways,* July 1899, xxx.

33. *Official Guide of the Railways,* August 1928, xxix.

34. *Official Guide of the Railways,* September 1900, xxv; J. W. Nourse, Passenger Traffic Manager, St. Louis–San Francisco Railway, *Proceedings of the Annual Conference of the American Association of Passenger Traffic Officers* (1935), 86. In addition to public timetables, railroads published special employee timetables intended for their operating personnel alone. These were no-nonsense publications that provided the essential facts and nothing more.

35. *Official Guide of the Railways,* September 1928, xxx.

36. *Official Guide of the Railways,* July 1907, xxxii.

37. For an extended discussion of this kind of railroad promotional activity, see Carlos A. Schwantes, *Railroad Signatures Across the Pacific Northwest* (Seattle: University of Washington Press, 1993).

38. K. Ross Toole, *Twentieth-Century Montana: A State of Extremes* (Norman: University of Oklahoma Press, 1972), 80; Jonathan Raban, *Bad Land: An American Romance* (New York: Pantheon Books, 1996).

3. Copper Connections and the Last Transcontinental Railroad

1. Wm. Prescott Smith, *The Book of the Great Railway Celebrations of 1857* (New York: D. Appleton & Co., 1858).

2. *American Railway Times* 21 (June 12, 1869): 190.

3. *Official Guide of the Railways*, June 1915, xxvii.

4. *Official Guide of the Railways*, May 1918, xxiii.

5. Ernest Howard, *Wall Street: Fifty Years after Erie—Being a Comparative Account of the Making and Breaking of the Jay Gould Railroad Fortune* (Boston: Stratford Co., 1923), 16.

6. *Official Guide of the Railways*, April 1902, xxvi.

7. John H. Rehor, *The Nickel Plate Story* (Milwaukee, Wis.: Kalmbach, 1965), 317–36 passim; Howard V. Worley Jr. and William N. Poellot Jr., *The Pittsburgh and West Virginia Railway: The Story of the High and Dry* (Halifax, Pa.: Withers Publishing, 1989).

8. Carl Snyder, *American Railways as Investments* (New York: Moody, 1907), 724.

9. John Leeds Kerr, "History of Western Railroads," *Railway & Marine News and Pacific Commerce* 23 (November 9, 1925): 17.

10. *Railway & Marine News* 28 (November 1931): 16–18.

11. *Official Guide of the Railways*, September 1917, xxiii.

12. *Official Guide of the Railways*, January 1918, xxiii.

13. *Official Guide of the Railways*, April 1918, xxiv, xxv.

14. *Official Guide of the Railways*, August 1914, xxix.

15. *Railway and Marine News* 22 (April 1924): 13; *Railway and Marine News* 22 (March 1924): 11.

16. Gregory Lee Thompson, *The Passenger Train in the Motor Age: California's Rail and Bus Industries, 1910–1941* (Columbus: Ohio State University Press, 1993), 31.

4. Roads Stretching from Farm to Market, but Seldom Beyond

1. James W. Abbott, "Transcontinental Highways," *Good Roads* 34 (August 1905): 531–33.

2. As quoted in Allan Nevins, *Ford: The Times, the Man, the Company* (New York: Charles Scribner's Sons, 1954), 256.

3. James W. Abbott, "Straw Roads," *Good Roads* 34 (June 1905): 376–77.

4. Charles Fuller Gates, "Touring in California [1901]," as quoted in Frank Oppel, *Motoring in America: The Early Years* (Secaucus, N.J.: Castle Books, 1989), 141.

5. Andrew McNally III, in *Proceedings of the Annual Conference of the American Association of Passenger Traffic Officers* (1955), 26.

6. As quoted in Phil Patton, *Open Road: A Celebration of the American Highway* (New York: Simon & Schuster, 1986), 61.

7. Charles Fuller Gates, "Touring in California [1901]," as quoted in Oppel, *Motoring in America*, 137.

8. Ibid., 143.

9. Ibid., 137–148.

10. H. P. Burchell, "The Automobile as a Means of Country Travel [1905]," as quoted in Oppel, *Motoring in America,* 277.

11. *Good Roads* 40 (November 1910): 410; Bruce E. Seely, "Railroads, Good Roads, and Motor Vehicles: Managing Technological Change," *Railroad History,* Autumn 1986, 34–63.

12. *Official Guide of the Railways,* September 1911, xxx.

13. Curt McConnell, *Coast to Coast by Automobile: The Pioneering Trips, 1899–1908* (Stanford, Calif.: Stanford University Press, 2000). Alexander Winton, maker of the first automobile to cross the continent, went on to found the Winton Gas Engine & Manufacturing Company in 1912, which came to specialize in building heavy-duty marine diesel engines. In the mid-1930s it was a Winton diesel that powered the streamlined Burlington "Zephyr" as it streaked across the Great Plains to set speed records and capture the public's fancy. By that time, the parent company for Winton diesel engines was a rapidly expanding enterprise called General Motors, which was seemingly interested in all modes of transportation powered by internal combustion engines—from automobiles and trucks, obviously, to railway locomotives and even early airlines.

14. H. P. Burchell, "The Automobile as a Means of Country Travel [1905]," as quoted in Oppel, *Motoring in America,* 277.

15. Mark Trester, "The Highway of Many Waterfalls," *Highway Magazine* 14 (December 1923): 278–80.

16. *Highway Magazine* 12 (December 1921): 10.

17. Samuel Christopher Lancaster, *The Columbia: America's Great Highway through the Cascade Mountains to the Sea,* 2nd ed. (Portland: Samuel Christopher Lancaster, 1916).

18. Nellie Barnard Parker, "Blazing the Oregon Trail," *Highway Magazine* 14 (October 1923): 2–5.

19. Ibid.; Merrill J. Mattes, "Scotts Bluff and the Old Oregon Trail," *Highway Magazine* 31 (November 1940): 255–58 (a reprint from *National Park Service Bulletin*).

20. Khyber Forrester, "Old 'Hell Trail' of the 'Forty-Niners,'" *Highway Magazine* 26 (August 1935): 172.

21. Charles Caldwell, as quoted in Joseph J. Corn, *The Winged Gospel: America's Romance with Aviation, 1900–1950* (New York: Oxford University Press, 1983), 46.

5. The Emergence of New Corridors of Power

1. Charles A. Lindbergh, *Autobiography of Values* (New York: Harcourt Brace Jovanovich, 1977), 8–9.

2. Albert Bond Lambert, "Early History of Aeronautics in St. Louis," *Missouri Historical Society Collections* V (June 1928): 237–55; Albert Bond Lambert Aeronautical Papers (two boxes at the Missouri Historical Society, St. Louis), and James J. Horgan, *City of Flight: The History of Aviation in St. Louis* (Gerald, Mo.: Patrice Press, 1984).

3. Dwight D. Eisenhower, *At Ease: Stories I Tell to Friends* (New York: Doubleday & Co., 1967), 159.

4. Ibid., 166.

5. Edwin A. Stevens, as quoted in the *Highway Magazine* 8 (May 1917): 1.

6. *Better Roads and Streets* 6 (May 1916): 22.

7. Ernest Flagg Ayres, "How the Idaho State Highway Department was Developed," *Highway Magazine* 16 (October 1925): 13–14.

8. Leland C. Lewis, "The West's Most Unique Highway," *Highway Magazine* 14 (August 1923): 6.

9. *Highway Magazine* 19 (January 1928): 8–10.

10. *Highway Magazine* 14 (March 1923): 2.

11. Aldo Leopold, "Conserving the Covered Wagon," *Sunset Magazine,* March 1925, in *The Early Sunset Magazine, 1898–1928,* ed. Paul C. Johnson, 213–15 (San Francisco: California Historical Society, 1973).

12. Drake Hokanson, *The Lincoln Highway: Main Street Across America* (Iowa City: University of Iowa Press, 1988), 6.

13. George R. Stewart, *U.S. 40: Cross Section of the United States of America* (Boston: Houghton Mifflin Co., 1953), 10–11; Hokanson, *Lincoln Highway,* 8–9.

14. As quoted in Tom Lewis, *Divided Highways: Building the Interstate Highways, Transforming American Life* (New York: Penguin Putnam, 1997), 50.

15. Hokanson, *Lincoln Highway,* 75.

16. Ibid., 76; Stewart, *U.S. 40,* 11.

17. *Proceedings of the First National Old Trails Road Convention* (1912), 21. A copy is preserved at the St. Louis Mercantile Library.

18. Stewart, *U.S. 40,* 12.

19. Hokanson, *Lincoln Highway,* 95, 106.

20. As quoted in ibid., 64.

21. *Highway Magazine* 16 (October 1925): 2.

22. The Lincoln Highway Association was reactivated in October 1992 to refresh the nation's collective memory of the original Lincoln Highway.

23. Michael Wallis, *Route 66: The Mother Road* (New York: St. Martin's Press, 1990), 1–2.

24. Ibid., 1.

25. *Better Roads and Streets* 6 (November 1916): 30; *Kansas Farmer* as quoted in *Highway Magazine* 7 (March 1916): 12.

26. Hokanson, *Lincoln Highway,* 82–83.

27. *Highway Magazine* 11 (January 1920): 34–35.

28. Ben H. Petty, "Road Signs of the Times," *Highway Magazine* 26 (February 1935): 32–33.

29. H. J. McKeever, "Wanted by American Farmers—Better Market Roads," *Highway Magazine* 19 (December 1928): 327–29; S. R. Winters, "Farm-to-Market Roads . . . A National Asset," *Highway Magazine* 30 (August 1939): 183–85.

30. Harry Byron Jay, "The Evolution of Road Location," *Highway Magazine* 20 (September 1929): 227ff.

31. Ibid.

32. Ibid., 227ff.; Baird H. Markham, "Highway Travel Develops into Big Business," *Highway Magazine* 31 (August 1940): 183–88.

33. *Highway Magazine* 31 (January 1940): 3.

34. Carl Crow, "'Uncle Ben' and the Caterpillar," *Sunset Magazine,* January 1917, in *Early Sunset Magazine,* ed. Paul C. Johnson, 169–72.

6. The Twentieth-Century Transportation Revolution

1. Walter P. Chrysler, *Life of an American Workman* (New York: Dodd, Mead & Co., 1937), 120.

2. As quoted in Vincent Curcio, *Chrysler: The Life and Times of an Automotive Genius* (New York: Oxford University Press, 2000), 124.

3. John R. Stilgoe, *Metropolitan Corridor: Railroads and the American Scene* (New Haven, Conn.: Yale University Press, 1983), 51.

4. Ibid., 54.

5. Allan Nevins, *Ford: The Times, the Man, the Company* (New York: Charles Scribner's Sons, 1954), 385.

6. On the jitney craze, see Carlos A. Schwantes, "The West Adapts the Automobile: Technology, Unemployment, and the Jitney Phenomenon of 1914–1917," *Western Historical Quarterly* 16 (July 1985): 307–26.

7. *Railway Age Gazette* 61 (December 1, 1916): 997.

8. *Railway Age* 87 (September 28, 1929): 755.

9. R. C. Henderson, "How the Automobile Has Built Roads," *Highway Magazine* 26 (December 1935): 292–95.

10. John W. Larimore, "The Changing Highway Picture," *Highway Magazine* 28 (July 1937): 153.

11. Robert R. Updegraff, "And Now—Mobility!" *Magazine of Business* 54 (August 1928): 161.

12. George R. Chatburn, *Highways and Highway Transportation* (New York: Thomas Y. Crowell Co., 1923): 203.

13. H. P. Burchell, "The Automobile as a Means of Country Travel [1905]," quoted in Frank Oppel, *Motoring in America: The Early Years* (Secaucus, N.J.: Castle Books, 1989), 273.

14. Gregory Lee Thompson, *The Passenger Train in the Motor Age: California's Rail and Bus Industries, 1910–1941* (Columbus: Ohio State University Press, 1993), 9, 22.

15. *Railway Age* 69 (August 6, 1920): 214–15.

16. Sinclair Lewis, *Main Street* (New York: Grosset & Dunlap, 1920), 20.

17. *Bus Transportation* 4 (January 1925), 27.

18. *Official Guide of the Railways,* May 1911, xxxi.

19. As quoted in Phil Patton, *Open Road: A Celebration of the American Highway* (New York: Simon & Schuster, 1986), 67.

20. Claude P. Fordyce, "Following the Highways for Health and Pleasure," *Highway Magazine* 16 (July 1925): 13.

21. *Railway Age* 86 (June 22, 1929): 1495.

22. Rollo Walter Brown, *I Travel by Train* (New York: D. Appleton-Century, 1939), 21.

23. Lewis R. Freeman, "From Chicago to Los Angeles on Common Carrier Lines," *Bus Transportation* 15 (June 1926): 295.

24. *Railway Age* 86 (April 27, 1929): 998.

25. *Railway Age* 86 (January 5, 1929): 107.

26. [Jack Rhodes], *Intercity Bus Lines of the Southwest: A Photographic History by Jack Rhodes* (College Station: Texas A&M University Press, 1988), 119.

7. The New Overland Route

1. The story of the first transcontinental telephone conversation comes from Phil Ault, *Wires West* (New York: Dodd, Mead & Co., 1974), 160–63. See also Robert Luther Thompson, *Wiring a Continent: The History of the Telegraph Industry in the United States, 1832–1866* (Princeton, N.J.: Princeton University Press, 1947).

2. Good accounts of the Rodgers flight appear in Sherwood Harris, *The First to Fly: Aviation's Pioneer Days* (New York: Simon & Schuster, 1970), 256–79; and Harry Bruno, *Wings over America: The Inside Story of American Aviation* (New York: Robert M. McBride & Co., 1942), 65–79.

3. For my discussion of early aviation in the inland Northwest, I am heavily indebted to my graduate student Daniel Rust and to his unpublished essay, "Nick Mamer and the First Century of Aviation in the Inland Empire," which he presented to a Phi Alpha Theta regional conference in 1999.

4. G. Thornhill, "System in the Industry," *Aero Digest* 16 (April 1930): 51.

5. Federal officials had grounded the Fokker's model F-10a as a result of a TWA crash in 1931 that killed Knute Rockne, Notre Dame's illustrious football coach. Its fatal flaw lay concealed within wings that consisted of a wooden framework covered with plywood, a design that proved highly susceptible to wood rot. See Robert J. Serling, "Clipped Wings: The Grounding of Airlines with Fatal Flaws," *Airliners* 15 (January/February 2002): 65–71.

6. As quoted in *Official Aviation Guide*, August 1938, 4–5.

7. Charles K. Field, "On the Wings of Today," *Sunset Magazine*, March 1910, as quoted in Paul C. Johnson, ed., *The Early Sunset Magazine, 1898–1928* (San Francisco: California Historical Society, 1973), 118–23.

8. Ibid.

9. Ibid.

10. Ibid.

11. Robert J. Serling, *Eagle: The Story of American Airlines* (New York: St. Martin's/Marek, 1985), 8.

12. Andrew McNally III, *Proceedings of the Annual Conference of the American Association of Passenger Traffic Officers* (1955), 26; as quoted in *Pilots' Directions: The Transcontinental Airway and Its History*, ed. William M. Leary (Iowa City: University of Iowa Press, 1990; reprint of the Post Office guide published in 1921), 62–63.

13. Herbert Hoover Jr., "The Function of Aircraft Radio," *Aero Digest* 16 (January 1930): 61.

14. When Congress enacted the Kelly Act, there were three modest passenger-carrying airlines in the United States, two of them located in the West: short-lived Ryan Airlines between Los Angeles and San Diego; and Pacific Marine Airways between Wilmington, California, and Catalina Island, founded by Sid Chaplin, the brother of movie comedian Charlie Chaplin.

15. *Aero Digest* 16 (May 1930): 153; George Svehla, "A Survey of Civil Aviation in the Southwest," *Aero Digest* 17 (August 1930): 58.

16. *Highway Magazine* 19 (May 1928): 133; *Highway Magazine* 20 (September 1929): 242.

17. *Official Guide of the Railways*, July 1, 1929, xxvii. *Official Guide of the Railways*, July 1929, 3; *Official Guide of the Railways*, August 1929, 11.

18. *Official Guide of the Railways,* July 1929, 3; *Official Guide of the Railways,* August 1929, 11.

19. *Official Guide of the Railways,* July 1, 1929, xxvii.

20. As quoted in Thomas Petzinger Jr., *Hard Landing: The Epic Contest for Power and Profits That Plunged the Airlines into Chaos* (New York: Three Rivers Press, 1995), 4; Joseph J. Corn, *The Winged Gospel: America's Romance with Aviation, 1900–1950* (New York: Oxford University Press, 1983), 25.

21. Ralph L. Woods, "The Grouping of Aircraft Companies," *Aero Digest* 16 (March 1930): 80ff.

22. Marcia Davenport, "Covered Wagon—1932," *Good Housekeeping* 95 (October 1932): 140–49.

23. Robert S. Clary, "The Next Ten Years of Flying," *Aero Digest* 16 (March 1930): 57ff.

24. As quoted in Robert J. Serling, *The Only Way to Fly: The Story of Western Airlines, America's Senior Air Carrier* (New York: Doubleday & Co., 1976), 114.

25. *Fortune* 9 (May 1934): 89.

26. R. Thompson, Passenger Traffic Manager, Chicago & North Western Railway, in *Proceedings of the Annual Conference of the American Association of Passenger Traffic Officers* (1934), 51.

27. Serling, *The Only Way to Fly,* 143.

28. As quoted in ibid., 171.

29. *Railway Age* 86 (May 25, 1929): 1190.

8. Hard Choices for Hard Times

1. *North Western Bulletin* of January 1909, as quoted in the *Official Guide of the Railways,* March 1909, xxvii. In another variation of this story, Vanderbilt responds to a reporter for the *Chicago Daily News,* Clarence Dresser, on October 8, 1882.

2. *Railway Age* 93 (December 3, 1932), 812; George W. Anderson, "Roads —Motor and Rail," *Atlantic Monthly* 135 (March 1925), 393–404.

3. *Official Guide of the Railways,* November 1911, xxxii; *Railway & Marine News* 22 (February 1924): 9.

4. *Railway Age* 89 (July 20, 1929): 187.

5. *Railway Age* 89 (December 7, 1929): 1317.

6. *Official Guide of the Railways,* November 1927, xxx.

7. *Official Guide of the Railways,* May 1930, 16.

8. *Railway Age* 81 (November 20, 1926): 967.

9. J. L. Hays, manager news bureau, Union Pacific System, in *Railway & Marine News* 27 (October 1930): 24–25.

10. Great Northern Railway, *Annual Report for 1925,* 8; Great Northern Railway, *Annual Report for 1926,* 8; Great Northern Railway, *Annual Report for 1930,* 7.

11. *Railway Age* 87 (December 28, 1929): 1462; *Railway Age* 87 (September 28, 1929): 755.

12. Albro Martin, *Railroads Triumphant: The Growth, Rejection, and Rebirth of a Vital American Force* (New York: Oxford University Press, 1992), 109.

13. *Railway Age* 94 (April 8, 1933): 501.

14. *Official Guide of the Railways,* August 1927, xxxi.

15. *Official Guide of the Railways,* April 1930, 20.

16. R. Thompson, Passenger Traffic Manager, Chicago and North Western Railway, *Proceedings of the Annual Conference of the American Association of Passenger Traffic Officers* (1934), 58.

17. Mark Reutter, "Building a Better Iron Horse," *Railroad History,* Millennium Special [2000]: 40.

18. *Official Guide of the Railways,* December 1939, 41; *Official Guide of the Railways,* October 1941, 52.

19. Paul J. Neff, Assistant Chief Traffic Officer—Passenger, Missouri Pacific Lines, *Proceedings of the American Association of Passenger Traffic Officers* (1940), 55.

20. Lloyd W. McDowell, "Westward Comes the Tourist," *Railway and Marine News* 21 (May 1923): 12.

21. *Official Guide of the Railways,* August 1905, xxx.

22. *Official Guide of the Railways,* August 1926, xxxii.

23. *Official Guide of the Railways,* March 1930, 15.

24. *Official Guide of the Railways,* June 1939, 29.

25. *Official Guide of the Railways,* April 1941, 39.

26. *Official Guide of the Railways,* May 1927, xxvi.

27. *Official Guide of the Railways,* March 1927, xxxi; November 1928, 6.

28. *Official Guide of the Railways,* December 1939, 41.

29. *Official Guide of the Railways,* April 1931, 45.

30. *Official Guide of the Railways,* August 1929, 12.

31. *Official Guide of the Railways,* December 1933, 42.

32. *Official Guide of the Railways,* June 1915, xxvi.

33. *Official Guide of the Railways,* February 1928, xxx.

34. *Official Guide of the Railways,* January 1905, xxix

35. From *Rocky Mountain Official Railway Guide,* February 1906 (reprinted by the Pacific Railway Journal, San Marino, California, 1960), 12, 15.

36. *Official Guide of the Railways,* December 1936, 43; *Official Guide of the Railways,* February 1937, 40.

37. Donald Magarrel, "Food Service on Air Lines," *Aero Digest* 30 (April 1937): 23.

38. *Aero Digest* 29 (July 1936): 67.

39. *Official Guide of the Railways,* September 1939, 36.

9. Is This Trip Necessary?

1. Tom Brokaw, *The Greatest Generation* (New York: Random House, 1998).

2. *Portland Oregonian,* April 6, 1941.

3. *Aero Digest* 16 (April 1930): 109.

4. For further discussion of wartime life in this corner of the United States, see Carlos A. Schwantes, ed., *The Pacific Northwest in World War II* (Manhattan, Kans.: Sunflower University Press, 1986).

5. *Highway Magazine* 33 (December 1942): 287.

6. Leon S. Wellstone, "Gasoline Rationing and Business," *Highway Magazine* 33 (October 1942): 231, 233.

7. *Railway Age* 114 (April 24, 1943): 816.

8. Ibid.

9. G. Lloyd Wilson, *Selected Papers and Addresses of Joseph B. Eastman* (New York: Simmons-Boardman, 1948): 89.

10. As quoted in the *Highway Magazine* 33 (October 1942): 232.

11. *Official Guide of the Railways,* July 1945, 14.

12. *Highway Magazine* 33 (April 1942): 82.

13. J. Monroe Johnson as quoted in *Official Guide to the Railways,* July 1945, 14.

14. Southern Pacific, *Public Timetable,* November 22, 1942.

15. Southern Pacific, *Condensed Public Timetable,* July 26, 1942.

16. R. H. Clare, General Passenger Agent, Pennsylvania Railroad, *Proceedings of the Annual Conference of the American Association of Passenger Traffic Officers* (1946), 82.

17. *Official Guide of the Railways,* January 1946, xv.

18. Ibid., xvi.

19. Ibid., xv.

20. As quoted in Carl Solberg, *Conquest of the Skies: A History of Commercial Aviation in America* (Boston: Little, Brown and Co., 1979), 318.

10. Auto Euphoria and Other Postwar Enthusiasms

1. John Steinbeck, *Travels with Charley: In Search of America* (New York: Viking Press, 1961), 81.

2. On the Pennsylvania Turnpike, see Dan Cupper, "The Road to the Future," *American Heritage,* May/June 1990, 102–11.

3. *Highway Magazine* 37 (December 1946): 243.

4. As quoted in Richard Longstreth, *City Center to Regional Mall: Architecture, the Automobile, and Retailing in Los Angeles, 1920–1950* (Cambridge, Mass.: MIT Press, 1997), 13.

5. All quotes for this section come from Jack D. Rittenhouse, *A Guide Book to Highway 66* (1946; reprint, Albuquerque: University of New Mexico Press, 1989), 5.

6. Tom Snyder, *The Route 66 Traveler's Guide and Roadside Companion* (New York: St. Martin's Press, 1990), xv–xvi.

7. Ibid., xvi–xvii.

8. *St. Louis Post-Dispatch,* February 20, 2001.

9. James Lehrer, *We Were Dreamers* (New York: Atheneum, 1986).

10. H. H. Dunn, "Plan High-Speed Motorways in California," *Highway Magazine* 16 (March 1925): 6–7.

11. Ibid.

12. C. F. Seifried, "Wyoming's Far Flung Highways Are Modernized for Defense or Tourist Travel," *Highway Magazine* 32 (January 1941): 15–17

13. *Highway Magazine* 38 (October 1947): 231.

14. For an extended examination of this subject, see Carlos A. Schwantes, "Anxiety and Affluence: The 1950s in Oregon and Washington," in *Jet Dreams: Art of the Fifties in the Northwest,* ed. Barbara Johns (Tacoma and Seattle: Tacoma Art Museum and the University of Washington Press, 1995), 34–45.

15. Dwight D. Eisenhower, *Mandate for Change, 1953–1956* (New York: Doubleday & Co., 1963), 501, 548.

16. Ibid., 501.

17. Ibid.

18. *Highway Magazine* 7 (October 1916): 12.

19. Eisenhower, *Mandate for Change,* 548.

20. Ibid.

21. Tom Lewis, *Divided Highways: Building the Interstate Highways, Transforming American Life* (New York: Penguin Putnam, 1997), ix.

22. Eisenhower, *Mandate for Change,* 549.

23. R. C. Henderson, "Our Roadsides Bloom," *Highway Magazine* 29 (May 1938): 116.

24. Roy A. Klein, "Preservation of Scenic Resources along Oregon Highways," *Highway Magazine* 16 (May 1925): 6–7.

25. Ibid.

26. William Least Heat Moon, *Blue Highways: A Journey through America* (Boston: Little, Brown, 1982).

27. Baird H. Markham, "Highway Travel Develops into Big Business," *Highway Magazine* 31 (August 1940): 183.

28. Ibid.

29. American Automobile Association, *Western Directory of Accommodations Listing the Better Hotels, Resorts, Inns, Courts, Cabins and Restaurants* (Washington, D.C.: American Automobile Association, 1941), 4.

30. S. R. Winters, "Cabins and Courts at 'America's Crossroads,'" *Highway Magazine* 37 (June–July 1946), 136.

31. Lewis, *Divided Highways,* 212–13.

32. Snyder, *Route 66 Traveler's Guide,* xvii.

11. The Sky's the Limit

1. St. Louis *Post-Dispatch,* March 13, 2001.

2. Edward V. Rickenbacker, *Rickenbacker* (Englewood Cliffs, N.J.: Prentice-Hall, 1967), 228.

3. As quoted in Frank J. Taylor, *High Horizons: Daredevil Flying Postmen to Modern Magic Carpet—The United Air Lines Story* (New York: McGraw-Hill Book Co., 1951), 142–43.

4. W. A. Patterson as quoted in Arch Whitehouse, *The Sky's the Limit: A History of the U.S. Airlines* (New York: Macmillan Co., 1971), 292.

5. Thomas Petzinger Jr., *Hard Landing: The Epic Contest for Power and Profits That Plunged the Airlines into Chaos* (New York: Three Rivers Press, 1995), 23.

6. R. E. G. Davies and I. E. Quastler, *Commuter Airlines of the United States* (Washington, D.C.: Smithsonian Institution Press, 1995), 262.

7. As quoted in R. E. G. Davies, *Rebels and Reformers of the Airways* (Washington, D.C.: Smithsonian Institution Press, 1987): 61.

8. Petzinger Jr., *Hard Landing,* 30.

9. *USA Today,* December 12, 2000.

10. As quoted in Donna M. Corbett, "Donald W. Nyrop: Airline Regulator, Airline Executive," in *Airline Executives and Federal Regulation: Case Studies in American Enterprise from the Airmail Era to the Dawn of the Jet Age,* ed. W. David Lewis (Columbus: Ohio State University Press, 2000), 153.

11. *Official Airline Guide,* December 1954, 477.

12. *Seattle Times* as quoted in *Railway & Marine News* 26 (November 1929): 66.

13. *Proceedings of the Annual Conference of the American Association of Passenger Traffic Officers* (1930), 52.

12. Reinventing the Railroads

1. *Official Guide of the Railways,* March 1955, 351–52.

2. I have recorded life's lessons learned this way in a lighthearted publication titled *Everything I Needed to Know about Life I Learned from the Pennsy* (St. Louis: John Barriger III National Railroad Library, a special collection of the St. Louis Mercantile Library, 2001).

3. *Proceedings of the Annual Conference of the American Association of Passenger Traffic Officers* (1968), 8.

4. Ibid.

5. *Railway Age* 140 (May 21, 1956): 94. These ranks are in terms of passenger-miles.

6. *Railway Progress,* 10 (May 1956): 8–9.

7. *Proceedings of the Annual Conference of the American Association of Passenger Traffic Officers* (1931), 47.

8. David P. Morgan, *Proceedings of the Interim Business Meeting of the American Association of Passenger Traffic Officers* (1958), 10.

9. Pierre Martineau, *Proceedings of the Interim Business Meeting of the American Association of Passenger Traffic Officers* (1958), 7.

10. Ibid., 8.

11. *Official Guide of the Railways,* April 1953, 14.

12. *Proceedings of the Annual Conference of the to the American Association of Passenger Traffic Officers* (1968), 16.

13. *Railroad Magazine* 86 (November 1969): 31; *Proposed Passenger Train Act of 1960,* Hearing before the Surface Transportation subcommittee of the Committee on Interstate and Foreign Commerce, United States Senate, 86th Congress, 2nd Session (Washington, D.C.: Government Printing Office, 1960), 59.

14. *Proceedings of the Annual Conference of the to the American Association of Passenger Traffic Officers* (1968), 7.

15. H. J. McKeever, "Wanted by American Farmers—Better Market Roads," *Highway Magazine* 19 (December 1928): 327–29; S. R. Winters, "Farm-to-Market Roads . . . A National Asset," *Highway Magazine* 30 (August 1939): 183–85.

16. *Official Guide of the Railways,* August 1932, 58.

17. As quoted in Frank N. Wilner, *Railroad Mergers: History, Analysis, Insight* (Omaha: Simmons-Boardman Books, 1997), 220. The statistics come from *Railroad History,* Autumn 2001, 17.

18. As quoted in John F. Stover, *American Railroads,* 2nd ed. (Chicago: University of Chicago Press, 1997), 246.

19. George W. Hilton, "The Demise of the ICC," *Railroad History,* Autumn 2001, 8–15.

20. In 1988 the ICC authorized the holding company Rio Grande Industries, which controlled the 2,250 mile Denver & Rio Grande Western, to acquire financial control of the ailing Southern Pacific, 13,800 miles, and become a

15,000-mile system in the same league as Union Pacific and Burlington Northern.

Conclusion

1. Francis Vivian Drake, "Pegasus Express," *Atlantic Monthly* 149 (June 1932): 669.

2. Edgar H. Felix, "Airport and Airway News," *Aero Digest* 13 (December 1928): 1138.

3. Ibid.

4. *Fortune* 143 (October 9, 2000): 22.

5. As quoted in George R. Chatburn, *Highways and Highway Transportation* (New York: Thomas Y. Crowell Co., 1923), 205.

6. Harris M. Hanshue, "Across the Continent in 12 Hours," *Aeronautics* 6 (June 1930): 463–64, 482.

7. Francis Vivian Drake, "Pegasus Express," *Atlantic Monthly* 149 (June 1932): 663.

8. Ibid., 665–66.

9. Ibid.

10. Ibid., 670.

11. *Birth of an Industry: A Nostalgic Collection of Airline Schedules for the Years 1929 through 1939* (Oak Brook, Ill.: Reuben H. Donnelley Corporation, 1969). Facsimile reprints of key issues of the *Official Aviation Guide*.

12. Midway ceased flying on September 12, 2001, the day following terrorist attacks on New York and Washington.

13. My area and population statistics come from *The New York Times Almanac 2002* (New York: Penguin Putnam, 2001). In calculating the population of the contiguous states of the West, I included all of Minnesota and Louisiana, though the Mississippi River bisects both states.

14. I originally discussed the concept of noncontiguous urban sprawl in a brief essay, "Our Western Landscape Is Shrinking," *Journal of the West* 39 (Summer 2000): 3–5.

15. Sam Bass Warner Jr., *Streetcar Suburbs: The Process of Growth in Boston, 1870–1900* (Cambridge, Mass.: Harvard University Press and MIT Press, 1962).

Sources of Images

The camera of
piercing the gloom
waning days as

The following bibliography seeks to guide readers to my sources as well as suggest opportunities for further study. Some sources are mentioned only in the chapter notes.

Prologue

Francaviglia, Richard V. *Hard Places: Reading the Landscape of America's Historic Mining Districts.* Iowa City: University of Iowa Press, 1991.

Johnson, Paul C., ed. *The Early Sunset Magazine, 1898–1928.* San Francisco: California Historical Society, 1973.

Malone, Michael P., and Richard W. Etulain. *The American West: A Twentieth-Century History.* Lincoln: University of Nebraska Press, 1989.

Meinig, D. W. *The Great Columbia Plain: A Historical Geography, 1805–1910.* Seattle: University of Washington Press, 1968.

———. *Southwest: Three Peoples in Geographical Change, 1600–1970.* New York: Oxford University Press, 1971.

Nash, Gerald D. *The American West in the Twentieth Century: A Short History of an Urban Oasis.* Albuquerque: University of New Mexico Press, 1977.

Stilgoe, John R. *Common Landscape of America, 1580–1845.* New Haven, Conn.: Yale University Press, 1982.

———. *Outside Lies Magic: Regaining History and Awareness in Everyday Places.* New York: Walter and Co., 1998.

1. Transportation Corridors Transform the West

Armstrong, Ellis L., ed. *History of Public Works in the United States, 1776–1976.* Chicago: American Public Works Association, 1976.

Billington, David P. *The Tower and the Bridge: The New Art of Structural Engineering.* Princeton, N.J.: Princeton University Press, 1985.

Bottles, Scott L. *Los Angeles and the Automobile: The Making of the Modern City.* Berkeley: University of California Press, 1987.

Brodsly, David *L. A. Freeway: An Appreciative Essay.* Berkeley: University of California Press, 1981.

Cook, Richard J. *The Beauty of Railroad Bridges in North America: Then and Now.* San Marino, Calif.: Golden West Books, 1987.

Cronon, William. *Nature's Metropolis: Chicago and the Great West.* New York: W. W. Norton & Co., 1991.

Fogelson, Robert M. *The Fragmented Metropolis: Los Angeles, 1850–1930.* Berkeley: University of California Press, 1967.

Frederick, J. V. *Ben Holladay, the Stagecoach King: A Chapter in the Development of Transcontinental Transportation.* 1940. Reprint, Lincoln: University of Nebraska Press, 1989.

Hudson, John C. "Railroads and Urbanization in the Northwestern States." In *Centennial West: Essays on the Northern Tier States,* ed. William L. Lang, 169–93. Seattle: University of Washington Press, 1991.

Hunter, Louis C. *Steamboats on the Western Rivers: An Economic and Technological History.* Cambridge: Mass.: Harvard University Press, 1949.

Larson, John Lauritz. *Bonds of Enterprise: John Murray Forbes and Western Development in America's Railway Age.* Boston: Harvard University Graduate School of Business Administration, 1984.

Lass, William E. *A History of Steamboating on the Upper Missouri.* Lincoln: University of Nebraska Press, 1962.

Lingenfelter, Richard E. *Steamboats on the Colorado River, 1852–1916.* Tucson: University of Arizona Press, 1978.

MacMullen, Jerry. *Paddle-Wheel Days in California.* Stanford, Calif.: Stanford University Press, 1944.

McShane, Clay. *Down the Asphalt Path: The Automobile and the American City.* New York: Columbia University Press, 1994.

Mills, Randall V. *Stern-Wheelers up Columbia: A Century of Steamboating in the Oregon Country.* 1947. Reprint, Lincoln: University of Nebraska Press, 1977.

Miner, H. Craig. *The St. Louis-San Francisco Transcontinental Railroad: The Thirty-Fifth Parallel Project, 1853–1890.* Lawrence: University Press of Kansas, 1972.

Moody, Ralph. *Stagecoach West.* New York: Thomas Y. Crowell, 1967.

Russel, Robert R. *Improvement of Communication with the Pacific Coast as an Issue in American Politics, 1783–1864.* Cedar Rapids, Iowa: Torch Press, 1948.

Schonberger, Howard B. *Transportation to the Seaboard: The "Communication Revolution" and American Foreign Policy, 1860–1900.* Westport, Conn.: Greenwood Publishing Corporation, 1971.

Scott, Quinta. *Along Route 66.* Norman: University of Oklahoma Press, 2000.

Steinbeck, John. *The Grapes of Wrath.* New York: Viking Press, 1939.

Taylor, George Rogers. *The Transportation Revolution, 1815–1860.* New York: Holt, Rinehart and Winston, 1951.

Vance, James E., Jr. *Capturing the Horizon: The Historical Geography of Transportation since the Sixteenth Century.* 1986. Reprint, Baltimore: Johns Hopkins University Press, 1990.

White, Richard. *The Organic Machine: The Remaking of the Columbia River.* New York: Hill and Wang, 1995.

Winther, Oscar Osburn. *The Transportation Frontier: Trans-Mississippi West, 1865–1890.* New York: Holt, Rinehart and Winston, 1964.

2. When Railroads Ruled

Armbruster, Kurt E. *Orphan Road: The Railroad Comes to Seattle, 1853–1911.* Pullman: Washington State University Press, 1999.

Athearn, Robert G. *Union Pacific Country.* Chicago: Rand McNally, 1971.

Bartky, Ian R. *Selling the True Time: Nineteenth-Century Timekeeping in America.* Stanford, Calif.: Stanford University Press, 2000.

Beebe, Lucius, and Charles Clegg. *The Trains We Rode.* 2 vols. Berkeley, Calif.: Howell-North Books, 1965–66.

Best, Gerald M. *Snowplow: Clearing Mountain Rails.* Burbank, Calif.: Howell-North Books, 1966.

Borchgrave, Alexandra Villard de, and John Cullen. *Villard: The Life and Times of an American Titan.* New York: Doubleday, 2001.

Colorado Midland Railway. *Official Time Tables and Connections, December 1902.* Reprint.

Deverell, William. *Railroad Crossing: Californians and the Railroad, 1850–1910.* Berkeley: University of California Press, 1994.

Douglas, George H. *All Aboard! The Railroad in American Life.* New York: Marlowe & Co., 1992.

Dubin, Arthur D. *More Classic Trains.* Milwaukee: Kalmbach Publishing, 1974.

———. *Some Classic Trains.* Milwaukee: Kalmbach Publishing, 1964.

Gordon, Sarah H. *Passage to Union: How Railroads Transformed American Life, 1829–1929.* Chicago: Ivan R. Dee, 1997.

Grant, H. Roger. *The North Western: A History of the Chicago & North Western Railway System.* DeKalb: Northern Illinois University Press, 1996.

Grant, H. Roger. "Seeking the Pacific: The Chicago & North Western's Plans to Reach the West Coast." *Pacific Northwest Quarterly* 81 (April 1990): 67–73.

Greever, William S. "Railway Development in the Southwest." *New Mexico Historical Quarterly* 32 (April 1957): 151–203.

Hidy, Ralph W., Muriel E. Hidy, and Roy V. Scott, with Don L. Hofsommer. *The Great Northern Railway: A History.* Boston: Harvard Business School Press, 1988.

Hofsommer, Don L. *The Southern Pacific, 1901–1985.* College Station: Texas A&M University Press, 1986.

———. "For Territorial Dominion in California and the Pacific Northwest: Edward H. Harriman and James J. Hill." *California History* 70 (Spring 1991): 30–45.

———. "Rivals for California: The Great Northern and Southern Pacific, 1905–1931." *Montana, the Magazine of Western History* 38 (Spring 1988): 58–67.

———, ed., *Railroads in the West.* Manhattan, Kans.: Sunflower University Press, 1978.

Klein, Maury. *Unfinished Business: The Railroad in American Life.* Hanover, N.H.: University Press of New England, 1994.

———. *Union Pacific: The Rebirth, 1894–1969.* New York: Doubleday, 1989.

Kratville, William W. *Steam, Steel & Limiteds: A Definitive History of the Golden Age of America's Steam Powered Passenger Trains.* Omaha, Neb.: Kratville Publications, 1983.

McFarland, Edward M. "Mel." *A Colorado Midland Guide and Data Book.* Golden: Colorado Railroad Museum, 1980.

MacKay, Donald. *The Asian Dream: The Pacific Rim and Canada's National Railway.* Vancouver, B.C.: Douglas & McIntyre, 1986.

McKee, Bill, and Georgeen Klassen, *Trail of Iron: The CPR and the Birth of the West.* Vancouver, B.C.: Douglas & McIntyre, 1983.

Malone, Michael P. *James J. Hill: Empire Builder of the Northwest.* Norman: University of Oklahoma Press, 1996.

Martin, Albro. *James J. Hill and the Opening of the Northwest.* New York: Oxford University Press, 1976.

Meeks, Carroll L. V. *The Railroad Station: An Architectural History.* New Haven, Conn.: Yale University Press, 1956.

Middleton, William D. *Landmarks on the Iron Road: Two Centuries of North American Railroad Engineering.* Bloomington: Indiana University Press, 1999.

Overton, Richard C. *Burlington West: A Colonization History of the Burlington Railroad.* Cambridge, Mass.: Harvard University Press, 1941.

Richards, Jeffrey, and John M. MacKenzie. *The Railway Station: A Social History.* New York: Oxford University Press, 1986.

Riegel, Robert Edgar. *The Story of Western Railroads: From 1852 through the Reign of the Giants.* New York: Macmillan, 1926.

Schivelbusch, Wolfgang. *The Railway Journey: Trains and Travel in the 19th Century.* New York: Urizen Books, 1979.

Schwantes, Carlos A. *Railroad Signatures Across the Pacific Northwest.* Seattle: University of Washington Press, 1993.

Scott, Roy V. *Railroad Development Programs in the Twentieth Century.* Ames: Iowa State University Press, 1985.

Stilgoe, John R. *Metropolitan Corridor: Railroads and the American Scene.* New Haven, Conn.: Yale University Press, 1983.

Stover, John F. *American Railroads.* 2nd ed. Chicago: University of Chicago Press, 1997.

Vance, James E., Jr. *The North American Railroad: Its Origin, Evolution, and Geography.* Baltimore: Johns Hopkins University Press, 1995.

Ward, James A. *Railroads and the Character of America, 1820–1887.* Knoxville: University of Tennessee Press, 1986.

White, W. Thomas, ed., "Railroads and the American West." Theme issue of *Journal of the West* 39 (Spring 2000).

3. Copper Connections and the Last Transcontinental Railroad

DeNevi, Don. *The Western Pacific: Railroading Yesterday, Today and Tomorrow.* Seattle: Superior Publishing Co., 1978.

Derlieth, August. *The Milwaukee Road: Its First Hundred Years.* New York: Creative Age Press, 1948.

Hilton, George W., and John F. Due. *The Electric Interurban Railways in America.* Stanford, Calif.: Stanford University Press, 1964.

Middleton, William D. *The Interurban Era.* Milwaukee: Kalmbach Publishing, 1961.

———. *The Time of the Trolley: The Street Railway from Horsecar to Light Rail.* San Marino, Calif.: Golden West Books, 1987.

———. *When the Steam Railroads Electrified.* Milwaukee: Kalmbach Publishing, 1974.

Mills, Randall V. "Early Electric Interurbans in Oregon." *Oregon Historical Quarterly* 44 (March 1943): 82–104; and 44 (December 1943): 386–410.

———. "Recent History of Oregon's Electric Interurbans." *Oregon Historical Quarterly* 46 (June 1945): 112–39.

Schwantes, Carlos A. *Vision and Enterprise: Exploring the History of Phelps Dodge Corporation*. Tucson: University of Arizona Press, 2000.

Signor, John R. *The Los Angeles and Salt Lake Railroad Company: Union Pacific's Historic Salt Lake Route*. San Marino, Calif.: Golden West Books, 1988.

Turbeville, Daniel E. *The Electric Railway Era in Northwest Washington, 1890–1930*. Bellingham: Center for Pacific Northwest Studies, 1978.

4. Roads Stretching from Farm to Market, but Seldom Beyond

Berger, Michael L. *The Devil Wagon in God's Country: The Automobile and Social Change in Rural America, 1893–1929*. Hamden, Conn.: Archon Books, 1979.

Fahl, Ronald H. "S. C. Lancaster and the Columbia River Highway: Engineer as Conservationist." *Oregon Historical Quarterly* 74 (June 1973): 100–144.

Finch, Christopher. *Highways to Heaven. The Auto Biography of America*. New York: HarperCollins, 1992.

Flink, James J. *America Adopts the Automobile, 1895–1910*. Cambridge, Mass.: MIT Press, 1970.

Holt, W. Stull. *The Bureau of Public Roads: Its History, Activities and Organization*. Baltimore: Johns Hopkins University Press, 1923.

Horn, C. Lester. "Oregon's Columbia River Highway." *Oregon Historical Quarterly* 66 (September 1965): 249–71.

Lewis, Sinclair. *Free Air*. 1919. Reprint, Lincoln: University of Nebraska Press, 1993.

Mason, Philip Parker. *The League of American Wheelmen and the Good-Roads Movement, 1880–1905*. Ann Arbor: University of Michigan Press, 1957.

Oppel, Frank, ed., *Motoring in America: The Early Years*. Secaucus, N.J.: Castle Books, 1989.

Preston, Howard Lawrence. *Dirt Roads to Dixie: Accessibility and Modernization in the South, 1885–1935*. Knoxville: University of Tennessee Press, 1991.

Proceedings of First National Old Trails Road Convention. Kansas City, Missouri, April 17, 1912.

Rose, Albert C. *Historic American Roads: From Frontier Trails to Superhighways*. New York: Crown Publishers, 1976.

Scharff, Virginia. *Taking the Wheel: Women and the Coming of the Motor Age*. New York: Free Press, 1991.

Sears, Stephen W. *The Automobile in America*. New York: American Heritage, 1977.

Wixom, Charles W. *Pictorial History of Roadbuilding*. Washington, D.C.: American Road Builders' Association, 1975.

5. The Emergence of New Corridors of Power

Belasco, Warren James. *Americans on the Road: From Autocamp to Motel, 1910–1945*. Cambridge, Mass.: MIT Press, 1979.

Cole, Terrence M. "Ocean to Ocean by Model T: Henry Ford and the 1909 Transcontinental Auto Contest," *Journal of Sport History* 18 (Summer 1991): 224–40.

Flink, James J. *The Automobile Age.* Cambridge, Mass.: MIT Press, 1988.

———. *The Car Culture.* Cambridge, Mass.: MIT Press, 1975.

Hokanson, Drake. *The Lincoln Highway: Main Street Across America.* Iowa City: University of Iowa Press, 1988.

Laux, James M. "Alexander Winton" and "Winton Motor Carriage Company." In George S. May, ed., *The Automobile Industry, 1896–1920,* a volume of *The Encyclopedia of American Business History and Biography,* 468–74. New York: Facts on File, 1990.

McConnell, Curt. *Coast to Coast by Automobile: The Pioneering Trips, 1899–1908.* Stanford, Calif.: Stanford University Press, 2000.

Manchester, Albert D. *Trails Begin Where Rails End: Early-Day Motoring Adventures in the West and Southwest.* Glendale, Calif.: Trans-Anglo Books, 1987.

Post, Emily. *By Motor to the Golden Gate.* New York: D. Appleton and Co., 1916.

Raitz, Karl, ed., *The National Road.* Baltimore: Johns Hopkins University Press, 1996.

Sadin, Paul. "Demon, Distraction, or Deliverer? The Impact of Automobile Tourism on the Development, Management, and Use of Mount Rainier National Park, 1907–1966." MA thesis, University of Idaho, 2000.

Schlereth, Thomas J. *US 40: A Roadscape of the American Experience.* Indianapolis: Indiana Historical Society, 1985.

Snyder, Tom. *The Route 66 Traveler's Guide and Roadside Companion.* New York: St. Martin's Press, 1990.

Stewart, George R. *U.S. 40: Cross Section of the United States of America.* Boston: Houghton Mifflin, 1953.

Tarkington, Booth. *The Magnificent Ambersons.* 1918. Reprint, N.Y.: Random House, 1998. Transportation plays a central role in this Pulitzer Prize–winning novel.

Wallis, Michael. *Route 66: The Mother Road.* New York: St. Martin's Press, 1990.

6. The Twentieth-Century Transportation Revolution

Cantelon, Philip L., and Kenneth D. Durr. *The Roadway Story.* Rockville, Md.: Montrose Press, 1996.

Chrysler, Walter P. *Life of an American Workman.* New York: Dodd, Mead & Co., 1950.

Curcio, Vincent. *Chrysler: The Life and Times of an Automotive Genius.* New York: Oxford University Press, 2000.

Donovan, Frank. *Wheels for a Nation.* New York: Thomas Y. Crowell, 1965.

Foster, Mark S. *From Streetcar to Superhighway: American City Planning and Urban Transportation, 1900–1940.* Philadelphia: Temple University Press, 1981.

Goddard, Stephen B. *Getting There: The Epic Struggle between Road and Rail in the American Century.* New York: Basic Books, 1994.

Henderson, James David. *Meals by Fred Harvey.* 1969. Revised ed., Hawthorne, Calif.: Omni Publications, 1985.

Karolevitz, Robert F. *This Was Trucking: A Pictorial History of the First Quarter*

Century of Commercial Motor Vehicles. Seattle: Superior Publishing Co., 1956.

Knowles, Ruth Sheldon. *The First Pictorial History of the American Oil and Gas Industry, 1859–1983.* Athens: Ohio University Press, 1983.

Meier, Albert E., and John P. Hoschek. *Over the Road: A History of Intercity Bus Transportation in the United States.* Upper Montclair, N.J.: Motor Bus Society, 1975.

Poling-Kempes, Lesley. *The Harvey Girls: Women Who Opened the West.* New York: Paragon House, 1989.

[Rhodes, Jack.] *Intercity Bus Lines of the Southwest: A Photographic History by Jack Rhodes.* College Station: Texas A&M University Press, 1988.

Schlisgall, Oscar. *The Greyhound Story: From Hibbing to Everywhere.* Chicago: J. G. Ferguson Publishing Co., 1985.

Thomas, D. H. *The Southwestern Indian Detours: The Story of the Fred Harvey/Santa Fe Railway Experiment in "Detourism."* Phoenix: Hunter Publishing, 1978.

Wik, Reynold M. *Henry Ford and Grass-roots America.* Ann Arbor: University of Michigan Press, 1972.

Wren, James A., and Genevieve J. Wren. *Motor Trucks of America.* Ann Arbor: University of Michigan Press for Motor Vehicle Manufacturers Association of the United States, Inc., 1979.

7. The New Overland Route

Allen, Oliver E. *The Airline Builders.* Alexandria, Va.: Time-Life Books, 1981.

Berg, A. Scott. *Lindbergh.* New York: G. P. Putnam's Sons, 1998.

Birth of an Industry: A Nostalgic Collection of Airline Schedules for the Years 1929 through 1939. Oak Brook, Ill.: Reuben H. Donnelley Corporation, 1969. Facsimile reprints of key issues of the *Official Aviation Guide.*

Breihan, John R. "From Amusements to Weapons: The Glenn L. Martin Aircraft Company of California, 1910–1917." *Journal of the West* 36 (July 1997): 29–38.

Bruno, Harry. *Wings over America: The Inside Story of American Aviation.* New York: Robert M. McBride & Co., 1942.

Corn, Joseph J. *The Winged Gospel: America's Romance with Aviation, 1900–1950.* New York: Oxford University Press, 1983.

Davies, R. E. G. *Airlines of the United States since 1914.* 1972. Revised ed., Washington, D.C.: Smithsonian Institution Press, 1982.

Davis, Kenneth S. *The Hero: Charles A. Lindbergh and the American Dream.* Garden City, N.Y.: Doubleday & Co., 1959.

Gordon, David G. *Wings over Washington.* Seattle: Museum of Flight, 1989.

Gottlieb, Robert, and Irene Wolt. *Thinking Big: The Story of the Los Angeles Times, Its Publishers and Their Influence on Southern California.* New York: Putnam, 1977.

Harris, Patrick. "The Exhibition Era of Early Aviation in Oregon, 1910–1915." *Oregon Historical Quarterly* 87 (Fall 1986): 245–76.

Harris, Sherwood. *The First to Fly: Aviation's Pioneer Days.* New York: Simon and Schuster, 1970.

Hatfield, D. D. *Dominguez Air Meet.* Inglewood, Calif.: Northrop University Press, 1976.

Heppenheimer, T. A. *Turbulent Skies, The History of Commercial Aviation.* New York: John Wiley & Sons, 1995.

Holland, Maurice, with Thomas M. Smith. *Architects of Aviation.* 1951. Freeport, N.Y.: Books for Libraries Press, 1971.

Hudson, Kenneth. *Air Travel: A Social History.* Totowa, N.J.: Rowman and Littlefield, 1972.

Komons, Nick A. *Bonfires to Beacons: Federal Civil Aviation Policy under the Air Commerce Act, 1926–1938.* Washington: U.S. Department of Transportation, 1978.

Launius, Roger D., and Jessie L. Embry. "The 1910 Los Angeles Airshow: The Beginnings of Air Awareness in the West." *Southern California Historical Quarterly* 77 (Winter 1995): 329–46.

Leary, William M. *Aerial Pioneers: The U.S. Air Mail Service, 1918–1927.* Washington, D.C.: Smithsonian Institution Press, 1985.

———, ed. *The Airline Industry.* New York: Facts on File, 1992.

———, ed. *Aviation's Golden Age: Portraits from the 1920s and 1930s.* Iowa City: University of Iowa Press, 1989.

———, ed. *Pilots' Directions: The Transcontinental Airway and Its History.* Reprint, Iowa City: University of Iowa Press, 1990. Reprint of the Post Office's guide in 1921.

Leary, William M., and William F. Trimble, eds. *From Airships to Airbus: The History of Civil and Commercial Aviation.* Washington, D.C.: Smithsonian Institution Press, 1995.

Lindbergh, Charles A. *Autobiography of Values.* New York: Harcourt Brace Jovanovich, 1977.

Neal, J. Wesley. "America's First International Air Meet." *Historical Society of Southern California Quarterly* 43 (December 1961): 369–414.

Roseberry, C. R. *Glenn Curtiss: Pioneer of Flight.* Garden City, N.Y.: Doubleday & Co., 1972.

Serling, Robert J. *Eagle: The Story of American Airlines.* New York: St. Martin's/Marek, 1985.

———. *Maverick: The Story of Robert Six and Continental Airlines.* Garden City, N.Y.: Doubleday & Co., 1974.

———. *The Only Way to Fly: The Story of Western Airlines, America's Senior Air Carrier.* New York: Doubleday & Co., 1976.

Shamburger, Page. *Tracks across the Sky: The Story of the Pioneers of the U.S. Air Mail.* Philadelphia: J. B. Lippincott Co., 1964.

Smith, Henry Ladd. *Airways: The History of Commercial Aviation in the United States.* New York: Alfred A. Knopf, 1942.

Solberg, Carl. *Conquest of the Skies: A History of Commercial Aviation in America.* Boston: Little, Brown and Co., 1979.

Spitzer, Paul G. "Seattle's First Aviators and Their Claims to a New Province of the Sky." *Pacific Northwest Quarterly* 92 (Spring 2001): 71–79.

Taylor, Frank J. *High Horizons: Daredevil Flying Postmen to Modern Magic Carpet—The United Air Lines Story.* New York: McGraw Hill, 1951.

Trimble, William F. "Jerome C. Hunsaker, Bell Labs, and the West Coast Model Airline." *Journal of the West* 36 (July 1997): 44–52.

Tweney, George H. "Air Transportation and the American West." *Montana, the Magazine of Western History* 19 (Autumn 1969): 68–77.

Whitehouse, Arch. *The Sky's the Limit: A History of the U.S. Airlines*. New York: Macmillan Co., 1971.

Whitnah, Donald R. *Safer Skyways: Federal Control of Aviation, 1926–1966*. Ames: Iowa State University Press, 1966.

8. Hard Choices for Hard Times

Aron, Cindy S. *Working at Play: A History of Vacations in the United States*. New York: Oxford University Press, 1999.

Bartlett, Richard A. "Those Infernal Machines in Yellowstone Park." *Montana, the Magazine of Western History* 20 (July 1970): 16–29. A study of automobiles entering the nation's first national park.

Jakle, John A. *The Tourist: Travel in Twentieth-Century North America*. Lincoln: University of Nebraska Press, 1985.

Kolko, Gabriel. *Railroads and Regulation, 1877–1916*. Princeton, N.J.: Princeton University Press, 1965.

Löfgren, Orvar. *On Holiday: A History of Vacationing*. Berkeley: University of California Press, 1999.

Martin, Albro. *Enterprise Denied: Origins of the Decline of American Railroads, 1897–1917*. New York: Columbia University Press, 1971.

Meinkle, Jeffrey L. *Twentieth Century Limited: Industrial Design in America, 1925–1939*. Philadelphia: Temple University Press, 1979.

Pomeroy, Earl. *In Search of the Golden West: The Tourist in Western America*. New York: Alfred A. Knopf, 1957.

Pulos, Arthur J. *American Design Ethic: A History of Industrial Design to 1940*. Cambridge, Mass.: MIT Press, 1983.

Reed, Robert C. *The Streamliner Era*. San Marino, Calif.: Golden West Books, 1975.

Robertson, Archie. *Slow Train to Yesterday: A Last Glance at the Local*. Boston: Houghton Mifflin, 1945.

Rollo, Walter Brown. *I Travel by Train*. New York: D. Appleton-Century Co., 1939.

Rothman, Hal K. *Devil's Bargains: Tourism in the Twentieth-Century West*. Lawrence: University Press of Kansas, 1998.

Runte, Alfred. "Promoting the Golden West: Advertising and the Railroad." *California History* 70 (Spring 1991): 62–75.

———. *Trains of Discovery: Western Railroads and the National Parks*. Revised ed. Niwot, Colo.: Roberts Rinehart, 1990.

Thompson, Gregory Lee. *The Passenger Train in the Motor Age: California's Rail and Bus Industries, 1910–1941*. Columbus: Ohio State University Press, 1993.

van der Linden, F. Robert. *The Boeing 247: The First Modern Airliner*. Seattle: University of Washington Press, 1991.

Wrobel, David M., and Patrick T. Long. *Seeing and Being Seen: Tourism in the American West*. Lawrence: University Press of Kansas, 2001.

9. Is This Trip Necessary?

Bauer, E. E. *Boeing in Peace and War*. Enumclaw, Wash.: TABA Publishing, 1990.

Biddle, Wayne. *Barons of the Sky: From Early Flight to Strategic Warfare—The Story of the American Aerospace Industry.* New York: Simon & Schuster, 1991.

Bilstein, Roger E. "From Colony to Commonwealth: The Rise of the Aerospace Industry in the West." *Journal of the West* 36 (July 1997): 8–20.

Denham, Athel F. *20 Years' Progress in Commercial Motor Vehicles, 1921–1942.* Detroit and Washington, D.C.: Automotive Council for War Production, [1942?].

Hungerford, Edward. *Transport for War, 1942–1943.* New York: E. P. Dutton & Co., 1943.

Launius, Robert D., ed., *The Aerospace Industry in the West.* An issue of *Journal of the West* 36 (July 1997).

Lotchin, Roger W. *Fortress California, 1910–1961: From Warfare to Welfare.* New York: Oxford University Press, 1992.

Mansfield, Harold. *Vision: A Saga of the Sky.* New York: Duell, Sloan & Pearce, 1956.

Nash, Gerald D. *The American West Transformed: The Impact of the Second World War.* Bloomington: Indiana University Press, 1985.

Wilson, G. Lloyd. *Selected Papers and Addresses of Joseph B. Eastman.* New York: Simmons-Boardman, 1948.

10. Auto Euphoria and Other Postwar Enthusiasms

Eisenhower, Dwight D. *Mandate for Change: 1953–1956.* New York: Doubleday & Co., 1963.

Jakle, John A., and Keith A. Schulle. *The Gas Station in America.* Baltimore: Johns Hopkins University Press, 1994.

Jakle, John A.; Keith A. Schulle; and Jefferson S. Rogers. *The Motel in America.* Baltimore: Johns Hopkins University Press, 1996.

Kay, Jane Holtz. *Asphalt Nation: How the Automobile Took Over America, and How We Can Take It Back.* New York: Crown Publishers, 1997.

Kerouac, Jack. *On the Road.* New York: Viking Press, 1957.

Lewis, David L., ed. *The Automobile and American Culture.* A special issue of *Michigan Quarterly Review* 19 (Fall 1980)/20 (Winter 1981).

Lewis, Tom. *Divided Highways: Building the Interstate Highways, Transforming American Life.* New York: Penguin Putnam, 1997.

McMurtry, Larry. *Roads: Driving America's Great Highways.* New York: Simon & Schuster, 2000.

Marsh, Peter, and Peter Collett. *Driving Passion: The Psychology of the Car.* Boston: Faber and Faber, 1987.

Patton, Phil. *Open Road: A Celebration of the American Highway.* New York: Simon & Schuster, 1986.

Rae, John B. *The Road and the Car in American Life.* Cambridge, Mass.: MIT Press, 1971.

Rittenhouse, Jack D. *A Guide Book to Highway 66.* 1946. Reprint, Albuquerque: University of New Mexico Press, 1989.

Robyn, Dorothy. *Breaking the Special Interests: Trucking Deregulation and the Politics of Policy Reform.* Chicago: University of Chicago Press, 1987.

Rose, Mark H. *Interstate: Express Highway Politics, 1941–1956.* Lawrence: University Press of Kansas, 1979.

St. Clair, David J. *The Motorization of American Cities.* New York: Praeger, 1986.

Seely, Bruce E. *Building the American Highway System: Engineers as Policy Makers.* Philadelphia: Temple University Press, 1987.

Steinbeck, John. *Travels with Charley in Search of America.* Philadelphia: Curtis Publishing, 1962.

Witzel, Michael Karl. *The American Gas Station: History and Folklore of the Gas Station in American Car Culture.* New York: Barnes & Noble Books, 1999.

Yates, Brock. *The Decline and Fall of the American Automobile Industry.* New York: Vintage Books, 1984.

11. The Sky's the Limit

Bailey, Elizabeth E.; David R. Graham; and Daniel P. Kaplan. *Deregulating the Airlines.* Cambridge, Mass.: MIT Press, 1985.

Barlett, Donald L., and James B. Steele. *Empire: The Life, Legend, and Madness of Howard Hughes.* New York: W. W. Norton & Co., 1979.

Bednarek, Janet R. Daly. *America's Airports: Airfield Development, 1918–1947.* College Station: Texas A&M University Press, 2001.

Biederman, Paul. *The U.S. Airline Industry: End of an Era.* New York: Praeger Publishers, 1982.

Braznell, William. *An Airman's Odyssey: Walt Braznell and the Pilots He Led into the Jet Age.* Columbia: University of Missouri Press, 2001.

Davies, R. E. G. *Rebels and Reformers of the Airways.* Washington, D.C.: Smithsonian Institution Press, 1987.

Davies, R. E. G., and I. E. Quastler. *Commuter Airlines of the United States.* Washington, D.C.: Smithsonian Institution Press, 1995.

Dempsey, Paul Stephen; Andrew R. Goetz; and Joseph S. Szyliowicz. *Denver International Airport: Lessons Learned.* New York: McGraw-Hill, 1997.

Eads, George C. *The Local Service Airline Experiment.* Washington, D.C.: The Brookings Institution, 1972.

Komons, Nick A. *The Cutting Air Crash: A Case Study in Early Federal Aviation Policy.* Washington, D.C.: Department of Transportation, 1973.

Lewis, W. David, ed. *Airline Executives and Federal Regulation: Case Studies in American Enterprise from the Airmail Era to the Dawn of the Jet Age.* Columbus: Ohio State University Press, 2000. This volume includes excellent bibliographical essays on the history of commercial aviation in the United States.

Lewis, W. David, and Wesley Phillips Newton. *Delta: The History of an Airline.* Athens: University of Georgia Press, 1979.

Mellberg, William F. *Famous Airliners: From Biplane to Jetliner—The Story of Travel by Air.* 2nd ed. Vergennes, Vt.: Plymouth Press, 1999.

Murphy, Michael E. *The Airline That Pride Almost Bought: The Struggle to Take Over Continental Airlines.* New York: Franklin Watts, 1986.

Nance, John J. *Splash of Colors: The Self-Destruction of Braniff International.* New York: William Morrow and Co., 1984.

Peterson, Barbara Sturken, and James Glab. *Rapid Descent: Deregulation and the Shakeout in the Airlines.* New York: Simon & Schuster, 1994.

Petzinger, Thomas, Jr. *Hard Landing: The Epic Contest for Power and Profits That Plunged the Airlines into Chaos.* New York: Three Rivers Press, 1995.

Rae, John B. *Climb to Greatness: The American Aircraft Industry, 1920–1980.* Cambridge, Mass.: MIT Press, 1968.

Rummel, Robert W. *Howard Hughes and TWA.* Washington, D.C.: Smithsonian Institution Press, 1991.

Sampson, Anthony. *Empires of the Sky: The Politics, Contests and Cartels of World Airlines.* London: Hodder and Stoughton, 1984.

Stroud, John. *Airports of the World.* London: Putnam, 1980.

12. Reinventing the Railroads

Brandes, Ely M., and Alan E. Lazar. *The Future of Rail Passenger Traffic in the West.* Menlo Park, Calif.: Stanford Research Institute, ca. 1966.

Burby, John. *The Great American Motion Sickness; or, Why You Can't Get There from Here.* Boston: Little, Brown and Co., 1971.

Daughen, Joseph R., and Peter Binzen. *The Wreck of the Penn Central: The Real Story Behind the Largest Bankruptcy in American History.* Boston: Little, Brown and Co., 1971.

Dorin, Patrick C. *The Domeliners: A Pictorial History of the Penthouse Trains.* Seattle: Superior Publishing Co., 1973.

Itzkoff, Donald M. *Off the Track: The Decline of the Intercity Passenger Train in the United States.* Westport, Conn.: Greenwood Press, 1985.

Kirkland, John F. *Dawn of the Diesel Age: The History of the Diesel Locomotive in America.* Glendale, Calif.: Interurban Press, 1983.

Lyon, Peter. *To Hell in a Day Coach: An Exasperated Look at American Railroads.* Philadelphia: J. B. Lippincott Co., 1968.

Martin, Albro. *Railroads Triumphant: The Growth, Rejection and Rebirth of a Vital American Force.* New York: Oxford University Press, 1992.

Ola, Per, and Emily d'Aulaire. "Freight Trains Are Back and They're on a Roll." *Smithsonian,* June 1995, 36–49.

Saunders, Richard, Jr. *Merging Lines, American Railroads, 1900–1970.* DeKalb: Northern Illinois University Press, 2001.

White, John H. *The Great Yellow Fleet: A History of the American Railroad Refrigerator Cars.* San Marino, Calif.: Golden West Books, 1986.

Wilner, Frank N. *Railroad Mergers: History, Analysis, Insight.* Omaha: Simmons-Boardman Books, 1997.

Zimmermann, Karl. *Amtrak at Milepost 10.* Park Forest, Ill.: PTJ Publishing 1981.

Conclusion

Conzen, Michael P., ed. *The Making of the American Landscape.* London: HarperCollins Academic, 1990.

Jackson, John Brinckerhoff. *Discovering the Vernacular Landscape.* New Haven, Conn.: Yale University Press, 1984.

Jakle, John A. *The Visual Elements of Landscape.* Amherst: University of Massachusetts Press, 1987.

Lobeck, K. *Airways of America: The United Airlines.* 1933. Reprint, Port Washington, N.Y.: Kennikat Press, 1970.

Longstreth, Richard. *City Center to Regional Mall: Architecture, the Automo-*

bile, and Retailing in Los Angeles, 1920–1950. Cambridge, Mass.: MIT Press, 1997.

Longstreth, Richard. *The Drive-In, the Supermarket, and the Transformation of Commercial Space in Los Angeles, 1914–1941*. Cambridge, Mass.: MIT Press, 1999.

Meinig, D. W., ed. *The Interpretation of Ordinary Landscapes: Geographical Essays*. New York: Oxford University Press, 1979.

Simmons, Jack, and Gordon Biddle, eds. *The Oxford Companion to British Railway History: From 1603 to the 1990s*. Oxford: Oxford University Press, 1997.

Vranich, Joseph. *Supertrains: Solutions to America's Transportation Gridlock*. New York: St. Martin's Press, 1991.

Warner, Sam B., Jr. *Streetcar Suburbs: The Process of Growth in Boston, 1870–1900*. Cambridge, Mass.: Harvard University Press and MIT Press, 1962.

This 1970 brochure highlighted the Indiana Toll Road as part of a network of such superhighways linking New York, Boston, and Chicago. Motorists who followed it all the way across the Hoosier State, a distance of 157 miles, had to pay $2.80. The toll roads of Illinois, Ohio, Pennsylvania, and New Jersey levied additional fees on travelers hurrying between Chicago and New York. Author's collection.

Kansas City, Missouri, 9, 46, 49, 172, 230, 312, 314, 322
Kansas City Southern Railway, 79, 204, 352
Kelleher, Herbert, 318–319. *See also* Southwest Airlines
Kelly Act (1925), 199, 201, 211, 382
Kuhler, Otto, 228

Labor, 54–55, 69, 73, 251, 252, 320
Lambert, Albert Bond, 140
Lancaster, Samuel C., 134
Las Vegas, Nevada, 6, 40, 67, 94, 203, 236, 317, 320, 333
Lead, South Dakota, 20
League of American Wheelmen, 123
Lewis and Clark Expedition, 189, 192
Lewis, Sinclair, 117, 125
Lincoln Highway
    evolution as a transportation corridor, 150, 193
    promotional activity by Lincoln Highway Association, 147–150, 155
Lindbergh, Charles A., 135, 137, 195, 204, 208, 247
Lindbergh Line, 205, 208, 211, 242
Lindblad Expeditions. *See* Tourism, cruise boats
Lockheed commercial aircraft, 196, 250
    Constellation, 261, 262, 267, 297, 304, 314, 316
    Sky Zephyr, 195–197
Lorenzo, Francisco A., 317–318
Los Angeles, California, xv
    commercial aviation, 202–203, 205, 206, 207, 247, 250, 322
    railroad transportation, 88, 90, 92, 101, 226–227, 236, 368
    roads and highways, 122, 165, 174, 273, 284
    suburban growth, xv, 3, 25, 40, 88, 174
Los Angeles International Air Meet (1910), 198–199
Loughead brothers, 250

McNary-Watres Act (1930), 211, 215
Mamer, Nicholas Bernard, 190–191, 194–196
Martin, Glenn, 199, 247
Metropolitan Corridor, 65, 324, 356
Mexico, 93
Milwaukee Road. *See* Chicago, Milwaukee, St. Paul & Pacific (Milwaukee Road)

Mining and transportation, 108, 172, 293
    copper and investment capital, 88–89, 91–92, 93, 94, 99
    general history, 7, 9, 16, 20–21, 33, 68, 91
    impact of California Gold Rush, 7
Minnesota, 98, 128–129
Missouri Pacific Lines, 43, 95, 137, 232, 234, 348
Missouri River, 13, 33, 89, 90
Model T Ford, 117, 125, 126, 137, 172
Moffat Tunnel, 98
Montana, 7, 13, 36, 85–87, 129, 195–196
Montana Rail Link, 352
Morgan, David P., 333, 338
Motels, 277–278, 290–291
Motor Carrier Act of 1935, 187, 220

Narrow-gauge railroads, 4–5, 16, 48
National parks and monuments of the West, 46, 52, 78, 80, 179–180, 186–187, 233, 278
    Carlsbad Caverns, 179, 182, 234
    Crater Lake, 85, 179
    Glacier Park, 179, 186–187, 235, 278
    Grand Canyon, 85
    Mesa Verde, 182
    Mount Rainier, 179, 278
    Olympic, 278
    Petrified Forest, 234
    Yellowstone, 84, 85, 151, 179, 180–181, 233–234, 278
    Yosemite, 84, 123, 233
Native Americans, 84, 187, 234, 235
Nevada, 34–35, 67, 148, 201
New Deal, 31, 246
New Mexico, 31, 41, 234
New Orleans, Louisiana, 46
New York Central Lines, 205, 219, 243, 328
New York City, 3, 147, 148
North Dakota, xviii, 129
Northern Pacific Railway, xviii, 12, 46, 76–77, 79, 84, 85, 233, 245, 253, 352
Northrop, John K., 250
Northwest Airlines, 195, 196, 204, 262, 268, 320

Oakland, California, 48, 89–90, 95, 242, 265, 274–275, 358
Office of Defense Transportation, 243, 253, 257, 259, 260, 263

CARLOS ARNALDO SCHWANTES is the St. Louis Mercantile Library Endowed Professor of Transportation Studies and the West at the University of Missouri–St. Louis. In addition to teaching classes on a variety of subjects, including Transportation in American Life, he is the author or editor of fourteen books. Schwantes, an avid photographer, has illustrated several of his books. A native of North Carolina, he received his Ph.D. in Amcrican history from the University of Michigan in 1976. Before coming to the University of Missouri–St. Louis he was professor of history at the University of Idaho.